FIELDENS OF TODMORDEN

FIELDENS OF TODMORDEN

A Nineteenth Century Business Dynasty

[signature: Brian Law]

BRIAN R. LAW

With an introduction by
STANLEY CHAPMAN
Professor of Business History
University of Nottingham

George Kelsall

To the generations of Todmorden people
who were associated with the Fielden family and business

First published in 1995 by
George Kelsall
22 Church Street
Littleborough
Lancashire OL15 9AA

British Library Cataloguing in Publication Data
Law, Brian R.
    Fieldens of Todmorden: Nineteenth Century
    Business Dynasty
    I. Title
    942.812
ISBN 0 946571 26 0 Hardback
ISBN 0 946571 27 9 Paperback

Designed by Roger Birch
Set in Imprint by RAP Limited, Rochdale

Printed and bound in Great Britain by Balding+Mansell

Frontispiece: Waterside Mill at the end of the nineteenth century.

CONTENTS

List of Tables and Appendices

List of Maps, Plans and Figures

AUTHOR'S PREFACE

My interest in the Fieldens reflects my upbringing in Todmorden, the mill-town which their business success in the nineteenth century had largely created, and to which their mills, homes and philanthropy gave prominent architectural features. A general but vague awareness of Fielden history, something which anyone living in Todmorden must share, was stimulated by a realisation that my own family had been closely associated with the Fieldens — as political allies in John Fielden's time and subsequently, in business, as tenants, and as overlookers and weavers in their mills. Of course many, if not all, Todmorden families would have similar associations.

When the opportunity came in retirement I began to explore Fielden history, guided by Stuart Weaver's book 'John Fielden and Popular Radicalism,' and by Stanley Chapman's 'Merchant Enterprise in Britain.' Both of these scholars had been down the Fielden trail; their accounts made me aware of the size and complexity of the Fielden business and its remarkable success in the early and mid nineteenth century. When I studied the Fielden papers in the John Rylands Library in Manchester and the business documents deposited in the West Yorkshire Archive I realised that there was enough material for a story about the business that had not yet been told. That view was strengthened and confirmed when I was able to see papers in the Fielden family's possession. These different sources form the basis of this history, supplemented by other original and secondary materials: my interpretation of the sources has drawn on insights gained from my own business career.

The course of the Fielden business perhaps epitomises that of the British economy over the period; a phase of remarkable enterprise and dramatic expansion succeeded by a decline in the industrial spirit and a failure to renew the business. 'Great profit has a tendency to produce a relaxation of exertion,' as one contemporary observed, and this was true of the Fieldens. The story of the family also illuminates many themes in social history, in paticular: the extent of social responsibility among the businessmen of the time; their changing relationship with local communities; the striving of those who had accumulated or inherited great wealth from industry and trade for social distinction and the values and lifestyle of the landed gentry; and the way in which that lifestyle was eroded in the twentieth century.

Business and social history lends itself to illustration which highlights its themes, places and personalities pictorially. Thus I have complemented my text with maps, paintings, photographs and documents to produce an illustrated history, relevant and substantial for the scholar on the one hand, but interesting and informative for the general reader on the other. I hope I have done justice to all the material and all the help I have received.

I am grateful to members of the Fielden family who have made papers and photographs freely available, given me generous and enjoyable hospitality in their homes, and much encouragement to complete the task on which I had embarked. I have to thank Mrs Ann Stevens and Mr and Mrs Jonathan Lovegrove Fielden of Longden Manor; Mr and Mrs John Anthony Fielden of Court of Hill; Mr and Mrs John Fielden of Odiham and Grimston Park; Mr and Mrs Phillip Fielden of Adlestrop; Mrs Patricia Villiers-Stuart and Mrs Electra May of Beachamwell.

Many people in Todmorden have also helped me, especially Jack Taylor with his own recollections of the Fieldens and his manuscript material, and Joseph Hirst, last company secretary of Fielden Brothers, a life-time employee, and still living at Waterside. There are many others, not least Betty Savage and Dennis O'Neill, with their great knowledge of Todmorden families and places and events, Douglas Wilson, for family history and Malcolm Heywood, the town's most recent historian. In practical terms my writing would not have been possible without the efficient support of Mary Villet and her word-processor.

What I have written has benefited from the encouragement and criticism of Negley Harte of University College, London, Professor Stanley Chapman and Dr Steve Toms of the University of Nottingham, and Professor Theo Barker of the London School of Economics.

Finally there is the collaboration and support of Roger Birch of Todmorden. Without his professional skills and without access to his photographic library, this book in its present form would not have been possible. The book is as much his as mine.

My wife and family have encouraged me throughout, sustained me when doubts or fatigue set in, and accepted exceptional inconvenience as papers and writing have intruded on normal living. They have 'lived with' the Fieldens for a long time. I hope that they will feel that the resulting book justifies their tolerance.

INTRODUCTION

Stanley Chapman
Professor of Business History
University of Nottingham

The name of John Fielden is familiar to everyone with an interest in British social and industrial history as one of the outstanding reformers of the early factory age. His political crusade has been the subject of several studies over the years, but the family fortune that sustained his arduous career in the vanguard of Industrial Revolution politics remains strangely unrecorded. Social and political historians have not been much interested in economic matters, and the dispersion of the Fielden records in half-a-dozen locations round Britain, both family and public, has required a business historian with exceptional persistence and dedication. Brian Law has now skilfully filled that role, drawing on his own family background in Todmorden and insights gained in his business career, as well as extensive reading and exhaustive research of the records.

The fortunes won by entrepreneurs last century have been the subject of much research in recent years. This work leaves no doubt that John Fielden's family enterprise, Fielden Brothers, accumulated more capital in business than any other cotton firm in Britain before the watershed of the American Civil War. In the next generation, three Fielden brothers were among the wealthiest nouveaux riches in Victorian Britain. Some of the explanations are pretty familiar from our knowledge of the period: the ascetic habits of the founder and John Fielden's generation, the Quaker self-discipline bred into the family, operation in a cheap and deferential labour area (in this case Todmorden), and capital accumulating from windfall gains in the French Wars. But Mr Law shows that this was only the beginning. From the early years Fielden Bros. developed quickly as a mercantile as well as manufacturing organisation, at first through brother Thomas in Manchester and their friends the Pickersgills in London, later through Wildes, Pickersgill and Co. in Liverpool. The development may sound obvious enough, but all the evidence goes not to show that only a handful of Lancashire enterprises were able to successfully unite the two functions. Guiding Fielden Bros. as an integrated enterprise was John Fielden, bargaining for machinery and buildings when costs were cheap, buying and selling when raw cotton was low and yarns and fabrics buoyant, always keeping a loyal Todmorden labour force in tow. His political status was not irrelevant, for when crisis overtook the firm in the early 1840s he was able to obtain a large loan from the Bank of England despite the prejudice of the Bank's Liverpool and Manchester branch agents (managers).

Historians have debated the emergence of class and class consciousness in the nineteenth century for many years. Whatever its significance elsewhere, Brian Law provides much detail to show that such notions were slow to emerge in Todmorden, and that Fieldens remained the patriarchs of the town to the fourth generation. Industrial relations continued to be moulded by the old master and servant tradition, with the addition that the family and their managers were mill martinets rather than fathers to their employees. There was, as one outsider observed, 'very harsh discipline' at the Waterside mills, the core of the Fielden enterprise. While the family drew huge incomes from the business, wages continued lower than in most of the rest of Lancashire — still as much as 5 — 10 per cent below that of the cotton industry a century after the business was first started in 1784. If there was tension and conflict in Victorian Todmorden, it was more likely to be over chapel rivalries than head-on conflicts between bosses and workers. Trade unions made very little impact on Fielden Bros. last century.

Factory colonies were a conspicuous feature of the early years of the Industrial Revolution, and those at Cromford (Arkwright), Styal (Greg), New Lanark (Robert Owen), and other locations are still much studied and visited. The Fieldens' great wealth came in the second generation rather than first, but there was more than enough of it to create something as spectacular as Saltaire or Ackroydon. Surprisingly for a family that always professed complete dedication to the best interest of its labour force, the Fieldens endowed their people with very little indeed, and that very late. The Unitarian Chapel (1869) was a family extravagance more akin to aristocratic self-indulgence than Nonconformist piety or service to others. Todmorden town hall (1875) was a magnificently expensive classical building, but more a symbol of Fielden pride than community endeavour. Apart from these two public buildings, there was only Robinwood Terrace, a late experiment in improved working class dwellings. Todmordians had to look to the chapels and friendly societies for community support while the third generation Fieldens spent huge sums on their Victorian palaces. Brian Law rightly recognises that Todmorden, like other mill-towns, was a harsh and dirty place throughout the nineteenth century. The Unitarian ideology embraced by the Fieldens was overlaid by self interest, an unpleasant contrast with more dedicated Unitarian families like the Strutts, Gregs and Ashtons of Hyde, and the commendable building records of some of Fieldens' other major rivals (such as the Ashworths of Turton and Whiteheads of Rawtenstall) featured in Cooke Taylor's *Tour of Lancashire* (1842).

The shift of industrial entrepreneurs to finance is a familiar feature of economic history but it has recently been embraced in a major re-interpretation of British history at large. Caine and Hopkins have coined the phrase 'gentlemanly capitalism' to develop a thesis in which London-based merchants and financiers, allied with the aristocracy, continued to dominate both the British economy and British economic policy, including imperial expansion into the present century. Successful provincial entrepreneurs, and more particularly scions of the second and subsequent generations, were drawn into the metropolitan network and were seduced to a lifestyle that drew its inspiration from aristocratic ease and extravagance.

Clearly the Fielden dynasty offers a most interesting case study to illustrate and refine the work of Caine and Hopkins. The radical politics of John Fielden and his brothers must appear as a powerful repudiation of any suggestion of 'gentlemanly capitalism' and its free trade. R.H. Greg, a rival cotton spinner with a strong commitment to 'Manchester School' politics, wrote in 1837, not unfairly, that John Fielden 'can scarcely have heard of the name of Adam Smith.' At the same time, John developed mercantile and financial connections that were crucial to the success of his business, and invested heavily in railways, shipping and property. And of course his election to Parliament introduced him to the British political elite in Westminster and life in the home counties, and established a family tradition of political activity. Never the less, the second generation were much closer to what one recent historian, Professor Theodore Koditschek, had identified as 'the self-denying entrepreneur' (*Class Formation and Urban Industrial Society: Bradford 1750-1850*, (CUP, 1990)).

It was only after John's death in 1848 that the family invested heavily in land, but, as Mr Law traces in some detail in Chapter 6, the three principal heirs to the business responded in rather a different way. After the cotton famine they became truly rich. They had already spent freely on large residences in the Todmorden area; in the early 1870s, at the peak of the mid-Victorian property boom, the two younger brothers (John II and Joshua), severed the first strand of the traditional Lancashire link by acquiring large estates in more rural parts of England, and for the rest of their lives they maintained a figurehead commitment to Todmorden's political and social life. More significantly, the third generation failed to give real leadership to the cotton business, which steadily contracted while the brothers became major money lenders to some of their contacts in the Manchester business community, a process that was very largely concealed from employers and workers in their industry. Consequently it was only in the fourth generation, whose members were brought up in rural England and sent to public schools and the ancient universities, that the family's real break with northern industry came.

The rise and fall of the Fielden enterprise evidently preceded that of the British cotton industry at large. Partly it was a matter of industrial structure. As Douglas Farnie relates in his *English Cotton Industry and the World Market* (O.U.P, 1979), the heyday of the firms that combined spinning and weaving ran from the 1830s to the early 1860s. Focused on coarse spinning and plain weaving, combined firms were overtaken by the faster-growing specialised producers, first in spinning in south Lancashire during the 1850s, then in weaving in north Lancashire during the 1880s as the power loom reached technical perfection. In the third generation, Fielden Bros.' problems were exacerbated by their autocratic management tradition, which made delegation difficult. The management culture required the continuous presence of the family partners who attended less and less often. The business lost momentum and slipped down the table of the industry's major firms.

Paradoxically, Fielden Brothers only survived as a limited company through the fourth generation because the family shareholders' trusted Chairman, E.B. Fielden, had an expensive upper class life-style, as a result of which he was more or less always in debt. He worked the old business hard to improve his own income, but also out of a sense of obligation to the family shareholders, and to the firm's workpeople and the Todmorden community. Meanwhile he continued to live in splendour on his estate in Shropshire, as well as meet his heavy commitments to public life. So, while 'gentlemanly capitalism' failed to renew and expand the business in the third generation, the fourth kept it struggling on beyond its expected life-span. The temptation to offer this pattern as a model of British industrial enterprise as a whole must be resisted, at any rate in this brief introduction.

Note on the Value of Money

Most of the money values expressed in what follows — wealth, incomes, profits, asset values etc. — relate to the early, middle or late nineteenth century. Throughout this period and indeed up to the first world war, the purchasing power of money was comparatively stable; if anything prices tended to fall. The first world war brought a sharp rise in prices but the inter-war years saw prices falling again. Inflation returned in the second world war and has continued at a variable rate ever since, quickening especially in the 1970s.

As a general guide **a multiple of sixty converts nineteenth century values to those of the present day**. Thus a weekly wage of 15 shillings, typical at Waterside in the 1890s, would be about £45 today; a business-man's fortune of £200,000 which John Fielden left in 1849, would be the equivalent of £12 million in today's money. This puts the wealth of the Fieldens' in context: if the wealth of the family as a whole accumulated to say 1890 is of the order of £4 million, this would compare with £240 million today, a huge fortune then and now.

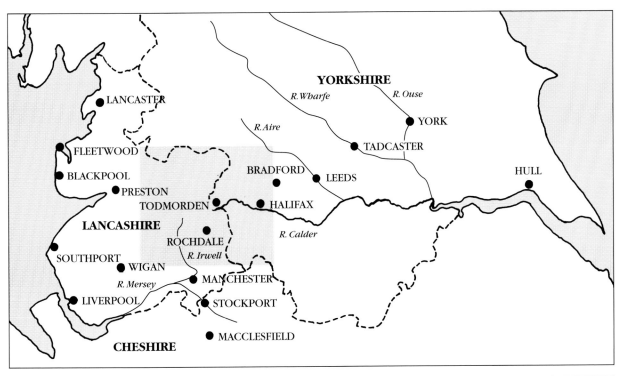

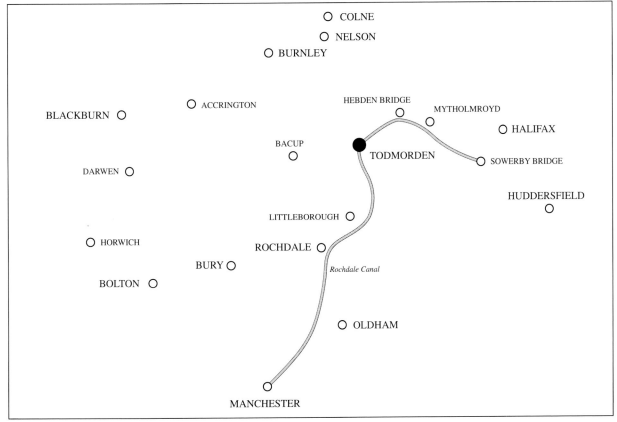

LOCATION MAPS OF TODMORDEN

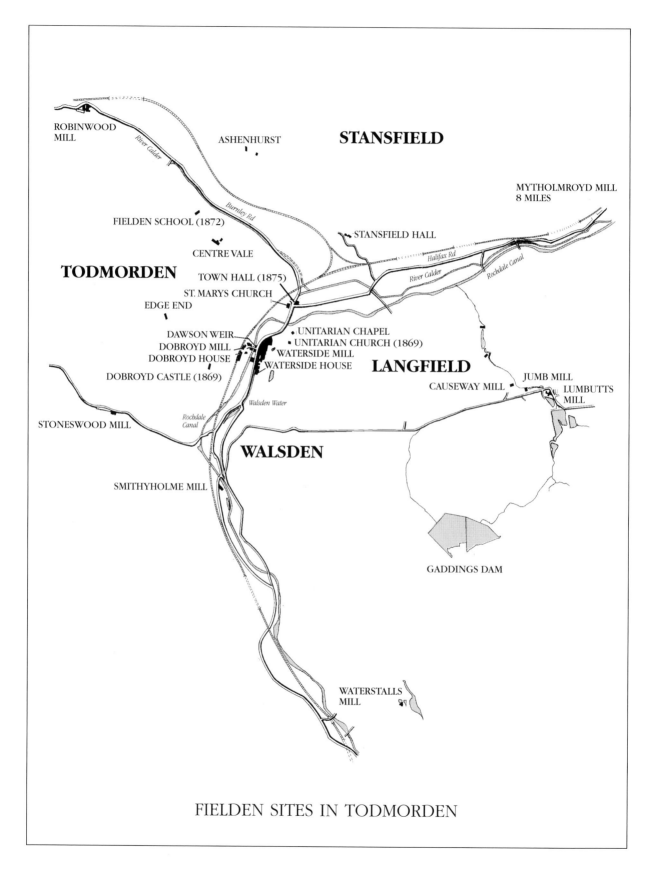

FIELDEN SITES IN TODMORDEN

JOSHUA FIELDEN'S FAMILY TREE

(to the third generation)

Joshua Fielden (1748-1811) m. (1772) — Jenny Greenwood

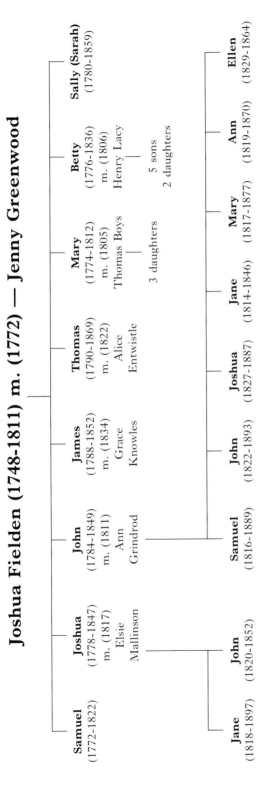

Samuel (1772-1822)

Joshua (1778-1847) m. (1817) Elsie Mallinson

John (1784-1849) m. (1811) Ann Grindrod

James (1788-1852) m. (1834) Grace Knowles

Thomas (1790-1869) m. (1822) Alice Entwistle

Mary (1774-1812) m. (1805) Thomas Boys — 3 daughters

Betty (1776-1836) m. (1806) Henry Lacy — 5 sons 2 daughters

Sally (Sarah) (1780-1859)

Samuel (1816-1889)

John (1822-1893)

Joshua (1827-1887)

Jane (1814-1846)

Mary (1817-1877)

Ann (1819-1870)

Ellen (1829-1864)

Jane (1818-1897)

John (1820-1852)

Edge End Farm, typical of
many small hillside farms in
the Upper Calder valley, was
owned and occupied by
Fieldens in the late seven-
teenth century. When Joshua
Fielden was born here in
1748 it had been sold, his
father being a tenant. Joshua
followed his father making a
living from the farm and
from his activities as a
clothier before leaving in
1782. Edge End then passed
out of Fielden occupation but
again became a Fielden property in the 1840s and is
owned by a Fielden today.

THE BEGINNINGS
Joshua Fielden and Sons

The romantic beginnings of the Fielden business have been described many times.[1] The particular family, for there were many Fieldens in Todmorden, can be traced back to the sixteenth century. They were no different from many others inhabiting the small farms and associated cottages in the upland townships of the Pennine parishes of Halifax and Rochdale. They made a living partly by farming, partly by weaving woollen cloth, whether for others or for their own account. Some members of the family in particular generations had more wealth than others, notably a John Fielden who died childless at Todmorden Hall in 1734, owning several farms and leaving a comfortable fortune. But generally the family were farmer-weavers, leading a hard, frugal and simple life.

Joshua Fielden, the founder of the Fielden business, does not appear to have been among the wealthier members of his family. He was born in 1748 at Edge End Farm, on the hillside above the Walsden branch of the Calder valley where his father was a tenant. He grew up there, married and began to raise his children, tenanting the farm from his elder brother. The farm itself, 38 acres, was larger than most in the district, although it occupied only part of his time. Documents survive which show that he was buying wool and yarn from a John Royds in Halifax in 1774 and 1775, spending as much as £61 on parcels of wool and £56 on parcels of yarn.[2] He may have prepared the wool for spinning and weaving in his own household but he was more probably

(Above)
Joshua Fielden (1748-1811) married Jenny Greenwood at the Friends Meeting House in 1771, and they began to raise their family at Edge End before moving to Laneside to take up cotton spinning in 1782. Jenny resisted the move at the time, preferring the fresh air and long views of the hillside. The cotton-spinning and manufacturing business of Joshua Fielden and Sons struggled during the Napoleonic period. Joshua withdrew in 1803 leaving the business in the hands of his sons; when he died in 1811 he left £200.

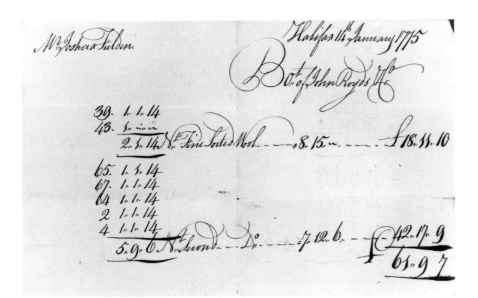

(Left)
Wool Bill dated 1775. Joshua Fielden, while still a clothier at Edge End, went to Halifax, 12 miles away, to buy wool or woollen yarn, which was then put-out for spinning and weaving to farms and cottages in the district. The woven cloth would be sold in the Halifax Piece Hall.

Laneside: the three cottages in the Walsden valley were bought by Joshua Fielden in 1782 with a mortgage loan. His family — there were eight surviving children — lived in one cottage, the other two being used to prepare and spin cotton. A third storey was added and the building enlarged to the rear, before the first mill, seven windows long and five storeys high, was built on adjacent ground in 1804. Members of the Fielden family continued to live in the Laneside cottages until the 1850s and they remain private residences to the present day.

putting it out to others, and taking back the woven cloth for sale in Halifax some 12 miles away. Joshua Fielden was recalled as a man of robust character who pursued his business as a clothier with untiring zeal; like other members of his family, he was a Quaker.

When cotton emerged as the promising new textile material, Joshua Fielden followed the many throughout East Lancashire who were taking it up. Like others he saw the opportunity, not only in the new lighter fabric but also in the improved means of spinning that were becoming available. In 1782 he moved with his wife and five small children from his hillside farm to three cottages at Laneside, by the turnpike and the river in the Walsden valley. He bought the premises at Laneside with a £400 mortgage loan at 5 per cent interest from Quaker friends. His grandson, Joshua Fielden, was later to write 'my grandfather being too poor to buy all three cottages, a friend lent him a portion of the money to complete.' He borrowed a further £250 on the same terms a few years later in 1790.[3] Good water power from the Walsden branch of the Calder was an attraction of the site, and here he began preparing and spinning cotton yarn. He may have had hand-looms at Laneside, but mainly he was putting out yarn, whether weft or warp, to hand-loom weavers scattered throughout the district. The small business gradually progressed, acquiring land, premises and water rights, enlarging the preparation and spinning operation, adding new machinery to the early spinning jennies, water-frames or throstles for warp, and mules for weft. Initially a third floor was added to the cottages and they were extended to the rear; then a small mill was built, five storeys high, seven windows long, to accommodate more machinery. In 1794 a small water-powered spinning mill was tenanted at Lumbutts, a hillside community in Langfield Township 2 miles away.

Joshua Fielden's five sons (Samuel born 1772, Joshua 1778, John 1784, James 1788, and Thomas 1790) worked in the business from an early age. The eldest, Samuel, took responsibility for the Lumbutts mill. The middle son who was to become most renowned, namely John, was later to describe his labours in the Waterside mill, as it now came to be called, from the age of ten and the ardours of accompanying his father on weekly visits to Manchester, 20 miles away, taking calico pieces for sale and returning with bags of cotton. The small business had the status to obtain credit and probably made full use of it, buying cotton on a three or four months bill. When the Rochdale Canal had been completed along the Calder valley, after 1804, canal boats were used to carry cloth and cotton, to and from Manchester, instead of carting by road.

The standing of the business at the time is indicated by early records relating to the Canal. The Calder valley millowners associated to protect their interests in the uninterrupted flow of the river and secure compensation water from the Canal Company. Joshua Fielden joined the Association but in 1803 he was among those members whose subscription was only three guineas, while eleven other local millowners including John Buckley at Ridgefoot, Christopher Rawdon at Callis Mill, and Thomas Edmundson at Mytholmroyd, lower down the Calder valley, were paying ten guineas.[5] Joshua's son John was to become Chairman of the Association in 1813 and it was virtually run by Fieldens thereafter.

Joshua Fielden himself seems to have retired from the business in 1803, leaving it to his sons, who continued to trade as Joshua Fielden and Sons. At, or about this time, Samuel bought the Lumbutts mill

Ridgefoot Mill or Buckleys, was the largest mill in the district at the time of the Crompton census in 1811 when 6,000 spindles were recorded. Buckleys derived their water power from the same stream as Waterside and they had a close understanding with the Fieldens on their respective rights. Their business failed in the trade depression of the 1840s, when Ridgefoot was taken by the Ormerod Brothers, rivals of the Fieldens.

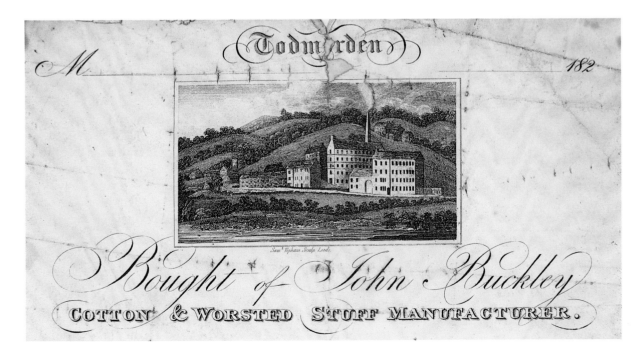

19

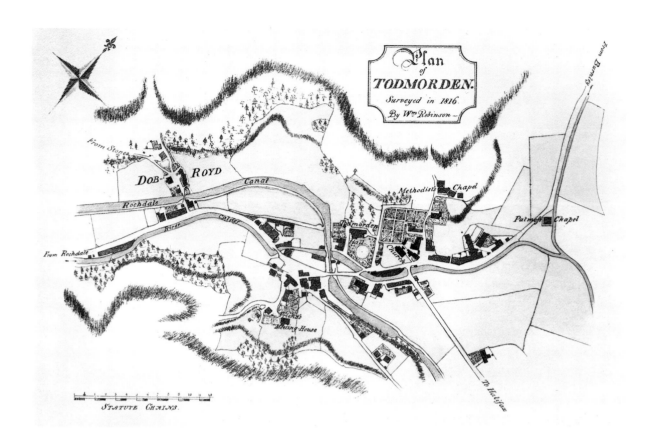

Todmorden in 1816. The cluster of Fielden buildings at Waterside remain a small affair but the gathering of houses, shops and inns near Todmorden Hall and St. Mary's church, where the valleys converge, is already the nucleus of a small town. Buckley's mill is also conspicuous.

as his own property although he probably ran it in association with the family concern, now managed by his brothers. The business cannot have flourished in the difficult period of the Napoleonic Wars. Its relative status is indicated by the Crompton Census of 1811: at that time Crompton found 2280 mule spindles and 864 throstles at Waterside; Samuel's mill at Lumbutts had 2400 mule spindles. The Crompton census identified fifty-six mills, of which forty-five were probably spinning cotton, in the upper Calder valley, with 124,000 spindles in total. (Crompton identified a total of 4,670,000 spindles in England and Scotland).[6]

In 1811, then, Joshua Fielden and Sons was still a small, struggling enterprise, not different from many others in the locality. The upper Calder valley, with its numerous small water-mills and scattered population, , hardly compared with the large concentrations of cotton spinning capacity and growing urban communities in Manchester, Stockport, the Tame Valley, Bolton, or Preston.

2

THE RISE TO PROMINENCE
Fielden Brothers 1816-1832

Crompton's survey was carried out in the year of Joshua Fielden's death in 1811. Joshua's interest in the spinning and weaving business had ceased and the buildings and machinery and other properties had passed to his sons. He apparently left no more than £200. Waterside, at the time, taking 17s 6d per spindle as the value for buildings, power and machinery, might be worth £3000; Lumbutts would be worth about £2000.[1]

On 3 May 1816, the business that was Joshua Fielden and Sons became a partnership, Fielden Brothers: Samuel, the eldest son, joined his brothers in the new concern, with the Lumbutts mill remaining his private property. Some of the other assets within the Partnership were probably owned by individual Partners but the detailed assessment of the Partnership assets or capital that had been made on 19 April 1816 has not survived. According to the first Partnership documents, the Partnership capital was divided into eight shares: Samuel, Joshua and John had two shares each; James and Thomas, the younger brothers, one each.[2] The document provided for the assets to be valued at 30 June each year, and the profit or loss 'gained or sustained' for the year to be determined. Unfortunately these early accounts have not survived and the first detailed inventory of the Partnership assets or capital is dated 30 June 1832, coinciding with John Fielden's election to Parliament. Fielden Brothers capital was then recorded as £307,366 and, after adjustment for private property within that figure, the Partnership's joint capital was £277,342.[3]

The Partnership Document of 1816. Written in John Fielden's hand, the first clause required that 'the whole of our time and attention that is applied to business ... shall be devoted wholly and solely to the care and management of the Partnership concern.' The second clause stated the Partners were not to 'transact any business or make and repair any kind of machinery or do any other kind of work,' unless all were in full agreement; 'any new work or alterations in building and machinery' also required full agreement.

The Partnership Document of 1816. Other clauses required all the Partners to consent to individual drawings; and for payment of £4 per week personal expenses to each Partner, a payment that was forfeit on failure to attend the weekly meeting without adequate excuse.

When the first Partnership was formed, Samuel, Joshua and John, the eldest brothers, each took one quarter of the capital and profits, James and Thomas one-eighth each. The Partners were to receive 5 per cent interest on their individual capital held in the concern.

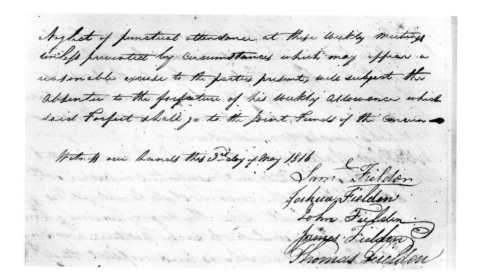

Thus by 1832 Fielden Brothers was a most significant enterprise, owning one of the greatest capitals in the industry. From its obscure status in 1811 the Partnership had become one of the largest combined spinning and weaving concerns. The 39,048 spindles and 684 power looms described in the 1832 inventory represented about one per cent of the capacity of the Lancashire industry. Additionally upwards of 1,000 dependent hand loom weavers were producing 2,000 to 3,000 pieces of cloth per week.[4] But the manufacturing assets in Todmorden, large as they were, represented the lesser part of the total capital of the concern. By 1832 what was described as 'Property abroad or in Manchester', amounted to £184,603, over 60 per cent of the capital.

Why, in this early period of the cotton industry, were Fielden Brothers so dramatically successful? How did they rise to so prominent a position as manufacturers, and accumulate so large a surplus capital that could be employed outside manufacturing?

Background of the Industry

Before addressing these questions it is relevant to describe some general features of the cotton industry at this time. Most noteworthy, of course, is its extraordinary expansion in the period following the end of the Napoleonic wars. Here the best indicator is consumption of raw cotton, which between 1815 and 1832 increased at a rate of 8 per cent compound annually; in the next twenty years to 1852 it was to grow at an annual rate of 5 per cent[5] (Figure 1). Such sustained rapid growth resulted from development of markets for cheap cotton cloth produced in the United Kingdom, initially in Europe, then in the Americas, the Ottoman Empire, and in a later period in India, China, and to a lesser extent, Africa. The availability of cheap cotton cloth to supply these markets was achieved by the coming-together of low-cost raw material from the American South, and the specialised enterprise and skill of Lancashire, applying the new technologies in cotton preparation, throstle and mule spinning and weaving, and selling the cloth wherever markets could be found. Competition rapidly brought prices close to costs, themselves falling: prices of yarn and cloth in the 1850s were about a quarter of those of 1814. Cotton cloth was not merely made widely available, it was very cheap in real terms. Cheapness, it came to be said, and to be believed, promoted consumption without any definite limit.

Sustained expansion of the industry did not guarantee success and prosperity to its participants. Competition was intense. Stimulated by periods of buoyant trade and the lure of fortunes to be made, capacity and the numbers of firms expanded as fast or faster than the needs of markets. Margins between the cost of cotton and the selling prices of yarn and cloth were lean or inadequate for much of the time. John Fielden was to complain, 'we have got mills and machinery to produce more than there is a vent for at a remunerative price.'[6] He was

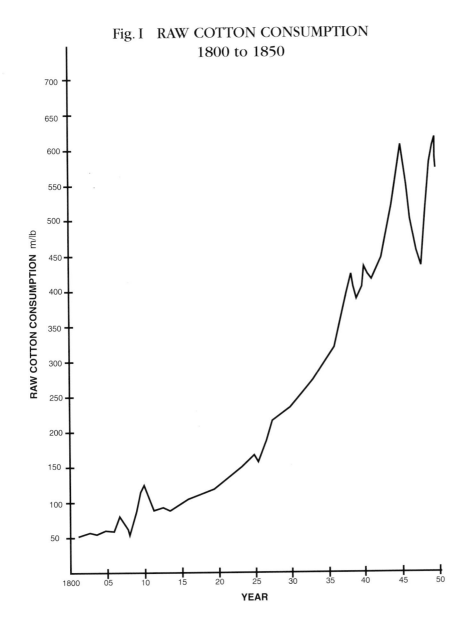

Fig. I RAW COTTON CONSUMPTION
1800 to 1850

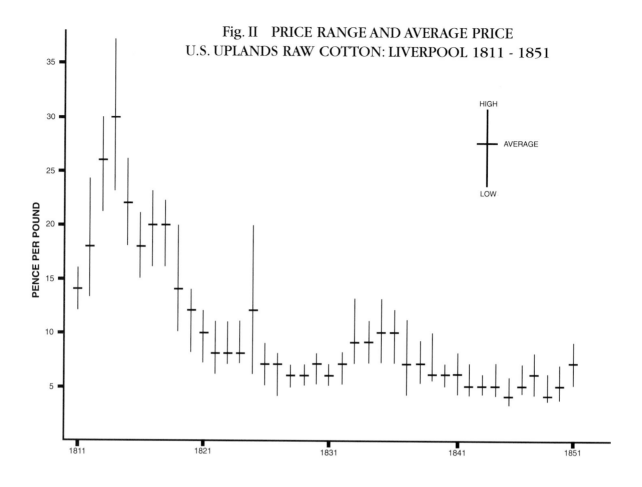

Fig. II PRICE RANGE AND AVERAGE PRICE U.S. UPLANDS RAW COTTON: LIVERPOOL 1811 - 1851

referring to the position in 1841, a year when business and margins collapsed, but his remarks would apply to many earlier and subsequent years when trade and capacity were pushed too far in a period of boom. One participant in the industry, in 1833, spoke of 'great extension, of a rapid sale and activity, but making very moderate returns of profit.' He went on to attribute this 'not to any want of demand — but to an extremely extensive production with reference to the demand.' Over capacity and competition led to weak selling as goods were pressed on an oversupplied Manchester market. The position was aggravated by the many small manufacturers of limited resources who purchased raw cotton on credit and speculated by holding off from sale of finished goods waiting for a rise in the market; all too frequently they eventually sold in distress to Manchester dealers. To Fielden and others, the Manchester Exchange was 'the slaughterhouse.'[7]

Rapid changes in technology, in the size and speed of mules, or the speed of looms, or in improved steam engines lowering fuel consumption in relation to the work load, for instance, while steadily reducing costs, resulted in a high rate of obsolescence and loss of competitive status if a firm could not keep abreast by replacing or modernising its machinery and sources of motive power.

Finally there were other hazards: participants in the industry had

24

to manage their exposure to the huge risks inherent in a highly volatile raw cotton market, a market that worked in a fog of uncertainty regarding crop prospects, shipments, arrivals, consumption and speculative participation (Figure II). At this period news from America would take four to five weeks to cross the Atlantic. Thus John Owens, commenting on the market in 1823, could say, 'It seems clear even the best informed know little about production and consumption and have not sufficient data to form an opinion.'[8] With raw cotton representing a large proportion of the value of yarn and cloth, the violent ups and downs of the cotton market were at once a source of huge risk and opportunity, a peril and a temptation, especially when the margin from trading with a balanced position was meagre or inadequate. To be on the wrong side of that market, for whatever reason, could eliminate a firm's margin, capital or credit. Whether he was net long or net short of cotton was at all times the manufacturer's principal concern, and even if the manufacturer got his own position right, sharp movements in cotton prices could lead to supplier or customer default. These were the inescapable hazards of the trade.

Fluctuating raw cotton prices imposed their own cycle on demand and activity within the industry. When prices were high, traders were inhibited in expectation of a fall. When prices began to fall no-one would make commitments until some kind of confidence returned. Such had been the bitter experience in the period 1825-1826 when at the top of a four year boom, raw cotton prices peaked at over 19d a lb to fall to a low of below 6d a lb in 1826.[9] A similar fall took place in 1836. On top of the cotton cycle, there was the general trade cycle: the recurrent phenomenon of exaggerated boom followed by commercial panic, anxiety to turn stocks and debts into cash, inability to discount bills, bank and business failure, frozen credit and widespread reluctance to enter into commitments . At times of panic business was usually at a standstill. Writing in March 1826 Fieldens' London agent could say 'produce of different sorts can now be sold — this was not the case a month ago for then there was no price.' Early in 1826 the Manchester Chamber of Commerce reported that 'many spinners and manufacturers were overstocked with goods for which no market could be found, and that even the goods for which there was a demand were being sold at a ruinous loss.' But at this stage in the industry's history such setbacks, or 'treacherous whirlpools' as they were described, tended to be shortlived; very brisk conditions had returned by 1827.[10]

Given these general circumstances however, and the fact that many new entrants had limited means and relied on debt for finance, it was not surprising that there were many more business failures than successes. 'Three men fall for every one that rises', it was said.[11] John Fielden speaking in 1833 of contemporaries in his youth who had accompanied him to the Manchester market, claimed 'three fourths of the manufacturers at least in the neighbourhood where I reside' were 'reduced to poverty.'[12] Allowing for the exaggeration in these statements, there is no doubt that mortality of firms in this turbulent early period was very high. But while many firms failed as each boom collapsed, new entrants moved in during the next upswing to carry the industry forwards.

Reasons for Fieldens' Success

And yet, in these difficult general circumstances, Fielden Brothers flourished. Can this be explained? Their location in the district that was becoming known as Todmorden was at some disadvantage, 20 miles from Manchester: whether by road, canal, or later railway there was a freight penalty. Understandably the Fieldens became eager supporters of the Manchester and Leeds Railway in the 1830s. The site at Waterside proved, fortuitously, to be a good one, affording flat valley bottom space on which to expand with a strong stream and good fall of water. It was close to the canal and when the railway came this was nearby. And there was plenty of water power elsewhere in the Todmorden district which the Fieldens were enterprising and resourceful in developing; there was also cheap local coal. Housing and provisions were cheaper than in the large towns, wages were lower. The community had little government and rates were low.

The particular line of cotton business Fieldens chose to pursue left them very exposed to competition. As manufacturers of coarse plain grey domestics, shirtings, T cloths and sheetings, from low counts of yarn, they were in the mass rather than speciality market; many others were in the same area of business and prices were fixed in the slaughter-house of the Manchester Exchange. Product differentiation gave no protection from competitive pressures: Fielden's cloth had no brand status. Concern for quality may have distinguished them and enhanced their reputation. That they were so concerned figured in the early correspondence. Thus in November 1819 John told Waterside 'to take care to have them as good as we have sent before as it is of the first importance to keep up the quality.' Again in August 1826 Thomas, writing to Waterside, said 'Everyone complains of our cloth being worse and there is reason.' He argued that they 'must keep the weavers up to their merits.' 'Inferior pieces' were 'no good, they must get them done well and look them carefully over.'[13]

The calibre and business skills of the Partners, the unique attributes of Fielden Brothers, were the main sources of their success. The five, subsequently four, brothers (following Samuel's death in 1822) were a harmonious unity who proved able to manage what became a very large and complex business. They complemented each other. Joshua, the eldest, had been apprenticed as a mechanic in Oldham; he was a capable engineer and his ability, coupled with that of his assistants, to make and improve machinery was of great importance to the business. James Fielden took the Partners' role with the workpeople in the mills on a day to day basis, but otherwise played a more passive role. Thomas, the youngest brother, although closely monitored at first by John, took over the market-man's role in Manchester and Liverpool, selling or marketing the cloth, buying the raw cotton. From the start he had flair and dedication, and emphatic, sometimes emotional views. Always, however, he deferred to John who had been trained in the arts of buying and selling by his father and preceded Thomas in this commercial role. Both of them were described as sharp and hard in business.

The Partners met at Waterside each Monday morning and no doubt all important issues were discussed at these meetings. There is no indication of any serious disagreements or antagonisms in their relationships. It is clear that the deciding voice, from an early stage, was that of John. He was described as the 'master spirit' and the other partners readily accepted the acumen, strong leadership and authority of this quite exceptional man.[14] Apart from his remarkable stamina, drive and ambition, he had a shrewd and confident strategic judgment, in his choice of business areas and his timing of investment and new ventures. His standing was evident not merely within the business but in the locality and before long in commercial and political circles in Lancashire and elsewhere.

The first Partnership agreement of 1816, in John Fielden's hand (as were most of the important business statements during his lifetime, for these were private, confidential and even secret papers), recorded the Partners' exclusive and dedicated commitment to the business, their intention to restrict their drawings, to pay themselves no more than £4 per week. Like other successful businessmen at this period they were for the most part self taught and their lifestyle was rough and frugal: they were tireless and drove themselves hard. John, who was best known, was singularly earnest, careful, painstaking, thorough and persevering in all he did. Contemporaries regarded the brothers as selfish and mean but respected their keen approach, their industry, honesty and integrity. Above all, but especially John and Thomas, they were bold and enterprising in their determination to build and diversify their business. And of course they would all share in the wealth that they created.

At an early stage the brothers developed some key relationships with other businessmen. One was with John Pickersgill, partner in 1812 in Hebden and Pickersgill, Manchester warehousemen in Cheapside, London. In that year Joshua Fielden invited Pickersgill to sell cloth on commission for the Fieldens.[15] This was the beginning of a long and fruitful association, that brought immediate market expertise and subsequently had a significant influence on the development of Fielden Brothers, and the firm's connection and its commercial judgment. Another important early relationship was with Colin Campbell a leading Liverpool cotton broker and eminent Liverpool citizen. Campbell, his younger brother, Daniel, his son John and their successors were to be Fieldens' eyes and ears in the Liverpool markets for most of the nineteenth century. Good trade intelligence and a well informed view of cotton prices, and the markets for yarn and cloth, allied to willingness to take large positions, were among the Partnership's key strengths. They knew, as did their competitors, that profits in cotton manufacturing had more to do with timely and bold buying and selling, than with efficient production, important as that was. John Fielden (and probably by extension his brother Thomas) 'united in a remarkable degree caution and boldness; never allured into speculation in the anxious hope of acquiring sudden riches, he seldom missed a favourable opportunity of profiting by the state of the market.' Perhaps of him it was said, as of Alexander Brown, that 'he kept himself informed of conditions wherever he traded, and armed with the facts he would buy, sell, or hold on, as the situation seemed to demand.' The shrewd and far-sighted John, it was said, had a wonderful sense of markets and was rarely at fault.[16]

Strong as the Partnership was, as the business developed it needed competent well-motivated managers. If they were members of the family, so much the better so far as the Fieldens were concerned, and the Partners, at various times, gave employment to relatives in a senior capacity so long as they proved their worth: Edmund Wrigley, his son Thomas Wrigley, Thomas Fielden Uttley, illegitimate son of Samuel Fielden, were examples. But others grew within the business: John Holt, manager at Waterside, was one, John Haigh another, both starting as young men in the mill. The Factory Inspectors, who did not usually single out individual managers, described Holt as 'a highly intelligent manager'; Haigh was 'a person of superior ability and intelligence, intimately acquainted with cotton spinning.' The Partners gave men such as these responsibility and authority and rewarded them well, in particular by giving them bonuses, commissions or profit participation.[17] There is no doubt too that Fieldens employed some gifted mechanics in the early years, not least John Lord and his seven sons, who in 1835, with Fielden financial help, left to set up their own successful engineering business.

The Fieldens had a stable, reliable, loyal, and some would say, deferential and docile workforce. Succeeding generations of the same family tended to work in their mills. Of course, in Todmorden at the time, they had factory labour almost at their command; there were few other employers and if a person got out of work at Waterside or the outmills, it would not be easy to find a job elsewhere. Dependence for work and livelihood was strengthened by the fact that many workpeople were living in cottages which the Partners or the concern had acquired; at Lumbutts, for instance, rents were deducted from wages for many of those working there. Work at the time dominated peoples lives.

A Carding Room in the 1830s. The successive processes of carding, drawing and roving which transformed laps of cotton into thick loose thread to be spun on mules or throstles, were carried out at all the Fielden spinning mills. Typically the operatives were girls or young women, earning wages of 7 to 9 shillings a week in the mid-nineteenth century.

Working conditions and discipline in Fielden mills were hard, as anywhere else; good order, regularity and punctuality were insisted upon. With limited competition for labour in a smallish isolated manufacturing community, at least in the early and mid-nineteenth century, Todmorden acquired and retained a reputation as a district of low wages. Fieldens had no wish to change the situation. When taunted with paying low wages for long hours, John Fielden is quoted as saying 'they paid the standard prices that others did for the work their hands turned off.' On another occasion their policy was described as being to pay 'the ordinary wages of the district.'[18] If anything the concern followed others in raising or lowering wages and, from time to time, enquired what other people were paying before charging their own rates. They became concerned if they were losing people who moved for higher wages and no doubt used their local influence to check such competition. Thus later in the century, Fieldens were to write to one local competitor, Firth and Howarth, complaining that their manager 'had been bidding for some of our workpeople inducing them to leave our employment.' They warned the party concerned and threatened retaliation.[19] As with other cotton manufacturers, a high proportion of the workforce were children, as the law permitted, or girls and young women: such a profile was maintained as marriage and child-bearing created turnover among the young women, and as young men left for other occupations when Fieldens could not advance them. Given generally poor margins on plain cloth, low labour cost was crucially important. There is some indication that Fielden Brothers' labour costs were lower than across the industry, as will be seen, and this was probably due as much to lower wages as to higher productivity.

Periods of short time working apart, and earnings fell when short-time was worked, Fieldens worked slightly shorter hours than the rest of the industry. John Fielden recalled that in the first mill, seventy-one hours weekly were being worked, at a time when seventy-two or more were the norm elsewhere. Charles Wing, a sympathetic visitor in 1836, noted a sixty-seven and a half hour week compared with sixty-nine hours in most mills; in 1844-46 Waterside was still working one hundred and thirty-five hours each twelve days, or allowing for Saturdays, virtually a twelve hour day. After the Ten Hours Act in 1847 hours were reduced to fifty-eight weekly, (five days from 6am to 5.30pm and Saturday 6am to 3.30pm with one and a half hours meal-breaks) while others in Lancashire worked sixty hours as the new law permitted.[20]

What distinguished the Fieldens as employers when they were established and successful (and could afford it) was their reluctance to cut wages when trade was bad, or to close their mills and put people out of work. In part this was a business view: there was no point in reducing wages and lowering prices to stimulate an artificial demand when work become scarce. The market would only stock up on cheap goods that would come back later and postpone its return to a healthy state. Rather, as John Fielden was to say, 'No-one can deny that it would be much better to reduce the quantity of work when there is not a demand to take off what is produced; and instead of reducing wages at such periods, the very opposite course should be pursued.'[21] But there was a more fundamental aspect. To the Fieldens the employer had a responsibility to maintain the livelihood of his workpeople, to give them 'constant work' and the means of subsistence however difficult times were. Thus their wealth and capital was a shield which protected their workpeople from many of the fluctuations in the market. Although they were quick to resort to short-time working, this was a policy the business followed on many occasions, at some commercial risk, at times when other mills were cutting wages or laying off their hands. As a grateful weaver wrote to John Fielden, 'we know by experience a reduction in wages will be the last thing you will resort to, your anxious desire being to see a well paid, well fed and happy people.' Such a policy was partly good commercial sense: as a contemporary Lancashire millowner, Henry Ashworth, said, 'the manufacturer had every inducement to keep skilled hands at a certain loss rather than let them be scattered. You cannot at any time gather together from an unselected mass of people that particular quality of skill that gives you excellence and reputation in the market.'[22] John Fielden put it another way. 'Good masters', he said, 'keep their hands together and wait for better times.'[23] But expediency apart, this policy was humanitarian responsibility, and unusual, given the circumstances of the time. Samuel Fielden was to call it 'a social and religious duty,' which was calculated to avoid 'that most difficult and dangerous of all questions, the relative rights of capital and labour,' or putting it another way, conflict and alienation.[24]

The Fielden paternal, almost patriarchal, style was reflected in other practices. As the business grew older, those who had spent their lives working for it were given modest pensions in their old age. Although the Partners individually and the Partnership owned many cottages near their mills, there was only a limited attempt to provide model or improved housing in the way that many successful Lancashire and Yorkshire millowners did. But the business went beyond what the law required in providing education, starting a factory school as early as 1827. The partners were concerned about safety and their genuine distress came through whenever serious accidents occurred. A partner was always present when the workforce was paid; any employee could take a grievance to a partner and was encouraged to do so; no one was dismissed except with a partner's agreement; in the early years the partners dealt with all applications for work.

The Fieldens, of course, were known throughout their business. For many years they lived and worked with their hands; they were visible, accessible, approachable, sympathising and friendly; they would know many of their workpeople by name. There were no trade unions, nor did the Fieldens play any part in organisations of cotton masters. There were seldom any differences between them and their workpeople; if any arose they would be settled directly. There were no recorded strikes or turnouts at Fielden mills, and few in Todmorden, in sharp contrast to the experience of other Lancashire mill-towns. Instead it was said of their relations with their workpeople, that there was a strong feeling of 'content and familiarity.' John Fielden could say, 'The interests of the employers and employed, were identical. It was the duty of every Master, to take care as far as he possibly could, that his hands were well-fed, well-sheltered, and well-clothed for moderate labour; and it was the duty of the workpeople to be diligent and prudent, and serve their Masters faithfully;' or, as Samuel Fielden put it later, there need be no conflict of interest between the 'employer who had risked his fortune in manufacture' and 'those upon whose industry and fidelity such fortunes depend.'[25] The well-being of the workpeople was essential to the firm's prosperity. Most Fielden employees were long serving, hardworking and committed, proud and grateful. When the plug-drawing mob came to Waterside in August 1842 John Fielden could say 'the arms of my people are protection': if his people would not preserve the mills, he would never appeal to the magistrates or the militia, and in the event he had no need. Industrial relations in the Fielden mills were personal relations and in these respects the firm was ahead of many in the industry, a condition which undoubtedly contributed to the Partnership's success.

All these considerations helped Fielden Brothers rise to prominence. But a fortuitous event seems to have figured in family recollections of how the business gained a significant early advantage. In 1812 their Manchester agent failed and they were left with a large stock of unsold cloth that had been drawn against. The market was unfavourable and a decision was taken to hold for better prices, difficult as that course was, given the shortage of cash and credit. The war of 1812 between England and the United States intervened. Cotton prices rose sharply, doubling between 1812 and 1814; cloth prices followed to a lesser extent. Joshua Fielden, describing the event in 1875, said 'our goods went up to fabulous prices' and this 'became the foundation of the firm.'[26]

It has to be inferred that the profit from stock appreciation (perhaps as much as £5,000) at this time gave the firm freedom from debt and a significant — for the period — capital. They seem to have traded profitably in the subsequent years: a Partnership document in 1819 refers to profits of £8,000 per year.[27] The succeeding years through the early 1820s saw a strong boom in Lancashire in which good profits could be made. Thus almost from the earliest years of the Partnership it is reasonable to suppose there was adequate capital to sustain and develop the business. That remained their situation subsequently, except for those few occasions when, whatever the Partnership assets, the business became short of cash.

A strong financial position was an enormous advantage. The firm's credit was good; it was seen as a reliable supplier or customer and people had no doubts about doing business with Fielden Brothers. The business could grow from its own cashflow, both by enlarging its mills and extending its machinery, and by acquiring other mills, that for whatever reason were available cheaply. Given funds, and a confident view, the business could buy new or second hand machinery cheaply in periods of bad trade. In particular, when the time came, it could afford to introduce steam-power and in due course power-loom weaving, both expensive investments. It could keep abreast of changing technology by replacing or modifying old-fashioned machines, or by upgrading its

31

steam engines. Generally, the business expanded its fixed assets in a well timed way — when trade was bad and poised to recover — and at low cost. Fieldens' buildings and machinery probably cost less in relation to capacity than those of their competitors: they had a cheap asset base. When trade boomed, they were not struggling to enlarge capacity, but had mills and machinery in place.

Adequate financial resources enabled the business to live through periods of falling prices and bad trade. As Thomas Fielden put it on one occasion, 'its no use to go on selling or rather giving our property away. Nobody of sound mind will do so that can hold.'[28] The Fieldens could usually afford to hold. In periods of poor trade it was their practice to avoid slashing margins by reducing prices, but rather to wait for margins to come back, and meanwhile 'weave for stock', keeping the workforce together and building inventory that would appreciate in value subsequently. 'Weaving for stock' remained a familiar expression throughout Fieldens' history. Their strong financial position enabled them to trade unprofitably for quite long periods, and at times take large write-downs, bad debts, and losses. Fieldens had the funds to build stocks of raw cotton if their view of the market warranted this. Most significantly, adequate funds were to enable the business to avoid the Manchester market, the slaughter-house, for the sale of its cloth. Thus while some cloth sales were always to be made in Manchester, Fieldens from an early period could become merchants themselves and secure a higher margin by consigning a large proportion of their goods abroad, albeit assuming large risks and waiting long periods for the proceeds, but able to employ their capital for this purpose.

These, then, are some of the reasons why Fielden Brothers succeeded in the period following 1815, rose to prominence by 1832 and flourished subsequently. That success was reflected in physical expansion of the spinning and weaving activity in Todmorden, and associated marketing activity.

Expansion in Todmorden

In 1811 the Fieldens had two small spinning mills producing warp and weft for putting out to some hundreds of hand-loom weavers who worked for them. With their enhanced capital after 1812, and trading profits of about £8,000 yearly, the enterprise appears to have grown rapidly by enlarging its spinning capacity, partly at Waterside where the first mill was extended, and partly by acquiring other small water-powered mills in the locality as these became empty and available, whether through the death, or business failure of the previous owners. Such outmills were bought cheaply, often at a fraction of their original cost, but there were other reasons for buying them. They all had a local workforce that was not available at Waterside. At this early period factory labour was still predominantly drawn from the hillside farms and there could well have been recruitment problems in the valley bottom. A town was beginning to develop where the Walsden valley joined the so-called Burnley valley, to form a main Calder valley leading towards Halifax, but not many people lived there. Moreover, the outmills had water power while Waterside had reached its limits in this regard. They gave a quick expansion of capacity. This was an opportunistic and a practical policy, right at the time, although in later years the resulting mill structure was to prove inefficient.

By 1819 four additional 'outmills' had been acquired: Causeway, Stoneswood, Smithyholme and Waterstalls. These could be enlarged and additional machinery introduced while their power sources could be enhanced by building dams and by introducing small steam engines. Causeway, on Lumbutts Clough, although occupied by the Fieldens from 1812, was bought in 1815 for £1,580.[29] Samuel's mill at Lumbutts, now rented by the Partnership, was higher up on the same stream. To supply these two mills the Fieldens were later to invest in an elaborate series of dams that linked up with the Rochdale Canal Company dam system on Gaddings Moor. A new road to give improved access to Lumbutts was also built. Stoneswood Mill in the tributary Dulesgate valley had originally been built to spin weft and warp by local farmer-weavers, Charles Barker, James Stansfield and Luke Hamer who then enlarged their putting-out operation and started a small hand-loom factory. When one of the partners died they gave up in 1815 and the mill stood empty until bought by the Fieldens in 1818. Smithyholme Mill, not far from Waterside, had been built by a local landowner, James Hardman, and let to the Law Brothers, two spinning entrepreneurs. Fieldens were able to buy the mill for £2,300 (including farm land and cottages) in 1819. When the Law brothers moved to a new and larger mill, Fieldens enlarged Smithyholme for their own use, adding a steam engine and manager's house.[30] Without exception the outmills were

Stoneswood Mill, an early water-powered spinning mill which, having stood empty for three years, was bought cheaply by Joshua Fielden in 1818. Steam power was introduced and the mill re-equipped for cotton preparation, throstle spinning and warping. It remained a Fielden mill, employing fifty to sixty people and working 5,000 or so spindles, until 1889 when it was sold. Joshua Fielden and his heirs also owned cottage property close by. The mill has remained in use to the present day

Smithyholme Mill, probably built about 1805 for James Hardman, local landowner and surgeon, it was occupied for cotton spinning by the Law brothers who moved to their own larger mill in Walsden in 1819. John Fielden then bought the mill and adjacent property for £2,300. A manager's house was built and a small steam engine installed and the Partnership equipped the mill for cotton preparation and throstle spinning for warp. There were 3,000 spindles and fifty employees in 1856, chiefly children and young women. Fielden's sold the mill in 1873, but it remained in use and most recently has been converted into a retirement home for the elderly.

bought by individual Partners — Joshua and John, in practice — who then received rent at 7 per cent of agreed value from the Partnership. Machinery in the mill would usually belong to the Partnership; exceptionally it might belong to an individual Partner.

The main expansion took place at Waterside. Bit by bit the early small mill was extended and new buildings added to house particular processes or functions. At the formation of the first Partnership in 1816 there were about forty workpeople. Steam power was introduced progressively according to need. It was first mentioned in May 1818 when John Fielden advised Thomas, in Manchester, that the mill had closed because the crank of the steam engine had broken; Stoneswood and the other mills were working at night until the repairs were completed.[31] Other mentions in correspondence in the early 1820s indicate a single steam engine at that time. In 1824 the Partnership spent £1,700 on a new 60 HP steam engine and boilers supplied by Richard Ormerod of Manchester, the engine house, chimney and other works being put up by local builders.[32] But the most important initiative was the decision to introduce power-loom weaving. By the 1820s the power-loom had been improved to the extent that it was relatively trouble free, although restricted to the production of plain calico. Fieldens proceeded cautiously: in January 1822 they were purchasing a few looms from Roberts Hill and Co. and impatient to get them started, saying they had hands waiting for the looms.[33] As their confidence grew they decided to push ahead more rapidly; they could afford to do so and no doubt they realised that the future lay in this direction. John Fielden's concern for the plight of the hand-loom weavers, including his own, is somewhat at variance with the Partnership's determination to take advantage of the opportunities that power-loom weaving afforded. And if machine-making in Lancashire was in its infancy then thrusting businesses like the Fieldens would build their own looms which they did in the late 1820s; the Ashtons of Hyde who had a foundry and a mechanics shop were doing the same at the time. Already by 1824 the first power-loom shed was being built at Waterside. Throughout this period, as their spinning capacity grew, Fieldens were also employing more hand-loom weavers and improving their facilities to put out warp and weft, and take-in pieces, over an enlarged spread of operations; they had weavers all over the upper Calder valley including some as far away as Shibden, near Halifax. All the hand-woven pieces were brought to Waterside to be 'looked over' and packed for loading on canal boats. The wages paid for weaving a piece held up until the mid 1820s but fell drastically thereafter. Fieldens had to follow the market as these wages came down and attempts led by John Fielden in April 1826 to organise minimum wages among competing manufacturers (i.e. putters-out) came to nothing.[34]

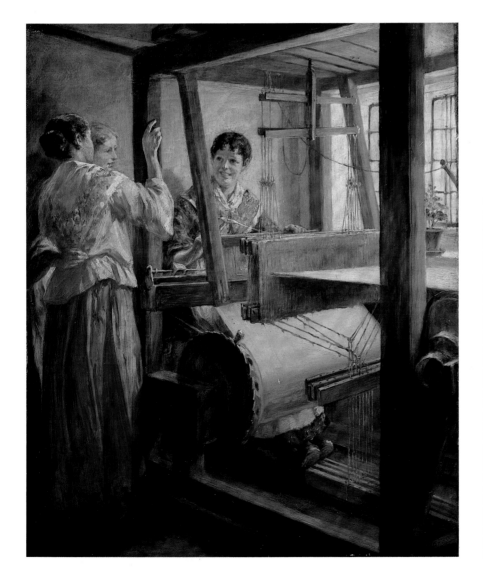

Hand-Loom Weavers: from a painting by A.W. Bayes of Lumbutts. Bayes, who was born in 1832, would have been familiar with such a scene as he depicts; in 1851, for instance, there were still a score or more hand-loom weavers in cottages around Lumbutts. Nonetheless the cheerful faces and youth of the participants can hardly have been representative of hand-loom weaving at the time or during its decline in the 1820s and 1830s. Fieldens probably employed 1,500 hand-loom weavers in the early 1830s but the numbers rapidly diminished as their power-loom capacity was enlarged. John Fielden campaigned strenuously for government to alleviate their plight but his business, and many others like it, were the main agents competing to destroy the home-weaver's livelihood. In February 1861, the last hand-loom weavers in Fielden employment, numbering thirty-nine, were given pensions of 2 shillings per week.

The Todmorden Business in 1832

The first account of the Partnership's manufacturing assets that survives is that of 30th June 1832. The Machinery Valuation at that date provides a detailed description of the spinning and weaving business in Todmorden as it stood at the end of the first phase of expansion. Particulars are also given of the working capital, and of the other properties in Todmorden, whether owned by the Partnership or individually. Tables I and II summarise the value of buildings and machinery both at Waterside and at the outmills. Table III summarises the total value of Todmorden assets at this time.

A clear picture emerges. The hand-loom weaving activity had not diminished and the value of work in progress with hand-loom weavers, some £1,650, suggests the Partnership was employing about 1,000-1,500 weavers, given the value of a woven piece. This figure is consistent with John Fielden's statement in 1835 that his firm's weavers produced 2,000 to 3,000 hand-loom pieces per week.[35] But the hand-loom capability was supplemented by the new Waterside power-loom weaving shed in course of completion: there were 684 power-looms in June 1832, but by 1835 the number had grown to 810 looms employing 405 weavers.[36]

The weaving business was supplied with weft and warps from spinning capacity at Waterside and at the five outmills. Each of the outmills was equipped to work from raw cotton, engaging in the preparatory processes (cleaning, carding, drawing, roving), but was then either specialised to weft (mules) or to warp (throstles) while Waterside had both types of spinning machinery. The age and provenance of the

Table I: Fielden Brothers: Waterside Spinning and Weaving 1832.

Department	Machinery	Power	Valuation Buildings/ Power	Machinery
Cotton Preparation and Spinning	Scutching, Carding Engines, Slubbing and Roving Frames. 114 Throstles/14,448 spindles at 4/- each 20 Mules/4,788 spindles at 2/- each 2 Self-Acting Mules/504 spindles at 8/- each Total: 19,740 spindles	5HP Water 3 Steam Engines (14,16,30 HP)	£10,800 Includes ancillary	£12,505
Weaving	684 looms at £10 54 looms making at £8	Steam Engine (60 HP)	£10,000	£9,480
Ancillary	Warehouses, counting house, workshops, foundry, taking-in rooms, school room, timber yard, stables etc.		Included above	
Gas Works			Included above	£1,500
			£20,800	£23,485

Source: WYAS C353/132 Machinery Valuation

Table II: Fielden Brothers: Outmills 1832.

Mill/Owner	Machinery	Power	Valuation Buildings/ Power	Machinery
Dobroyd/Partners	Cotton Preparation 1,512 mule spindles at 2/3 each	1.5 HP Water 1 Steam Engine	£950	£489
Lumbutts/Joshua	Cotton Preparation 20 mules/4,944 spindles at 1/6 each	7 HP Water	£2,700	£1,142
Causeway/John	Cotton Preparation 18 mules/5,208 spindles at 1/6 each	6 HP Water	£2,400	£1,030
Stoneswood/Joshua	Cotton Preparation 42 throstles/5,148 spindles at 4/- each	Water Wheel 2 Steam Engines	£3,000	£1,777
Smithyholme/John	Cotton Preparation 16 throstles/2,016 spindles at 6/- each	3.5 HP Water 1 Steam Engine	£1,770	£1,335
Waterstalls/John	Not in use	—	£500	—
	Total Spindles in all Mills: 19,308	—	**£11,320**	**£5,773**

Source: WYAS C353/132 Machinery Valuation

mules and throstles is indicated by their valuation. The range is considerable with the most modern equipment, two self-acting mules at Waterside, costed at 8s per spindle compared with old mules valued at 1s 6d per spindle. Not all the mills had steam-power; dams, goits or man-made water-courses, and waterfalls are significant elements in the valuation of the buildings.

Waterside itself was already a labyrinth of buildings; apart from cotton preparation rooms, spinning and weaving rooms or sheds, there were many attics, stores, warehouses and workshops described in the inventory. The mill had become the principal taking-in shop for the work of the hand-loom weavers. It was also, and importantly, a workshop that supported the spinning and weaving operations. Thus the foundry and mechanics workshop had the capacity to make looms and no doubt improve and maintain all kinds of machinery and mill work. The extraordinary self-sufficiency of the business is evident in the fact that it was making its own pickers, reeds, healds and shuttles. This is not to deny that Fieldens gave business to an increasing number of tradesmen in the growing town — engineers, builders, millwrights, carpenters, carters as well as suppliers of coal and other materials. Some of these local suppliers, (Wilson, the bobbin maker who, starting in 1823, built up an international business, being the best example), received not merely business support but timely loans from the Fieldens. For specialised equipment — steam-engines, boilers, mules and throstles — the Partnership had, at the time, to look outside Todmorden. Gas was made at Waterside, at first in 1827 to light the factory, but subsequently to supply on commercial terms, cottages, public houses, chapels and the like.

Table III: Fielden Brothers — Todmorden Assets 1832

	£
Waterside Spinning and Weaving	44,285
Outmills	17,093
Stocks of Materials, Finished Goods including Work in Progress	36,552
Other Properties	25,490
Other Assets (Debtors, Turnpike Roads, Cash etc.)	14,930
Less: Balance of Trade Debtors less Creditors	(15,617)
Less: Owing on properties	(7,336)
Less: Properties individually owned	(22,658)
Joint Partnership Assets in Todmorden	**£92,739**

Source: WYAS C353/132 Machinery Valuation

Working assets, as distinct from buildings and machinery, were considerable. The inventory was meticulous; it seems as if every tool, every nail, was recorded. Spares, materials, raw cotton, stocks of weft and warps, hand and power-loom pieces in warehouse, work in progress in the mills and materials in the possession of hand-loom weavers are all identified. A total value of £36,552 is given to these inventories, of which £24,553 was piece goods stock, and £5,033 raw cotton, about two weeks supply. Notable in 1832 was the use of suppliers credit with trade creditors exceeding debtors by £15,617. That this was not the normal position is suggested by the fact that on 1 January 1836 and 1 January 1837 debtors exceeded creditors by £12,428 and £7,162 respectively Most probably the largest debtor/creditor entries relate to sums owing either way between Todmorden, and the Manchester operation, which maintained separate accounts.

Finally there were the other properties in and around Todmorden in Partnership or individual ownership by 1832. Here, there were the homes of the Partners (Dawson Weir, Waterside House and Wellfield); various farms that had been acquired, whether as investments, to protect water supplies or for sentimental reasons; and worker's cottages adjacent to or nearby the mills. It was John Fielden in particular, and to a lesser extent Joshua, who sought to place part of his individual wealth in local property or in the outmills which were then let to the Partnership.

What was described in 1832 was a formidable, significant and highly competitive capacity. It was in place when the cotton trade was again leaping forward and would yield exceptional profits in the years that followed.

Commercial Activities

Important as the mills in Todmorden were, as the manufacturing operation, the business was also about buying cotton and selling cloth. In its early period this was accomplished by the weekly visit to

Manchester with horse and cart carrying woven pieces and at times yarn or warps for sale, and returning with bags of cotton bought from dealers there. For how long the family walked is not recorded but it was later said of John 'when he got a horse it made him a man, when he got a gig it made him a king.'[37] The early Manchester transactions may have been for cash; alternatively bills of exchange may have been used on both sides, but more particularly on the cotton purchase side. Thus in February 1811 the firm bought six bags of cotton from Boulton and Ramsden, weighing a total of 1862 lbs, costing £108.12s.4d; they paid on a two-months bill.[38] Probably this remained the pattern of Joshua Fielden and Sons' commercial activities until the first Partnership was formed. In these early years, it was John Fielden who involved himself most closely in the commercial side: he was the 'market-man', spending much of his time in Manchester, and in Liverpool, as the cotton market began to develop there. The all important commercial activities — getting the best prices for the cloth, holding off the market or selling forward, buying cotton keenly, waiting to buy, and buying cotton for stock — were the responsibility of John Fielden. Although he kept his brothers informed, he seems always to have been in control, giving detailed instructions by letter when he was not in Manchester or Liverpool.

Like other Lancashire manufacturers of cotton cloth Fieldens needed representation in London as well as Manchester. In 1812, they had approached Hebden Brothers and Pickersgill of Cheapside, in the City,

Waterside Mill: this photograph, although taken in the 1860s, shows the mill as it must have looked in 1832. The first small mill built in 1804 adjacent to Laneside cottages can be clearly distinguished as well as subsequent extensions to accommodate throstle and mule spinning and all stages of cotton preparation; the foundry lay behind the tall buildings while the Mechanics shop was the low building in front; the first power-loom weaving-shed with 810 looms in 1835 lay beyond these buildings on the left. Waterside House to the right of the photograph, was added to the cottages as the residence of Joshua Fielden, the oldest Partner, and his family. The buildings across the road at right angles to the mill, were the counting-house, warehousing and from 1827 the Factory School: these buildings are still there. About 840 persons worked at Waterside in the mid 1830s.

Waterside, and the out-mills, gave Fieldens a significant capacity and made them one of the largest combined spinning and weaving businesses in the industry at the time.

to act as their agent. Hebden and Pickersgill (John Pickersgill was the principal at that time) described themselves as Manchester Warehousemen; they were among a large number of Cheapside merchants stocking and dealing in cotton cloth to the domestic and continental markets. The letter of instruction from Todmorden in May 1812 asks them to sell 'four or five hundred pieces per week on commission.' On 12th June the first 300 pieces were consigned. Hebden Brothers and Pickersgill reported on 20 June saying 'every exertion has been made to sell the calicoes but hitherto without success, for such is the state of the market that no quantity can be pushed without making a sacrifice, such as we fear you would not approve, instead of an advance of sixpence, or more, as you expected.' They go on 'of this you may rely, that we shall on no occasion make sales to cover our advances by sacrificing your goods, at the same time we trust you will not tie us so close as to prevent sales when a small deviation from your instructions would effect them.' Business at the time was slow, less brisk in London than in Manchester, although both markets were being influenced by deteriorating relations between Britain and the United States. A year later, in August 1813, London was complaining about 'the manner of bleaching and the system of sending goods here.' Some cloths 'have been so badly got up, our friends have refused them.' Communications by letter were slow and there were frequent requests from London for meetings to discuss the state of the market and the discretion that was to be exercised. The Fielden-Pickersgill association did not have an easy start, but in December 1817 Pickersgill was sending oysters to Todmorden by coach, as a Christmas gift. Relations with John Fielden by then were warm and personal. In August 1818, 461 pieces of cloth were sold for £489-8s less commission of 5 per cent.[39]

As the Fielden business grew after 1812, with enlarged spinning capacity supplying growing numbers of hand-loom weavers, and subsequently the power- looms at Waterside, so the scale of commercial involvement increased. Like other growing firms, instead of visiting Manchester weekly and transacting business from an inn, the Partners opened a small warehouse in the Manchester commercial district, in their case at 5 Peel Street. Thomas, the youngest of the brothers, began to share with John the market-man's role, selling the yarn, warps and cloth and buying the cotton. Thomas lived close to the warehouse, in Great Ducie Street, Hunts Bank, but divided his time between Manchester, Todmorden and Liverpool. Apart from his weekly visits to Todmorden, Thomas seems to have written to his brothers almost daily, setting out market intelligence and gossip, his opinions and actions, instructions for delivery of woven pieces and supplies of cotton, family news and movements and his views generally. Thomas took care of the Partnership's banking arrangements with Cunliffe Brookes Bank in Manchester. He also purchased in Manchester or Liverpool any materials the Todmorden factories might need, whether this was picker hides, seal oil, paint, tallow for size and candles, wire, screws, lead pipe, hinges and so on. At some stage Thomas had assistance in the Peel Street office but in the early stages this was a modest affair. A letter to John in August 1814 tells him that in Thomas's absence he

Peel Street. When their Manchester agent failed in 1812 Fieldens took their own warehouse in what was then the commercial district close to Market Street and the Exchange. Peel Street, and other premises in Cannon Street nearby, remained the base for the commercial operations supervised by John and Thomas Fielden. Cloth pieces were held here and sold to the Manchester trade or consigned overseas: if they had to be finished they would be moved to the Bowker Bank print works in nearby Crumpsall. In the 1850s the Partnership bought more modern premises in Norfolk Street, close to the new Royal Exchange.

would find the key to the warehouse with Jepson's, a neighbour.[40] By 1819 Fieldens had taken a second and larger warehouse nearby at 9 Cannon Street. John, meanwhile, continued to make frequent visits to Manchester; it was probably only by the late 1820s that Thomas assumed full responsibility for the commercial role.

During this early period, movement of woven cloth to Manchester or Liverpool was by canal and likewise transport of cotton from Liverpool. James Veevers was the canal contractor whom Fieldens generally used, maintaining warehouses in Todmorden, Manchester and Liverpool and providing fast regular boats along the Rochdale Canal and on to Liverpool. Ten hours was the normal journey to Manchester. But these services were not without interruptions. Thomas complained of delays due to frost in March 1814, and due to prolonged drought in April 1826. The canal was reported closed in September 1837 with a fortnight's rain being required before it could be opened again. At times like these, movement of goods fell back on the road carrier, where Wilson and Brooks, among others, provided a service from Manchester. Uncertainties and delays in carriage between Todmorden and Manchester made it necessary to hold piece-goods stock in Manchester, and raw cotton stocks at the mills or with the carriers. From time to time individual mills closed for lack of cotton. The brothers themselves, of course, travelled by coach or by gig. By the 1820s the *Perseverance* was providing a daily coach service to and from Manchester while on market day, Tuesday, a market coach left Todmorden at 5a.m.

A regular item sent from Manchester to Todmorden by coach was gold coin or bank notes. The proceeds of sales of cloth, including bills that were held to maturity or sold or discounted, were banked with the Manchester bank, Cunliffe Brookes. In 1812 Fieldens appear to have been paying their workforce by 'notes of hand' (or shop notes as they were sometimes called) which were accepted by local tradesmen as payment for goods and endorsed as they were spent: these notes were then redeemed for bills of exchange or for sovereigns at Waterside.[41] But this practice, widespread as it was at the time, did not continue; the hand-loom weavers were being paid in sovereigns in 1822 and probably the workforce generally. Thus, for example, in July 1822 John Fielden requested £500 in sovereigns from Manchester to pay the weavers at Frieldhurst; on 29th March 1826 Thomas sent £300 in sovereigns, £30 in silver and £30 in bank notes by coach to Todmorden; on 28th April he sent £200 in Bank notes from Cunliffes and on 29th August £200 in sovereigns.[42] The emphasis on gold may have reflected John Fielden's distrust of paper money; no risk seems to have been attached to sending cash by coach. Of course, as the scale of operations in Todmorden grew, so did the cash needed to pay wages (these were paid fortnightly) and the need to balance the collections in Manchester in respect of local sales and the irregular remittances from abroad, with the cash sent by coach to Todmorden or the drafts against cotton and other supplies. This commercial task was managed in Manchester: in effect the Manchester office managed the sales ledger and the cotton purchase ledger. No records of the early years survive, but judging by the position in 1832 and subsequently, the Partnership seems to have made only limited use of supplier's credit. There is no record of loans or advances from banks in the early years.

A strong connection with the rapidly developing Liverpool cotton market was essential to an ambitious manufacturing concern. Apart from their visits, the Brothers engaged two prominent Liverpool cotton brokers to inspect and select and buy, to instructions, the particular grades and qualities they required and to provide them with the intelligence and advice that would provide the basis for a sound buying policy. Thus Godfrey Barnsley and Colin Campbell both served Fielden Brothers as an important client in this early period. Barnsley was writing to the Brothers daily in 1814. He seems to have dropped out later but the association with Colin Campbell and his family, as has already been noted, was to prove a long and fruitful one.

The Partnership had no explicit buying policy. It is most likely that there was a willingness to take a bold view from time to time, and presumably successfully. Thus there would be many times when they would not immediately cover sales of cloth with cotton purchases, but would wait for prices to fall. If they expected prices to rise they would buy cotton for stock. Writing to Fieldens in March 1826, John Pickersgill gave his advice: 'was I a manufacturer and spinner and I could see a fair prospect of disposing of goods after they were made, I certainly should purchase cotton without loss of time. Given the low price as it is the foreigners are not such fools as to send cotton to be sold for nothing.' No doubt the Fieldens acted on that kind of opinion. As the leader of the Partnership, and the bolder spirit, it would be John Fielden who took these decisions, critically important as they were. In May 1814, on the advice of Barnsley, John went to Liverpool 'to buy as much as wanted,' since Manchester dealers were asking excessive prices. He needed cheap cotton to make a margin on the prices being bid for cloth. In October 1814, and again in December 1814, John, writing from Liverpool, describes his intention to stay and wait a few more days for lower prices and for the right qualities from ships that were expected

The Old Manchester Exchange, built in 1809; John and Thomas Fielden were both members in 1819 and the Partnership would sell much of its grey cloth to merchants on the Exchange. But John Fielden, with others, regarded the Exchange as a 'slaughter house' where for much of the time competing weak sellers on an over-supplied market were exploited by the merchants, and prices and margins were depressed. Rather than 'put money into the pockets of the Jews,' as John Fielden put it, Fielden Brothers began to merchant much of their cloth to overseas markets themselves, using their capital for the purpose; there were large risks in such business but the profits made by the Partnership in the 1820s and 1830s suggest it was very successful.

to arrive. Thomas, as he assumed the responsibility, would also frequently wait in Liverpool for several days for the market to fall or a ship to arrive with new offerings. In September 1820, John writes of his intention to visit Liverpool where 'if cotton be low and flat and you have any money to spare as I expect you will now that goods sell so well, we can perhaps pay a little attention to that article with a view to meet our expenses.'[43]

Sales and Marketing

What of selling the cloth? Certainly at an early stage sales were being made through commission merchants. As the business grew in confidence, and as an organised cloth market developed in Manchester, sales were being made on an outright basis to merchants, whether for immediate or forward delivery. Thus on 5th September 1817, a typical market day, 'white supers' were sold to S. Thorp and Sons, London (to be forwarded from Manchester by Pickford's boat); grey No. 4s were offered to Thomas Potter but refused; and Nash and Mitton paid 17/6 for 2nd 74s, a high price which the buyer agreed because Fielden cloth 'finished very well.' Their orders were to be 'got up in the best manner.'[44] The Brothers were selling grey hand-loom cloth at this period, to a variable specification as to widths and counts, although predominantly of the grades described as Supers 70s and 74s. Fustian was made and sold occasionally. Warps (and yarn) were probably only sold when more were being produced than the weaving operations required. Immediate discretion whether to make sales and on what scale gradually passed from John to Thomas but significant policy questions would be discussed by the brothers and approved by John. Thus John instructed Thomas in September 1817, 'you will act as you think for the best in accepting any offer you may have made for any goods that we have.'[45]

This kind of discretion was exercised on a day-to-day basis: that is, whether to sell forward, sell hand-to-mouth or hold off and wait. In taking these decisions the Partners sought the best advice available to them. Often they turned to John Pickersgill, still their London agent, but becoming more than a customer, rather a trusted friend and associate. As early as August 1820, John Fielden was telling Thomas to 'get Pickersgill's opinion before we sell.'[46] And again, in this early period, when difficult market conditions persisted, the firm reduced its sales and resorted to short-time or weaving for stock. Thus in July 1822 John told Thomas, 'I do not think it would be wise to force the sale at present. Let us grin and abide and hope for more prosperous and profitable adventures in the future.'[47]

The significant policy initiative taken by the Partnership about 1820 was to go round the Manchester merchants and sell part of their output directly to merchants or agents in markets overseas, not to firm priced orders, but on a consignment basis, that is, to be sold at the best price attainable on arrival. Leaving aside the question of feasibility, the incentive to do this was two-fold. On the one hand, by consigning cloth abroad, the firm could avoid those periods when trade was at a standstill in Manchester because of a crisis of confidence or inadequate margins.

Thus in 1826 Thomas Fielden wrote, 'unless things mend we have no prospects. All the manufacturers say they are worse and worse. There is no chance of a sale at present: however disposed I may be to sell I cannot find buyers.' In September of that year there were over 15,000 pieces in hand at Waterside.[48] Or as the *Manchester Gazette* in 1829 put it , 'you can sell neither cloth nor twist at any price that will cover your expenses, you cannot make profits; you cannot save yourselves from loss. Your eyes are wandering over the map of the world for new markets.'[48] More generally, and given the tight margins prevailing on sales in Manchester, a direct exporter could augment its margin by taking for itself the merchant's profit, albeit also assuming the merchant's costs and the merchant's risk. John Fielden could say in 1834, 'manufacturers have had to add to their own business that of a merchant with a view to make out of both the profit they had on manufacturing only.'[50] In valuing goods consigned abroad, 10 per cent above Manchester market prices was expected, or 20 per cent for shipments to the West Coast of the Americas. Extra margin apart, a further consideration may have been the decline in sales through Pickersgill in the 1820s as the London market failed to keep pace with Manchester.[51]

But to go round Manchester and consign woven cloth abroad to distant destinations, assuming the merchants role, had several implications. The routine of procuring freight for the consignment or insurance presented no difficulty. Crucial was having a trusted agent in the key markets abroad; an agent who would dispose of the consignment skilfully, holding for better prices if his judgment so inclined; who would choose customers whose credit was good; and above all who could be relied on to remit the proceeds or use them wisely. But probably of greatest importance was the knowledge of foreign markets and the judgment where to consign; irrespective of the merits of the agent, there was no certainty that cloth would be saleable in distant markets at prices that were rewarding, or even saleable at all. Arrivals could meet glut or shortage. Markets were frequently oversupplied but if they were 'starved' a killing would be made. Writing of the 'small easily saturated markets of Latin America, where after independence there was a mad rush to sell', D.C. Platt comments, 'the timing of a speculative consignment was all important: one cargo alone might fill the market for months or years at a time, and a late arrival find no market at all.'[52]

Intelligence on the state of trade at different destinations travelled only at the speed of the fastest ship — perhaps four to six weeks from North America, three to four months from South America. In January 1822 Thomas wanted John's decision on 'what goods were to go to New York, Buenos Aires or Lisbon.'[53] He was not enthusiastic about New York where he believed the market was overstocked; he favoured Lisbon. John's decision can hardly have been an easy one, but he developed a very high reputation for judging world markets correctly over the years, identifying those where the best prices and speediest returns could be achieved.

All too often the value realised depended on whether the cloth was so stowed that it was first to leave the hold and get ashore, or its landing was delayed. John Fielden was to complain of the activities of weak

74

competitors; Manchester exporters who were soliciting goods for consignment, offering up to three-quarters of their value and then sending the goods 'to markets where few are wanted and are sold at considerable sacrifices to cover the advances made on them.'[54] Another problem was the lack of warehouse facilities at some of the destinations to store unsold goods which were frequently damaged; Fieldens lost a consignment landed at Tacna in a typhoon. As an additional hazard, the proceeds that would eventually be realised from sales of cloth were at risk from movements in foreign exchange values, generally in the wrong direction in trade with South America in this period. Argentine dollars, for instance, were particularly prone to depreciation; John Fielden was complaining in 1834 of the dollar falling from a value of 44d to 7d over a few years.[55]

On top of performance risks and market risks inherent in these adventures in trade, was the financial implication of consignment business: even if the sale on arrival proceeded smoothly and at remunerative prices, working capital was tied up throughout the voyage, until the goods could be sold, throughout the period of credit given to the customer and then throughout the voyage home, when specie or collateral was returned. For some destinations, funds could be tied up in stocks afloat or abroad, and debtors or remittances, for well over a year. John Fielden was to express it starkly: 'only the richer neighbour has the capital and opportunity to ship to a foreign port, the poorer has to force his goods immediately on the home market.'[56] But even the rich companies would be stretched for returns and find themselves illiquid and there were many examples of insolvent exporters whose assets on paper exceeded their debts.[57] To assume the merchant's role successfully required judgment and expertise, good connections, substantial working capital and a measure of good fortune in what can only be described as a highly competitive and speculative business. In the event Fielden Brothers seem to have had those qualities as well as good luck. It has to be presumed that their merchanting role was successful. It would not have been continued otherwise, nor would they have flourished in the way they did.

The merchanting activity had two other consequences. The first was an involvement in finishing, since the overseas' agents required not only grey cloth but also finished cloth, whether bleached, dyed or printed. The Manchester merchant secured these services to his specification by putting finishing out on a commission basis to a host of specialist finishing concerns. Fielden Brothers behaved in the same way. In particular they contracted with a firm whose works were on the river Irk, at Bowker Bank, Crumpsall, near to Thomas Fielden's home. No doubt Thomas had a close relationship with the proprietor of Bowker Bank and could keep a close eye on what was being done. The association with Bowker Bank and its successive owners, continued throughout Thomas's lifetime.

Secondly, the merchant needed the facility to sell the produce he might receive in payment for his consignment, whether because his cloth was sold on a barter basis, or because the proceeds from sale were used to purchase produce at his risk or at his agent's risk. When produce was received in payment, in contrast to bills or specie, there was always the chance of a double profit — one on the calico exported and one on the produce returned in payment. In this early period the Fieldens had to rely on others to dispose of whatever produce they received against their consignments. After all, they knew nothing of the market for hides, horse-hair, timber or ashes. In particular they worked closely with Daniel Campbell, Colin Campbell's brother, who was a General Broker in Liverpool. Later, the need to dispose of return cargoes of produce, shipped as payment for Fielden cloth, was to lead them into direct participation in the produce markets.

Fieldens' early merchant enterprise was directed at markets in North America, especially New York, and the Canadian maritime provinces, Quebec, Nova Scotia and New Brunswick. John Jacob Astor's American Fur Company was a large customer, with payment being made by bills drawn on Astor's London agent, C. H. Lampson who sold Astor furs in the London market. It was not all plain sailing: in April 1822 John Fielden complained of a bad debt in New Orleans and concluded 'there is no luck for us yet in the trade to North America but we must persevere in hopes of better success.'[58] By the 1820s, however, many of Fieldens' consignments of cloth were directed at the emerging markets in South America. The newly independent republics were eager to trade with Britain and offered significant commercial advantages to British goods. Agents or partners of Liverpool and Manchester houses were quick to establish themselves. One such was Hodgson and Robinson in Buenos Aires. Fieldens and John Owens, the Manchester merchant, were probably their largest suppliers. Thus as early as August 1820 Fieldens were shipping 'prints and white goods' to Hodgson and in September 1821 a letter from Hodgson refers to a shipment of tallow to Fielden Brothers as part payment for cotton shirtings. In October 1821 Hodgsons was shipping bullion via Rio, horse hides and horse hair to pay for goods.[59] In September 1831 Hodgson was instructing John Fielden regarding a shipment of salted and dry ox hides to 'dispose of this shipment at the best market prices which can be obtained' but to 'use your discretion in holding it for some short time if you think it best.'[60] From the proceeds of this shipment, $20,000 (Argentine dollars) was for the account of Fielden Brothers and the balance to other creditors. Barter or contra-trade of this kind was no doubt customary at the time. Less usual was the transfer to Fieldens of mortgages on two estancias on the Argentine pampas, valued at $120,000, to cover balances due. What eventually happened to these cattle raising properties is not recorded, although they remained part of the assets of Fielden Brothers for many years.[61]

These were the normal risks and characteristics of overseas trade at the time, at least to remote destinations where the potential returns were largest. Fieldens dealt with agents in many of the South American ports, agents who were connected usually with Manchester or Liverpool merchants, enterprising young men seeking to make a fortune and willing to endure the privations of living and working in remote and strange locations. The agent's role, would be to receive the consignment, to sell it on the best terms attainable, giving credit where necessary, and to return to their principal the proceeds in one form or another, bills, specie or collateral produce. A commission of up to 3 per cent was charged for this service. On this basis Fieldens appear to have made consignments all around South America, from Pernambuco, Bahia, Rio de Janeiro, the Plate and on the Pacific side to Valparaiso, Callao, Lima, Tacna and Arequipa. At the same time they were making consignments to the Levant when that market developed. The Bank of England agent in Liverpool was exaggerating when he wrote, at a later date, of the Fieldens, 'they sell little or nothing for home consumption, but ship out to various parts of the globe nearly the whole of what they produce.'[62] But he did convey their enterprise. Samuel Kydd was to put it another way when he wrote in 1857, 'In every market of the world where cotton or cotton fabrics were bought or sold, the name of Fielden was known; it was synonymous with probity and confidence; it was England representing honest dealing and courageous enterprise.'[63]

The Partnership in 1832

1832 marked a significant event. John Fielden was elected Radical MP for the Oldham constituency in the Reform Parliament. If this was the threshold of a political career it also implied some lessening of the energies he could devote to the business. But that business had by then achieved a significant standing in the expanding cotton industry, a standing that seemed secure.

The Partners made a detailed assessment of their capital in June 1832. Their manufacturing assets in Todmorden have already been described. The overall position is summarised in Table IV, Partnership Capital in 1832. Regarding the breakdown of the £184,603 described as 'Property Abroad and in Manchester' no detail has survived. £23,406 was piece goods stock in Manchester and possibly with the finishers at Bowker Bank. There would be some raw cotton in Liverpool. Moneys would be owing from Todmorden, in respect of cotton purchases, less what was owed to Todmorden in respect of sales of cloth. There would be trade debtors in Manchester but large assets were described as 'adventures in trade', that is cloth on consignment, in warehouses overseas and debts due from overseas agents.

Table IV: Partnership Capital in 1832.

To Property Abroad and in Manchester	184,603
To Estates, Mills, Machinery	86,868
To Stock	36,552
To Other Assets: Turnpike loans/Pickersgill/Cash	14,930
	322,953
Less Balance of Trade Debtors/Creditors	(15,617)
Capital in Trade	307,336
Less Private Property and Payments due for property	(29,994)
Partnership Capital	**£277,342**

Source: WYAS, Machinery Valuation, C353/132

Clearly at this stage in the evolution of the business all the assets are committed to cotton manufacturing and trade. This is still a highly focused concern in its use of funds. And for the most part the assets are not liquid: there is little cash, and should the need arise, cash would not be easy to realise quickly. Against that consideration, however, a profitable business would be generating a strong cash flow to fund investment in growth and new ventures, as well as drawings by the Partners for their own use. These were the characteristics of a bold ambitious business.

Such, then, was the wealth and character of the business in 1832. The individual Partners had been sparing in their drawings and their individual investments were local and closely linked to the business. Thus some of them owned their homes; outmills had been purchased by either John or Joshua; they had bought farms and cottages. But clearly in 1832 the greater part of the brothers wealth was in the business and collective. They were all deeply involved. The individual shares were calculated very precisely and collective agreement carefully recorded as summarised in Table V.

Table V: Shares in Partnership Capital 1832.

	Partnership Capital	Private Property
Joshua Fielden	£70,750	£9,250
John Fielden	£87,592	£12,408
James Fielden	£60,000	—
Thomas Fielden	£59,000	£1,000
	£277,342	£22,658

Source: WYAS, Machinery Valuation, C353/132

All signed their assent. The 1832 document, painstaking as it is, was written by John Fielden. The Partners did not take equal shares of the joint property: part of it, mainly the Todmorden assets, was divided equally, but the balance, including the assets in Manchester and abroad,

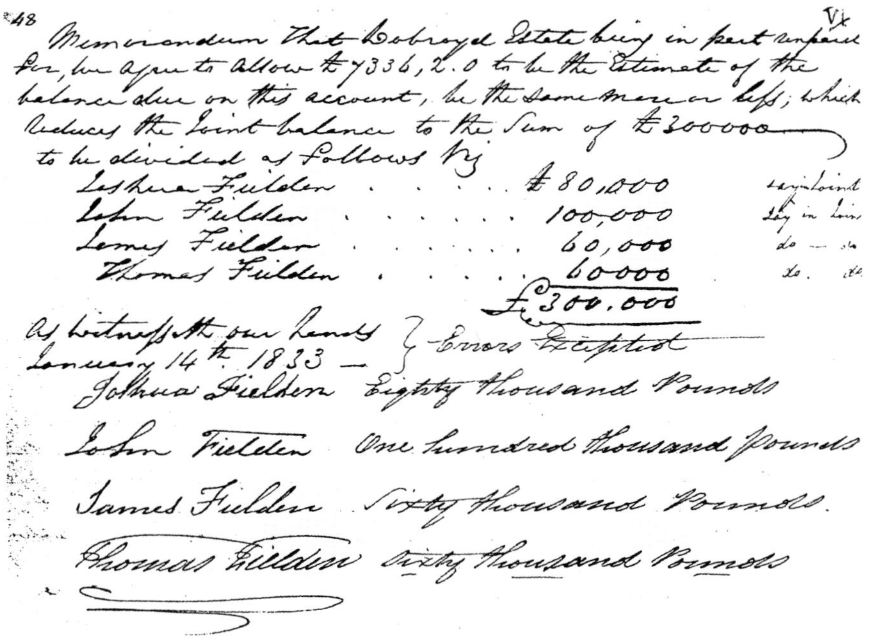

48

[Handwritten ledger document reading:]

Memorandum That Dobroyd Estate being in part unpaid for, we agree to allow £7336,2.0 to be the estimate of the balance due on this account, be the same more or less; which reduces the Joint balance to the Sum of £300000 to be divided as follows Viz

Joshua Fielden £80,000
John Fielden 100,000
James Fielden 60,000
Thomas Fielden 60,000
                        £300.000

As witness the our hands January 14th 1833 — Errors Excepted

Joshua Fielden Eighty thousand Pounds
John Fielden One hundred thousand Pounds
James Fielden Sixty thousand Pounds.
Thomas Fielden Sixty thousand Pounds

Partnership Capital in 1832. The Private Ledger, written in John Fielden's hand, shows that Fielden Brothers had become 'one of the richest houses in Lancashire.' In this signed statement, the detailed valuation of Partnership capital was simplified as a total of £300,000, shared by the Partners as shown

were divided in fifteen shares, four to Joshua, five to John, and three each to James and Thomas. The Partners agreed that henceforth rental be paid to the owners of any property occupied by the firm,' and also that the share of profit or loss in the business of the Concern, be from the 1st June 1832, divided in equal proportions'[64]

Family and Public Life to 1832

The Fielden partners had a hard upbringing. The old cottage mill at Waterside was their home and they were helping or working there at an early age. Their formal education, such as it was, came from a man recalled as 'Long Sam', who taught reading, writing and rudimentary grammar in his home. Joshua Fielden, the boys' father, seems to have objected to Long Sam's Jacobin views in the 1790s and this source of education was cut off. Thereafter the boys or youths would be self taught.[65]

The business was struggling when the father withdrew and indeed when he died, but made rapid progress after 1812. The first Partnership agreement in 1816 provided for the Partners to withdraw £4 weekly for personal expenses. Their drawings increased thereafter to the extent that mills and farms had been bought as private property, but there is nothing in the early records or correspondence that survives to suggest comfort or leisure in their lifestyle; rather these were lives given over substantially, if not entirely, to business, to family, and to matters relating to religion or public life.

Samuel the eldest brother, never married. Supervising and eventually owning the Lumbutts mill, he was a frequent visitor to that place. He fathered at least two natural children there; brought up by their mothers in Lumbutts, both of them found employment or support from Fielden Brothers in later years. He collapsed and died suddenly in 1825

(Overleaf top)
Jenny Fielden, née Greenwood (1749-1825), old Joshua's widow, lived with her unmarried children at Laneside until her death in 1825.

(Centre)
Sally (Sarah) Fielden (1780-1859) lived unmarried at Laneside and remained a Quaker all her life. She was closely involved with her brothers' business activities, helped to resolve differences between them and was a steadying influence at times of difficulty such as 1812 and 1842.

(Bottom)
Joshua Fielden (1778-1847) was the oldest brother, after the death of Samuel in 1822. Although taking an equal share of the Partnership profits, he deferred to the authority of John, concerning himself with the machinery and motive power arrangements of the mills.

demonstrating stone-breaking to workmen building a new road. His personal estate was less than £5,000 and his interest in the Partnership passed to his brothers, and his mill at Lumbutts to his oldest brother Joshua.[66]

The other surviving children of Joshua Fielden of Edge End remained at the Laneside cottages until they married. Thus two sisters, Mary and Betty, were married in 1805 and 1806 respectively; despite their Quaker upbringing, they married Anglicans in Halifax Parish Church and their children, named from their fathers Boys and Lacey respectively, were to benefit by inheritance from the subsequent wealth of their uncles, some of whom were to be childless. Joshua's other surviving daughter Sally, or Aunt Sarah as her nieces and nephews were later to call her, remained unmarried and lived at Waterside, all her life. She, alone among the family, died a Quaker. Following the death of her mother in 1825, Aunt Sarah managed the old family home. She retained a strong hold over her brothers throughout her lifetime (she died in 1859 aged 79) and at periods of crisis or critical decision was a steadying influence.[67]

Joshua, the second brother, born in 1778, seems to have taken the leadership role for a while following his father's withdrawal in 1803. At least he was corresponding on behalf of the firm in 1811 and 1812. At Waterside he supervised the Mechanics Department, at the time making much of the machinery; he dealt with suppliers of steam engines and other equipment. Although Joshua's profit participation in the early Partnership was equal to that of John and larger than that of his younger brothers James and Thomas, he seems to have moved into the background as John, who held the commercial responsibilities of the business, assumed the dominant leadership position. By 1820 people in Todmorden, and probably to a greater extent in Manchester and Liverpool, regarded John Fielden as the personification of Fielden Brothers. But if Joshua was in the background, he remained an independent and at times strong-minded individual. He was quite a character in Todmorden, enjoying a drink with his lifetime friends and recalling the early days of the firm, their limited capital, hard fare, long hours, and many rebuffs; if they had few friends in the early years, when they achieved success there was no lack of friends at all.[68]

Joshua had a natural son, Nathan Firth, born in 1805, for whom he made generous provision in his will. He married in 1817 Else Mallinson, daughter of John Mallinson, farmer of Horton-in-Ribblesdale. How and where they met is not recorded. She was an Anglican, and her brother Richard, from 1828, was the vicar of Arkholme in the Lune Valley. Thus began the Mallinson connection with the Fielden family which was to continue throughout the nineteenth century. Joshua and his wife continued to live at Waterside: a small house was added to the extended cottages for their use. They had two surviving children, Jane born in 1818 and John born in 1820. As the family grew, a second larger house, called Waterside House, was added and Joshua was to spend the rest of his life there. The two houses, valued at £1,200 in 1832, remained the property of the Partnership, the occupants paying rent.

Of the younger brothers James, born in 1788, is a more obscure figure, quiet and unpretentious. He lived as a bachelor at Waterside, probably with his sister Sarah, until his marriage in 1834, taking responsibility as a Partner for the day-to-day management of the mills. He shared his brother John's political opinions but lacked his stature; nonetheless he took on a public role in Todmorden and was actively involved in the Todmorden Political Union in 1831. Thomas, shrewd, down-to-earth, hard and unsympathetic, volatile and emotional in his views, moved to Manchester by 1820, living on top of his job, close to the Peel Street warehouse, in Hunts Bank. He married Alice Entwistle in Liverpool in 1822 and moved to Rose Hill or Wellfield, in Crumpsall, on the fringe of Manchester at the time, and some three miles from the warehouse, where his house, garden and stables was valued in 1832 at £1,000. He stayed there for the rest of his life. His marriage had no surviving children. Thomas's correspondence suggests that except when he was ill, he was driving himself all the time, whether in Manchester, Todmorden or Liverpool. Perhaps even more than John, he was totally dedicated to the business

John, the second eldest surviving brother, married Ann Grindrod, daughter of a Rochdale grocer who also owned cottage property in that town, in 1811. On or before his marriage the Partnership bought for his use a recently built inn at Dobroyd Bridge, Waterside; enlarged and modified this became Dawson Weir. For some years, thereafter, as well as a dwelling, Dawson Weir was the counting house where the partners met every Monday morning: it also seems to have been used to take in hand-loom pieces. The property was valued at £850 in 1832. John Fielden's three sons and five daughters were to be born and raised there and it remained the family home until 1842 when the more spacious

(Above)
Thomas Fielden (1790-1869) succeeded John as 'the market man' and made his home at Wellfield in Crumpsall, Manchester. He played an important role in directing the commercial activity of the Partnership in Manchester and Liverpool from the late 1820s.

(Left)
Dawson Weir was originally an inn. John Fielden bought the house on his marriage in 1811. His family of eight children were born and raised there — one daughter died in infancy. Opposite the Waterside mill, and surrounded by workpeople's cottages and shops, Dawson Weir was at the heart of the Waterside community. In the early years it was used to take-in woven pieces and the Partners would meet there each Monday morning at nine o' clock to discuss the state of the business. By 1840 John Fielden's children were complaining of lack of room to entertain their friends and in 1843 the family moved to Centre Vale. For many years thereafter mill-managers at Waterside were given free occupation of Dawson Weir as part of their reward.

and prestigious Centre Vale estate was acquired. Dawson Weir faced the growing Waterside mill; it was adjacent to shops and workers' cottages; the canal and later the railway lay behind. It was at the heart of the Fielden community and when John Fielden vacated the house, it was to be occupied by successive Fielden managers.

As his children grew up John Fielden was becoming a man of substantial property as well as public renown. Nevertheless, his way of life remained simple and unostentatious, although some way removed from that of his workers. In 1822 he was asking Thomas in Manchester, to send 'a small salmon, some nice cherries or other fruit and two or three of your nice cabbages.' In August 1826 he was to take his wife and children to Blackpool, then more exclusive and fashionable than it was to become subsequently. They stayed at Fish's Hotel, bathed and drank salt water, and felt better for the change. Occasionally there were concerts in Manchester. Meanwhile John Fielden's children received a private education. Samuel, the eldest son, born in 1816, was sent to a school run by a John Hathersage on the south side of Ardwick Green, Manchester. In his youth, young Sam would get to know this part of

Samuel Fielden's School Bill. The bill for half-year's fees and expenses came from the Unitarian School at Stand outside Manchester. On leaving this school, Samuel studied at Manchester College in York, also an establishment for dissenters, before joining his father and uncles at Waterside at the age of eighteen in 1834. He quickly became involved in most aspects of the business but especially mill-management where he was in the mill at 5 o'clock each morning, and aware of every detail of its operations.

Manchester well; in later life he was to invest in property there. A school bill from Ardwick Green dated 27 December 1824 survives: the eight year old Samuel received a half year's boarding and instruction at a cost of £17.10s with pens, ink and writing books 4s 6d additional. After Ardwick Green, Sam went to a school in Stand, near Manchester, run by a Unitarian Minister, where in 1827 his half-year fees were £27.17s including washing, shoe-making, haircutting, and dancing lessons. It was at Stand that he first encountered the young William Gaskell, newly appointed to Cross Street Chapel in Manchester, and a large influence on Sam's later life. In 1829 his pious father was writing to him at Stand expressing concern at Sam's illness and reminding him that 'afflictions are not joyous but grievous and are sent to remind us of the instability of all things and the necessity of observing the rules, enjoined on us by the author of our being.' Finally, completing his education, Sam studied at Manchester College, York, then primarily a training centre for Dissenting ministers, from 1831 to 1834. At the age of eighteen he joined the business.[69]

The middle son, John Junior, (Jack as he was called at the time), went to St Domingo's House, a school in Everton, Liverpool run by a Mr Voelker, fashionable to the sons of nonconformist Lancashire businessmen. He was joined there by his cousin John, son of Joshua Fielden of Waterside House. Thomas Ashton of Hyde was also a student there. In 1839 Voelker seems to have returned to Switzerland taking some of his pupils with him; the young John Fielden was one of these, although his father had doubts especially at the suggestion that the boys should take guns. The younger brother, Joshua, born in 1827, seems to have studied locally before he too went to Switzerland, along with his older brother.

John Fielden's daughters went to private schools run for young ladies of similar background.[70] Ann Fielden, born in 1819, was at school with the Misses Leigh, at Castle Mere, at the end of 1830: a half year's charges amounted to £22.4s, to include music, painting and drawing. She then joined her older sister Mary at Dr. Carpenter's school in Bristol in late 1831. They were visited there at various times by their father, Aunt Sarah, Uncle and Aunt Thomas. The family were close. In later years the sisters and their brothers were to correspond frequently and affectionately; but in the early years it was John Fielden who wrote the family letters, passing on the news and sending gifts. In 1832 he was sending his daughters at school in Bristol, 'parkin' made by Aunt Sarah. Jane the oldest daughter, born in 1814 was epileptic: she lived at home with nursing care and was to die in 1846. Another daughter, 'my dear little Sarah', died in 1826 aged two, of whooping cough. John Fielden was to describe her illness and medication in great detail, in his letters to the family. His last child, Ellen, born in 1829, 'a dear little creature' to her father and older sisters, was also frail, not only as a child but throughout her lifetime.

John Fielden's wife Ann, whom he described as an 'excellent and beloved mother', died tragically in June 1831 following the shock of seeing a child drown in the nearby canal. His deep religious faith and piety came through strongly in letters he was to write at this time.

Although he had been brought up a Quaker, he was probably finding their quiet contemplative practice too conservative for his radical instincts. His son was later to recall that his father's sisters persuaded him to become associated with the Methodists in 1801, principally because of their enthusiasm for Sunday School teaching in which he had then become involved. But he seems to have differed from the Methodists after a time and briefly attended the Anglican church, St Mary's, probably with his brothers. He then came into contact with Joseph Cooke, who had broken away from Methodism to form a new sect called the Methodist Unitarians, attracting followers in the district around Rochdale. Their practice and belief was said to combine the simple piety of the Methodists, with the freedom from dogma associated with the Unitarians, believing as they did in 'One God in One Person.' John Fielden was particularly attracted to the preaching of Richard Wright, one of Cooke's followers. Fielden was to say, 'their views harmonise more with my ideas of what Christ himself has taught than any other I have yet heard.' This was 'the truth of Christianity.' Wright was invited to Todmorden to preach in 1818 and subsequently, when he attracted significant congregations. John Fielden actively supported the cause and saw to the provision of preachers whenever meetings could be held. By 1822 the Todmorden Unitarian Society was formed and were holding a fortnightly meeting in a rented room and in 1824 they built a Meeting House or Chapel and School at a cost of £990. Unable to raise that money in full, they had a large debt which was relieved in 1828 when John Fielden bought out the Society. The Chapel, School, burial ground, furniture etc. became his personal property, valued at £800 in the 1832 valuation. He, and subsequently his sons, were to pay the greater part of the expenses of the Chapel and School, including the Minister's salary, for many years thereafter. With his family he attended chapel regularly, acting as Superintendent of the Sunday School where he had a reputation for 'severe but wholesome discipline.'[72] He impressed on his sons the particular importance of

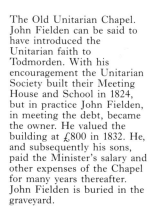

The Old Unitarian Chapel. John Fielden can be said to have introduced the Unitarian faith to Todmorden. With his encouragement the Unitarian Society built their Meeting House and School in 1824, but in practice John Fielden, in meeting the debt, became the owner. He valued the building at £800 in 1832. He, and subsequently his sons, paid the Minister's salary and other expenses of the Chapel for many years thereafter. John Fielden is buried in the graveyard.

John Fielden MP. This portrait in oils by George Hayter in 1834 was one of a series showing members of the Reform Parliament. At the time John Fielden was probably at the height of his powers. A man of exceptional industry and stamina, aside from his active leadership of the large and complex Partnership business, his political activity was widening rapidly.

regular Sunday worship and study of the bible.

Outside his business life, his family, his religious faith and involvement, John Fielden's main interest in his youth and young manhood was in the education of the working poor. With his brother Joshua he began teaching in a Methodist Sunday School at the age of seventeen in 1801, scripture followed by reading, writing and arithmetic. He started his own Sunday School in 1803 at Gauxholme and later was to be instrumental in forming the Todmorden Sunday School Union in 1816. Three new schools were then provided which, by 1818, had 700 pupils. John Fielden taught in all these schools; he contributed to the cost of schoolrooms and furniture and secured on-going support from the Township Poor Rate to the extent of £21 per annum. He was also active in supporting and contributing to the large Methodist Sunday School at York Street, in the middle of Todmorden, which was opened in 1821. Meanwhile, at the Unitarian Meeting House, in the summer of 1825, a Free Day School opened for poor children of all denominations from the age of four up to the time (age eight or nine) when they went to the mill. John Fielden was to pay the salaries of those who taught there. Finally, in 1827, a Factory School was opened at Waterside, the first teacher, a Thomas Stewart, also being the resident minister at the Unitarian Chapel. This Fielden Factory School took part-time young children from the mill in three sessions daily; in periods of short-time working it was also used to provide instruction to full-timers in the evening.[72]

John Fielden, recognised as head of the firm of Fielden Brothers both locally and within the industry, quickly emerged as a leading figure in public life in Todmorden and more gradually beyond. He followed his father in participating in the affairs of Todmorden and Walsden Township. Although the population was increasing rapidly, there was not much local government at the time beyond provision for the poor and some road maintenance. As an Overseer, Fielden was characteristically most conscientious and painstaking in sifting the facts and judging the merits of pauper settlement cases; his laboriously hand-written notes survive from the early 1820s. A large employer of hand-loom weavers himself, John Fielden was deeply concerned at their plight and the inexorable competitive pressures which were forcing down the work-payment they received. Thus he was active during the period of severe distress in 1826, in attempting to organise an agreement between employers of hand-loom weavers to fix minimum rates of payment. Loom-breaking was spreading across Lancashire at the time; it took place at Whitehead's mill in Rossendale but, obstructed by the militia, the mob did not reach Waterside, although Joshua and James, in John's absence, were sufficiently alarmed to hide some new looms in the nearby mill dam. If attempts at wage-fixing came to nothing at the time, Fielden was not to abandon the idea: he was petitioning Home Secretary Peel on the condition of the weavers in 1829, and subsequently, when he became an MP, he was to plead their plight in the House of Commons and through the Select Committee of which he was a member.

In 1831 Fielden was actively involved in early attempts to promote a Manchester and Leeds Railway Bill. Requesting him to join a deputation to the Parliamentary Committee because of his 'great local knowledge', the Directors urged his participation to help take his mind off the heavy affliction of his wife's recent death. He joined the deputation and stayed with the Pickersgills in London early in July 1831. Writing to his brothers, characteristically, he asks to be informed about 'what you are doing in Manchester and how the cotton market is', and gives James detailed instructions as to which warps to use for a particular order and the length of the cuts.[73]

The political agitation for reform of Parliament deeply engaged Fielden in national politics for the first time. He was a founding member of the Manchester Political Union and organised, with others, and led the Todmorden Political Union, early in 1831. Like the other Unions in the Midlands and elsewhere, that in Todmorden organised mass petitions and meetings demanding Reform. It encouraged among the poor unrealistic expectations of the benefits that would derive from reform of Parliament. And when Reform was achieved, Fielden, like other large employers at the time, organised a great celebration and feast which was remembered in Todmorden for many years thereafter.[74] Some outside Todmorden saw Fielden as a benevolent despot there, at least with regard to his own work-people. Certainly his work-people were completely under his influence and, from time to time, were to be mobilised by managers and overlookers to demonstrate or support issues for which he campaigned. But his following in the town, at this time and for the rest of his life, was a function not merely of being head of a conspicuously successful business, and the provider of work for a large number of people, but also of his character, his sincerity, his devotion to good causes, his quiet simplicity and his piety. He had no sense of self-importance but was seen as plain, true, faithful, one of the ordinary people, who was 'never ashamed to admit the rock from which he was hewn.'[75]

John Fielden's public life outside Todmorden, his political activity, and the major causes for which he campaigned so earnestly and effectively, have been fully described by several scholars.[76] That he became a member in the Reform Parliament in 1832 indicates his regional political standing and established reputation. Without his business success and the prominence this gave him, his political influence would have been doubtful. As it was in July 1831 his name was being recommended in the Manchester press for Parliament as a 'man of excellent character, ample fortune, enlarged and liberal views.' In July 1832 he was adopted, with William Cobbett, as a Radical candidate for Oldham. In his address to the electors there he made the point that a seat in Parliament would subject him to 'a great personal disadvantage.' He continued, 'nothing but an anxious solicitude to see the people restored their just rights, and especially the condition of the labouring portion of society greatly improved, could induce me to make the sacrifice.'[77] Thereafter, Parliament and the large causes with which he was associated, took more and more of Fielden's time. With his large and motherless family; with the affairs of the business, which he was reluctant to delegate, with his Parliamentary duties and political involvements, with wearying travel and lodgings in Central London for part of the year, Fielden's life after 1832 was fully committed. In the end his health gave way under the strain. But in 1832 he was in his prime and on the threshold of the national political career that made him famous.

3

A VAST AND COMPLICATED BUSINESS
Fielden Brothers 1832-1850

Progress to 1836

With the power-loom shed approaching completion, and with spinning capacity enough to meet requirements of both the power-looms and the hand-loom weavers, Fielden Brothers were in a strong position to benefit from the booming cotton trade of the early and middle 1830s. As well as 2 to 3,000 hand-loom pieces weekly, they now had capacity for up to 4,000 power-loom pieces, mainly domestics, that is, shirtings and T cloths from narrow looms. As the power-looms came into production, there was some decline in the number of hand-loom weavers employed: by 1836 the number had fallen by one-seventh compared with 1832. But meagre as the financial returns were, hand-loom weaving was to continue for a further period; the new power-looms were operated mainly by young women, working two looms per weaver.

In 1833 the power-loom shed was brought to its capacity of 810 looms. Although extension of the first shed began in 1836 and additional looms were installed taking the total number to 1,058 in 1841, depressed trade brought hesitation and the next big step forward in power-loom capacity was to wait until the late 1840s. Fieldens were by no means the first among the power loom concerns. Their 810 looms compared with an estimated industry total of 108,000 in 1835,[1] and there were certainly larger concerns in Manchester, Stalybridge, Stockport and Hyde. But Fieldens were among the largest combined spinning and weaving firms in the industry; thus in 1841 there were 321 combined firms in Lancashire, but only 22 had more than 1,000 hands, while the average combined mill had 349 hands, 65 HP and employed £24,500 fixed capital.[2] Fieldens valued their fixed assets at £95,000 at that time. They were employing 840 people at Waterside when Charles Wing visited in 1836, and probably close to 1,100 at all their mills, a number that would have grown beyond 1,200 by 1841. And of course, Fieldens dominated Todmorden's industry at this time.[3]

If a further major stride forward in power-loom capacity was to be postponed, spinning capacity continued to be modernised and enlarged. Thus the small mill at Waterstalls that had been acquired earlier had been refurbished, a new dam added, and was producing water twist by 1834. Twelve new throstles with 1,296 spindles were installed at Stoneswood in 1835, at a cost of 7s.6d per spindle. Following a protracted legal dispute with other millowners, principally over the basis on which

(Opposite)
Waterstalls Mill in its extraordinary situation high on the hillside above the Walsden valley. Water power was available augmented by small reservoirs and, in the early nineteenth century, there would be local labour from the nearby farms. The Mill had 1,200 spindles at Crompton's Census in 1811. It was bought by the Fieldens for £500 in 1832, probably because it was close to Bottomley where that branch of the family had lived for many generations. New machinery was installed in 1834 and a small steam engine and the mill — employing about 25 people, chiefly children and young women — continued to produce throstle yarn for warps until 1860 when it was closed and the machinery sold; others worked the mill for some years subsequently.

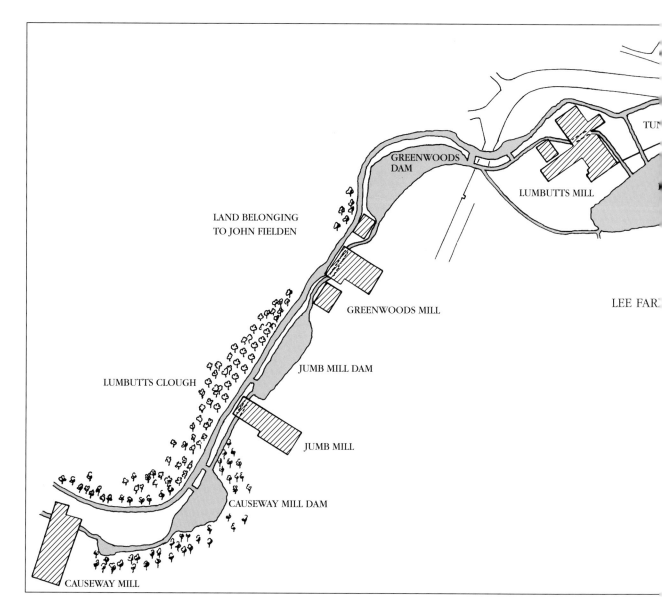

Lumbutts Dams. Lumbutts Clough, with its strong flow from the Langfield hillside augmented by compensation water from the Easterly Gaddings dam, supported several water-powered spinning mills. Disputes between the mill-owners were inevitable, in particular over the basis on which the costs of dam construction should be shared. Uttley and Greenwood, who owned the smaller mills, argued that they did not need the additional water which new dams would provide. Fieldens, owning Lumbutts

the costs of dam construction and maintenance should be shared, major dam construction to enhance water power in the Lumbutts valley took place between 1833 and 1838. Westerly Gaddings dam was built on the Langfield moor above, adjacent to and augmenting Easterly Gaddings, built earlier by the Rochdale Canal Company. The Company was obliged to fill the easterly dam with water from its own system of drains once a year, to compensate millowners on the Calder for water abstracted and used by the Canal. A tower holding two overshot 30 foot water wheels was already a feature of Lumbutts Mill; as the new and higher dams were completed the tower was enlarged to take three water wheels, one vertically above the other, with water being introduced on each wheel at three levels. This unusual arrangement gave 14 HP; it was supplemented by a steam engine, also of 14 HP. The mill itself was enlarged at this time.

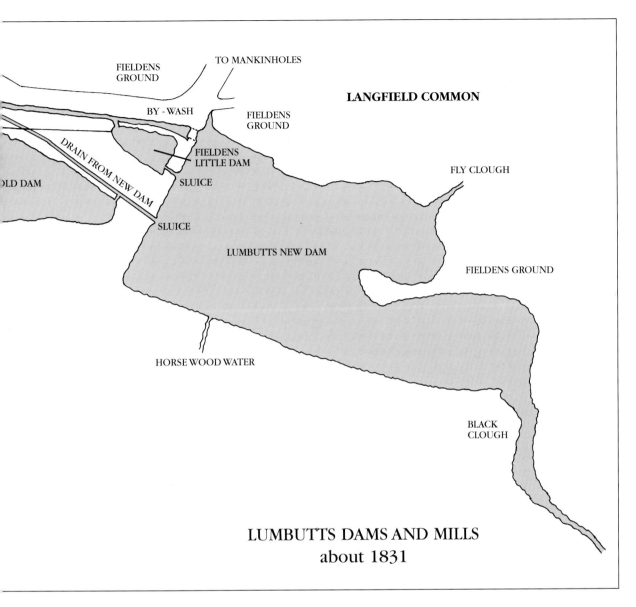

LUMBUTTS DAMS AND MILLS
about 1831

Substantial investments were made at Waterside in new warehouses, sizing rooms, in carding capacity and in spinning where eighteen new self-acting mules, larger in size and providing 6912 spindles at 4s 6d per spindle, replaced 4788 old mule spindles in 1835 (Appendix I). Provision for a further major increase in spinning capacity took place with the purchase at auction, at the end of 1836, (following the death of the owner), of Mytholmroyd Mill, lower down the Calder valley and about 8 miles from Todmorden. Built in the 1790s and used for the preparation and spinning of worsted, Mytholmroyd took the full flow of the river to give 30 HP from three water-wheels. After acquisition, as Joshua Fielden's property, the worsted machinery was sold and cotton preparation machinery and throstle spindles installed. This large mill, which was eventually to take 13,000 spindles, was valued at £8,500 with steam engines; it was bought at a time of boom in Lancashire and was

Mill and Causeway Mill, took the issue to arbitration and won a ruling that the cost of dam construction would be shared, with Fieldens paying two-thirds. The chart, used by the arbitrator, shows the arrangement of the dams and mills in 1831. Following the ruling Fieldens built Westerly Gaddings and Healey and Pearson dams above the existing Lee dam; subsequently they were able to add another level and third water wheel to their unusual tower arrangement at Lumbutts Mill.

61

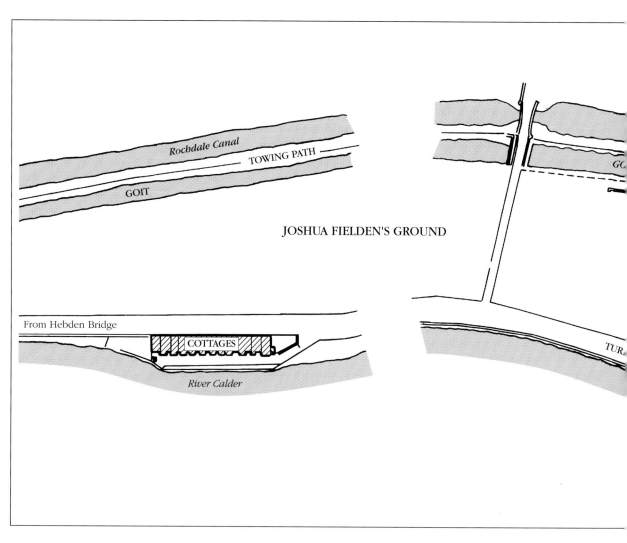

expensive compared with other Fielden mills.[4]

Given conditions in the industry the crucial question was the efficiency of the enlarged, modernised but fragmented spinning capacity, and how this compared with the industry as a whole. The mills generally had been bought cheaply. Capital costs per spindle seem to have been on the low side. Thus writing in 1840, James Montgomery gives costs of 9s 6d for throstle spindles and 5s 6d for mules; Ure quotes figures slightly lower, 9s 0d for throstles and 5s for mules, but gives costs at the Orrell mill in Stockport as 10s 6d for throstles and 4s 9d for hand-mule spindles. Costs at Bailey's mill at Stalybridge point to mule spindles at 5s 9d each. Fieldens paid less than these indications, 4s 6d for mules, down to 8s 6d for throstles (Appendix I). Another contemporary yardstick for fixed capital was £500 per horsepower employed; again, Fieldens' investment was closer to £360 per horsepower at Waterside, less at the outmills.[5]

Wage costs also seem low, although wage comparisons are not easy to make. Job definitions varied and the available data is sparse and generalised. But taking one representative situation, a four-side throstle-

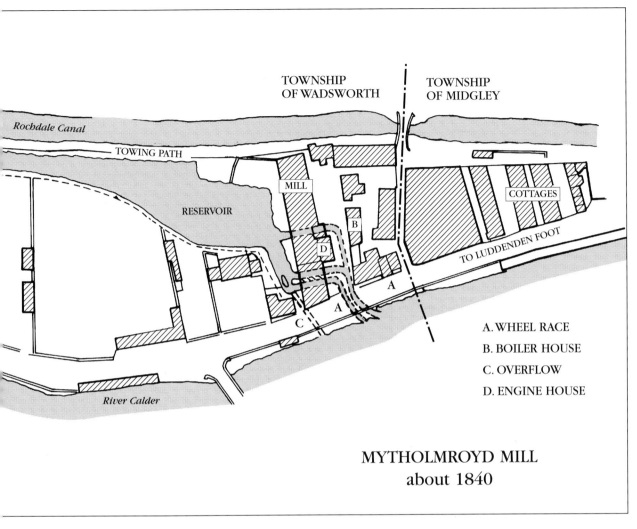

TOWNSHIP
OF WADSWORTH

TOWNSHIP
OF MIDGLEY

Rochdale Canal

TOWING PATH

MILL

RESERVOIR

B

D

A

A

C

COTTAGES

TO LUDDENDEN FOOT

A. WHEEL RACE

B. BOILER HOUSE

C. OVERFLOW

D. ENGINE HOUSE

River Calder

MYTHOLMROYD MILL
about 1840

spinner, typically a young woman, Fielden mills were paying between 6s 9d and 7s 6d weekly around 1850: quoted wages for Lancashire at the time range from 7s 6d/8s 6d in the 1830s to 8s 6d/9s 0d in the 1850s. Productivity within the mill is even more difficult to judge and compare. Fieldens looked at these matters closely, comparing practice across their mills. To attempt an outside comparison, at the Greg mill at Styal in 1840, for a spindleage of 11,360 and a loomage of 165 there were 435 employees, a total that had fallen to 396 by 1845 when there were 303 looms. At Waterside in 1836, 840 employees were operating close to 22,000 spindles and 810 looms. This would suggest labour productivity was about 5 to 10 per cent greater at Waterside than at Styal, a conclusion that is confirmed by a similar comparison for the mid-1850s. Baines in 1835 cites national figures giving one operative per 52 spindles, and 0.57 operatives for each power loom: the Waterside ratios for 1836 are at least 5 per cent better.[6]

Wage payments and labour productivity would determine wage costs per unit of output. An assessment over twelve weeks made by Fieldens in the summer of 1842 indicate spinning labour costs of 0.94d per pound

Mytholmroyd Mill had the advantage of substantial water-power from the river Calder. The drawing shows how the flow could be diverted to three water wheels at the mill, probably under-shot since the fall would be limited: in 1856 water power was giving 28 HP. The mill, six storeys high, had been built in the 1790s for worsted spinning. Bought by Joshua Fielden in 1836 it was then re-equipped with 13,000 throstle spindles. It was sold in 1871 when Fieldens were reducing their capacity and concentrating on fewer sites to reduce costs and improve profitability.

63

of yarn at Waterside. Lord Ashley gave the House of Commons a figure of 1.3d per lb of yarn labour costs as typical for the industry in 1844. Probably more reliably, John Fielden, quoting Kenworthy of Blackburn in the same debate, said that direct (i.e. variable) costs of spinning 36 count yarn were about 1.25d per lb. Fieldens' total variable mill costs (that is including stores and coal as well as labour) were 1.13d per lb of yarn at Waterside with the newest mill, Mytholmroyd below that figure although some of the small outmills were well above it. Weaving labour costs at Waterside, including preparation, supervision and packing were calculated as 1.27d per lb of cloth and total variable costs 1.60d per lb. Fieldens' work, was low counts of yarn and plain calico, at thecheaper end of the industry. Fieldens' total labour costs for spinning and weaving were 2.21d per lb of cloth, and total variable costs 2.73d per lb of cloth. Montgomery calculates a figure of 4.7d per lb of cloth, including all spinning and weaving variable costs, overhead labour, insurance and depreciation of capital at 7.5 per cent, but not interest or profit, while Merttens, writing in 1894, suggested that labour costs per lb of cloth in 1844-46 were 3.5d.[7]

There were other elements in cost, not least those of raising power. The horsepower needed to drive a mill was a material consideration, reflecting design and layout and the competence of the millwright's work. The Fielden mills seemed to have less horsepower per 100 spindles or 100 looms than the figures quoted by Ure as typical for the industry. Given the horsepower requirement, steam-engine design and boiler efficiency would determine coal consumption. There are no indications of Fielden's comparative standing in these areas, although all their mills continued to use water-power, as well as steam, until late in the century. Local coal was cheap in Todmorden but was supplemented, at least when the railway came, with coal from Barnsley or Wigan.

It is reasonable to conclude that Fieldens' costs were below those typical for the industry at the time; its mill margins, accordingly, would be somewhat higher. To the extent that its asset costs were also lower, its return on capital would have been significantly higher than that of the industry. In practice, of course, the realised mill margin and return on capital would also depend heavily on skill in buying cotton and selling yarn or cloth.

The expanding concern was using more cotton, producing on a larger scale, and selling more cloth, (up to 7,000 pieces weekly,) as well as yarn and warps. John Fielden was giving a significant proportion of his time to his parliamentary and constituency affairs, especially between February and July, although when in London he remained in close touch through correspondence. The other brothers presumably enlarged their roles and Thomas in particular flourished on the commercial side. He took assistance in Peel Street, particularly John Bone, who proved an able deputy, transacting business, advising Waterside daily of market conditions, of the quantities and qualities sold and the despatches to Manchester required to meet them. The Partnership was now selling freely to merchants in the Manchester market, A.S. Henry, Lascardi, Ralli Brothers, Butterworth and Brooks being among the names mentioned, as well as on consignment to its agents abroad, and especially in South America. At this time a close association was formed with Richard Rostron, a highly respected Manchester merchant, whose branches in the main Brazilian ports acted as Fielden agents. Rostron was about the same age as Thomas Fielden and had come to Manchester from Edenfield, near Bury, where his father was a calico-printer at Rosebank; Fieldens may have had cloth finished there. John Reid, the Bank of England's Manchester agent, was to report favourably on Rostron's standing and credit when a bill was questioned.[8]

So the Partnership flourished; its joint assets rose from £277,342 in June 1832 to £472,708 at the end of 1835, an increase (or profit) of £195,366 over forty-three months representing an annual return on average capital of approximately 15 per cent (Tables VI and VII). These years, and the following two, were to be among Fielden Brothers most profitable in terms of return on capital employed, the more remarkable given the fall in gross cash margins and John Fielden's persistent complaints of lower profit margins at this time. A profit return of 10 to 15 per cent on capital, would be regarded as highly satisfactory for the industry: that Fieldens were close to the top of this range reflects their low asset base relative to turnover and their higher mill margin. Fieldens' figures, of course, were the result of merchant enterprise as well as cotton spinning and weaving, with the greater part of the increase in the Partnership assets being employed in 'stock in Manchester, Liverpool, Bowker Bank and abroad.' On a much more focused business, the Ashworths during this period were averaging 8 to 9 per cent and this was the range Henry Ashworth was to quote to a House of Lords Committee in 1846. R.H. Greg of Styal was to suggest to the samecommittee that 7.5 per cent was a representative return, probably

Table VI: Fielden Brothers: Employment of Capital 1832-1849 (£000).

Date	Total[1]	Todmorden[2]	Manchester[3] & Abroad	Wildes[4] Pickersgill/ Fielden Bros & Co	Other (Loans, Property)
1st June 1832	277	93	184	—	—
1st January 1836	473	122	351	—	—
1st January 1837	527	127	201	199	—
1st January 1838	603	143	251	209	—
1st January 1839	644	199	225	220	—
1st January 1840	652	206	215	231	—
1st January 1841	694	273	178	243	—
1st January 1842	645	308	82	255	—
1st January 1843	610	377	94	139	—
1st January 1844	641	403	88	150	—
1st January 1845	694	352	177	165	—
1st January 1848	782	131	255	271	121
30th June 1849	829	117	271	295	145

Source: Longden MSS, Private Ledger.
Notes:
1. Prior to Drawings, except 1848 and 1849. (For Drawings see Table VII).
2. Excludes private property, mills, farms, houses, etc.
3. Includes Liverpool prior to 1836.
4. Fielden Brothers and Co. from 1st January 1842.

Table VII: Fielden Brothers: Capital Employed, Profit and Drawings 1832-1849.

Period Ending	Opening Capital	Profit[1] (Including interest)	Drawings	Retained Profit
	£	£	£	£
1st January 1836	277,342	195,366	30,624	164,742
(43 months)	(1st June 1832)			
1st January 1837	442,084	85,446	14,205	71,241
	(1st January 1836)			
1st January 1838	513,325	89,529	31,198	58,331
1st January 1839	571,656	72,085	18,971	53,114
1st January 1840	624,770	26,923	18,248	8,675
1st January 1841	633,445	60,424	19,484	40,940
1st January 1842	674,385	(29,153)	10,023	(39,176)
1st January 1843	635,209	(25,508)	11,922	(37,430)
1st January 1844	597,779	43,257	2,987	40,270
1st January 1845	638,049	56,325	6,737	49,588
1st January 1848	687,637			
(36 months)	(1st January 1845)	205,849	110,941	94,908
30 June 1849	782,387			
(18 months)	(1st January 1848)	114,813	68,580	46,233

Source: Longden MSS: Private Ledger.

Notes: 1. Before determining profit, the Partners charged interest at five per cent on opening capital. This was distributed according to the respective shares in that capital. Profit was then shared equally between the Partners. Profit as set out in the Table includes both interest, and profit.

reflecting his own experience.[9] Given lower returns on merchanting it is reasonable to conclude that in the period to 1850, Fieldens achieved much higher returns on their manufacturing assets than they did on the total. That they were outperforming most of the industry is not in doubt.

Profitable, competitive, well-established in an expanding industry, the Partnership could now afford to lessen their focus on manufacturing and direct marketing, and look for opportunities to employ its growing surplus capital in different if contiguous and related business areas.

Wildes Pickersgill

The association with John Pickersgill went back to 1812. Pickersgill himself had flourished; he had married a daughter of John Cunliffe of Addingham, an influential early Yorkshire worsted spinner. His correspondence with John Fielden indicates a very cordial relationship in which their families were involved, indeed, as Pickersgill put it in 1838, 'all the Fieldens old and young, big and little ' were his welcome guests.[10] John Fielden and his children and Thomas Fielden and his wife became regular visitors at Pickersgill's home in London's Tavistock Square. In 1826 Pickersgill had moved in the City from Cheapside to 19 Coleman Street; here he shared offices with George Wildes whom he had known for ten years or so. By the 1830s he described himself as a merchant and probably conducted a small banking business.

Wildes was one of a number of emerging merchant bankers who specialised at the time in financing the booming Anglo-American

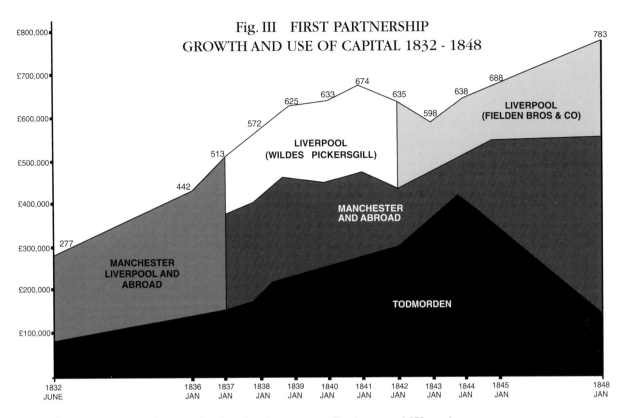

Fig. III   FIRST PARTNERSHIP
GROWTH AND USE OF CAPITAL 1832 - 1848

trade.[11] The strongest houses in that business were Barings and W. and J. Brown, both established in Liverpool and the main United States ports. Newer entrants included Morrison Crowder, and especially the so-called 'Three W's', that is George Wildes, Timothy Wiggins and Thomas Wilson. The 'Three W's' were aggressive in their approach, accepting or guaranteeing the bills of United States importers buying in the United Kingdom, and making advances to United States exporters on a scale that was large in relation to their own resources; they were also less circumspect in choosing the parties to whom they extended credit than the more established firms such as Barings. But the North Atlantic trade was booming in the 1830s and using credit at a rapidly increasing rate; no doubt a mood of euphoria and boldness was also in evidence. Wildes wanted an establishment in Liverpool where so much of the North American trade was conducted. At the same time Fielden Brothers, consigning cloth abroad on a growing scale, were more and more involved in receiving produce in exchange, consigned for their account, or to be sold by them for the account of an overseas debtor. John Fielden would have met George Wildes through John Pickersgill; certainly both he and brother Thomas knew Wildes in 1831 and in 1835 the three saw mutual benefit in creating a joint Liverpool venture.

This was the genesis of Wildes Pickersgill. In announcing its formation on 15th September 1835, Fielden Brothers stated they had 'connected themselves with our old and valued friends, Messrs George Wildes and Co. of London, for the purpose of opening an Agency and Commission House at Liverpool.' George Wildes' announcement refers

That these Articles of Partnership shall be deposited with the said John Fielden — and any or either of the parties hereto shall be at liberty to peruse and take extracts therefrom or a Copy thereof in his presence at any time during the continuance of this Copartnership. In Witness whereof the said parties have hereunto set their hands and seals the day and year first above written

The Wildes Pickersgill Partnership agreement, signed by the major partners, and witnessed, interestingly by the young Samuel Fielden and by Aunt Sarah, the unmarried sister of the Fielden brothers. Wildes Pickersgill was an important diversification for the Fieldens, to which they committed a large part of their capital: it took them into the bulk trades of Liverpool, into ship-owning, and into merchant banking operations where their competitors included Barings and Browns.

to a 'Branch House' in which Fieldens will be 'mutually interested.' They said that the firm at Liverpool 'will also be used by our several partners in London.'[12] Fieldens took a 7/20th share in the Partnership, that is in the profits or losses. Apart from John Pickersgill and his son William, and George Wildes, who together took a 8/20th share, other Partners who would manage the Liverpool activity included Fielden's nominee, Daniel Campbell, younger brother of Colin Campbell, (the trusted Fielden cotton broker), who had been in business as a General Broker since the 1820s and had worked for the Fieldens in that capacity, and William Bowman, who was a Wildes' employee; Campbell and Bowman were salaried but had a 3/20th and 2/20th share respectively. Fielden Brothers were to introduce capital to the concern, initially up to £200,000, on which they were to receive interest at 5 per cent. The new business took an office and warehouse in Peter's Place, off Rumford Street, in the heart of Liverpool's commercial district, and a short walk from George's and Prince's docks.

From the outset there appears to have been some conflict of purpose in the enterprise. For Fieldens, Wildes Pickersgill was a means of using their capital to earn interest and profit by broadening their activities in a contiguous and complementary business area, that is direct involvement in the foreign trade of Liverpool, especially as a merchant selling consigned imports on commission, As the Bank of England was to put it a few years later, 'having had a large surplus capital they became partners in Wildes Pickersgill who receive and dispose of all their produce which is imported on account of shipments made by the manufacturing firm to all parts of the world.'[13] Wildes, on the other hand, was interested in financial business associated with the North American trade; the Liverpool branch was to be an extension of his London activity.

Wildes Pickersgill had another Partner, namely William Cunliffe Pickersgill, the eldest son of John Pickersgill. Born in 1811, William went to the United States in 1834 to broaden his experience before joining his father's business. He worked with the firm of Riggs and Griffith, tobacco and cotton merchants in Baltimore, with whom his

Partnership Announcement: a similar letter with different emphasis was circulated by George Wildes.

MANCHESTER, 15th SEPTEMBER, 1835.

We beg leave to inform you, that we have connected ourselves with our old and valued Friends,

Messrs. GEORGE WILDES & Co. of London, for the purpose of opening an Agency and Commission House at LIVERPOOL,

under the Firm of WILDES, PICKERSGILL & Co.

We refer to the Circular letter annexed for further particulars,

And are, very respectfully,

Your obedient Servants,

Fielden Brothers.

father and George Wildes had trading connections. While there he met and fell in love with Anna, the second daughter of George Washington Riggs, the senior partner, also born in 1811; the two were married in December 1835.[14] William became the American partner of Wildes Pickersgill. He was to manage that side of the business, in particular either himself or through agents, soliciting customers for the firm. Much of the business was with merchants or factors in the southern ports of Charleston, Savannah, Mobile and New Orleans who were selling cotton to Liverpool on consignment terms, that is to be sold on arrival for their account; they would need advances against the expected sale value. Other North American produce would be negotiated on the same consignment basis, although some would be an outright purchase, paid for by a bill drawn on Liverpool. Other customers would be American importers who needed their bills to be accepted in Liverpool or London so as to finance purchases of cloth and dry goods in the United Kingdom. William would assess the credit standing of potential suppliers and customers, and as business materialised arrange the credits to American merchants, collect the acceptances, and transact the foreign exchange. Describing the business as a 'Commission House,' Pickersgill & Co. opened an office in Hanover Street in the Wall Street district. On their marriage, the Pickersgills lived in nearby Washington Square, and later on Staten Island.

Whatever energy and acumen the young William Pickersgill brought to the Wildes Pickersgill business, could only be augmented by his marriage into the Riggs family. His new wife's uncle was Elisha Riggs, by this time established as a widely respected merchant and banker in New York, Philadelphia and Baltimore. Elisha Riggs had enormous influence on the commercial and financial affairs of the United States at the time; he would be known to everyone. Moreover he was in partnership with the young George Peabody who in 1838 was to move to London and develop the merchant banking business that in time became Morgan Grenfell. Elisha Rigg's son, another George Washington Riggs, also achieved eminence as a banker in partnership with Thomas Corcoran; Corcoran and Riggs, of Washington DC, the predecessor of today's Riggs Bank, was subsequently to play a major role in handling the debt of the Federal Government.

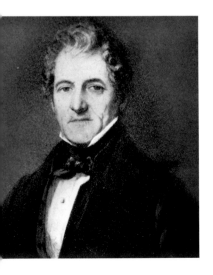

At the end of 1835 and throughout 1836 John Fielden and his brothers must have felt comfortable with the extension of their enterprise to Liverpool and the new network they had joined. Quickly going beyond the original intention to dispose of produce received in payment for cloth consigned abroad, Wildes Pickersgill entered the main Liverpool trades with North America, importing not only cotton, but also tar, turpentine, Indian corn, flour, ashes and other commodities. UsingPickersgill connections with maritime Canada, Wildes Pickersgill also began to import Canadian timber. Like other Liverpool merchants in the North American trade, Wildes Pickersgill acted as ship agents generally taking care of a ship's business while in port. All these activities were conducted for the most part on a commission basis and since commodities were rarely bought outright the firm, as agents rather than principals, were not assuming price risks in volatile markets; these risks lay with the shipper or his plantation supplier, for instance, in the case of cotton. At 3 per cent commission on produce consignments, a commission agency with a large volume had a very lucrative business.

The importing business, in cotton at least, was based upon the assumption of a different kind of risk, namely the credit risk implied by the advance to the shipper (or his supplier) of at least a proportion of the anticipated realisation of the eventual sale of the consignment in Liverpool. The ability to make such advances on liberal terms and for extended periods, had become a condition of receiving the business. So long as cotton prices remained firm and the contracted shipper was financially sound and reliable, this was good business. And the same could be said of the other side of the business in which Wildes participated, namely the provision of credit by accepting bills drawn by United Kingdom suppliers on United States importers who had purchased goods in Lancashire, the Midlands or the like. After all, this business put Wildes Pickersgill side-by-side with houses like Baring and Brown, the foremost names of the time in trans-Atlantic commerce.

1836 was another very successful year for Fielden Brothers, probably the best year in their history thus far. Profit was £85,466, a return of 19.3 per cent on the capital at the beginning of the year (Table VII). The partners felt able to increase their Drawings to £14,205 during the year. The available records do not make clear what part of the 1836 profit was contributed by the Wildes Pickersgill partnership. The Ashworths also had an exceptional year in 1836, averaging about 25 per cent return on capital employed of £92,000 at their two mills.[15] At the end of 1836 Fielden Brothers capital had increased to £513,325; Todmorden assets were £126,938 of which £38,819 were work in progress and stocks of cloth and raw cotton; Manchester assets were £201,375, mainly supporting the consignment sales of cloth; £199,215 had been committed to Wildes Pickersgill, this mainly financing advances to overseas suppliers or trade debtors to whom the firm had extended credit (Table VI). It is not clear what, if any, finance was being provided by the other partners in Wildes Pickersgill but Fieldens were committing nearly 40 per cent of their capital. It was important that the venture should succeed.

The Panic of 1837

1837 was to be a dramatic and frightening year. Trade with North America had boomed but the boom had gone too far. Freely available credit had supported not only rapidly expanding trade but speculation in land and other assets. Cotton prices had risen sharply reaching a peak of 12d a pound in April 1836. They then fell abruptly, reaching a low of 4½d early in 1837, precipitating a collapse of business confidence. A series of United States bank failures followed which lead to widespread suspension of payment by American debtors. The effects spread swiftly to the United Kingdom where those banks who had advanced credit incautiously and on too large a scale were immediately in trouble. They were called upon to meet their acceptances but found it impossible to call in debts in the United States; the flow of payments from America almost ceased temporarily while cotton consignments were realised on

(Opposite above)
William Pickersgill (1811-1892) was the eldest son of John Pickersgill, the London merchant with whom the Fieldens formed a close association in 1812. Pickersgill married Anna Riggs, niece of the influential American merchant banker, Elisha Riggs. He established a Commission House in Hanover Street, New York, in 1835, and as a partner, developed the North American business of Wildes Pickersgill and its successor, Fielden Brothers and Co., Liverpool. He was described as 'the most conservative banker in the city of New York,' perhaps because he followed John Fielden's advice when he left for America, "never a bad debt William." Having made a large fortune he returned to the United Kingdom in the late 1860s and lived in semi-retirement in Bexley, Kent.

(Opposite below)
Elisha Riggs (1770-1853). William Pickersgill married into the Riggs family, wealthy and powerful in banking and merchanting in New York, Baltimore and elsewhere. The connection must have helped his own, and the Fielden business.

terms which yielded receipts well below the prior advances made to shippers.

The 'Three W's' had no alternative but to approach the Bank of England for assistance to meet their obligations. George Wildes, in particular, early in March 1837, had acceptances due over the period through May exceeding £1,300,000 with cash and bills in hand of only £120,000.[16] Wildes' ability to meet his engagements, that is to pay thebills he had accepted, was completely dependent on remittances from the United States, short of Bank of England assistance. Wildes asked the Bank for £240,000 and gave as security what he described as 'certain friends'; their names included Wiggins and Wilson, themselves in similar trouble, and with more substance, Brown, Overend and Gurney, and Baring. But the largest guarantees for £30,000 each came from Fielden Brothers and A.& S. Henry, the largest merchant in the Anglo-American trade. These names were to cover the Bank should Wildes fail to repay any loan.

The Bank had made an advance of £100,000 to Wildes on 9th March, and on 21st March agreed to discount bills drawn in favour of Wildes. In the succeeding weeks the Bank monitored his affairs very closely, concerned as it was with the consequences of him suspending payment; Wildes, for instance, was required to cease accepting any further bills. By June 1st the Bank had advanced £703,727 against which it was holding bills valued at £561,323 and other security of £53,000. At that point the Bank decided to give no further assistance to Wildes, nor to Wilson and Wiggins. All three banks went into liquidation; the Bank of England had sufficient collateral for its advances not to call upon Wildes' guarantors; Fielden Brothers, accordingly, did not have to make good their security of £30,000. Baring Brothers, prudent and well reserved as they were, could weather the American panic. Others received help; W. and J. Brown (in 1837, Brown Shipley in the UK) were not in so strong a situation but given their importance and standing, and the petitions to support them raised by Liverpool and Manchester merchants, the Bank was willing to provide loans to the extent of nearly £2 million; Morrison Crowder was also helped by the Bank to the extent of £325,000. Despite the fact that the 'Three W's' all suspended payments, the crisis was contained.[17]

What of Wildes Pickersgill? A principal Partner had failed and whatever capital Wildes had committed to the Partnership was presumably exhausted. More seriously, Wildes Pickersgill had been involved in the same business as Wildes and was similarly exposed to the shortfall of American remittances. Fortunately the scale was smaller. On 31st May 1837, Wildes Pickersgill had £179,487 worth of acceptances in circulation; as these acceptances fell due, with virtually no remittances, and having endorsed bills drawn on Wildes, Wildes Pickersgill had problems in meeting its obligations. Fielden Brothers stood behind it but, perhaps for the first time, the partners realised that substantial as their resources were they were illiquid and short of cash. Their assets were in buildings and machinery and in unsold cloth consigned to distant destinations and in debts owing by merchants or agents round the world. On 20th June 1837 John Fielden himself turned to the Bank of England for help writing as follows:[18]

> 'Messrs. Wildes Pickersgill of Liverpool, with whom we are partners, have applied to us for assistance to meet their acceptances falling due and the returned bills they have endorsed drawn upon Houses in London and Liverpool who have recently suspended payment. We are desirous to give the assistance required.'

To enable such assistance to be given, that is for Fieldens to introduce more capital to Wildes Pickersgill, John Fielden asked the Bank to discount bills drawn by Fielden Brothers upon Manchester and Liverpool merchants with establishments abroad who 'have property of ours under their care on which no advances have been made.' He listed some of the principal debtors; thus Richard Rostron of Manchester owed £14,570 in respect of goods consigned to Rostron, Dutton and Co. in Rio de Janeiro and Rostron Hall and Co. in Bahia; Joseph Green of Liverpool owed £27,137 in respect of consignments to Green, Nelson of Valparaiso; Clegg and Christie of Manchester owed £5,833 against goods consigned to the same firm's offices in Beirut, Aleppo and Damascus. John Fielden asked for an advance of £75,000 upon such security.

The Governor of the Bank of England met John Fielden on 22nd June. He was not happy about the security offered but he was prepared to help. He instructed the Bank's adviser, James Freshfield, to assess what other security Fielden Brothers could afford. Freshfield reported that the land, buildings and machinery in Todmorden were worth more than £70,000 and that the Fieldens had property individually worth £40,000. And although he cast doubt on the value of such assets as security 'if Fieldens were unable to work them', he regarded the brothers as 'persons in good credit and of undoubted property', while Wildes Pickersgill's 'engagements are comparatively small.' On Freshfield's report the Bank were willing to advance £50,000.[19]

The end of the Wildes Partnership

No more is mentioned of the affair. The crisis passed and although 1837 was a bad year for the industry, it proved another excellent year for Fielden Brothers with a profit of £89,529, higher in absolute terms than any previous year. Drawings in the year were high at £31,198, including £23,454 taken out by Joshua to pay for Mytholmroyd Mill and other properties. The brothers' investment in Wildes Pickersgill rose to £209,301 at the end of 1837 (Table VI). But they were no longer comfortable with their exposure to its kind of business, especially with the scale of advances to parties in North America and the potential for bad debts. When John Fielden looked at his enlarged involvement and the large sums owing he expressed his concern. With regard to 'the parties your have accepted for', he told Bowman in July 1837, 'their engagements are either something or nothing,' and if the latter, 'what a business it is that we have got hold of.' 'You must rely upon yourselves,' he said, 'and you must not expect much more from Fielden Brothers.'[20] Some indication of the nature of the business and its risks is provided by a surviving balance sheet (Table VIII).

Clearly Fielden Brothers, following Wildes failure, were providing all the capital. Part of the liabilities were a firm short-term obligation (namely the acceptances) while the assets were a long line of debts from the United States, Canada and places such as Leghorn, Trieste and Buenos Aires, mainly advances on produce, that is, cotton, timber, wool, even rags, or payments due in respect of accepted bills. Debts due from Sundries included £36,585 owing by George Wildes and Co. while the Sundries Liability indicated further sums owing to Fielden Brothers and John Fielden personally.

Table VIII: Wildes Pickersgill: Financial Position 31st March 1838.

	£
Assets	
Debts due from the United States less amount received for produce	226,899
Debts due from Colonies less amount received for produce	159,663
Debts due from Other places	10,514
Debts due from Sundries	69,476
Advance on Mediterranean Produce	1,200
	£467,752
Liabilities	
Capital (Fielden Brothers)	£209,301
Stock held for others to be sold	£20,000
Debts Due to United States, Colonies & Other Places	£18,210
Debts due to Sundries	£51,021
Acceptances	£169,220
	£467,752

Source: Taylor MSS.[21]

John Owens (1790-1846), the Manchester merchant who did an extensive business in Lancashire cloth and other articles of manufacture with South America and elsewhere. Fieldens would sell to him and on occasions engaged in joint ventures with him but they would also be his direct competitor in consigning cloth abroad. Like him, they speculated in railway shares and lent money to others, with railway shares as security. On his death most of his fortune endowed Owens College, established in 1851 in central Manchester.

JOHN OWENS

The firm retained, however, the position it had established in the Liverpool import trades and as a ships agent,[22] Thus in 1839 it imported 15,325 bales of cotton, 1.5 cent of total Liverpool imports but well below W & J Brown (48,238 Bales), Dennistoun (42,234 bales) Baring Brothers (29,000 bales), or Brown Shipley (25,638 bales), although greater than Rathbones. The cotton business was quite independent of Fielden Brothers in Todmorden; as John Reid, the Bank of England agent in Manchester was to report in 1839, 'they are not at all in the habit of making any purchases from them.'[23] In the timber trade Wildes Pickersgill accounted for 11.8 per cent of Liverpool imports, some 20,618 tons, giving them second place to Gibbs and Bright (24,568 tons), the Anthony Gibbs associate. Other significant imports in 1839 were 7303 barrels turpentine and 3187 barrels flour, both from New York. In the same year Wildes Pickersgill were agents on eighty ship entries, mainly sailings from Maritime Canada, New York or the American cotton ports; in most cases the firm had an interest in the cargo. B.W.Clapp describes a joint venture between Fieldens and John Owens where Liverpool would be involved. The two merchants chartered a ship the *D'Arcy*, in August 1840 to pick up cargo in Buenos Aires following the blockade of that port: the *D'Arcy's* return to Europe with wool and tallow was delayed until November 1841 but the commodities sold at very full prices.[24]

Despite this business and aside from the risks, Wildes Pickersgill was not apparently making any worthwhile profits. Its credit standing was low, although it had a discount facility of £20,000 with the Bank of England (Fielden Brothers had negotiated a similar discount facility at the Manchester branch of the Bank in December 1839; the Bank was concerned that the two should be distinct enterprises). There were rumours in 1840 that attempts to secure advances against American bills — no doubt debts owing — were refused by other financial houses, and that Fielden Brothers themselves were pressed for money.[25] No doubt, assessments of the firm were influenced by the involvement of George Wildes and recollections of the events of 1837. John Fielden and his friend John Pickersgill had made attempts to introduce better control over lending, putting limits on William Pickersgill's advances and cotton purchases. In April 1838, although gloomy about American business, Pickersgill was 'happy to say we are getting our acceptances paid quite as fast as I expected.' In trying to reassure Fielden he could only say 'all we want is time and patience', but Fielden's confidence remained low.[26]

A statement of debtors and creditors in November 1841 shows the same heavy reliance on Fielden Brothers' capital to support advances and credits given to debtors all round the world. Fielden Brothers are shown as a creditor for £247,778. But Colin Campbell is now contributing £38,407 as a creditor. Pickersgill & Co. is shown as a large debtor (£253,760) and creditor (£169,405) indicating the scale of their involvement. Although the debtors were merchants throughout the United Kingdom, in New York and the United States cotton ports, there are especially large accounts with John Kirk and John Wishart in St. John, both timber shippers and the St. John Whaling Company, suppliers of sperm oil. Finally the Astor concern, the American Fur Company owed £60,128, partly offset by £27,112 owing to C.M Lampson, their agent in London.[27]

The Partnership was restructured at the end of 1841, when the original agreement expired. Wildes Pickersgill ceased to trade and its assets and liabilities were assumed by a new company, Fielden Brothers & Company, in which the Fieldens, William Pickersgill and Daniel Campbell were Partners; George Wildes, John Pickersgill and William Bowman withdrew. There is no indication that Fieldens had lost heavily in Wildes Pickersgill; it had been a source of risk and anxiety that yielded no commensurate return. The documents prepared at the time of the wind-up indicate that in six years profits of not less than £50,000 after interest on partner's capital were made. The wind up document clearly anticipates that most of the money owing to the Partnership would be paid and this seems to have been the case and Fieldens made no subsequent provision for bad debts incurred by Wildes Pickersgill.

Fielden Brothers and Company

The new company began to trade on a more restricted basis. As overseas debtors repaid their advances or bills, and this form of financing was not renewed, the capital employed was sharply reduced, partly it is true

The Flags, Exchange Buildings, Liverpool. Here, throughout the nineteenth century, buying and selling brokers, acting for shippers, importers and manufacturers, transacted business in actual raw cotton, "arrivals" or futures. Twelve o'clock noon was the important time for Change — and a top hat and frock coat the required dress. Fieldens would not trade themselves here, but through brokers, and especially Colin Campbell.

to support the stock position that was developing in Todmorden, to the partners' deep concern. The new business concentrated on cotton and produce imports through Liverpool, advancing finance to the extent necessary to secure consignments that would be sold on a commission basis. Fielden Brothers remained the main providers of capital. William Pickersgill in New York, trading as Pickersgill and Co., but also as Fielden Brothers & Co., handled the American side of the business as before. Daniel Campbell took charge in Liverpool where he seems to have been highly regarded. Thomas Ellison was to describe him as 'a man of very good presence; tall, erect and dignified, and in all matters an ideal British merchant.'[29] Both Pickersgill and Campbell, as partners, put in some capital. New York and Liverpool were now to be involved with William Pickersgill's youngest brother Thomas, who had established himself as a commission merchant in Buchanan Street, Glasgow; Thomas in turn was in partnership with James Tibbits in Quebec to trade there as Pickersgill Tibbits. On Thomas's death in 1847, his father's company, John Pickersgill and Co., in which the other older brother John was involved, took over the Glasgow operation.

Application was made to the Bank of England for the Wildes Pickersgill discount facility of £20,000 to be transferred to the new company. The Bank's Liverpool agent, Samuel Turner was against this; he clearly had doubts whether Fielden Brothers were as safe as they seemed but the Court granted the facility nonetheless. Turner, and others in Liverpool, retained their suspicions; in May 1842, referring to the general view that Fieldens were 'men of large property and that the House was quite undoubted,' he 'had not quite that confidence that others express'; if the credit of the firm 'stands as quite first rate', his impression was that 'it really is not so strong as is generally believed.'[30]

Fielden Brothers & Co. was a general importer but the greater part of its business remained in cotton and timber. In cotton it maintained the strong position Wildes Pickersgill had developed. There was a close relationship with Andrew McDowall and Co., cotton factors in

George's Dock, Liverpool. This early photograph shows the congested shipping in the old eighteenth century dock: the Goree warehouses are on the right. The Liver and Cunard Buildings now occupy the site. George's Dock in the 1830s handled most of the general trade of Liverpool such as cotton, hides, provisions and exports of cloth, hardware and the like, in which Wildes Pickersgill and later Fielden Brothers and Co. were involved. Princes Dock, which was adjacent, opened in 1821 and would provide berths for the sailing packets. As the trade of the port boomed many other docks were built, including the first specialised timber dock, Brunswick Dock, in 1834.

Charleston, South Carolina, based on family and friendship ties — the young John Fielden had been at school with a McDowall — but Pickersgill or Fieldens had agents in each of the main cotton shipping ports. For a while in late 1842 and 1843 Fielden Bros. and Co. appeared to be the largest Liverpool importer surpassing both Barings and Brown Shipley and Rathbone: the scale of its business, (184,392 bales or about 8 per cent of total imports) on a falling market, caused the Bank of England some concern.[31] But for the most part the cotton was not at Fieldens' risk. On arrival the consignments were sold through brokers on the best terms for the account of the shippers and found their way to the spinning concerns in Lancashire. Again at this time, there is no evidence that the Liverpool house was importing cotton for the account of the manufacturing business in Todmorden; the relationship was much the same as with Wildes Pickersgill, that is the two were distinct separate businesses; the main business between Liverpool and Todmorden was in flour (for size) and in timber.

Timber remained the other large import business; this was still a rapidly expanding bulk trade between the United Kingdom and the Canadian Maritimes, with Liverpool, through Brunswick and later Canada Docks, the main port of entry. Squared logs and deals (3 inch planks) of White and Red Pine made up the bulk of the trade which was carried in specially designed timber ships, built for the most part in St. Johns or Quebec. The trade was a volatile one, up and down, with the Canadian merchant, financed by advances from Liverpool, taking the risks; on arrival the timber was generally auctioned by the

Charleston, South Carolina, a major cotton shipping port where Fielden's agent was A.G. McDowall. Wildes Pickersgill, and then Fielden Brothers and Co., had a significant share of the Liverpool trade in new cotton, importing, on commission terms, from all the major American cotton ports, New Orleans, Mobile, Savannah, as well as Charleston. These imports were sold on the Liverpool market; Fielden Brothers in Todmorden bought their mill requirements quite separately.

importer to inland dealers on the dockside. The Fieldens had anotherCanadian concern when John Fielden became involved in the affairs of the whaling business, the Mechanics Whale Fishing Co., partly no doubt to better source whale and sperm oil which were important lubricants used in Lancashire mills at the time, but mainly because the Company was a debtor to Wildes Pickersgill for £12,000.[32] But Liverpool continued to trade a whole range of other commodities including, as earlier, Indian corn, American flour, bacon and lard, hides, ashes, turpentine, New York apples, rice, red clover seed and flax seed, tallow and whalebone. All these are among the items of produce mentioned in Bills of Entry arrivals for Fielden account, or in market letters and correspondence.[33] Continuing the Wildes Pickersgill business, the firm acted as ships' agent to several ship owners, usually but not always figuring as the principal importer of cargo on the vessel.

Both Barings and Brown Shipley had become Liverpool agents to the booming packet lines owned by New York companies which serviced the passenger, mail and fast cargo traffic between New York and Liverpool. The sailing packets were at their peak in the late 1830s and 1840s; traffic volume was growing strongly, with emigration providing a means of filling the space below decks on the westbound journey, while competition from steam had not yet asserted itself. No doubt because of William Pickersgill, in 1842 Fielden Brothers & Co. were appointed agents for the New Line, owned in New York by Woodfull and Mintum. They had four ships to service, including *Queen of the West* (1334 tons)

A Sailing Packet of the 1840s, similar to the *Queen of the West* and the *Independence* which were among the ships which Fieldens managed as the New Line. The Liverpool — New York crossing against the prevailing wind, took 35 days, and more in winter when it was an ordeal for passengers and crew alike. The westward crossing, at about 20 days was much shorter. Steerage accommodation was crowded and primitive but full-fare paying passengers had individual cabins, a saloon, salt water baths, and fresh meat provided by the farm, live animals being carried for slaughter on the voyage. The cabin fare was £25, a large sum at the time.

New York Packet Ships.				
Days of sailing from Liverpool.		Days of sailing from New York.		
Jan. May Sept.		Mar. July Nov.		
1 1 1	Monteruma—*Lowber* Baring	16 16 16		
6 6 6	Hottinguer—*Bursley* Fielden	21 21 21		
11 11 11	Roscius—*Collins* Brown	26 26 26		
		April Aug. Dec.		
16 16 16	Europe—*Furber* Baring	1 1 1		
21 21 21	Independence—*Nye* Chapman	6 6 6		
26 26 26	Samuel Hicks—*Bunker* Sands	11 11 11		
Feb. June Oct.				
1 1 1	New York—*Cropper* Baring	16 16 16		
6 6 6	Liverpool—*Eldridge* Fielden	21 21 21		
11 11 11	Siddons—*Cobb* Brown	26 26 26		
		May Sept. Jan.		
16 16 16	Columbus—*Cole* Baring	1 1 1		
21 21 21	Ashburton—*Huttleson* Chapman	6 6 6		
26 26 26	Stephen Whitney—*Thompson*			
		Sands 11 11 11		
Mar. July Nov.				
1 1 1	Yorkshire—*Bailey* Baring	16 16 16		
6 6 6	Queen of the West—*Woodhouse*			
	Fielden	21 21 21		
11 11 11	Sheridan—*De Peyster* Brown	26 26 26		
		June Oct. Feb.		
16 16 16	Cambridge—*Barstow* Baring	1 1 1		
21 21 21	Washington—*Allen* Chapman	6 6 6		
26 26 26	United States—*Britton* Sands	11 11 11		
Apl. Aug. Dec.				
1 1 1	England—*Bartlett* Baring	16 16 16		
6 6 6	Rochester—*Britton* Fielden	21 21 21		
11 11 11	Garrick—*Trask* Brown	26 26 26		
		July Nov. Mar.		
16 16 16	Oxford—*Rathbone* Baring	1 1 1		
21 21 21	Patrick Henry—*Delano* Chap-			
	man	6 6 6		
26 29 26	Virginian—*Allen* Sands	11 11 11		

launched in 1842 and the largest sailing ship of the day, and the *Liverpool* (1139 tons) launched in 1843, which, with its sixty first and second class cabins, state-rooms, bathing room, smoking room and 183 foot upper deck, provided new standards in passenger accommodation; up to 500 steerage passengers were kept entirely separate. The *Liverpool* could also carry 1,500 bales of cotton. Other ships on the line at the time were the *Rochester* and the *Hottinguer.*[34]

The Fielden agency ships made three double crossings a year and thus provided a monthly service leaving Liverpool on the 6th of each month and New York on the 21st. With Barings, Brown Shipley and others, in 1843 the several agencies were offering six Liverpool — New York sailings each month, at five day intervals. The fare at the time for cabin journeys was £25, without wine and spirits; dogs were charged £6, and steerage passengers £3.10s. The westward passage took on average thirty-five days, longer in winter and shorter in the summer, while the eastward crossing was shorter, averaging twenty-five days and sometimes as swift as fifteen days. Sailing times could be delayed by unfavourable winds, especially in Liverpool, where the prevailing westerly blew straight down the Mersey, but the packets stuck to their schedule whether full or not. The winter crossings, needless to say, did great damage to the ships and were an ordeal to the crews and passengers alike. Each ship had a farmyard, a cow for milk, sheep, pigs and chickens to provide food during the crossing. Cargo was carried as well as passengers and mail, cloth from Liverpool, and from New York cotton and provisions such as flour, cheese, lard and tobacco.

To Fieldens, as to Barings and Brown Shipley, being a sailing packet agent brought fees for providing services, booking passengers and gathering or distributing cargo, as well as servicing the ship. The real benefits, however, lay in the commissions on sales of cotton or produce consignments carried on the ship which were usually sold through its agent. And secondly there was intelligence; being first with the news

(Above)
Timetable for the Liverpool — New York Packet 1844. The several packet lines provided sailings from each port every five days. Each ship made three round trips yearly which allowed plenty of time for contingencies and refurbishment. Fielden's competitors in the business included Barings and W & J Brown, both to become famous names in merchant banking.

(Above left)
Princes Dock, Liverpool. The New York sailing packet with St Nicholas's Church behind.

ROCHESTER, of N York, P Woodhouse, NEW YORK, 24 m, 845 t, Fielden Brs & Co, W D	
Turpentine 300 brls	do
136	Order
Cotton 397 bls	do
191	Collmann & Stolterfoht
124	Phipps & Co
58	Hunt & Tyndall
319	Rathbone Brs & Co
13	Mitchell, Tooker & Co
204	J & D Stuart & Co
100	Bancroft & Co
1 brl ore	do
1 bx conts unkn	Master
1 bx seeds	Brown, Shipley & Co

Liverpool Bill of Entry: the *Rochester* was one of the Fielden packets. In addition to passengers, cotton and turpentine were among the cargo for Fielden account when the arrival from New York was entered on 11 March 1843. The *Rochester* sank with all hands in 1847.

South Street, New York, where the sailing packets between New York and Liverpool found berths. Fieldens' corresponding New Line agents, Woodfull and Mintum would have a small office here or nearby.

from America on the latest packet, which could frequently be a large advantage in the Liverpool markets. The Fielden agency did not last; the New Line was sold to the larger Blue Swallowtail Line in 1849 and Barings took over the agency. But by then Samuel Cunard with his Royal Mail Steamship Company was providing a fast service to New York, twice-weekly and a fifteen day crossing. The sailing packets lowered their fares but lost their business; in the 1850s most of the ships became carriers of emigrants.

The timber ports of Canada, Quebec and especially St. John, were also great shipbuilding centres and this, the 1830s and 1840s, was the great period for cheaply built Canadian softwood sailing ships. Many of the new ships, designed to carry timber, were loaded with timber in St. John when completed, and sailed to Liverpool where both cargo and ship was sold. These were probably the circumstances in which Thomas Fielden bought St. John-built ships for Wildes Pickersgill, the *Ben Nevis* (956 tons) in 1840, the *Britannia* (769 tons), the *Edinburgh* (942 tons) and the *Mountaineer* (870 tons) in 1841. These ships seem to have been sold back to St. John shipowners like John Kirk and John Wishart in the years that followed. In 1847 Fielden Brothers & Co. went into shipowning more seriously when they bought mainly from Tibbits, Kirk or Wishart as many as twenty-one ships, most newly built, others older, including ships like the *Edinburgh* and *Mountaineer* that had been bought and sold earlier. Of the ships now registered, in the name of Samuel Fielden, one was named *John Fielden* (916 tons) and another *Thomas Fielden* (904 tons). Typically these ships cost £7 to £12 per ton new, depending on the quality of the wood and the extent of the outfit; the *Ben Nevis,* for instance, had cost £7,588. The Fielden investment, at its peak in the late 1840s, must have been considerable, hardly less than £100,000.[35]

The Fielden ships were only part of a much larger fleet with over 400 ships carrying timber from the Canadian Maritimes to Liverpool at the climax of the trade. Each ship carried about its own weight in timber on two crossings between May and October, but this was not the only eastern cargo: the ships would carry cotton or other bulk cargoes from ice-free ports in winter. Thus in April 1850 the Fielden ship *Lord Wellington* arrived from New Orleans carrying for Fielden Brothers 1,000 bales of cotton and 8,903 sacks of Indian Corn as well as 7630 staves. Cargo for the westward crossing was far more difficult but in the middle and late 1840s the timber ships would carry the most impoverished emigrants, typically Irish, after the famine, who could scarcely afford to pay 30/- for the crossing, with no food or bedding supplied.

MOUNTAINEER, of L'pool, J Bogart, QUEBEC,	
27 m, 869 t, Fielden Brs & Co, River	
200 ps oak, 246 ps r & 170 ps w pine & 15 ps ash timber, 9157 staves, 2766 deals, 10½ cords	
lathwood	Fielden Brs & Co
1 brl apples	J S de Wolf
51 tcs beef	W Rose & Co
342 brls flour	C Cusack & Son
1439 50 kgs butter, 253 brls pot ashes, 1 birch canoe	Order
FRANCIS, of Peterhead, W Russeil, CEPHALONIA & ZANTE, 8 m, 148 t, J Heap&Sons, — D	
From Cephalonia	
40 bts 23 crtls 300 bxs currants, 1 t fustic do	
From Zante	
106 bts 82 crtls currants do	

Liverpool Bill of Entry, 18th December 1843.
The Fielden timber ship *Mountaineer*, 869 tons with a crew of twenty-seven, arrived in Liverpool from Quebec carrying a cargo mainly of red and white pine and oak logs, staves and deals which were sawn timber planks. While the timber was for account of Fielden Brothers and Co., provisions carried on the ship were for other Liverpool merchants. The timber would be off-loaded and sold at Brunswick Dock, Fieldens taking a commission on the sale value; their ship would also have received freight.

(Left and overleaf)
Timber Ships at Quebec in the mid nineteenth century. Quebec and St. John, New Brunswick, were the principal ports from which Canadian softwood timber was shipped to Liverpool in a season lasting from April to October. Rafts of timber were floated down to these ports in the spring; men selected the cargo from the floating timbers which were then lifted by chain and shoved through the ports near the ship's bow and stowed away. 'Deals' or sawn timber planks would be brought alongside in barges. Fielden Brothers and Co. had a significant share in this trade, owning at one time as many as twenty-one timber ships, two being named *John Fielden* and *Thomas Fielden*.

Conditions, needless to say, were wretched, with 400 or 500 people of all ages and all conditions crowded below deck for a crossing which in winter might take over fifty days. Many of the passengers remained at sea; in the worst year, 1847, one in six of those crossing to Canada died on board or in quarantine on landing. But this was the business of the time; there was a huge demand for passage at an affordable price. Many of the timber ships were diverted to the Australian trade after 1851 when gold discoveries there created an insatiable demand for passage.

The Brothers were comfortable with the new Liverpool firm, and especially with Daniel Campbell and William Pickersgill. In 1847 they reported profits of £157,500 over the five years since its formation; the capital employed in Liverpool, although sharply reduced between 1842 and 1845, was allowed to rise to £271,000 at the end of 1847 with the purchase of the timber ships (Table VI). The four Fielden brothers were now pleased to call themselves not merely manufacturers but also merchants 'of Manchester, Liverpool, and New York.' The name of Fielden was established and respected in North American commerce.

Todmorden and the Crisis of 1842

After the prosperous years of the early and mid 1830s, which continued into 1838, the Lancashire cotton trade was plunged into deep and prolonged depression between 1839 and 1842, a depression that went beyond the range of anyone's calculations. There were general causes: a succession of poor harvests, high food prices and the fall in railway investment. In Lancashire poor trade was also the result of falling raw cotton prices and over capacity, the consequence of headlong expansion during the boom; a long period of poor or inadequate margins followed. Falling prices and over-supply discouraged demand, the whole chain of distribution destocked and for long periods business in Manchester was at a standstill.

Writing to his brothers in December 1838, Thomas Fielden complained of 'constant uncertainty, whether to buy, whether to sell, what to pay, what to accept. It is not worth paying present prices for cotton and going on producing.' He urged to stop a few extra days at Christmas and take stock.[36] In the event, in late 1838 and during 1839, like other manufacturers, Fieldens worked short time for at least part of the year. Profits were sharply lower in 1839 following a write-down of 10 per cent in the value of stocks in Manchester and abroad.[37] Trade remained lifeless in 1840 and in April 1841 the Manchester agent of the Bank of England was reporting that 'few mills can at present be doing any good for their owners;'[38] there were mill closures and business failures across Lancashire in the year. Conditions worsened in 1842. Fielden Brothers & Co., in their first trade circular in March, reported 'a contracted, depressed and unprofitable trade in goods and yarns, together with crippled finances.'[39] Leonard Horner's Factory Inspector's reports in 1842 catalogue 'a state of extreme depression without any distinct prospect of improvement' and 'unexampled difficulty and distress in the manufacturing communities.' Mill property, Horner reported, was being sold at a fraction of its former value or was unsaleable.[40] John Bright was later to comment that between 1839 and 1842, one half of the cotton manufacturers of Stockport were 'wholly ruined.'[41]

These were the circumstances in which stocks of piece goods in Todmorden began to rise sharply. That this was allowed to happen was partly a reflection of the Partners' initial view that the recession would not last too long; trade and prices would recover, as they had done in the past, and cloth woven for stock would, in due course, be realised at a profit. Such a confident view of the future was reflected in a continued high level of investment in extended buildings, especially at Waterside where preparation of a second loom shed continued in 1839, and at Mytholmroyd where the large mill acquired by Joshua Fielden was extensively refurbished and carding engines and a comprehensive throstle spinning facility installed (Appendix I). In total £11,949 was spent at Mytholmroyd between 1838 and 1841. Two new 60 HP steam engines linked by one fly-wheel and costing £3,351 were installed at Waterside in 1841, the completion of an order placed some time before. The recession led to many cheap disposals of mill premises and machinery. Fieldens spent £1,645 at machinery sales in 1840.

As the depression continued, short time working, unemployment, and high food prices were causing acute distress among working populations throughout Lancashire. Reflecting these circumstances, the Chartist agitation was at its height and while John Fielden shared the peaceful objectives of the Chartist movement and with other Radicals had been associated with its early stages, he and his brothers were now concerned with the threat to good order and the peace of society. Their fears were to be justified as mob violence and disorder manifested itself in 1842. Fielden was deeply conscious of his obligation to his workpeople; without the work he gave them, and their wages, they would be destitute. As his son was to put it later, he would have accepted 'a social and religious duty' to protect his people. The Poor Law offered only a limited remedy to the distress of the time, not least because outdoor relief, exceptional and improper as it now was, depended in the last resort on poor rates levied on property owners, tradesmen and manufacturers, themselves in poor financial condition because of poor trade. Expenditure on outdoor relief in the Todmorden Union had risen from £3,025 in 1837 to £5,029 in 1840 and £5,836 in 1841; it was to riseto £9,039 in 1842.[42]

Fielden also believed strongly that the appropriate manufacturer response to depressed trade was not to reduce wages but to reduce output by short time working. In March 1841, for instance, he was aware of the local pressure to reduce wages. Inghams, for instance were doing that and making their weavers provide their own shuttles. In Burnley, mills were standing as masters and hands disputed a wage reduction of 1½d in the shilling, as the masters proposed, or 1d in the shilling, as the hands would accept. 'When', he asked 'will the masters learn wisdom and do less time rather than reduce wages.'[43] The course he followed and advocated was 'to do less time', whether by taking longer shutdowns at Christmas, Whitsun or Fair time; by working a shorter week; or by working shorter hours, for instance, the hours of daylight, or less. As in other periods of bad trade, actual practice may have been a combination of these. Invariably the mill would sustain losses at these periods because fixed costs would not be covered; but the workforce received some wages and lower output, if sufficient firms followed the policy, would hasten the eventual recovery.

Fielden's concern at the time is evident in an emotional speech on the Sugar Duties he had printed in May 1841, and in the representations he made to Sir Robert Peel at an interview on 4 October 1841. He then urged extraordinary help to the poor and government initiatives to regulate production.[44]

He had explained his position in a speech to the House of Commons in September 1841,

> 'The distress of the manufacturing population in his neighbourhood, and other manufacturing districts, was so great that they could not get bread to eat; they were begging about the streets in crowds and unable to get relief from the Unions sufficient to alleviate their wants. So severe was the distress in Lancashire that it was found impossible to raise sufficient means in the locality to support the poor, much less to pay the increased expense of a rural police. Were it not for the mill-owners the distress of the people would be even greater than it was; but out of sympathy for their workmen they gave them partial employment to keep them from starving. That was the case with regard to his own firm; they employed their men four hours a day, only to enable them to obtain food, not for any profit to themselves.'[45]

When William Dodd visited Waterside in November 1841, the mill was working in daylight only, that is eight hours.[46] But such was the state of trade that even reduced output was unsaleable on satisfactory terms. Fielden had demonstrated the collapse in margins that took place in 1841 in his meeting with Peel. A clerk in his Manchester office writing in March 1842 spoke of sales of cloth 'being a rare occurrence these

TODMORDEN FROM THE NORTH.

days.'[47] As Fieldens continued to weave, albeit on a reduced scale, without making sales, they were committing more and more of their capital to stocks of finished goods. Stocks of woven pieces, both power-loom and hand-loom, had now been increasing since late 1838 and the build up continued without respite. Dodd found nearly 300,000 woven pieces in stock, all ready for market. So large a quantity would represent about one year's production from the power-loom shed and hand-loom weavers combined. The brothers were well aware of the cash flow implications: as John Fielden had written in November 1840, 'The state of business is such in the cotton branch that I and my partners find it necessary to stop all outlets of money — in order that we may be able to continue our hands at work.'[48]

This policy, sensible and humane as it was for a firm with adequate capital — it would not have been feasible for less wealthy concerns — was all-right so long as the depression in trade was not too prolonged. In 1841 and 1842 the Fieldens miscalculated the duration of the recession and its severity. The financial implications of what they were doing are evident from the figures in Table IX. Such a huge unsold stock, which had to be written down in value as prices continued to fall, represented a significant risk. More importantly, as more and more of the Partnership's capital was absorbed in stock, the policy became difficult to sustain. Funds employed in Manchester and Liverpool had to be diverted to Todmorden to meet the raw cotton and wages bills implicit

Tait's view of Todmorden, one of the series of views along the line of the Manchester and Leeds Railway, published in 1840. The industrial town is still comparatively small, settlement predominantly on the hillsides rather than the valleys. The chimneys of Waterside and of Buckley's Mill at Ridgefoot are prominent. The scene is peaceful but the period, the early 1840s, was one of distress and hardship throughout the manufacturing districts of Lancashire.

Piece Stocks at Waterside 1840s. Weaving for stock was a policy regularly followed by the Fieldens in the troughs of cotton trade activity. It usually made good commercial sense and protected the livelihood of their work-people. But the trade depression of the early 1840s was more severe and prolonged than anticipated, and the huge accumulation of unsold cloth at Waterside, over one-year's output of power-looms and hand-loom weavers, nearly exhausted the substantial capital of the Partnership and brought it close to insolvency.

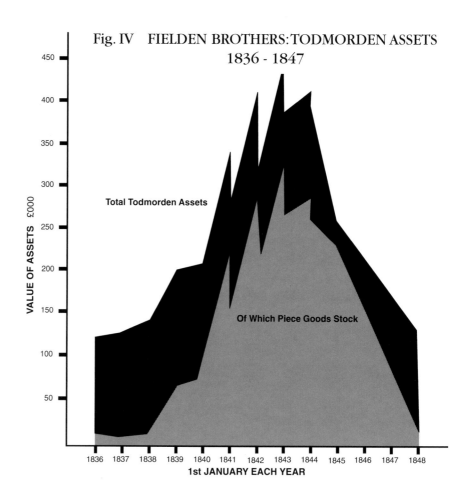

Fig. IV   FIELDEN BROTHERS: TODMORDEN ASSETS 1836 - 1847

Table IX: Fielden Brothers: Todmorden Assets and Stock 1832-1845.

Date	Total Todmorden Assets (£)	Of Which Stock (£)	Piece Goods Stock (£)
1 June 1832	92,739	36,552	24,553
1 Jan. 1836	121,616	22,007	9,945
1 Jan. 1837	126,938	38,819	7,468
1 Jan. 1838	143,608	26,119	11,107
1 Jan. 1839	199,344	86,280	62,260
1 Jan. 1840	205,849	93,749	72,039
1 Jan. 1841	272,870	147,039	124,165*
1 Jan. 1842	307,832	202,439	183,973*
1 Jan. 1843	376,727	274,342	258,269*
1 Jan. 1844	402,904	307,042	281,021*
1 Jan. 1845	351,949	251,059	228,715*

Source: WYAS, Machinery Valuation, C353/132.

*Note *:* Stocks of piecegoods were written down by 5 per cent (£6535) on 1 January 1841; one-sixth (£36,795) on 1 January 1842; by 10 per cent (£28,697) on 1 January 1843; by 12½% per cent on 1 January 1844 (£40,142) and by 12½% per cent on 1 January 1845 (£32,674).

in the expanding inventory. Most pronounced was the withdrawal of capital from the Manchester activity, that is from direct marketing of cloth abroad. Funds tied up in Wildes Pickersgill were not released until the partnership was dissolved at the end of 1841: a sharp reduction in Liverpool capital employed followed in 1842 (Table VI). With a savage deterioration in cash flow, investment in mills and machinery virtually ceased (Appendix I). The crisis point was reached in the spring of 1842 when, no doubt, there were no longer the liquid resources within the Partnership to continue their policy. At that time at the several mills wages amounting to £580 per week were being paid, and about 65,000 lbs cotton costing say £1,300 weekly being used.[49] Without cash to pay for cotton, or to pay wages, the Fieldens would have to close. Abraham Ormerod, a local rival mill owner, was to talk in Manchester of rumours sweeping Todmorden that this was going to happen and that Fieldens would have to suspend their works. Indeed without help they might have become insolvent.

These were the circumstances in which John Fielden made his second approach to the Bank of England for help. On 8th June writing from his London lodgings in Panton Square, John Fielden described how his firm were

'holders of a very considerable stock of cotton goods of our own manufacture, all made at low prices but not low enough to command a sale at present except at a sacrifice such as we cannot willingly submit to as we cannot replace them at the prices we should have to accept. And we are also employers of some thousands of hands for whom we have a sincere regard and should deeply regret being under the necessity of throwing them out of work,'

Fielden asked the Bank to advance £50,000 for 6 months at interest on the same security as it had accepted in 1837. The Governors agreed to the loan at 4 per cent interest, subject to a further report from James Freshfield on the collateral.[50] So Freshfield visited Todmorden again and confirmed the security. The Bank's loan was not in the event needed, but with this backing the firm survived. Fortunately trade revived in the autumn. The approach to the Bank of England was no doubt a last resort when other sources of credit proved abortive: the Bank was not in the business of baling out failing businesses and the exceptional assistance it offered clearly indicates the standing, respect and influence which John Fielden then commanded.

1841 and 1842 had brought losses, (Table VII) due to unprofitable trading and heavy write-downs of piece goods stock and abnormal depreciation of machinery. Thus the firm's normal practice was to depreciate buildings by 5 per cent, machinery by 10 per cent annually: these were higher rates of depreciation than normally practised by Lancashire firms, typically 5 or 7½ per cent. All expenditure on building and machinery, much of it carried out by Fieldens' Mechanics Department and much of it repairs and maintenance rather than additions to fixed assets, was capitalised rather than expensed; aggressive depreciation in the circumstances was prudent and appropriate. The effect was to reduce profits and write down the value of fixed assets, understating their true worth, but the Partners were the only parties affected. At the end of 1841, at a time when mills and machinery were unsaleable or selling at a fraction of their cost, Fieldens depreciated their machinery by 33 per cent; a further large write down of about 15 per cent took place following revaluation at the end of 1842. Over the same years, the Ashworths depreciated machinery at 7½ per cent or 10 per cent, and seem to have made no provision in the worst years 1839-1842.[51]

Speaking in February 1844 John Fielden said that:[52]

'he and his partners, instead of a profit on the three years preceding, had sustained a heavy loss; they held a heavy stock of goods which had been accumulating over that period, and the value of their stock upon the same quantity of goods had been less and less every succeeding stock-taking; that the raw material used had fallen lower and lower until July last; that they had kept up wages which, had they been reduced, would have caused much suffering among their workpeople; that they had made bad debts to a considerable amount; and that the capital employed had diminished in amount at the end of that period.'

The actual losses, were £29,153 and £25,508 in the two years 1841 and 1842 (Table VII). These were easy for the Fieldens to take: this had been a cash crisis rather than a profit crisis. Fortunately 1842 was to prove the lowest ebb. The firm, unlike many others, had survived. It closed 1842 with a huge inventory of cloth, written down to market levels or below and with enlarged and improved physical assets, realistically revalued and probably undervalued. As trade recovered it could again view the future with confidence.

Recovery in the 1840s

Trade began to pick up in November 1842. The stoppage of mills in the summer of 1842 that followed the Plug Drawers riots, reduced mill output and hastened the turn-round. Cotton prices remained low but there was a strong revival of business in 1843 at improved margins. Partly stimulated by cheap cotton, the industry again began to increase its turnover; cotton consumption after falling in 1841 and 1842, increased by 19 percent in 1843 and by a further 17 per cent by 1845. At the end of 1844, *The Economist* was to write of 'better prospects than for several years past.' These were again busy years with renewed mill building in Lancashire and mills long unoccupied being taken up by new tenants; in 1845 and 1846 it was difficult to find hands. There were severe checks in 1847, when a sharp rise in cotton prices and weak yarn and cloth markets combined to depress the cotton industry, and again in 1848 when the revolutions across Europe paralysed commercial transactions for a time, but there was a further strong recovery in 1849.

Fieldens could now exploit their enlarged facilities and complete the next phase of their expansion at Todmorden. They had survived the severest recession to date. Their own analysis of their costs in Todmorden spinning and weaving no doubt demonstrated that their labour costs and overheads were more than competitive with the industry. At this time the fact that they had several mills, under different managers, with similar equipment and performing similar processes, provided another advantage; namely the opportunity to compare the manning levels and performance of one mill with that of another. The Partners seem to have done this frequently, and used the exercise to improve performance across the business.[53] 'Periods of depression have always been periods of progress,' as Thomas Ellison was to write much later. As in other businesses, the recession had stimulated Fieldens to search for economies in operation to be achieved by improvements in spinning and weaving efficiency, (machine speeds, manning levels) and by savings in fuel use and the like. Engineering skills and investment were partly directed to these ends. The newly opened Manchester and Leeds Railway, with sidings and Fieldens' own warehouse adjacent to Waterside, could only help their competitiveness within the industry.

There was now a further source of impetus: the next generation. Of the four brothers in the first Partnership, James and Thomas were childless. Joshua had a son and a daughter: the son, John, was stricken with syphilis and was to take no part in the business, eventually moving away from Todmorden. It was the three sons of John who were now to assume an increasingly active role before succeeding to leadership in the second Partnership. The eldest, Samuel, having completed his

The Rochdale Canal at Waterside, close to the mill, and heavily used by the Partnership before the railway came. With the opening of the Manchester and Leeds, Fieldens built warehouses at their own siding, these being connected with the mills by an overhead walkway; this photograph shows the walkway where it crosses the canal.

Young Sam. Samuel Fielden, born in 1816, having completed a very Unitarian education and been through the mill, took charge as a junior partner of manufacturing activities in Todmorden in the late 1840s. He looks confident, authoritative but not arrogant or overbearing in this engraving of the time.

education, joined the business in 1835. A letter from his sister dated May 1836 makes the point that 'Sam is so industrious you cannot think — he often gets up at five-o-clock in the morning and goes into the mill.'[54] Young Sam, as he was known, was to prove able, masterful and assertive and to dominate the business in the future. In the 1840s he gradually took control of Waterside and the outmills, although he communicated with his father, involved as the latter was with Parliamentary Affairs and the Ten Hours Bill, at every stage. In June 1840 he wrote to London to say that he had let a farm and to report progress on the loom shed extension and new steam engines, as well as family and local news. In July 1845 Sam was asking his father, 'how and where you intend the twist for the coarse drills to be spun and warped.' He went on 'there certainly is as much winding as they well can manage, if they could do more. We have three weeks stock of warps for the present make of drills, and it will be time to stop warping them 'ere long.'[55] John Fielden, involved in the detail, was not a delegator, but his eldest son was also demonstrating his involvement with the business.

John Junior, the second son, was gregarious and outgoing; he joined the business as assistant to Thomas in the Manchester warehouse. In July 1845 he is writing confidently to his father about the market in Manchester, 'I have not sold any more yarn, as I think I may probably get a little more than 9½d for 24s in the course of another week.' But he had sold 3870 pieces of cloth as he reported.[56] He became the firm's representative on the Exchange on market days. Joshua, the third son, on completing his schooling, seems to have gone to work in the counting house at Waterside. Many of the firm's letters in the late 1840s and subsequently are in his hand, as are the confidential ledgers. But illustrative of the close involvement in detail that John Fielden retained, Joshua is corresponding with his father in April 1845 about the digging of goits and the wheel race at one of the mills, as well as family matters.[57]

Samuel and his younger brother John were admitted to the Partnership along with the senior manager, John Holt, in 1845, Samuel receiving 10 percent of the profits, his brother and Holt 5 per cent each. Joshua had to wait for his participation until the second Partnership was formed in the early 1850s.[58] The management resources were further strengthened by Thomas Fielden Uttley, the illegitimate son of the eldest brother, Samuel, who had died in 1822. Uttley had a close relationship with his 'uncles'; after working under John Haigh, he was placed in charge of the newly-acquired and refitted mill at Mytholmroyd. Edmund Holt, related to John Holt, the Waterside manager, was put in charge at Lumbutts. Some of the able Fielden managers left to start on their own. John Lord, the machine maker and his sons, have been mentioned; John Firth and William Howarth were two others to leave Waterside to start as cotton manufacturers, Firth and Howarth, and succeed on their own account; another was John Lacy who established himself at Callis Mill.

Thomas Fielden Uttley (1817-1862) was the natural son of Samuel Fielden (1772-1822) the oldest of the second generation. His uncles provided for him and he became manager of the Mytholmroyd Mill and then, in the 1850s, of Waterside when he lived at Waterside House. His health failed and he moved to Stones where he died in 1862. He had been given a share of Partnership profits like his predecessor at Waterside, John Holt, and he died a comparatively wealthy man. This picture shows Uttley and his family rowing on the mill dam at Mytholmroyd.

Fielden Brothers returned to modest profitability in 1843 and 1844, despite further write downs in the value of stocks of piece goods. Profits for the whole enterprise were £43,257 in 1843 and £56,325 in 1844. Short time working ended in 1843 although the physical stock of piece-goods continued to rise: it was only in the following year that in addition to sales of current output, the piece-goods inventory could be reduced substantially. By the end of 1847, however, the inventory had been reduced to normal levels. Never again would Fielden Brothers take quite the same bold course they had followed in 1841 and 1842. As capital was released by disposal of the Todmorden stock, and the firm returned to profitability, the funds employed in Liverpool and in Manchester were enlarged (Table VI). The allocation of the firm's assets returned to the pattern of the late 1830s; Liverpool, in particular, now trading profitably, was using funds on a large scale, with investments in ship-owning the new feature.

Meanwhile, the Partnership now had capital surplus to the needs of its core businesses. In Manchester, apart from adventures in trade, the partners became willing to use their wealth to purchase property, and to make loans to other businessmen whom they knew and could trust, with mortgage or other security; in effect the Fieldens were becoming financiers. At the end of 1847, for instance, £129,000 was loaned out to various but unidentified individuals on the security of railway shares, possibly to finance calls on other railway shares, or new purchases. Others, like John Owens, the successful Manchester merchant, were doing the same thing. The rate of interest charged is not recorded, but was probably 6 or 7 per cent. The fall in the value of railway shares left the status of these loans highly uncertain, as was recognised at the probate valuation in June 1849.

1847 was a bad year for the Partnership with heavy losses in the second half when there were a succession of cotton trade failures in Manchester. 1845 and 1846 had been strong years with very good mill margins but the period 1845-1847, although yielding an average annual profit of £68,616 , was not comparable to the very high rates of return achieved in the early and middle Thirties. The 18 months to 30th June 1849, when the Partnership assets were valued for probate, yielded gross profits of £114,813 (Table VII). The Ashworth mills showed a similar pattern during this period.

Expansion Resumes

The trade recession had left two major casualties in Todmorden. The one was the long-established firm of Buckley Brothers in the heart of the town, using the same strong Calder tributary as Waterside, and adjacent to the railway. The Buckley mill at Ridgefoot was acquired by a rising Todmorden business, Abraham Ormerod and Brothers; thereafter, Ormerods became significant in the town. The other casualty was James and Thomas Ramsbotham and Co., in business as cotton spinners and machine makers in Todmorden and Manchester. Thomas, a wealthy man for the period, had put together the Centre Vale estate in Todmorden's Burnley valley and built a small mansion there in 1826. He and his family had a business and social relationship with the

Fieldens and his second son, James, had married Jane Fielden, daughter of Joshua of the Partnership, in April 1837. The Ramsbotham business fell into financial difficulties in June 1837, following the failure of a Manchester cloth merchant, without becoming insolvent. After the death of Thomas in April 1839, his young sons (who had been educated at Cambridge) had no wish to continue and the firm's assets, and Thomas Ramsbotham's private property, were subsequently sold. Among the assets was the recently built but unfinished and unoccupied large six-storey mill at Robinwood in the Burnley valley. When this was offered for sale, in November 1844, John Fielden bought it for £3,900, an exceptionally low price, as his personal property, but to be rented by the Partnership as was the established practice for outmills.[59]

Robinwood was a major acquisition. Built to drawings by William Fairbairn, the leading mill architect of the day, its site exploited large water power (30 HP. for much of the year) and had access to local coal for its steam engines. In the next several years enlargement and completion of the mill and its equipment with the latest cotton preparation and spinning machinery represented a further significant expansion of Fielden's yarn-making capacity. Spending on building work and on machinery took place over several years: between 1844 and 1853 over £34,000 was put into Robinwood, part by John Fielden and his sons, the rest by the Partnership (Appendix I). £8,465 of the total was spent with Fairbairn on waterwheels, a steam engine and millwrights' work, but much of the work went to local builders and the greater part of the machinery, carding engines, intermediate processing, and throstles were supplied by the Fielden offshoot, John Lord and Sons, which had become Lord Brothers following the father's death. The Lords were now enjoying great success in developing and improving textile machinery and took out many patents in the 1840s; Fieldens would benefit from their association over many years. Robinwood began

Robinwood Mill, bought by John Fielden in 1843 for £3,900, newly built but empty of machinery. In the next ten years Fielden Brothers spent £34,000 on completing the mill, installing steam engines and equipping it for cotton preparation and spinning of warps yarn. In 1856 it had close to 24,000 spindles and employed over 300 workpeople, again predominantly children under 13 or young women. This aerial photograph was taken in July 1930.

Lumbutts Mill: the photograph shows the mill as it must have been after it was enlarged in 1845-47; it was then re-equipped with 6,528 throstles to spin warp yarn. The tower holding three water wheels with water from the dams being introduced at three levels had been completed earlier. In the 1850s the mill employed about 100 work-people, mainly half-timers and young women. Typical wages were 9s. per week and since many workers lived in Fielden cottages, rents were deducted from wages when these were paid each fortnight.

spinning on a limited scale in 1848 but did not reach its full capacity until 1854.[60] As the mill got going, employing many half-time young children, the Fieldens provided a factory school; workpeople's cottages grew up in the immediate district, many of which the Partnership eventually acquired.

Two other sites were the focus of the investment thrust of the late 1840s. Lumbutts Mill attracted £5,007 new investment between 1845 and 1847; the mill was enlarged, the old mules being removed and replaced with throstles; at this time Joshua Fielden passed his interest in the mill to his brother John. In 1845 Greenwood's Mill, using the same stream in the Lumbutts valley, was acquired by John Fielden from its owners Uttley and Greenwood, as was another nearby small mill, Jumb, in 1847; he appears to have paid a high price of £4,528 for Jumb with its associated dams and water courses.[61] As at Robinwood, the partners provided a small factory school for their half-timers.

Developments at Waterside were more important. Between 1845 and 1847 £7,230 was spent on upgrading the spinning mill, installing some new throstles and additional self-acting mules. Spending at Waterside included the enlargement of silk spinning, a small venture which was eventually was given up, but which, almost certainly, was encouraged and helped by the association with John Fielden's fellow MP, John Brocklehurst of Macclesfield. Spinning of waste silk was taking place at Waterside in 1836 but in 1845 a 5 HP steam engine was installed in the 'silk mill' and £1,587 spent on machinery.[62] The second cotton weaving shed had been partially built before the cash squeeze of 1841 and 1842 brought development to a halt. Completion of this facility now went forward, although only slowly, a further £6,162 being spent between 1845 and 1847. It was not until 1849 that additional looms were being bought at £6.13s each from William Hudson in Burnley; most of the new looms, however came from Lord Brothers in the following years, their price coming down from £6.10s to £5.5s. per loom.[63] The second weaving shed, and a third 80 HP steam engine, was completed in 1854; the concern then had 1,600 looms. By then hand-loom weaving had virtually ceased although there were still fifty-three weavers in service as late as 1861 when the oldest were pensioned off.

All these large investments in modernisation and enlargement, were state of the art and benefited from significantly lower machine prices. They serve to indicate the commitment of the next generation and its confidence that the industry, and Fieldens' place in it, had a buoyant future. Meanwhile, the first Fielden Brothers Partnership was drawing to a close.

Changing LifeStyles 1832-1850

The Fielden brothers, however humble their origins, had become substantial self-made men of property, in Todmorden and in Lancashire and beyond. Their success, wealth and standing inevitably influenced their lifestyle.[64] They were also getting older and their children were completing their formal education and growing up. John had assumed a national role as a radical politician, committed to parliamentary duties for part of the year and deeply involved in those issues which, in his view, were closest to the interests of the working poor: the plight of the hand-loom weavers; opposition to the new Poor Law; Chartism and the need for further reform of Parliament; and the Ten Hour Movement.

Absent from Todmorden, and deeply engaged, as he was, John Fielden did not neglect his family. He had married again, Elizabeth Dearden of Halifax, in 1834. She would manage the family home to which Fielden returned whenever he could. When not in Todmorden John corresponded regularly, almost daily, with wife and children, but he missed Todmorden, and was always eager for news, and was never happier than in the family circle at Dawson Weir. He took holidays with his family when he could; in 1837 they joined together in New Brighton, the following year in the Isle of Man; in 1839, he and his wife visited his two younger sons who were schooling in Switzerland. As the children grew older and completed their education, new interests and preoccupations emerged. They were all brought up as Unitarians, and the Sunday School and Chapel took part of their time, although the congregation had languished after John Fielden became an MP. Apart from their participation in the business, all the sons became deeply involved in their father's political activities but especially and passionately so, Samuel and Joshua. In particular they helped to lead the Factory Movement in the years after John Fielden's death, as it campaigned for further changes in the law to achieve the Ten Hour Day.[65]

The Fielden children had other interests and preoccupations than work and politics. The boys learned to ride and were keen about horses,

Samuel Fielden's letter to his sisters in Todmorden, dated May 1839, describes his social activities in London, but shows his concern for the welfare of his horse and his interest in 'the cricket.' He was a leader in the formation of the first Todmorden Cricket Club in 1835 and a keen player himself. In later years, as owner of Centre Vale, he was the Club's landlord, and relationships eventually became less cordial.

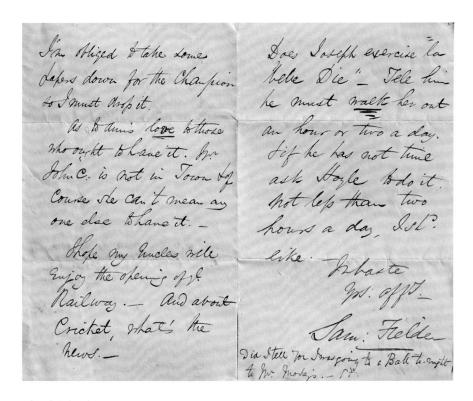

John Brocklehurst, (1788-1870), wealthy silk manufacturer of Macclesfield who, like John Fielden, was elected to the Reform Parliament. They became close friends and their families inter-married.

of which they seemed to have owned several; they were demanding judges of their quality and traded horses between themselves and their friends. They learned to shoot; in 1837 Samuel and John Junior, for instance joined the Mallinsons in North Lancashire to shoot partridge. Already by the 1840s the family rented or owned farms and moorland near Todmorden in Cragg Vale and Blackstone Edge where grouse afforded excellent seasonal sport. Samuel became enthusiastic about cricket and football; his letters to his sisters from London are full of repeated requests for news of the cricket; he helped to form the Todmorden Cricket Club in 1835 and for some years played for them.

The other preoccupation for the young Fieldens was marriage partners. Given their new status, suitable matches were not easy to find in Todmorden or the district around, either for the girls or the young men. Joshua's daughter, Jane, developed a feeling for one local young man of property, James, son of Thomas Ramsbotham; staying at the time with her uncle, the Revd. Richard Mallinson, at the parsonage in Arkholme in the Lune valley, young Ramsbotham seems to have been at the centre of her thoughts late in 1836. The feeling was evidently reciprocated and the two were married at Todmorden Church in April 1837; this was the first marriage within the third generation.

To widen his children's friendships and experience John Fielden introduced them to his own particular friends outside Todmorden. Thus his friendship with John Brocklehurst clearly led to their respective families meeting and mixing. The two had much in common; they were successful businessmen; they were simple and unostentatious in their personal life; they shared a strong sense of duty and obligation to their work people; they were Unitarians. The same was true of Fielden's

96

relationship with the Pickersgills in London. Samuel Fielden, in particular, as well as his sisters were often visiting London and mixing with John Pickersgill's family in the 1830s, staying with them in Tavistock Square, joining them at dinners, balls and at public entertainment. Samuel and John Junior seem to have spent some time in John Pickersgill's City office; certainly Samuel met George Washington Riggs there in 1839. From letters it is clear that the older Fielden sisters had an eye for the younger Pickersgills, Thomas and John Cunliffe. The close friendship between John and Thomas Fielden and John Pickersgill is evident in the continental holiday they and their wives took in September 1845, together with John's daughter Ann, his wife's unmarried sister Susan, and William Cobbett's son, John. They crossed from Folkestone to Boulogne and travelled over a period of twelve days across Northern France and Southern Belgium ending their tour in Fontainebleu and Paris. An account of the joint expenditure on the holiday survives: meticulously detailed by John Fielden, the total for nine persons was 2519 francs (equated to £99) plus English expenses including railway and boat fares of £26. William Cobbett's sons, John Morgan, Richard and James, remained in the Fielden family circle. Indeed, following their father's death in 1835, John Fielden became something of a surrogate father and this particular family friendship continued over many years: John Morgan Cobbett was eventually to marry Mary Fielden in 1851, while John Fielden's sons remained involved with Richard Cobbett, a Manchester barrister, throughout their lives.

With a widening circle of family friendships and involvements, as well as the need to entertain his political allies in Todmorden, John Fielden's home at Dawson Weir became increasingly inadequate. It was not merely cramped; it was surrounded by millworkers cottages and local tradesmen and much of the mill and town traffic would pass the door. In February 1841 the daughters were complaining of the difficulty of entertaining friends and asking permission to hold 'a good large party and dance, for young and old' at Uncle Joshua's more substantial house at Waterside. At the Census in that year, John Fielden, Samuel, and Jane, Mary and Ann were living at Dawson Weir together with three servants: half the family was away. These problems were resolved in 1842 when, after lengthy negotiations over a period of at least two years, John Fielden acquired the Centre Vale estate from the Executors of Thomas Ramsbotham - in effect from his niece Jane and her husband James Ramsbotham. The Classical style house, built in 1826, if not large, was comfortable and prestigious and the park, which had been built up by acquiring farms and other land over the years, was in the quiet and unspoiled part of the Burnley Valley but yet convenient for the town. Rumour at the time suggested John Fielden bought the estate for as much as £15,000, a figure likely to be exaggerated, but no reliable record survives although John Fielden's drawings in 1842 were £12,310; notwithstanding the firm's problems at the time he found the cash.

Centre Vale was to receive and entertain Fielden's political associates and others, Lord Ashley, Richard Oastler, Parson Bull, Lord John Manners of Young England. It was from there that John Fielden's third

daughter, Ann was married to Henry Brocklehurst, the second son of John Brocklehurst, in May 1848; whether or not this was an arranged marriage is not clear, but it was an obvious alliance. The Brocklehursts came to Todmorden from Macclesfield for the wedding in strength, staying at Centre Vale, in Joshua's house at Waterside and indeed, in other Fielden houses in the locality. The Brocklehurst connection was to be strengthened some years later when Joshua Fielden, John's youngest son, married Ellen Brocklehurst, daughter of Thomas Brocklehurst of Fence, the banker and brother and partner of John, the silk manufacturer and MP. This marriage took place at the twelfth century Prestbury Church, near Macclesfield in May 1851, and a wedding tour took the couple to Paris, Marseilles, Genoa, Florence and Venice. During John Fielden's lifetime his epileptic eldest daughter, Jane, was to die in 1846. His other daughters remained unmarried as did his sons. In 1851 Samuel and John Junior, aged 34 and 28 respectively, and their youngest sister Ellen were living at Centre Vale while Henry and Ann Brocklehurst and their daughter Mary Ann were visiting with a nurse and friend; Centre Vale had four living-in servants, while a coachman and gardener were living at Platts House on the estate.

Centre Vale marked a somewhat grander lifestyle but throughout his life John Fielden remained a man of plain, simple, unostentatious tastes. There was little evidence in his way of living of his great wealth nor of any search for status. Not that he was embarrassed by his wealth; to him it was a legitimate reward for frugality, ability and industry. He resented paying taxes, as did his brothers. At the end of his life his family and personal expenses were about £1,500 to £2,000 per year. There was little philanthropy beyond maintaining the Unitarian Chapel and paying its parson, and the occasional contribution to another Sunday School. The major acts of public giving were to be for the next generation. The

Fieldens had acquired a reputation for being mean; their benevolence found expression in their solicitude for their workforce and John's dogged untiring campaign for the interests of the working poor.

John Fielden's energy and stamina as well as his determination, willpower and sense of public duty, were remarkable. His political involvements imposed constant travel between Todmorden, Oldham, Manchester and other manufacturing centres, and of course London. Coach travel between Manchester and London was a twenty-four hour affair; the railway may have made this easier and more comfortable although in 1840 the train from Manchester to London still took ten to eleven hours. In London he lived in lodgings, for many years in Panton Square, off the Haymarket, then in Arundel Street, off the Strand, and late in his life in Wilton Place, Belgravia. More or less continuously, Fielden's political activity and his leadership role in particular causes, Anti-Poor Law, early Chartist activity and particularly the Ten Hour Movement, imposed the demands of public meetings, dinners, Parliament, Parliamentary Committees, speeches, the preparation of books and pamphlets and substantial political correspondence. From his own pocket he assisted political allies, like Richard Oastler, and financed several radical newspapers but especially the Ten Hour Advocate, the main organ of the Factory Movement, as well as meeting many of the Movement's operating expenses. On top of this he retained a close, if not continuous, control of a 'vast and complicated business,' as the *Manchester Guardian* was to describe it, and in the period 1837-1843, his business worries and the risk that Fielden Brothers could fail, must have been matters of deep concern.

Not surprisingly his health began to fail. He complained of shortage of breath; letters from family and friends urged him to take things quieter or seek medical advice. Perhaps for this reason, as well as to reflect his standing, and to make appropriate future provision for his daughters, he bought a modest country estate, Skeynes, near Edenbridge

John Fielden kept a notebook to remind him of the things he had to do. On 25 February 1846 one entry reads: 'P. looms. What to weave and what to spin and where'. Busy as he was, he did not let go of the details.

Skeynes Park. The house, park and small estate near Edenbridge in Kent was bought by John Fielden in 1845. He spent increasing periods there in the last years of his life when his health was breaking down. He died at Skeynes in May 1849.

John Fielden, towards the end of his life, an oil portrait now in the Bankfield Museum in Halifax. He looks aged and frail although sharp and perceptive. He was hard at work until a few days before his death. When his son Samuel visited him on 25 May he found him 'very restless, no appetite but taking a little rice pudding and mutton'. Following his death on 29 May his body was taken back to Todmorden and buried in his Unitarian Chapel, with many hundreds of working-men from Oldham, Manchester and elsewhere, attending the funeral.

in Kent, in 1845. Apart from a small (seven bedrooms) but dignified house and thirty-five acre park, the Skeynes estate had three tenanted farms and extended to 357 acres, yielding a rental of £750. Fielden probably bought it for about £18,000 and in 1845 spent £1,295 on furniture and chattels. Towards the end of his life, and especially in the winter months, he spent long periods at Skeynes where he would be joined by his wife and daughters. He had lost his Parliamentary seat in Oldham in the 1847 election, splitting his Radical supporters by his insistence that John Morgan Cobbett should be his running partner; Cobbett was regarded as a Tory. It was at Skeynes that Fielden died in May 1849, some were to say worn out by the work load and concerns that he maintained to the end, and disappointed that the Act of 1847 had not accomplished its full objective. In December 1848 he had written 'I have at present so many irons in the fire, some of them are left to burn.' Richard Oastler, at the end of February 1849, had begged him, 'do be careful to preserve that precious life of yours.' But to no avail.

On his death his body was brought back to Todmorden for burial in a simple grave at the Unitarian Chapel where he had continued to worship and teach in the Sunday School whenever the opportunity arose. Apart from his workpeople and his many friends in Todmorden, as well as business associates such as the Campbells, Pickersgills, Brocklehursts and Cobbetts, large numbers of working men walked to Todmorden from Oldham and Manchester, in particular, to honour their 'friend and political representative' as he was regarded, on this last occasion. As the Annual Register was to say in its obituary, 'John Fielden was essentially the zealous, persevering, tenacious advocate of the cause of the labouring classes. Once a labouring man himself, his sympathies were with them always.' His achievements as a business man attracted little comment.[66]

John Fielden's brothers do not seem to have shared his deep commitment to radical political causes. They were supportive but with the exception of Thomas, not closely involved. They had become Anglican and probably conservative in their politics. On one issue, however, the family was completely united, namely resistance to the new Poor Law. Their particular objections were to the workhouse principle in replacement of outdoor relief; it is likely also that they shared the fears of other employers that labour would move away from the district in periods of trade depression, rather than enter the workhouse. All the brothers played their part in rousing and leading feeling in Todmorden and closing their mills (probably without loss of pay) to assist protest and demonstration. Many of their workpeople, including overlookers and managers, participated and indeed led the local agitation; they held special positions in the concern thereafter. All this activity in 1837 and 1838 was conspicuously successful: no workhouse was built in Todmorden for another forty years while the new Guardians were able to continue the payment of outdoor relief in periods of trade distress as they had done in the past. But the ease with which roused public feeling turned into mob violence, even in Todmorden, which in turn was a threat to life and property, deeply worried the Fieldens, John included. A few years later he was to disassociate himself from the more physical aspects of the Chartist agitation. Concerned as John was with the condition of the labouring poor, he was also a firm believer in the rights of property and the need to safeguard them. Mob violence had no role in his political campaigning.[67] When it came to the Factory Movement, Joshua and James, living in Todmorden, would be aware that the cause which John was helping to lead was not a popular one with other employers. Indeed most Todmorden millowners, including the Ormerods, the Inghams and the Hinchliffes, were to sign petitions to Parliament against the Ten Hour Bill of 1847 which John Fielden, in the end, successfully introduced. When the Bill passed through Parliament, his son wrote that 'the masters here are very gruff about it'[68].

Of the brothers, least is known of James. In 1834 he had married a widow, Grace Knowles, she having been born an Ormerod at Todmorden Edge, a farm adjacent to Edge End. The circumstances of the Ormerods were similar to those of the Fieldens. At Todmorden Edge they were putters-out; they went into cotton spinning at the rented Gorpley Mill in 1804 and later into power-loom weaving and had taken Buckley's mill at Ridgefoot in 1844. But while the Fieldens were dramatically successful, the Ormerods had only modest success and no

James Fielden (1788-1852) had a passive role in the business and probably supervised the counting-house and manufacturing operations working through competent mill-managers such as John Holt and John Haigh.

Dobroyd House, built for James Fielden on his marriage to Grace Ormerod in 1834. Following his death and his widow's death in 1861 it became the home of John and Ruth Fielden who left it when Dobroyd Castle was completed. It was then rented by Charles Thorp, prominent doctor in Todmorden, and friend of the Fieldens.

doubt some feeling of envy. Certainly they clashed with the Fieldens from time to time on political and other issues. On their marriage, James and his wife lived in Dobroyd House which was built for them by the Partnership at a cost of £500; it was close by the canal, railway and the small Dobroyd Mill, and like Dawson Weir, right at the heart of the Waterside community, if somewhat more private. They paid a rent of £25 yearly for the house. James had his role as the partner present at the mills, but this would diminish as Young Sam became active. He and his wife had a quiet and comfortable lifestyle, two servants, a gardener and a coachman. Gardening, with a large hot house, seems to have been a keen pastime and invoices survive showing regular seed and plant purchases. The couple took long holidays in Blackpool, the Lake District and Scotland. Grace Fielden became a Baptist and worshipped regularly at the Baptist chapel, but both were to be buried at Todmorden Old Church. She outlived James, who died in May 1852.

Thomas, although he maintained his roots, belonged to Manchester rather than Todmorden. He lived very simply and apart from a 'salary' of £208, raised in the 1830s to £300, seems to have drawn very little from the business except to invest in railway shares; the dividends from these were for the most part reinvested. There are no extravagances, indeed no records of any holidays, other than the visit to France with his brother in 1845. It was possibly Thomas who attracted the epithets 'selfish and mean', even miserly, for the Fieldens at this time. He was well known in the Manchester market and had a wide circle of business associates. He would meet with them in the evenings, getting fuddled in simple taverns, he and his friends, rough and ready veterans of the early years, all successful, all committed to self-help. Although homely and modest, at all times shrinking from display and glitter, he was reserved, rarely showed enthusiasm and could be hard and unsympathetic. He showed what was described as 'the Fielden manner.' He was respected for his carefulness, diligence and shrewd common-sense. Of all the brothers, Thomas, although genuine and unostentatious, was proud and conscious of Fieldens' success and respectability and sometimes inclined to make others aware of it. His peremptory very lofty tone did not impress the Manchester agent of the Bank of England when Fielden Brothers sought a discount facility in 1839.[69]

Others were angry at or jealous of the Fieldens at this period, not least because of John Fielden's persistent earnest advocacy of causes with which many successful cotton manufacturers had little sympathy, or opposed, and his criticism of their practices. The influential millowner Robert Hyde Greg, for instance, no doubt speaking for many, attacked Fielden's views with some vigour in his tract, *'The Factory Question'*, printed in 1837. Fielden's opinions, he said were 'not only extremely erroneous but violent' and showed 'that he can scarcely have heard of the name of Adam Smith.' In March 1844, Fieldens were pursued, for unpaid income taxes, and bailiffs, having failed in an attempt to take possession of the Waterside premises, mainly because of resistance from the workpeople, then occupied the Manchester warehouse and seized the stock of calico pieces there. John raised the matter in Parliament and the affair created much interest in Manchester where Thomas would feel the smirks of satisfaction which rivals would display. Many of the most prominent business names in Lancashire, Horrocks Miller, Birley Brothers, Henry Ashworth, Thomas Ashton, Hugh Mason, Thomas Harrison, Joshua Hoyle, John Bright were among the 438 who signed Memorials against the Ten Hours Bill in 1847. Thomas, no doubt, took the weight of this feeling within the Manchester business community. There is no evidence that it concerned him, conscious and proud as he was of his firm's wealth and standing; as the *Guardian* said, Fieldens were 'one of the richest houses in Lancashire.'[70]

Joshua, the oldest surviving brother, remained independent and increasingly eccentric or wild, as his nephew Samuel was to put it. Following the death of his first wife, he remarried but was a widower again in 1840. His daughter Jane had married in 1837 and in 1841 he was living with his son, John, with servants, in Waterside House; his neighbours in the older Laneside cottages included his sister Sarah, and on occasion the Unitarian Minister or the teacher at the nearby factory school. Joshua's son, another John, created problems; whether or not by inclination he never seems to have been involved in the family business; at some stage he travelled in France and, it was there, the family story has it, that he contracted syphilis. But that apart, the presence of two Johns in the third generation, John the son of Joshua and John Junior the son of John, appeared to present problems. The argument developed, at Centre Vale at least, that there were too many Fieldens in Todmorden, and not room for all of them. John Fielden meanwhile had an affair with an attractive young woman, Sarah Cockcroft, thedaughter of a Dobroyd butcher, George Cockcroft. A child was born, christened Mary Alice Cockcroft, and the couple married in January 1847 having had another child which died in infancy. Joshua died, aged 69, in November 1847, to be buried in Todmorden Old Church. In March 1848 John and his wife Sarah, had a son, Joshua. Their inheritance was in the control of Joshua Fielden's executors, his brothers

Joshua Fielden who died at Waterside House in November 1847. He was the most approachable of the second generation brothers, who continued to mix with men he had known all his life in the Todmorden district. His son John, still living with his father at the time of his death, was encouraged to leave subsequently by the other Fieldens and took his wife, Sarah (née Cockcroft) and infant children to live in North Lancashire in 1848.

Sarah Fielden (née Cockcroft), the daughter of a Dobroyd butcher, had a rather public affair with John Fielden of Waterside House. Having had two children outside wedlock the couple married in January 1847 and a son, Joshua, was born in March 1848. John was encouraged to leave Todmorden and eventually settled at Caton in North Lancashire, where he died in 1852 (he was buried in Todmorden). He left his small son a substantial fortune, in the control of his Fielden cousins as Trustees. Sarah remarried but Joshua was sent by his Fielden relatives to Eton and Cambridge and a landed estate property in Norfolk, Beachamwell Hall, was purchased for him.

Thomas and James, and nephew John Junior. None of the executors approved of the match with Sarah Cockcroft, probably because she was a tradesman's daughter with a pert flirty manner. In 1848, the ailing John Fielden, with his wife and two small children, decided to leave Todmorden. No doubt influenced by his uncle, Richard Mallinson, Vicar of Arkholme, he went to live at Wenning Cottage in nearby Tatham, a remote but beautiful district in North Lancashire.[72]

Encouraged by their success and the rapid increase in the profits and capital of the Partnership, the Brothers had begun to withdraw funds on a significant scale in the 1830s (Table VII). High drawings continued in 1840 but then fell away sharply over the period through 1844, to rise again to £110,941 in the three years 1845-1847. Between 1832 and 1847 the Partners took £275,340 out of the business. A further £68,580 was withdrawn between 1 January 1848 and 30 June 1849, mainly by Joshua's Executors and by John Fielden.

Table X: Fielden Brothers Drawings 1832-1847.

Joshua	£84,611
John	£146,046
James	£19,469
Thomas	£25,214
Total	**£275,340**

Source: Longden MSS, Private Ledger.

The enhanced drawings, of course, supported a less frugal if scarcely grand or opulent lifestyle. In John's case his parliamentary and political activity would be an additional expense. He had to provide for his large family, and make an appropriate marriage settlement for his daughter Ann in 1848. Both John and Joshua had made important investments in private mill property, John at Lumbutts and Robinwood, Joshua at Mytholmroyd. John had bought Centre Vale and Skeynes; he also committed funds to Wildes Pickersgill and Co. and to Fielden Brothers & Co. in a personal capacity. But all the brothers were attracted to the fashionable investment of the period, namely the railways. Partly this reflected their obvious interest in the Manchester and Leeds Railway; John and Thomas were both active in the circles that promoted the line, and both along with Joshua and James, became substantial investors, Thomas becoming a Director. But the Manchester and Leeds apart, like many others at the time, they saw railway shares as a worthwhile investment; in particular, like their ownership of farms and cottages, it was a means of establishing private wealth and a source of income that was independent of their business. No doubt they were also caught up in the speculative boom in railway shares. John Pickersgill was buying shares in the North Midland for the account of John Fielden in November 1835. 'I did not like for him to be left out, as they are at a premium,' he wrote, but went on 'people are railroad mad here — several no doubt will burn their fingers.'[72]

Following John's death in 1849, his estate included railway shares with a nominal value of £50,233 paid, but a market value at the time of only £25,930. His fully and partly paid shares in the Lancashire and Yorkshire Railway (formerly the Manchester and Leeds) were then nominally £38,726, but with a value of £20,361; some of his other holdings, for instance in the Midland, had lost value to a greater degree, while those in the London and North-Western had held their value. Joshua's estate reflected the same situation: his shares worth a nominal value of £30,533 were valued for probate at £22,208. In the context of their large wealth, this slump in share value was hardly significant. In any event, the shares were not to be sold; passing to their heirs they would eventually recover their value and yield a stream of dividends.

The First Partnership Ends

The death of the three older brothers between November 1847 and May 1852 inevitably brought changes to Fielden Brothers. Joshua's death had little immediate effect: he had relinquished his participation in a formal agreement with his brothers in 1847. That of John was the effective end of the first Partnership. Following his death, a full valuation of Partnership capital was made for probate purposes, summarised in Table XI. The distribution of this capital between the Partners is shown in Table XII. John Fielden's share had been reduced by his substantial drawings, much of course, invested in private property and other assets. John's estate, together with James and Thomas, his surviving brothers, were each entitled to one third of the doubtful assets of £143,657.

Table XI: Partnership Capital 30 June 1849.

		£
Mills, farms, buildings, power sources		55,666
Machinery, as valued by Tweedale less 20%		48,850
Stocks at Waterside		12,601
Manchester and abroad		271,279
Fielden Brothers & Co.		294,855
Total, firm assets		**683,253**
Plus		
Loaned on Railway Securities	129,081	
Dormant Accounts	16,286	145,367
Total, including doubtful assets		**£828,618**

Source: Longden MSS, Private Ledger.

The deaths of Joshua and John had obvious implications. The leadership of the Partnership had to change; in particular the wisdom, experience, authority and connection of John Fielden was removed. His sons, or at least the eldest sons, Samuel and John Junior were now to assume the active leadership role while their uncles and especially Thomas, would become father figures although perhaps for a time the ultimate authority. Thus in June 1849, Samuel and John Junior took equal shares with their uncles Thomas and James in the profits of the Partnership, with 5 per cent remaining with John Holt, the Waterside manager. The other large implication was the withdrawal of Partner's capital from the business.[73] Most of the wealth of the deceased Fieldens was represented by their equity in the Partnership; they were to leave a large part of that wealth to children or relatives who in many cases had no participation in the concern. This had less serious implications than might be supposed. To the extent that Samuel Fielden or his brothers inherited, they could leave their inheritance within the Partnership. But in other cases, where the wealth passed to the next generation or to relatives, control lay with Executors or with Trusts that were managed as a rule by John Fielden's brothers or his sons, Samuel, John Junior and, in some instances, Joshua. The Executors or Trustees could use their discretion to make payments to the beneficiaries, to purchase homes for their use, to purchase income yielding assets such as railway shares, mortgages on property, or to leave part of the inheritance as a Private Family Account with Fielden Brothers. In practice, at the time of transition and for many years subsequently, Private Family Accounts provided substantial continued funds to the Partnership. They did not share in profits but they received interest at rates that varied from time to time between 5 and 3.5 percent. Where real property in mills used by the Partnership was passed down, its status was not changed; Fielden Brothers were merely to pay rent to the new owners, rather than to partners as previously.

As for the individual deceased partners' estates, that of Joshua's was substantial. With his railway shareholdings, chattels and private property — mills, farms, cottages — he must have been worth at least £250,000: at the end of 1847 following his death, his share in the Partnership was £195,768. His will provided for his real estate, that is the properties including the mills, to be shared between the natural son, Nathan Firth, and the Trusts established for Jane Ramsbotham and his son John. Mytholmroyd Mill, and its associated properties, for instance passed eventually to John Fielden's son Joshua, while Stoneswood Mill was part of Jane Ramsbotham's inheritance. Nathan Firth's mother, probably a mill girl in her youth, was given an income of £10 per year. John was to receive an income of £1,000 per year but the balance of the personal estate was held by the Executors for the eventual benefit of Jane Ramsbotham and John or his family. In June 1849 the Executors still had £196,282 in the Partnership, although as a Private Family Account earning interest.

The Executors decided initially to make what seemed appropriate provision for Jane. In 1849 they purchased Crowborough Warren, an estate in Sussex on the edge of Ashdown Forest: the substantial Georgian house, park and farmland extending to 1,300 acres cost £22,000; it was not far from John Fielden's house at Skeynes. Jane and her husband moved to Crowborough, raised a large family of children and eventually died there. The estate remained in the Ramsbotham family until the First World War; the approach to the Warren is still called Fielden Road. A similar provision was made for Joshua's son, John, and his wife Sarah, living at the time at Wenning Cottage on the income of £1,000 yearly. The Executors looked for a better property and in March 1850 purchased for £3,625, Greenbank, a small estate in Caton Green, 7 miles from

Lancaster, described by Thomas Fielden as 'the prettiest place in the whole of Lancashire.' John Fielden died there in September 1852 but not before his father's Executors had purchased another property, whether to set him up as a country gentleman or to create a sound investment for his wife and small children. This was the Beachamwell Estate, 4341 acres, much of it Breckland, near Swaffham in Norfolk, purchased for £35,000 in August 1851 and yielding a gross rental of about £2,200 yearly. At about the same time, again probably to create income, the Executors bought an Oxfordshire estate at Reading Bank for £18,000. The rents, some £960 per year, went to Jane Ramsbotham, and the property, never lived in by the family, was eventually to form part of Jane Ramsbotham's estate. Despite these outgoings, and benefiting from interest and rents received, the Executor's loan to Fielden Brothers was still as high as £166,952 by the end of 1851.

John Fielden's personal estate was eventually assessed at about £203,000, only part of which was equity in the Partnership, to which can be added his properties. Of the properties, Samuel received Centre Vale and Dawson Weir, while the Lumbutts mills and farms passed to John Junior, the second son; Smithyholme Mill and Walsden farms went to the youngest son, Joshua; Robinwood Mill and the Unitarian Chapel passed to the three sons equally. Skeynes went to his three daughters, although Mary lived there on her marriage. Various substantial legacies from the personal estate provided for Elizabeth, John Fielden's wife, and his daughters. Of the residue, about £149,000, two thirds went in equal shares to the sons, and one third to the daughters. Most of his reduced equity in the business passed to the sons to meet their share while the daughters' shares were met from free assets, mainly railway shares, but partly cash from the business. The Trusts established for the daughters, continued to lend to Fielden Brothers as a Private Family Account.

Restructuring

If the Partnership was not embarrassed by withdrawal of capital, the death of John Fielden and the succession to leadership roles of his sons, Samuel and John, caused a particular difficulty. Their shares in the profits of what can be called the Second Partnership were equal to their elderly uncles, but their share in the equity was far less. The apparent position in June 1849 was one where James and Thomas each had more than £190,000 in the Partnership, Samuel and John Junior, prior to their father's estate being distributed, only a few hundred pounds. To rectify this it was decided that Fielden Brothers & Co. Liverpool, which had a Fielden capital in trade of £294,855 (Table XI), should become a separate concern where James and Thomas should take equal shares valued at £147,427 each. Presumably William Pickersgill and Daniel Campbell retained a separate share. The capital of James and Thomas in the second Fielden Brothers Partnership was significantly reduced accordingly.

A further change was to remove the jointly owned Freehold properties in Todmorden, valued at £55,666 in June 1849, from the Partnership assets which also had a balancing effect since Thomas and James now owned a high proportion of these. The new position of the Partnership is summarised in Table XII. Together with the loans from Private Family Accounts, the greatly reduced capital of £73,938 financed the Todmorden Spinning and Weaving operations and the activities of Manchester. Fielden Brothers & Co., meanwhile, now outside the Partnership, was to remain a separate concern until the death of Thomas in 1869.

James and Thomas assumed responsibility for the doubtful assets identified in June 1849, eventually paying into John Fielden's estate his third share as debts and loans were repaid. As the estate was proven, augmented in this way and distributed, his sons were able to introduce more capital into the Partnership. The Private Ledger accounts lose their continuity at this stage but gross profits over two years from June 1849 appear to have been approximately £90,000, most of which stayed within the business. Thus in June 1851 a Partnership capital in trade of £232,553, together with Private Family Accounts providing additional funds of £275,542, financed assets of £78,905 at Todmorden (machinery and working capital) and £429,190 in Manchester (Table XII, Appendix III). Large retained profits in 1851-1852 increased the capital in trade to £268,684. Finally, the transition to the Second Partnership was completed following the death of James Fielden in May 1852. Practically all his wealth was in the Partnership, in the joint Todmorden Freeholds, or in Fielden Brothers & Co. He had no children and, after providing for his wife and elderly sister, Sarah, he willed a succession of legacies to his nieces and nephews, the sons and daughters of his deceased sisters who had not participated in the great wealth of the Brothers. But of the residue, Thomas the surviving brother and the heirs of James' dead brothers Joshua and John, took equal shares.

James's death precipitated withdrawal of his capital in Fielden Brothers & Co. in Liverpool, as well as his capital in Fielden Brothers. The capital employed in the Liverpool business was then to be sharply reduced, in part by the sale between 1851 and 1853 of the timber ships which had been acquired a few years earlier, and which may not have been very profitable. Some complicated transactions ensued with Thomas taking £100,000 from his capital in Liverpool, from which he took £36,055 into his personal wealth — buying railway shares — transferring the balance to the Partnership. Joshua, John's youngest son, was to introduce £22,196 into Fielden Brothers and now became a Partner taking the same share of profits as his brothers and uncle. (7½ per cent of total profit was meanwhile given to John Holt and Thomas Fielden Uttley, the senior managers.) The net result in the 18 month accounting period to end 1853 was only a modest withdrawal from Fielden Brothers capital compared with profits of £63,500; Partnership capital was to rise by £45,828 to the end of December 1853 when it stood at £314,511 which was augmented by Private Family Accounts totalling £204,239 (Table XII, Appendix III).

Thus although the equity in the Partnership was heavily reduced by the deaths of the second generation, and the spread of its activities changed, following restructuring its main asset base was not disturbed, merely financed in a different way. As the second Partnership of Fielden

Table XII: Transition to Second Partnership — Shares in Capital of Individual Partners.

	30 June 1849 (before restructuring)	30 June 1849[2] (after restructuring)	30 June 1851[2]	30 June 1852[2]	31 December 1853[2]
Executors Joshua Fielden	£196,282	—	—	—	—
Executors John Fielden	£94,823	—	—	—	—
James Fielden	£199,083	£33,100	£78,821	£86,214	—
Thomas Fielden	£191,029	£25,046	£68,008	£73,695	£154,229
Samuel Fielden	£1,473	£10,648	£44,161	£55,643	£68,300
John Fielden Junior	£353	£5,144	£41,563	£53,130	£67,017
Joshua Fielden	—	—	—	—	£24,965
Partnership Capital	£683,253[1]	£73,938	£232,553	£268,682	£314,511
Private Family Accounts	—	£258,792	£275,542	£185,584	£204,239
Total Capital in Trade	—	£332,730	£508,095	£454,266	£518,750

Source: Longden MSS, Private Ledgers.
Notes:
1. Firm assets described in Table XI.
2. Fielden Brothers and Co. no longer within the Partnership. Jointly owned freehold properties in Todmorden, mills, farms, cottages valued at £55,666 in June 1849 were also excluded.

Brothers moved into a period of high profits in the 1850s, the retained equity of the new partners and their uncle built up rapidly and the need for private family loans from Executors or Trustees greatly diminished. These loans were gradually to be reduced as the Executors/Trustees distributed income or bought other assets, but this was scarcely an event of significance (Appendix III). In effect the new partners bought out the descendants of the old. Family loans following a change in ownership from one generation to another played a similar, if more modest part in the Ashworth cotton enterprise.[74]

In all these ways, the transition to the second Partnership was a smooth one. Fielden Brothers had, for a time, reduced equity but no lack of finance; it had a substantial low cost manufacturing base completing a second phase of enlargement and modernisation; it had an established name and reputation; it had re-focused its activities on manufacturing and the cotton trade; and its new leadership combined a mature experience and wide trade connection with a renewed vigour and will to succeed. And the industry in 1850 was again on the threshold of a strong decade of expansion which Fieldens were in an excellent position to exploit.

4

BOOM AND FAMINE
The Second Partnership 1851-1865

Climax in the Fifties

The decade of the 1850s was the climax of the Lancashire cotton industry; in absolute terms the growth of capacity, output and cotton usage was not exceeded in any comparable period, whether prior or subsequently. Numbers of mills, installed spindles and looms, the workforce employed, all grew by more than 50 per cent. Likewise cotton consumption rose from an average of 613 million pounds in 1849-51 to an average of 1,023 million pounds in 1859-61. These were for Lancashire the golden years; the world wide demand for cheap cotton cloth seemed inexhaustible and Lancashire enterprise and skill, and expanding American cotton production, was able to supply it, without, at the time, significant competition.

These were also golden years for Fielden Brothers. As the decade began, the business was completing the phase of heavy investment in new and modernised capacity that began in 1845. In the 10 years 1845-1854 over £57,000 was spent on machinery, aside from substantial private expenditure on mill buildings and power sources. With the completion of Robinwood and the second weaving shed at Waterside, the partners brought capacity to its mature peak; it would be rationalised subsequently, but not enlarged. The mill capacity and structure as it then existed is described in Table XIII. About 100,000 spindles and 1,600 looms were available for cotton spinning and weaving providing work for a total of 1,925 people, about one fifth of Todmorden's textile workforce. Many workers were involved with Fieldens indirectly, as tradesmen, with local suppliers of services and materials, or as servants in Fielden homes. Indeed it could be said that at least 20 per cent of Todmorden's population depended at the time on Fieldens, one way or another.

Despite substantial growth, the firm was not so large relative to the industry as they had been in the 1830s, and in the next decade, as the industry continued to expand rapidly, Fieldens share fell further. But they remained one of the very largest concerns, say one of the top thirty. With 450 HP from steam engines, depending on activity, the mills were burning 700 to 900 tons of coal monthly. They could spin up to 400 bales of cotton a week and when working at this level, as they were in the busy periods, subject to weavers being available, they could weave up to 8 million pounds of calico a year. This was a peak output: 6 or 7 million pounds of cloth would be more normal. Depending on the level of activity and cotton prices and margins, the annual turnover of the spinning and weaving business in Todmorden in the 1850s would

Table XIII: Fielden Brothers: Cotton Spinning & Weaving: Capacity and Structure 1856.

		MACHINERY		Looms	POWER (HP)		WORKFORCE			
		Spindles			Steam	Water	Under 13	Women	Men	Total
		Throstle	Mule							
Waterside[1]:	Cotton Spinning and Weaving	15,080	20,824	1,641	273[2]	5	106	499	497	1,102
Dobroyd:	Breaking Up	—	—	—	3.5	0.5	—	—	3	3
Smithyholme:	Spinning	3,096	—	—	12	4	14	27	9	50
Stoneswood:	Spinning	5,184	—	—	14	5	19	25	10	54
Waterstalls:	Spinning	1,584	—	—	6	5	11	10	5	26
Lumbutts:	Spinning	6,528	—	—	14	14	39	42	16	97
Greenwood	Spinning	576	888	—	—	4	3	6	5	14
Jumb	Spinning	—	2,640	—	—	3.5	4	3	8	15
Causeway	Spinning		6,000	—		5	6	—	9	14	23
Mytholmroyd:	Spinning	13,440	—	—	30	28	69	99	32	200
Robinwood:	Spinning	23,712	—	—	90	10	106	154	49	309
Totals		69,128	33,224	1,641	451.5	85	377	880	668	1,925

Source: Rylands MSS, Return of Mills, 14 May 1856.
Notes:
1. Waterside had 2872 spindles engaged in silk spinning, giving work to 32 people, including 20 men.
2. Waterside had three large steam engines: 60 HP, 80 HP and 120 HP.

lie between £300,000 and £450,000. In round figures the cotton bill would be around £150,000/£250,000 and the direct wage bill between £60,000 and £80,000 per year. Fuel costs were also variable with output and with fluctuating coal prices but were a much smaller item at say £3,000 to £5,000 yearly. Then there were wage costs that were indirect overhead which in the Fifties were of the order of £13/14,000 per year; these included the wages of mechanics, masons and other craftsmen, ancillary staff whom Fieldens described as odd-fellows (carters, gate men, watchmen, engine tenters, gas-works men), warehouse clerks and management. Finally other expenses included mill stores, rents paid, rates, depreciation, carriage and selling expenses. Irrespective of what work was done, the workpeople were given New Year gifts (6d per head) and Fairings (about the same) and this was another overhead. Although many of the costs — and especially factory wages — were variable with output, the overall financial result was very dependent on the level of activity and the margin realised.

The decade of the Fifties began very strongly. In 1852 Leonard Horner, the Factory Inspector, was to write 'At no time in the last seventeen years — have I known such general prosperity — the activity in every branch is extraordinary.' He goes on to refer to 'a great scarcity of hands', with 'machinery standing idle for want of people to run it.' New mills were being built 'on all sides and machine makers are said to be overwhelmed with orders.' In these circumstances margins were very favourable to established concerns who had capacity in place. Not

Table XIV: Fielden Brothers: Capital Employed and Profit in Todmorden Spinning and Weaving 1851-1865.

Period Ending	Joint Todmorden Properties[1] £ Start of Period	Machinery in the Mills & Working Capital[1] £ Start of Period	Total Todmorden Capital Employed[1] £ Start of Period	Profit[2] £	Return on Todmorden Capital (Per Cent)[3]
30 June 1852	58,075	78,905	136,980	60,262	44.0
31 Dec 1853	54,000	64,222	118,222	41,400	23.3
31 Dec 1854	55,421	204,616	260,037	28,325	10.9
31 Dec 1855	53,429	208,373	261,802	18,037	6.9
31 Dec 1856	51,649	278,993	330,642	42,199	12.8
31 Dec 1857	54,655	70,447	125,102	(7,108)	(5.7)
31 Dec 1858	52,087	88,752	140,839	58,020	41.2
31 Dec 1859	49,600	153,009	212,609	74,878	37.0
31 Dec 1860	47,173	108,118	155,291	97,736	62.9
31 Dec 1861	44,977	187,090	232,067	62,467	26.9
31 Dec 1862	43,770	295,834	339,604	150,065	44.2
31 Dec 1863	43,650	435,384	479,034	127,148	26.5
31 Dec 1864	41,776	198,872	204,648	(15,398)	(6.5)
31 Dec 1865	39,933	133,466	173,399	18,904	10.9

Source: Longden MSS Personal Ledgers, WYAS Machinery Valuation
Notes: 1. For definitions see Appendix III
2. Profit includes interest on Working Capital, and rents on Property and Machinery less depreciation, plus profits (losses) on trading during the financial period.
3. Return on Capital compares Profit with value of Joint Property, Machinery and Working Capital (i.e. Total Todmorden capital employed) at the start of the financial period.

surprisingly Fielden Brothers were able to make quite exceptional profits in spinning and weaving in the early Fifties. In the twelve months July 1851-June 1852, the return on capital employed at Todmorden exceeded 40 per cent (Table XIV). The industry generally did well at the time, as the Ashworth results, for instance, indicate.[1]

Business results in the Fifties were, however, subject to wide variations from one year to the next. The sensitive indicator would be the mill-margin, a function of market conditions. Approximate representative mill-margins can be calculated from data published weekly in *The Economist;* these are a rough but fair guide to what was available in the market Of course, the actual mill-margin achieved would be determined by the commercial skills of the enterprise in timing its cloth sales and its cotton purchases, so enhancing the available margin. As James Watts was to put it, 'the results in the cotton trade have depended so much more upon skilful buying and selling, than upon the daily margin between the raw material and the finished article'[2]

When margins were poor, mill activity would fall, as short time was introduced. It was at times of high margins that Fieldens worked their capacity to the full, always provided they could find and hold their weavers, for weavers became scarce in busy periods and moved around for better pay. For a typical mill output of 7 million pounds of cloth, the middle of the Fielden output range, 1d on the mill-margin would add £29,000 to profit.

The boom of the early Fifties went too far. Trade fell off in the course of 1853, the year of the bitter and unsuccessful Preston strike for higher wages. Horner was to attribute falling prices and diminished margins 'to the very great increase in the number of mills, causing production to go far beyond the demands of existing markets.' Although activity picked up in the period 1855-56, profits remained under pressure. 1857, the year of the Indian Mutiny was a year of depression and distress in Lancashire, with high raw cotton prices, the result of a poor American crop, aggravating a period when general trade was affected by extensive bank and business failures, and bill refusals, spreading from the eastern United States to Liverpool and the North of England and Midlands as a whole. Towards the end of the year, there was a sharp rise in Bank Rate and a brief but severe panic.[3] Fieldens like others, worked extensive short time in the summer and autumn, when margins collapsed between high cotton prices and markets that would not pay more for cloth. They showed a loss of £7,108 for the year.

As confidence returned in 1858, the decade closed with a renewed extraordinary boom, fuelled by the huge surge in exports to India once the Mutiny was over and by cheaper cotton. Mill-margins again rose sharply, especially in 1860. Fieldens were running at full capacity for much of the period, using 350 to 400 bales of cotton a week, equivalent to 7 to 8 million pounds of cloth or warps a year, allowing for waste and for sizing.[4] Their spinning and weaving profits recovered sharply in 1858, rising in the two following years to reach £97,736 in 1860. Taking the Todmorden assets in that year, including freehold property, at £155,291, this represented a return on capital employed of over 60 per cent (Table XIV).

Fielden Brothers were, of course, not alone in enjoying such exceptional conditions. Labour became scarce in Lancashire. Cottage

Table XV: Approximate Representative Mill-Margins for Cotton Cloth.
   (pence per pound of cloth)

1848	6.2
1849	7.2
1850	6.3
1851	6.4
1852	7.5
1853	7.1
1854	6.8
1855	6.2
1856	6.7
1857	5.9
1858	6.7
1859	7.4
1860	8.6

Source and Note: The Economist published weekly raw cotton, yarn and cloth prices. Mill-margins are calculated for one representative grade of cloth, namely 27 inch printer, 72 reed, 29 yards per piece, piece weight 5lbs 2oz. Price of good fair US cotton is compared with price per pound of cloth to establish the margin, which for each year is the average of the first price given for each month. *The Economist* data was used by G.T. Jones to analyse efficiency change in the Lancashire cotton industry (*Increasing Returns*, Cambridge, 1933). His Diagram II clearly indicates a period of high margins in the early 1850s and in the period 1858-1861.

rents began to rise. Major strikes for higher wages were a feature of the weaving districts between 1858 and 1861, and by the latter year wages were as much as 25 per cent higher than a decade earlier. Fielden managers began to complain of unreasonable demands and insubordinate behaviour, and hands leaving for better wages; wages were raised by about 1d in the shilling across all Fielden mills in 1859. Fieldens' size and performance at this period can again be compared with that of Henry Ashworth and Sons.[5] The results at Ashworth's New Eagley Factory, also a combined spinning and weaving enterprise, if on the fine cotton side, show for the years 1854 to 1861 an average capital employed of £70,298, and an average profit of £7,174 after paying interest of 5 per cent on the capital. These results represent an average return on capital of about 15 per cent, comparable to that achieved by Fielden Brothers in much the same period of 24 per cent on a much larger capital (Table XIV).

The boom could not last. 1861 saw a return of the familiar condition of overstocked markets and falling margins with Lancashire mills reverting to short time working, and weaving for stock; cotton consumption fell during the year. Poor trade in 1861 was overshadowed by events in America. The Southern States had seceded from the Union in December 1860. Few people in Europe anticipated armed conflict as a consequence and the event had little immediate effect on the cotton market which was absorbing the large American crop harvested in 1860, the second large crop in succession. Cotton prices only began to rise in July 1861, some months after the first shots were fired at Fort Sumter in April. Cloth prices in an over-supplied market did not follow and by June, mill-margins began to fall. By December when cotton reached 12d a pound, cloth prices were showing some response but the mill-margin got down to 5d and business in Manchester was at a standstill. Only then, and as the conflict deepened, and the blockade of the South became effective, did Lancashire and the world realise a bitter struggle had begun and that a severe shortage of cotton would result.[6]

Fieldens in the Famine

Fieldens had good intelligence from the United States, given the Pickersgill connection. Whether they anticipated a Cotton Famine is not clear but they were certainly buying cotton for stock and filling available warehouses at the end of 1860.[7] In 1861, given the sharp fall in mill-margins, they were weaving for stock. Todmorden working capital, mainly stock, rose from £76,000 at the end of 1859 to £154,000 at the end of 1860 and £264,000 at the end of 1861. These figures represent a large real increase and the presumption is that when the American conflict began to bite, Fieldens, like other large cotton manufacturers who had the funds, had large stocks of cotton and also large stocks of unsold cloth. At the prices prevailing in early 1861, a stock of three months cotton would have cost about £60,000 and three months unsold cloth would represent a value of about £100,000. Stock levels of this magnitude at least are consistent with the increase in Todmorden assets in 1860 and 1861.

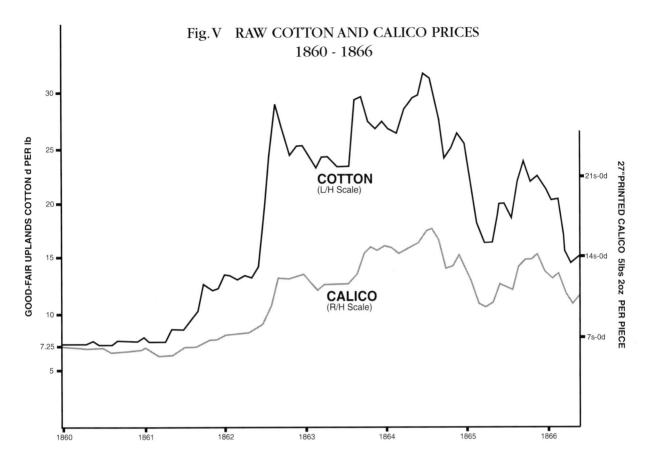

Fig. V   RAW COTTON AND CALICO PRICES
1860 - 1866

COTTON
(L/H Scale)

CALICO
(R/H Scale)

As the blockade on supplies of cotton from the American South took hold, the Liverpool market advanced sharply, attracting frenzied speculation. Figure V illustrates the trend of both cotton and representative cloth prices. Not only did cotton quadruple in price, remaining above 20d per pound for most of the three years 1862-1864, but prices became dangerously volatile, responding to each report of the progress of the struggle, the likelihood that one side or other would prevail, and 'peace scares' when the possibility arose that supplies lying in warehouses in the Southern ports would quickly reach the market. The rise in prices rationed supplies; cotton was always available, whether from stocks accumulated before shipments ceased, from resales by those who preferred to take profit rather than spin at very poor margins, from smuggling or blockade evasion and increasingly and especially from other sources such as India and Brazil. Meanwhile, throughout 1862, cloth prices responded inadequately to the advance in cotton, partly because of trade resistance and destocking, partly because many mills had large inventories of unsold cloth in 1861. Thus mill-margins which had fallen to below 5d at the end of 1861 and remained at about this inadequate level in the first half of 1862, disappeared with the sharp rise in cotton prices that followed the defeat of the Union Army at Bull Run at the end of August. The market now realised that this was going to be a long war. In the period August 1862 through early 1863, there

115

were many weeks when American cotton per pound was much the same price as calico per pound. 'To manufacture cotton bought now into goods now sold can only entail a very heavy loss', wrote *The Economist* on 27 December 1862. This was the time when mills throughout Lancashire stopped, or went on sharply reduced working.

Once destocking was over and reduced output took its effect, given strong overseas demand, cloth prices began to reflect expensive cotton and mill-margins came back to more adequate levels. And in 1863 more cotton began to arrive from non-American sources. On paper this was cheaper cotton, especially Surat, but that advantage diminished when waste losses and the difficulty of working were taken into account. None-the-less the worst of the Cotton Famine was over by the summer of 1863. Consumption that year was 508 million lbs, nearly half the pre-war level. Given the volatility of prices and the enormous uncertainties and risks, even as Lancashire mills returned at least to partial working, all participants in the market lived on a tentative and hand-to-mouth basis. Business was a lottery, but a lottery in which the participants had no choice but to engage.

Fieldens experience was probably not representative. They had good intelligence and large resources. In 1861 they were long of cotton and long of cloth. With many others they would welcome the rise in prices late in the year. It is not clear what they did as the situation developed, but certainly in August 1862 and until early 1863 they virtually ceased to work their mills except on a very occasional basis. Over a period of about 9 months of limited working they paid their workpeople half their normal week's wage whether they worked or not, thus setting an example that won the praise of the Factory Inspectors and earned the Partnership the enduring gratitude of their employees. The Partners had 'ordered' on 11 August 1862, 'that the workpeople, including overlookers .... shall be paid 6 days wages for the fortnight ended 13 August.' The practice continued thereafter so long as the stoppage of trade continued. For the Fieldens, the experience of the firm in protecting its workpeople from destitution in 1841 and 1842 was a precedent. Interestingly in Macclesfield during the silk trade slump in 1863-65 the Brocklehurst mills were kept going at a loss to the firm of £70,000; John Brocklehurst is reported as saying 'I have made my money in Macclesfield and I will spend it to the last sixpence before I will see the workpeople starve.'

Partnership Minute, 1862, records the decision to pay half-wages at the Fielden mills when operations ceased during the most difficult period of the Cotton Famine. The Fielden example was well-publicised in Lancashire, and was well-remembered in Todmorden. The total wages paid would be about £750 per week. The Partnership made a profit of £224,575 in 1862, principally due to the appreciation in the value of its stocks of cotton and cloth with the huge rise in cotton prices at the time, so the cost of wages without work would not be a heavy burden; more significant was the huge Rostron bad debt.

Throughout Lancashire, of course, during the worst period of the Famine the stronger companies, many of whom had taken large profits from the sharp increase in prices, were making some wage payments or otherwise helping their work-people with gifts of food, fuel and clothing. Apart from concerns of humanity, employers wanted to keep their labour force together with their self-respect maintained. It was the many smaller firms, especially on the weaving side, who, when they closed their mills, could do nothing for their hands. And the hands, eventually and reluctantly, had to turn to the Guardians or Relief Committees.[8]

After their extended closure, Fieldens resumed an irregular operation with limited working, two, three or four days, perhaps daylight hours only, and with extended shutdowns at holiday periods. One way or another a determined effort was made to find work and to provide the work-force with sufficient means to avoid destitution. And if machinery was not being worked the mill could be cleaned, walls whitewashed, woodwork painted, property and roadways repaired. For some mill-hands, seasonally, work was found on the Fielden-owned farms, making hay and the like. Idle mills or limited working, also provided an opportunity to upgrade machinery. Stoneswood had been modernised in 1860. Between 1861 and 1865 over £8,000 was spent on replacing all the old mules at Waterside with self-acting mules supplied by McGregor at prices which got down to 3s 6d a spindle. As a first step in rationalising the mill structure, the tiny ill-suited Waterstalls mill ceased operations in 1860 when the machinery was sold; the mill was subsequently let, and sold in 1864. The small mills acquired at Lumbutts were closed and demolished at this time and a new Jumb Mill built, although it was not to be fitted with machinery until some years later in 1871.[9]

Other concerns were behaving in much the same way as the Fieldens, doing limited work but keeping their hands together. By 1863 most firms in Lancashire had learnt to use short staple Indian Surat cotton which accounted for about half the supplies available. Fieldens had been using some Surat in the 1850s as part of their blend, mainly because, despite high waste, it was cheaper. Now it became the principal if not the sole part of their mix. And if at first there were universal complaints about dirt and waste, damage to machinery and loss of throughput and earnings because of yarn breakages, gradually the experience to use Surat cotton with greater facility was developed. It was at this period that in order to lessen breakages and improve colour, as well as replace expensive cotton for a given weight of cloth, many weaving firms, it seems in Todmorden in particular, increased the application of size (or Lancashire cotton as it came to be called) to the warp, raising the proportion from a typical 20 per cent, to as much as 60 or even 100 per cent. Cheaper whiter china clay was also substituted for flour in the sizing process.[10] Fieldens were among the firms who resisted these expedients which, in their view, would only cheapen and adulterate their cloth and destroy its reputation.

Although the Todmorden spinning and weaving operations in the period 1861 through 1863 must have been unprofitable, given discontinuous working and inadequate margins, the appreciation in the value of stocks of cotton and cloth resulted in exceptionally large profits in 1862 and 1863 as these stocks were sold. (Table XIV). Whether the cotton stock was resold, rather than worked, in either of these years is not known; probably it was made into cloth and the cloth put into stock; as cloth prices increased, especially in 1863, the stocks were sold and increased value realised. Todmorden assets which had risen sharply, then fell sharply, although they were still above normal. Whatever the costs of paying wages without work, and they were reported to have been about £750 per week, they were clearly small in the context of massive stock appreciation.

But after the exceptional stock profits of 1862 and 1863, 1864 brought problems. For much of the year margins were inadequate. Thus in August 1864 Fieldens were writing to Campbell in Liverpool.

> 'As we cannot dispose of our goods at anything like a price that will cover cost with present prices of cotton in your market, it is our intention to close our works in about a week. We must have either cotton down or goods up to induce us to go on working.'

Throughout 1864 prices were lurching dangerously, one way or the other, as news from America reached the market, but over the year they fell sharply. The overriding fear now was of being caught with cotton purchases or unsold goods on a falling market. Consignment to distant markets where goods would arrive long after advice of lower prices was especially imprudent. Most businesses, including Fieldens, had to write down stock or work-in-progress and many failures occurred in Lancashire. Fielden Brothers had a bad year in 1864 with a loss of £15,398. 1865 was a little better but operations remained hand-to-mouth. In January Campbell was told

> 'We feel almost inclined to stop our mills as we think it not at all impossible that cotton may fall to the extent of 1d or 2d per lb within a very short time. With the present excess of stock of cotton over this time last year, and the probability of large importation of last year's growth we cannot see how the present prices can be maintained.'[11]

Rather than pay up for American they were then buying Comptah, Smyrna and Japanese cottons as well as Surat. Confidence slowly returned and by September 1865 Campbell was sending 300 bales weekly, including 30 bales American and the rest Comptah and Surat. By then Fieldens, like many other employers, were short of hands. Thus, although difficult because of falling prices, 1865 brought some return towards normality. The industry's cotton consumption rose to 723 million lbs. In Todmorden, Fieldens could achieve a modest profit of £18,904. The period 1862-1865 had shown an average return on a swollen capital in spinning and weaving of 19 per cent: in the same period the Ashworths averaged 14 per cent at New Eagley. Watts regarded 12.5 per cent as the average profits of the trade at the time.[12] Taken as a whole, from a business point of view, the period 1850 to 1865 was one of extraordinary success. Although there were bad years, exceptional profits were made and the American war was a bonanza. The Todmorden activity, spinning and weaving, the core business, had been able to perform handsomely. To the Partners, overwhelmed by their success, the rest hardly mattered, provided it paid for its keep.

Liverpool

When the Partnership was restructured on John Fielden's death, Fielden Brothers & Co.'s capital became separately owned by Thomas and James. Together the brothers provided £294,855, with William Pickersgill and Daniel Campbell participating to an extent that is not recorded. Upon James's death in 1852 the greater part of his capital in the Liverpool business was withdrawn. About £27,000 passed to Thomas to meet his third share of James's residual estate. Thomas then in 1852 withdrew £100,000 from Fielden Brothers & Co. to increase his capital in Fielden Brothers and, in part, to add to his railway investments. This left him with about £75,000 in the Liverpool concern.

These changes in the Fielden capital employed in Liverpool coincided with but also contributed to a change in its role. For whatever reason it must be concluded the Fieldens lost interest in Liverpool. They were probably right. They lacked the critical mass and market share which would make for success, whether in ship-owning or the merchant trade. They had better uses for their funds. But the commercial opportunity had also changed while the youthful talent to maintain and develop the business was no longer there. Thus the scale of Liverpool activity was run down. The shipping interests were all sold between 1851 and 1853, partly to release capital. The trade in produce, cotton, timber and other commodities was much reduced but still substantial in 1850; thereafter it seems to have dwindled away. In the 1858 Bill of Entry Records the name Fielden appears rarely, although some cotton continued to be imported. The markets themselves were changing, especially in cotton where the fast steam packets facilitated the growth of 'arrivals' trading which gradually replaced the consignment business that had been the raison d être of the commission merchant. Cotton was now sold 'to arrive', even before it was shipped. The merchant's functions were assumed by the wharfinger on the one hand, who landed and warehoused, and especially by the selling broker, acting for the shipper, who traded with the buying broker, acting for the Lancashire spinners. The coming of an efficient trans-Atlantic cable in 1867 finally killed the consignment business, not merely for Fieldens, but for Barings, Brown Shipley and others.

Changing market circumstances probably did not prevent Fielden Brothers, like many others in Liverpool, making and retaining useful profits in the turbulence of 1862-1865. But thereafter the business withered away. Daniel Campbell died in March 1867, leaving about £90,000. His eldest son, appropriately named Thomas Fielden Campbell seems to have maintained a presence in the firm and so long as Thomas Fielden was alive, a Liverpool office was retained. But when Thomas died in December 1869, the presence of Fieldens in Liverpool also died; there is no mention of Fielden Brothers & Co. thereafter, in Directories or elsewhere.

New York

If Liverpool slowly declined, William Pickersgill with his strong Riggs connections, was developing a significant banking business in New York. It ceased to serve the Liverpool house and acquired an independent activity and status. But Pickersgill maintained the Fielden connection, not least because the Fielden reputation and reputed wealth strengthened his standing. How the equity in Liverpool was distributed between William Pickersgill and Thomas Fielden in the 1850s is not clear. So far as the New York activity is concerned, the bulk, if not all, of the equity must have belonged to Pickersgill.

The Pickersgill business in the 1850s in Wall Street and then at 29 William Street was a free standing merchant banking business, accepting, buying and selling bills, making loans or advances on shipments of commodities or other approved collateral, dealing in foreign exchange, and buying/selling or placing Federal government bonds and other stocks. In 1851, R.S. Dun could comment:

'Fielden Bros. and Co. of Liverpool and W.C.Pickersgill and Co. are the same, they are a very good firm and their Bills pass as freely as those of Brown Bros. and Co. Pickersgill manages the house here and his course of doing so convinces one that he will never get the house into trouble; he is cautious, attentive and energetic, and if he errs at all it is from being too cautious.'

Wall Street in the 1850s Pickersgill and Co. (Fielden Brothers and Co.) had offices at number 46 and later moved to 29 William Street, nearby. Already this was the heart of the New York financial district and Pickersgill was one of the most respected names in the city.

In 1858, Dun reported Pickersgill's personal capital at $500,000 and described him as 'the most conservative banker in the city, and his bills command as high a price as any in this city; he can command a large amount of money at the shortest notice; is shrewd, prompt, and highly esteemed; he represents and draws on Fielding (sic) Bros. and Co. who are worth 'tis said £2,000,000 sterling.' By 1868 it was said that Pickersgill had belonged to the banking elite for a quarter century and was now thought to be worth $1-2 million (£200-£400,000).[13]

Pickersgill would have been able to provide Fieldens with good intelligence on the commercial situation in America and in particular, on the course of the Civil War. Perhaps this was the basis of the statement by the author of *Fortunes Made in Business* that 'a large part of the prosperity of the firm is due' to 'the untiring energy and ability' of Pickersgill.[14] That would seem to overstate the contribution of the relationship, important as it was. Although Pickersgill and Co. continued in New York until 1868, William must have made his fortune by 1863 for in that year he bought Blendon Hall, a small estate in Bexley, Kent. His eldest and only surviving son had died in 1868 and this probably prompted him to return to England and take up residence in Blendon Hall about 1870. He spent the rest of his life there. When he returned to England, he shared offices with John Pickersgill and Co., the family bank, at 15 Leadenhall Street, and continued a modest investment business there under the name Fielden Brothers & Co. That firm had ceased to trade in Liverpool, but with its limited capital again became part of the Fielden Brothers Partnership following Thomas's death in 1869 when the greater part of his wealth passed to his nephews. The name Fielden Brothers & Co. first appears in the London Directories in 1871. By 1873 the office had moved to 7 East India Avenue and William Pickersgill was joined by Theodore Lodge who had been a cashier in the Liverpool business. Lodge now became the confidential clerk who handled the private affairs of the Fielden family for the next 30 years.

Manchester

Selling cloth and buying cotton on behalf of Todmorden, remained the chief Manchester activity after 1850. Consignment business continued with shipments to India and the Far East as well as those to the traditional South American markets. But speedier communications which enabled news to travel faster than goods reduced the opportunities for 'adventures in trade.' If a particular market was short of goods that would be known very quickly to all suppliers. The scale of direct selling diminished, and more of Fieldens' business went through the Manchester trade houses. A close business association between Thomas Fielden and his kindred spirit, Sam Mendel, the large and bold Manchester merchant specialising in grey cloth to India and China, probably developed during this period.[15] In consequence a smaller capital was employed in 'adventures in trade,' to be replaced by receivables from the Manchester trade houses.

These commercial activities would use most, if not all, of the capital in trade in Manchester in the early 1850s, financed partly by Partnership

The Irwell from Blackfriars Bridge.
Thomas Fielden would walk across one or other of the Irwell bridges most days when he was in Manchester and see this view which catches one aspect of the face of the nineteenth century city. In the foreground, cotton mills, an iron works, a tannery, a timber yard and other old workshops and warehouses line the river; in the background is Manchester Cathedral, Chetham School, Hunts Bank and the railway, and in the distance the Manchester Union workhouse

capital, partly by Family Accounts (Appendix III). But the Manchester Accounts, that is the capital in trade there, grew rapidly as profits were retained in the business, especially in 1859 and subsequently. Thus at the end of 1859 Manchester Accounts totalled £643,350 of which £468,384 was Partnership capital, the rest family loan. Surviving records do not make clear how so large a total was being used. The partners had started to lend to other business men, with some form of collateral, in the 1840s and this had continued. Almost certainly in the late 1850s they were lending to Manchester merchants like Sam Mendel, James Watts, Richard Rostron and others, and probably to Warner and Page, a leading Manchester stockbroker.[16]

Fieldens also began to invest in property. Their assets at end of June 1852 include freehold land at Longsight and residential property described as the Carpenters Estate, both in growing areas of Manchester, valued at £13,762. Additional land in Plymouth Grove and Hope was then acquired and an estate of building land at Queens Park, Chester, had been bought by the Trustees of Mary Cobbett in 1853 for £21,000. In 1857 this was acquired by the Partnership for the same sum. It was subsequently to be worth much more, but was held at this value in the portfolio for many years. 'Estates near Manchester' were valued at £60,000 in the Partnership Private Ledger in 1859 and each year subsequently to 1865. In later years the investment in property was to be increased substantially.

The objective of both the loan activity and property investment was presumably a safe yield. The partners were achieving high if irregular returns on their capital in Todmorden at the time and there were apparent limits to their enterprise. The interest and profits earned in Manchester were modest in comparison and in most years in the range from 3 to 7 per cent (Table XVI). There were good years, however, especially 1856 and 1862/1863 which saw gains on stocks of cloth and cotton. Over the whole period to 1865 Manchester achieved an average return of 7.7 per cent. Given the boldness implicit in the Todmorden activities a degree of caution with regard to other business may have seemed appropriate. A more conservative policy that now began to guide the business, in contrast say to the bold enterprise of the 1830s, was to become the distinguishing feature of the second Fielden Brothers Partnership. They were not alone in this. A not dissimilar business, John Foster and Sons of Black Dyke Mills, Queensbury, after spectacular success in the late Fifties and early Sixties chose to invest heavily in bonds and stocks quoted on the London Stock Exchange, rather than new forms of enterprise; by 1865 over 50 per cent of their capital was invested in this way.[17]

Fieldens, and this would be Thomas, retained the long standing connection with Richard Rostron and with South America; they had been dealing with Rostron and his agents in different Brazilian ports since the 1830s; his Manchester standing was high and it is reasonable to suppose Thomas Fielden could trust his friend. The Rostron association was now to yield another passive investment opportunity, that is one that required no active management, but could be expected to yield good returns. This was the Pernambuco Gas Company.

Table XVI: Fielden Brothers: Capital Employed and Profits in Manchester Business 1851-1865.

Period Ending	Partnership Capital[1] Employed in Manchester Accounts	Profits[2]	Return on Manchester Capital
	£ Start of Period	£	%
30 June 1852	153,648	5,254	3.4
31 Dec.1853 (18 months)	204,461	22,100	7.2
31 Dec. 1854	109,895	3,373	3.1
31 Dec. 1855	131,195	12,600	9.6
31 Dec. 1856	102,266	17,893	17.5
31 Dec. 1857	370,859	22,480	6.0
31 Dec. 1858	365,136	25,713	7.0
31 Dec. 1859	374,344	23,422	6.3
31 Dec. 1860	468,384	23,568	5.0
31 Dec. 1861	514,925	34,995	6.8
31 Dec. 1862	496,857	74,525	15.0
31 Dec. 1863	497,204	44,898	9.0
31 Dec. 1864	820,044	66,570	8.1
31 Dec. 1865	911,361	54,446	6.0

Source: Longden MSS, Private Ledger.

Notes:
1. Total Manchester Accounts less that part financed by Private Family Accounts, at start of financial period. In 1864 and 1865 net loans to Family members are added. (Appendix III).
2. Interest on capital employed plus trading profit on 'our other business', during the financial period.

Investment to provide public utilities in South American cities — gas, water, tramways and the like — began to attract British capital on a large scale in the 1850s. Some of the projects were financed by share issues in the London market, some privately. A few of the investments were to prove very lucrative, but all seemed to offer safe and attractive returns. A concession to supply gas in Pernambuco would have obvious appeal. The Partners understood gas, and Rostron not only knew Brazil but had a branch in Pernambuco — Rostron Rooker. Income would be assured by government, at least for the life of the concession, once the utility was completed. Engineering and management skills to implement the project were readily available in Manchester.

This was the genesis of the Pernambuco Gas Company. In 1857 a thirty year concession was negotiated and a contract was announced to erect buildings and machinery for the manufacture of gas, for 30 miles of mains, for street lamps etc. Edward Bellhouse, a consulting gas engineer of Manchester contracted to carry out the first part of the works at a cost of £53,000. Fielden Brothers and R. Rostron and Co. were to finance the project. Its eventual capital came to nearly £150,000, and if the intention at the outset was that the two participants would take equal shares, it seems that in the end Fieldens put up all the money. This £150,000 overseas investment was part of the Manchester business. The completed gas-works are described in a British Consulate report in 1864: there were then 1,110 public lights and 4,500 private fixtures, 40 miles of mains and two gasholders. The appalling living conditions in Pernambuco and its hinterland are vividly described by the Consul; a population of about one million were engaged in cotton and sugar cultivation or commerce; there were nineteen British merchants in the port, handling imports of about £1 million a year from the United Kingdom, of which between £600,000 and £900,000 might be cotton cloth, brought mainly in British ships out of Liverpool. This was the kind of market that Fieldens had been supplying for close to fifty years. Now it had given them a different business opportunity. Whether it was to bear fruit would only be evident in later years.[18]

Whether or not Richard Rostron ever put any money into the Pernambuco Gas Company, his main business and his various associated partnerships (Rostron Dutton, Rostron Rooker), failed early in the 1860s. Probably, judging by the date, this was a consequence of virtually complete inactivity in the Manchester market in 1862 but possibly because of wrong exposure to a rising cotton market. He seems to have owed Fielden Brothers no less than £134,349, part loans, part for cloth supplied on a consignment basis or on credit to Rio de Janeiro, Bahia and Pernambuco. Initially this was regarded as a good debt; then the decision was taken to write most of it off. To most businesses, this would have been a completely crippling loss. Indeed, even for Fieldens, to be so heavily involved with one trade house, could only represent a massive error of judgement, presumably by Thomas. The records are silent on the point; and fortunately the disaster, whatever its cause, coincided with the huge stock profits of 1862 and 1863. The Partnership accounts for 1862 write off £84,549 from a profit of £224,572 in that

The Rostron Mill at Edenfield. The Fieldens had a long commercial association with the respected Manchester merchant, Richard Rostron, selling through his agencies in Brazil and joining in the Pernambuco gas venture. It was said of Thomas Fielden that he had 'unbounded trust in those who once gained his confidence; sometimes this resulted in considerable loss.' Rostron's business failed in the early 1860s, leaving Fieldens with a huge bad debt, only partly secured by Rostron's assets in Edenfield, a print works, cotton factory and farms and cottages. These properties were owned by Fielden Brothers until 1889 and eventually passed to Samuel Fielden and then to his son.

Table XVII: Fielden Brothers: Partner's Capital Employed, Profit and Drawings 1851-1865.

Period Ending	Partners Capital Employed[1] £ start of period	Profit[2] £	Return on Partners Capital[3] Per Cent	Drawings[4] £
30 June 1852	290,628	65,516	22.5	33,461
31 Dec.1853 (18 months)	322,683	63,500	19.7	16,251
31 Dec. 1854	369,932	31,698	8.6	8,633
31 Dec. 1855	392,997	30,637	7.8	(9,274)
31 Dec. 1856	432,908	60,092	13.9	(2,961)
31 Dec. 1857	495,961	15,372	3.1	5,358
31 Dec. 1858	505,975	83,733	16.5	12,755
31 Dec. 1859	576,953	98,320	17.0	51,598
31 Dec. 1860	623,675	121,104	19.4	(2,203)
31 Dec. 1861	746,992	97,464	13.0	7,995
31 Dec. 1862	836,461	224,572[5]	26.8	246
31 Dec. 1863	976,238	172,046	17.6	87,592
31 Dec. 1864	1,060,692	50,971	4.8	26,903
31 Dec. 1865	1,084,760 1,116,709[6]	73,350	6.8	41,401

Source: Longden MSS, Private Ledger

Notes

1. Includes Joint Todmorden Properties, Capital Employed in Todmorden spinning and weaving, Manchester Accounts and Loans from 1863 (Appendix III).
2. Includes rents on property and machinery, interest and profits (losses) on trading.
3. Profits as per cent of Partners' Capital at the start of the period.
4. Drawings reflect depreciation of Joint Todmorden properties, and will be somewhat greater than the sums actually taken out by the partners.
5. Bad debt of £84,549 written off in 1862.
6. Partners Capital, including Joint Todmorden Properties, at end of 1865.

Private Ledger 1865. The last entry, signed by all the Partners, records the capital of the Second Partnership at its peak, following the profitable years of the 1850s and the more speculative profits made during the Cotton Famine period. At this point Joshua had reduced his share by drawings to finance Stansfield Hall and the expenses of his large family. The largest share was held by Thomas who, when he died in 1869, was to leave his stake in the Partnership and much of his considerable private wealth to his nephews.

year. In making this write-off, they assumed that £49,800 would be realised from assets remaining in Rostron's estate, chiefly farms, cottages, a print works in Edenfield, some shares and a life policy.[19]

Managing the Rostron assets (rents were collected, the print works were leased), developing the loan business, supervising Pernambuco, developing a property portfolio, buying cotton and selling cloth, remained the activities of the Manchester office. But after the Rostron affair, and as Thomas Fielden ceased to be active, the initiative passed to Todmorden and whatever happened in Manchester, large as the capital employed there may have been, was decided by the partners in Todmorden.

The Golden Years

It is convenient to summarise the achievement of this mid-Victorian period, when the third generation and their aging uncle took full opportunity of the cotton boom and its sequel in the Cotton Famine. As shown in Table XVII and Appendix III, the Partnership achieved a total profit between 1851 and 1865 of close to £1.2million of which approximately over £750,000 could be attributed to Todmorden Spinning and Weaving and the balance to other business. This was an average rate of return on Partnership capital in excess of 14 per cent, a high figure, although that earned on the Todmorden manufacturing activities at about 26 per cent, was far higher than that achieved in Manchester (about 7.7 per cent). Bad debts of at least £84,549 were written off and the Partners withdrew over £275,000 from the business for their personal use; they had other private income from rents and dividends on personal investments. The assets of the Partnership, including jointly owned properties, rose from £290,628 in 1851 to £1,116,709 at the end of 1865.

This was the proud position of 1865: Fielden Brothers was probably the most successful business in Lancashire at the time, the Partners were among the wealthiest people in Great Britain, and much of their wealth was outside the business. Fielden Brothers now entered its final period, until it ceased to exist as a business partnership. It was to be a conservative period and one of decline in a Lancashire that retained its vigour, notwithstanding a changed business environment. 'Great profit has a tendency to produce a relaxation of exertion' had been remarked by an earlier Lancashire entrepeneur.[20] Perhaps this was now to be true of the Fieldens.

MATURITY AND DECLINE
Fielden Brothers 1866-1889

With their fortunes made, it is not clear what the partners were now looking forward to. Most probably it was to relax and enjoy, in different ways, their new wealth, status and power. Their intention was not, apparently, to drive the business forward, whether by further expansion in the cotton trade or by new ventures in other business areas; rather their interest seems to have been to preserve their capital, let it grow in safe investments, and use the income to support a different and more lavish lifestyle.

Problems at Todmorden

They cannot, however, have been expecting the performance in Todmorden that emerged for the remainder of their business lives, that is until the end of the Second Partnership, shortly before Samuel Fielden's death in 1889. Between 1866 and 1889 the spinning and weaving business in Todmorden made a loss in thirteen out of the twenty four years (Table XVIII). Over the period the Partnership derived no income from Todmorden, whether as rent, interest or profit. Rather, to keep the business going they had to put back part of their capital, as much as £45,000 over the period. In the decade of the 1870s a loss was made in seven years with five consecutive loss making years beginning in 1875. The next ten years were slightly better, a loss in only five years and approximately neither loss or gain over the decade as a whole. Todmorden, to quote Farnie's words about the industry, may have remained 'a vehicle of power and status, but became less remunerative in economic terms and served increasingly as a machine for the payment of wages rather than of profits.'[1]

The magic touch, it would seem, had gone. Why, it may be asked, assume these risks, devote so much time and trouble, for no return, when the capital employed could be earning a safe 5 per cent in good railway stock and perhaps more in other slightly riskier equity investments. Not that such an alternative was considered, at least while Thomas was alive (he died in 1869), or subsequently by Samuel and John. Joshua, as will be seen, took a different view, as did the next generation. But certainly Samuel and John were too proud of their heritage and achievement, too loyal to their workforce, too conscious of the sacred trust, to consider giving up. They had no urge to develop the business but closure and sale was unthinkable, and probably not feasible. In the context of their wealth the losses in Todmorden were trivial and disappointing; frustrating, even humiliating as the situation was, not many people knew. The results were shared among a trusted few; the workforce and

Table XVIII: Fielden Brothers: Todmorden Spinning & Weaving: Capital Employed & Profit 1866-1889.

Period Ending	Freehold Property (Mills, Farms, Cottages)[1]	Machinery in the Mills	Working Capital[2]	Capital Employed	Profit[3]	Return on Capital[1]
	£	£	£	£	£	£
31 December 1865	39,557	31,338	162,228	233,123		
31 December 1866	37,579	28,961	240,278	306,818	5,673	2.4
31 December 1867	36,322	26,253	335,768	398,343	(86,234)	(28.1)
31 December 1868	35,000	23,652	415,021	473,673	24,674	6.2
31 December 1869	33,500	21,646	236,125	291,271	27,362	5.8
31 December 1870	32,000	19,212	206,253	257,465	(20,355)	(7.0)
31 December 1871	30,500	18,701	168,655	217,855	17,693	6.9
31 December 1872	29,000	17,186	144,700	190,886	(8,968)	(4.1)
31 December 1873	28,000	15,569	132,440	176,009	7,584	4.0
31 December 1874	27,000	15,061	176,936	218,997	15,103	8.6
31 December 1875	26,000	19,201	246,040	291,241	(6,714)	(3.1)
31 December 1876	25,000	21,842	218,520	265,362	(2,851)	(1.0)
31 December 1877	24,000	24,049	124,560	172,609	(9,487)	(3.6)
31 December 1878	23,000	31,839	92,566	147,405	(14,739)	(8.5)
31 December 1879	22,000	29.394	81,305	132,699	(3,061)	(2.1)
31 December 1880	21,000	29,987	66,811	117,798	(1,404)	(1.1)
31 December 1881	20,000	27,835	39,408	87,243	6,390	5.4
31 December 1882	20,000	27,219	52,356	99,575	(4,339)	(5.0)
31 December 1883	20,000	26,970	57,162	104,132	5,173	5.2
31 December 1884	20,000	26,570	68,264	114,834	4,031	3.9
31 December 1885	20,000	28,850	43,671	92,521	(11,162)	(9.7)
31 December 1886	20,000	26,768	21,778	68,546	1,882	2.0
31 December 1887	20,000	24,462	26,775	71,237	6,938	10.1
31 December 1888	20,000	22,728	37,070	79,798	(1,814)	(2.5)
31 December 1889	—	—	—	—	(3,123)	(3.9)

Source: Longden MSS, Stock Account; WYAS, Machinery Valuation, C353/132.
Notes:
1. Book value of Freehold property (owned by the Partners, outside the Partnership) is estimated after 1867, and assumed to be £20,000 from 1881. When the Partnership was wound up in 1889, the freehold properties, including steam engines etc., were valued at £159,700. (Appendix II).
2. Working Capital would include year end balances held at Waterside, in part financing stocks of cotton, work-in-progress, stocks of yarn, cloth and trade debtors, including Manchester. This last item, especially until the late 1870s, seems to have fluctuated in a way unrelated to the needs of the spinning and weaving business.
3. Profit includes interest at 5 per cent on Waterside Working Capital, rents on freehold property, rents on machinery less depreciation, and profit/loss on trading.
4. Profit as per cent of Capital Employed, end previous year.

townspeople could only judge the situation by their awareness that mills were being closed, capacity reduced, and earnings made uncertain and diminished by frequent short time working and by occasional wage reductions.

The period subsequent to the Cotton Famine was difficult for the whole industry. The end of the war left cotton prices very high. They were to fall, erratically, for the next five years, sharply in 1866 and especially in 1867. Falling prices inhibited confidence and invariably presented problems to the stockholding spinner or weaver. 1867 was a year of widespread recession and business failure, not merely in the

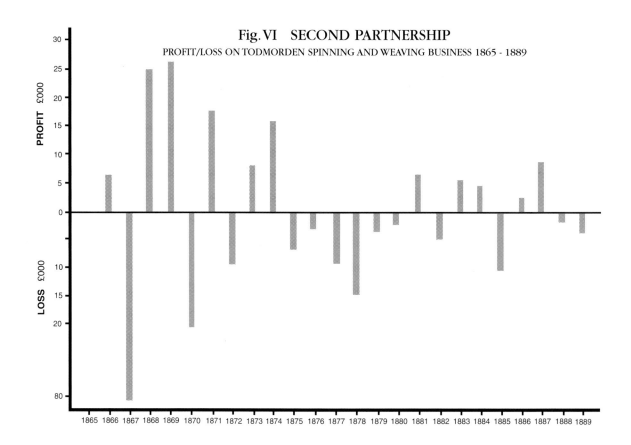

Fig. VI   SECOND PARTNERSHIP

PROFIT/LOSS ON TODMORDEN SPINNING AND WEAVING BUSINESS 1865 - 1889

cotton industry, but throughout the economy, partly due to the commercial difficulties precipitated by the collapse of Overend and Gurney in October 1866. At the height of the mid-century boom, in 1859 and 1860, mill-margins had averaged about 8d per pound of cloth. Between 1865 and 1870 they averaged 5½d. It was not until 1870 that cotton consumption in the United Kingdom recovered its pre-war level. But these were years of adjustment and perhaps not a cause of great concern at Waterside or elsewhere in the industry. The early 1870s were better years, with rising activity throughout Lancashire and mill-margins returning towards 7d per pound. Ellison was to describe 1871 as reaching or surpassing the profitable conditions that immediately preceded the Civil War. But this did not last. Ellison quoted an average margin of only 4½ per pound in 1872. The next two years brought recovery but from 1875 each year brought deterioration. This was the beginning of the great depression. To Ellison 1878 was 'a year of unparalleled commercial depression' with firm cotton prices after a poor crop but a weakening cloth market. Mill-margins fell below 4½d and in the following year, 1879, they averaged 4d although some sort of recovery started by the autumn. 1880 through 1882 were better years but margins averaged only 4d in 1883-1885, falling to 3¾d in 1885; Ellison wrote of 'wails of complaint from all quarters' in 1882, 'unbearable chronic over-supply' in 1884, and 'partial or entire disappearance of profits' in 1885.[2]

The problems of these years were not peculiar to Fielden Brothers nor in some respects to the cotton industry. Perhaps there had been an over-expansion of capacity; perhaps the world market was ceasing to grow; perhaps and more significantly the predominance and supremacy of Lancashire was being challenged by competition, competition from Continental Europe and the United States, and from indigenous industry as this developed in India and elsewhere.[3] But other long-established Lancashire firms, like the Ashworths were still managing to make a positive return, albeit on a smaller capital, year by year in the 1870s. Between 1865 and 1879 they seem to have averaged 12.8 per cent; over the same period the Fieldens averaged a loss of 2.3 per cent in Todmorden (Table XVIII), heavily influenced by the large loss in 1867. Elsewhere in Lancashire there was bold enterprise in this period; large powerful and profitable combines emerged, notably John Rylands and Sons, with 200,000 spindles and 5,000 looms in seventeen mills, 'the recognised and undisputed head and leader of the cotton trade,' powerful not merely in manufacture, but in finishing and in distribution; Horrocks Crewdson which had 200,00 spindles and 6,600 looms at the merger in 1887; and Tootal, Broadbent and Lee which had 172,000 spindles and 3,500 looms in the same year and average profits of over £17,000 a year between 1862 and 1885, with a loss in only two years.[4]

Long established combined spinning and weaving concerns in the plain cloth business like Fieldens had particular problems. For a variety of reasons, including the age of buildings and plant and the mill-structure of comparatively small scattered spinning facilities, they were losing their competitiveness within the industry. On the one hand, the rash of new large and specialised spinning enterprises in the Oldham district, aggressively managed as limited liability companies on quite different lines to the older family enterprises, were able to supply yarn at prices the Fielden spinning mills could not match. Samuel Fielden complained in 1881 of competition from 'modern mills, arranged and equipped for producing yarn of the best quality cheaply.' Burnley spinners spoke of Oldham yarn being 1d a pound cheaper. This inevitably put the Waterside weaving business at a disadvantage compared with specialist weaving concerns in North East Lancashire supplied from Oldham who, yarn costs aside, were probably more efficient weavers as well. In the market for plain cloth, Indian competition was also making itself felt. There were also those at Waterside who felt that Fieldens reluctance to size their cloth heavily was putting them at a disadvantage. If Fieldens had become high cost in an intensively competitive market, their results could only compare unfavourably with those of other businesses. But throughout Lancashire many long-established large combined businesses remained viable, as the Worrall Directories of the time show; Ashton Brothers in Hyde, for instance, were still working 145,000 spindles and over 3,000 looms; Hoyles in Bacup, Dugdales in Blackburn or Garsides in Ashton are other examples. Even locally, in Todmorden, as Fieldens limped along, unprofitably, although there were many business failures, younger enterprises — Maden and Hoyle, Luke Barker and Sons, Ormerod

Brothers, and other lesser concerns — appeared to flourish and indeed challenge Fielden's local ascendancy. By 1886, with Fieldens having reduced their spinning capacity since the 1850s, their 56,000 spindles, and a total of 1,450 looms, not all working at any time, compared with 283,358 spindles and 16,307 looms in Todmorden which had become mainly a weaving town with plenty of weaving firms, several with 1,000 looms or more, who offered alternative employment and were regular customers for surplus Fielden yarn.[5]

The Waterside business problem was compounded by a leadership and management problem, and this was the main cause of bad performance and decline. Old Thomas Fielden remained involved until the day of his death, in the Manchester office almost daily, in Todmorden at least once a week. Whether he contributed effectively is not clear but with his death the business had no comparable commercial acumen, flair or connection, either in buying cotton or selling cloth. Samuel would assume that responsibility but would be less closely involved, less on top of the market; the Manchester activity was delegated to staff who, however reliable and trustworthy, were cautious rather than bold, safe rather than enterprising. In Todmorden, the Fielden presence was less evident, with adverse effects on performance. Joshua, who was never deeply involved, became a Member of Parliament in 1868 and shortly thereafter ceased to live in Todmorden. John, approachable, genial, liked and respected by Fielden workers and townspeople alike, was an easy-going figurehead rather than a highly driven dedicated entrepreneur. When in the mill he would take decisions about hiring young men, wages, gifts to pensioners, short time working and holidays, but he rarely exercised strong authority. He was happy to spend much of his time as a Magistrate on the Bench, as Chairman of the Local Board, and, following his purchase of the Grimston Estate near Tadcaster in 1872, as a country gentleman. Even Samuel, the dominant, overbearing, and senior partner, although deeply concerned, was less than single-minded. He had his involvements in railway affairs, and increasingly enjoyed travel, to France and Germany, to Italy, to the Nile. Notwithstanding Samuel's contribution in the Forties and Fifties, the failure of the firm after the Famine must be attributed in large part to the slackening of his strong involved leadership. The dedication and drive of his early years gave way to an irregular presence and a more delegated approach and the day-to-day detailed management passed outside the family.

Perhaps this was inevitable. A feature of the Fielden style had always been close and continuous involvement of the family, not merely being visible, and accessible, but taking all the important decisions, on people, on operations, on investment, on buying and selling. This was not a culture where these responsibilities were readily assumed by subordinates, however long-serving, loyal, and experienced. Some of the managers — Joseph Hirst, in charge of Waterside weaving, was an example — had worked with Fieldens all their lives and had been deeply involved with the campaigns against the Poor Law and the Factory Movement; they were past their best. Younger mill-managers emerged, notably the Midgleys at Lumbutts, Thomas Wrigley at Robinwood, and John Lord (not to be connected with the Lord family that had become

Lord Brothers) at Waterside. Supervising all the managers was John Haworth, a Fielden employee all his life. In his case, dedicated as he was, as the years passed and he remained in post, his vigour could only diminish; he died in 1887 at the age of 77, still in the mill at six every morning. Thomas Wrigley succeeded him; he was related to the family, his father having married a niece of John Fielden; he joined the firm as a boy aged eight at Waterstalls Mill in 1842 and progressed from there. No doubt the family link helped and the fact that Wrigley was an active Freemason, as was Sam Fielden, probably helped too. John Lord, who compiled the deferential and respectful mill diary over many years was active in the Cricket Club where Sam was President, and was also Warden at the Unitarian Church. These men, and the senior warehouse clerks, such as William Hollinrake, living in Fielden houses, enjoying privileges of various kinds, were not likely to initiate change or challenge the existing order. Their experience and vision was narrow and limited: what they were good at was running the mills in the traditional way, achieving efficient routine. Factory discipline, for instance, was a prime concern, rooting out lax performance and minimising poor time-keeping (a constant problem on Monday mornings and after the infrequent holidays and especially the seasonal fairs), dealing with insubordination, keeping everyone 'up to their marks,' doing the right thing when there were accidents, or when long-serving employees were ill or died. And there were the day-to-day technical and commercial problems: cleaning goits, filling the dams, buying coal, avoiding waste, minimising and correcting breakdowns in the steam engines or in machinery throughout the mills. Always, they had to watch every penny. At their best the managers were on top of all these concerns; if they were lacking in zeal, slackness set in. Thus even in their routine functions, they had to be pushed and disciplined from time to time. This was the master's role: with his brisk authoritative manner and sharp tongue, Samuel did this admirably whenever he was in the mill. He had an eagle-eye for shortcomings, for waste and dirt, loafing, poor work, accident and fire hazards, breaches of discipline and failure to enforce the old rules. But his presence was occasional, the more so as the years went by.

The Fielden culture required the constant presence of the family, not merely to enforce standards, give leadership and take commercial decisions but to provide reassurance both to the workforce and to other stake-holders, that is suppliers and customers. A youthful member of the family who would guarantee succession was now essential. The business needed another 'Young Sam', who took control in the 1840s as the second generation began to step back. Sadly there was no 'Young Sam': the young men of the fourth generation, for whatever reason, did not wish to become involved. The eldest, Thomas Fielden, Joshua's son, born in 1854, educated at Wellington School and briefly at Trinity College, Cambridge, was clearly intended to join and lead the business. Following his marriage in January 1878 he lived at his father's house, Stansfield Hall, and in March came into the mill. Judging by the mill diary, compiled at the time by the Waterside manager, John Lord, that produced a lifting of hearts, a feeling of confidence for the future.[6] But Thomas did not take to the mill or the business. He moved round

William Hollinrake (1842-1901), typical of many Fielden senior employees. His father, Henry, died in 1871 after thirty-seven years with the Partnership, mainly as Cashier. William followed him as a warehouse clerk and later Cashier. For most of his adult life he was organist, Trustee and Treasurer of the Unitarian Church. He seems to have lost the confidence of Samuel Fielden in the 1880s and left the company in 1893 although he continued to live in a Fielden house at Waterside and for a while was tenant and then owner of the White Hart Hotel, a Fielden property. He was remembered in the Fielden wills, Samuel leaving him £100 and John £300.

133

the various departments, paid wages in the counting house, began buying cotton, giving instructions for warps and discussing 'poor and idle hands.' His attendance became increasingly spasmodic with long absences in 1879. His involvement ceased late in that year when his father, Joshua, left the Partnership. Things were at a low ebb at the time. Given the situation, Thomas probably decided that he preferred, as with his expectations he could afford, the life of a country gentleman. He moved with his family in due course as a tenant to Stockeld Park, an attractive country estate near Wetherby, not far from Uncle John's Grimston estate. Following his father, Thomas then began to cultivate the possibility of a Parliamentary seat which he eventually found in the local Middleton constituency in 1885.

At this critical time, the late 1870s, no other young Fielden was interested or available. Samuel's only son, John Ashton Fielden, fresh out of Harrow and Cambridge in the early 1880s, had been a frequent visitor to the mill during his vacations and acquired, probably from his father, a close knowledge of the business. But he did not take to the mill environment or to Todmorden, pleading, at the time, health reasons. He was more frank in later years. Todmorden he wrote was 'damp, dirty and dull; it has no society; it is a humdrum place which deadens the spirits.'[7] Clearly the young men of the fourth generation, prospective heirs to great wealth, perhaps influenced by the values of the English public school, had no wish to follow the lifestyle of their fathers or grandfathers. The family tried other relatives but their name conferred no magic nor did their motivation or performance display competence. Harry Hoyle, a relative of old Thomas Fielden's second wife, had a spell at Waterside and Robinwood; he was spoiled by John and became a frequent visitor to Grimston for the shooting. More significant was Richard Hugh Ramsbotham, son of Jane (née Fielden) and James Ramsbotham of Crowborough Warren. He became the day-to-day general manager at Waterside in 1870, and continued until the 1890s, living at Waterside House and then at Stansfield Hall. But however well connected or worthy, Ramsbotham never won the confidence of the family; he lacked stature and authority and Samuel, on his mill visits, would frequently over-rule him; having no significant wealth or anticipated inheritance, he could not behave as family, but resented having to behave as the hired-hand. He was not diligent, was not willing to be in the mill at six in the morning, nor to account for every absence or for his extended holidays. The business continued to languish in his immediate care.

Thus to review, during a period of changing, difficult, competitive trading conditions, the Fielden family had lessened their grip on the business which was managed by subordinates whose motivation , authority and skills were not adequate to the task. Samuel, or 'Black Sam' as he was now known in the town, increasingly short-tempered, would brutally upbraid the managers for shortcomings, but that made them more cautious or disheartened. What choices did the partners have? They were not going to close or sell the business. They had to retain the hope that a leader would emerge from the next generation. The option of bringing in non-family senior management does not seem to have been considered.

The main response to poor business results was to work at well below capacity, whether by short-time or by leaving spindles and looms idle. This, indeed, was the feature of the period. In 1867 for instance Waterside was entirely stopped for twenty-five days and worked short hours (usually eight hours) on a further sixteen days; on average 190 looms were standing. 1875 was busier with only sixteen days stopped and with an average of 170 looms standing; 1887 averaged 310 looms standing. All the years after 1865 featured short-time working in some degree, with severe loss of earnings to the workpeople and, unsurprisingly, a high turnover of weavers. In the worst years, in the late 1870s and for much of the 1880s, the mills took extended holidays at Christmas and at Fair times, and for long periods would work only for four days and then only in daylight hours. As John Lord noted in 1883 it had become 'quite unusual to work Monday these days.' The total wage bill in 1878 had fallen to about £40,000, materially lower than the high days of the 1850s. Compared with annual output that varied between 6 and 8 million pounds of cloth (about the same as cotton consumption) in the late 1850s, output and cotton usage was 4.2 million pounds in 1867, fell below 3 million pounds in the darkest year, 1878, and averaged just over 3.5 million pounds in the three years 1886-1888. Subsequent to the Cotton Famine, drawing on the experience gained then, and the need to meet low margins with lower costs, a high proportion of Surat cotton was being used, in 1868 more than half of all usage, but by the 1870s American cotton again predominated. Notwithstanding reduced operations, large unsold stocks of cloth built up in the most difficult years, notably in 1876 when the year ended with 235,589 pieces in stock, about six months output given the piece weights at the time; a year later the stock was still 155,838 pieces, and at the end of 1878, 127,460 pieces. 1883 and 1884 were other years when Waterside was 'adding to the stock and can't sell at all.'[8]

More positively, the business, while contracting, was restructured by concentrating production on fewer mills, themselves upgraded. Thus mills were closed, their machinery sold for what it was worth or moved to other mills, and the premises let or sold or demolished. From close to 100,000 spindles in 1856, spinning capacity had been reduced to about 56,000 spindles by 1886; the work-force had fallen to about 1,300 people. Interestingly, out of pride rather than oversight, the firm continued to report a capacity of 100,000 spindles to Worralls Directory. Smithyholme and Mytholmroyd Mills had been sold, Dobroyd and later Causeway closed and pulled down; mule spinning ceased at Waterside. But with two mills in Lumbutts, Robinwood, Stoneswood and Waterside, the business over much of the period was still taking in cotton, preparing it and spinning weft or warp at four sites, the whole to be woven at Waterside. Overheads, cartage, coal use, and direct labour costs must have been augmented by this fragmentation which persisted mainly because of inertia and reluctance to abandon long-serving employees. Stoneswood was kept going until 1889 when it was sold; indeed in 1880 some of its carding machines were replaced and in 1885, ten new ring throstles were put in at a cost of £2,028. There were more significant capital expenditures at what might be regarded as the core sites,

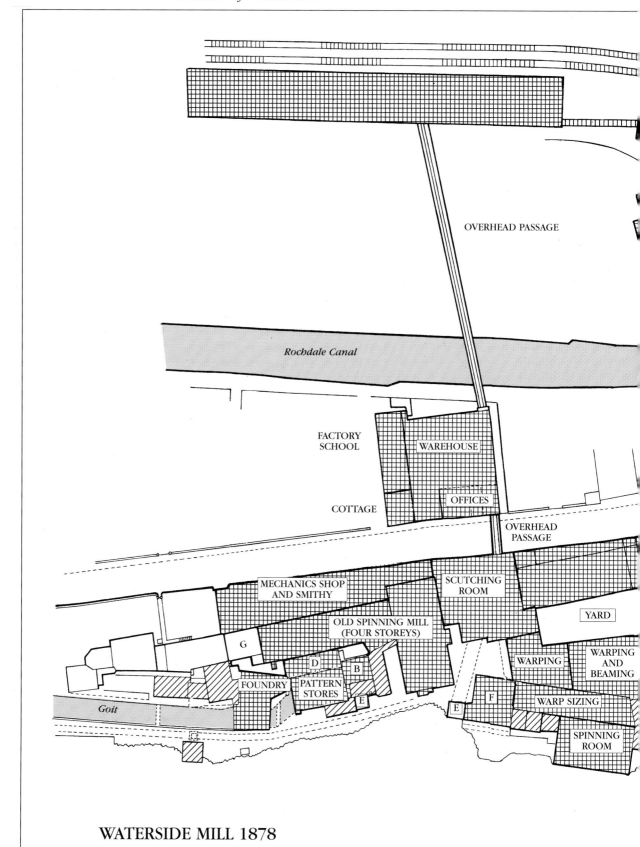

OVERHEAD PASSAGE

Rochdale Canal

FACTORY
SCHOOL

WAREHOUSE

OFFICES

COTTAGE

OVERHEAD
PASSAGE

MECHANICS SHOP
AND SMITHY

SCUTCHING
ROOM

YARD

OLD SPINNING MILL
(FOUR STOREYS)

G

D

B

WARPING

WARPING
AND
BEAMING

FOUNDRY

PATTERN
STORES

E

E

F

WARP SIZING

Goit

SPINNING
ROOM

WATERSIDE MILL 1878

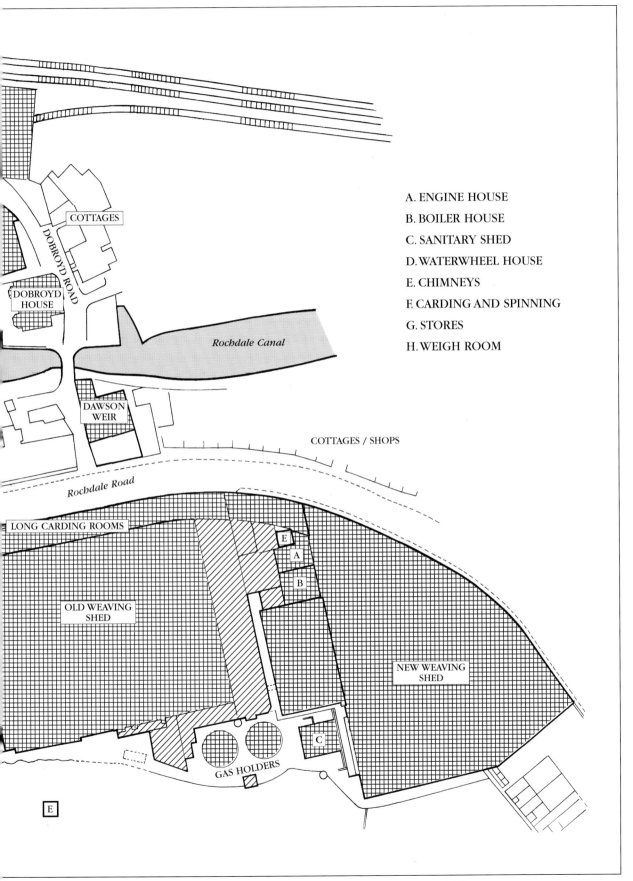

A. ENGINE HOUSE

B. BOILER HOUSE

C. SANITARY SHED

D. WATERWHEEL HOUSE

E. CHIMNEYS

F. CARDING AND SPINNING

G. STORES

H. WEIGH ROOM

Edward Lord (1812-1875). John Lord was a mechanic at Waterside who, with Fielden encouragement set up on his own at Clough Mill in Walsden in 1835, moving in 1837 to Canal Street in Todmorden where six of his seven sons carried on the business as Lord Brothers. Edward the senior partner, self-educated, was a gifted mechanical engineer who, it was said, could improve any machine he touched. He took out many patents, especially for cotton preparation machines (scutching, etc.) but the business made all kinds of textile machinery for carding, spinning and weaving. At one time or another they put their machines in all the Fielden mills, at very competitive prices. Lords went into cotton spinning in 1850 and later into weaving. Edward, who remained closely associated with the Fieldens, died in 1875 leaving about £80,000; the firm lost much of its vigour thereafter, was bought out in 1920 and closed in 1930.

(Above right).
Bill head of Lord Brothers, Canal Street Works.

(Previous page).
Waterside Mill, 1878. The mill plan shows a complex of related activities as they had evolved over close to eighty years; far from an ideal layout, but workable, if not as low cost as it had been compared with the modern specialised spinning and weaving mills of the Oldham district and Burnley-Blackburn respectively.

Robinwood, Lumbutts and Waterside. In particular, the depression of the late 1870s gave the opportunity to purchase spinning machinery and looms at low cost. Most of the Robinwood throstle spindles were replaced in this period, as well as over 1,100 Waterside looms with new looms being acquired at less than £5 per loom, after allowing credit for the old looms removed. Following the investment at Robinwood between 1875 and 1878, Wrigley, the local manager, could report twist production at .44 hanks per spindle hour, an improvement of over one-quarter since the early 1850s when the mill opened. Significantly, in 1884 and 1885, ring spindles were installed at Lumbutts, as at Stoneswood, and on a trial basis at Waterside and Robinwood (Appendix II); the firm was then spinning with a combination of rings, throstles and mules, the rings making both weft and warp.

These investments, substantially greater than depreciation, were an indication of determination to continue, willingness to experiment, confidence that Fielden Brothers had a future, as well as taking an opportunity to buy machines cheaply. But financial results did not improve. Samuel and John meanwhile grew older, and no successor emerged. The years went by; the age consideration alone was to impose change in leadership and in business form at the end of the 1880s.

Industrial Relations

Relations with the workpeople had become an additional source of concern throughout this period. Hitherto, the situation of local dependence on Fieldens for employment, and the family's paternal style had resulted in trouble-free industrial relations. The business had the people and the skills it required and their attitudes were loyal, grateful, obedient, disciplined. Fieldens, along with others, had benefited from Todmorden's out-lying status within the industry; wages had remained different from district to district, indeed from mill to mill; Todmorden was a low-wage district. The firm's protection of its workpeople during the early 1840s and more recently during the Cotton Famine, was well remembered, as was its policy of paying modest pensions to aged

138

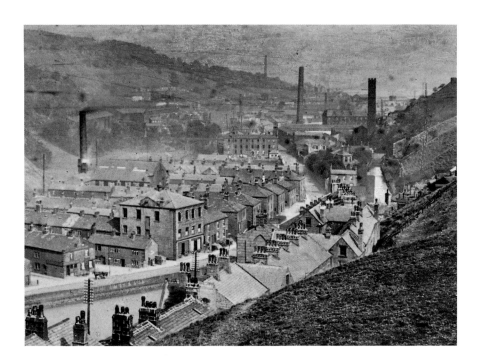

(Left).
Shade and Waterside, late nineteenth century. A large part of the Waterside workforce lived in the closely packed streets of Shade, many of the properties being owned by Fielden Brothers. The mill, within easy walking distance, is in the background.

(Below).
Lydgate, like Shade was another Fielden community that grew around Robinwood Mill, employing 300 or so workpeople. As at Shade and Lumbutts, many of the cottages were owned by Fielden Brothers. Lineholme Mill, in the background, had been bought for the Partnership, as an investment, in 1874.

Lumbutts, the third Fielden community, centred on Lumbutts and Jumb Mills, the latter, replacing smaller older mills, built in the Cotton Famine, but not equipped with mule spindles until 1871. Jumb Mill, like Lumbutts, was the personal property of John Fielden (1822-1893). He owned most of the cottages and farms around and built the village school at his own expense in 1878.

long-servers. Many of those in the mills were tenants of Fielden owned cottages. But changes were taking place. The Unitarian congregation in Todmorden, in which Fielden overlookers and workpeople were well represented, held an annual New Year party, usually in the schoolroom at Waterside. These were occasions when one of the brothers, and it was usually John, could speak about the business situation. During the Cotton Famine he could call for patience, making the point that manufacturers were suffering in the interests of their workpeople.[9] He expressed his regret that for the first time a pawnshop had opened in Todmorden. In 1867 and 1868 he was expressing concern at the stirrings of trade union organisation in Lancashire; weavers associations had been set up with varying success in many of the mill towns of North-East Lancashire in the late 1850s, mainly in the Preston and Blackburn areas. Their progress was mill by mill, town by town, but by the late 1860s they were coming closer to Todmorden, as attempts were made to organise the weavers in Rossendale, Burnley and Nelson, establishing where possible town lists defining rates of payment, and as the general objective, adoption of the Blackburn List. John Fielden saw the unions as a threat to prosperity; urging 'mutual confidence between employer and employed,' he warned of the danger of 'driving trade away.'

Large wage increases were given across Lancashire when the industry boomed in 1871. In March and April of that year Fieldens gave advances across all mills, generally of the order of 1d in the shilling, but for warpers as much as 2d in the shilling. Wage lists at this time show that young women employed as throstle spinners, winders and drawers were generally receiving 1s 11d or 2 shillings per day, 11s 6d or 12s per week. These rates were increased again by 1d in the shilling in 1876.[10] In 1872 John Fielden, whose income was not less than £20,000 a year, was to complain that he had 'never known workpeople so bad to manage or so unreasonable in their demands.' There had to be 'rules and regulations for well-working,' and while he would always listen to complaints, if 'they could not be settled, then they would remain unsettled.' He was not willing to submit to arbitration or that any club or union 'should step between him and his servants.' The local press carried an anonymous letter in reply, arguing that 'workmen never were so sensitive of the wrongs imposed on them by their masters' and that trade unions were needed 'to bring about a better state of things.' The letter complained of 'very harsh discipline' at Waterside, 'swearing and petty tyranny' from the 'middlemen.' At his son's coming of age in 1875, Joshua used the occasion to speak of his pride that there had been no

Wages at Robinwood. The workpeople at the mills were paid fortnightly: they were either on piece-work like the weavers, or on daily rates like the majority of spinning mill workers. When short-time was worked, and this was frequent in the 1870s and 1880s, earnings would fall in proportion. Fieldens were reluctant to cut wages although they did so in the worst years like 1879. In the boom years when wages moved higher across the industry, Fieldens would follow. The wage list for Robinwood in 1871 shows the increases in daily rates authorised by John Fielden.

Statement of the Wages paid at Robinwood Mill for the different kinds of work March 25th 1871

	Wages p. week		Remarks
Overlookers.	24/. 4/-	4/4 . —	
Steam tenter ·	20/. 3/4	3/6 ·	advanced
Steam Engine man.	22/. 3/8	4/-	May 18/71.
1st Stripper & Grinder	17/6 2/10	3/-	
2nd — " —	16/6 2/9	2/11 .	
Engine Men	15/. 2/6	2/8	2/9
Scutching Room men	15/. 2/6	2/8	2/9 J.F.
Warp Weigher .	18/. 3/-	3/4 .	
Drawing frame hand	12/. 2/-	2 at average of dyers frames. —
Dyers — — —	12/. 2/-	3¾ p: 10 s 2½
Engine Setts.	10/6 1/9	2/.
Hoist —	10/6 1/9	1/11
VI Side Spinners	11/. 1/10	2/-
III — " — — " —	9/. 1/6	1/8
Doffers . —	3/6 -/7	These pay 2½ p. week for school.
Winders.	11/. 1/10	by the piece @ 2⅛ p: throstle for 11s.
Warpers.	by Warp List and 1 p /. added	advance pscentage to 2 in the 1/-

		"Piece"
Winders work now for		
+ 68 15/15 throstles p: week	* 14s 2⅜	
△ 62½ — " —	16s 2¼	
# 60 — " —	18s 2⅛	

turn-out at Fielden mills throughout their history; he attributed this record to the fact that anyone with a grievance could 'bring it to the master,' and that there was no place for any middle-men. Clearly the brothers were concerned.

Bad trade and short-time working throughout Lancashire led to attempts to reduce wages by 10 per cent in 1878 resulting in bitter and sometimes violent industrial disputes in many of the weaving towns, notably in Blackburn. Todmorden had its first serious strikes, particularly at the Derdale mill of the rising concern Maden and Hoyle. The 10 per cent reduction became general across the industry, and at all Todmorden mills including Fieldens. Further wage reductions took place in the following year, including 5 per cent at Fieldens in August. Attempts to organise the workforce were strengthened in these circumstances, although success was patchy. In Todmorden meetings were held to form a local weavers association in 1878 but it was not established until February 1880. After a house-to-house canvas, the Todmorden Weaver's Association had 438 members at the end of that year.

Cotton Mill Operations. These illustrations by H.E. Tidmarsh depict typical operations such as were carried out in the Fielden mills in Todmorden. Except in mule-spinning, half-timers (aged nine to thirteen) and young women made up the greater part of the workforce. By the early 1880s the working week had fallen to fifty six and a half hours, ten hours daily and six and a half hours on the short Saturday. There were no paid holidays and normally the mills only closed at Christmas, Whitsuntide and Fair times, but as one Todmorden employer said, 'when they want a holiday they take it.'

The Fieldens were disturbed, not least at the effects of short-time working on their workpeople 'too many of whom live, sadly, too much hand to mouth,' as Samuel Fielden put it. Early in 1881, a typical paternalist remedy was adopted; large treats were given to those working at each of the mills, 1,523 workpeople (without wives or husbands) receiving a knife-and-fork tea, followed by entertainment, ostensibly to fulfil a promise made by John Fielden on his remarriage four years earlier. John Fielden, his wife, his nephew Thomas, and local managers visited each treat to be received with enthusiastic cheering. A banner described Fieldens as 'the best friends to the working class.' Thomas Wrigley, at Robinwood, praised the 'liberal employer' with a 'gentle public face', 'a good and steadfast friend to the working class,' who had 'by the liberal use of their capital benefited all classes.' Wrigley said everyone should be grateful, and called for increased zeal and endeavour to do their duty to their employer. For 'unless profit attended their work it could not permanently continue and the loss would fall heaviest on

143

the workforce.' He exhorted them, 'in whatever position they might be, to do their work well and effectively, to be united and all pull together.' A similar message was communicated at each gathering.

By such means, the advance of labour organisation was restrained, at least so far as Fieldens were concerned, unrest and dispute elsewhere in Lancashire not-withstanding. A public meeting in February 1882 had reminded Todmorden weavers that they were underpaid compared with other districts, as much as 5 to 10 per cent, emphasising that would remain the situation unless they organised themselves. It was not just the Fieldens; other employers, Ormerods in particular, were poor payers; their mills were on strike at the time. People in Todmorden were sleeping, it was alleged, and hurting other towns. The local press was hostile to the union organisers, 'paid agitators who are too lazy to work and too mischievous to be quiet; who rant against all constituted authority and break homes, slave whole families and ruin men who have to strike against their better judgement.' The Weavers Association made little if any progress: in 1887 its membership had fallen to 320 and its funds were as low as £123. Respect for the employers, fellowship at work and chapel among a predominantly female weaving workforce, and conservative attitudes were all obstacles, while by the late 1880s the mills were busier, wages were advanced, provisions were cheaper, the working week was shorter and life was easier. A feeling of well-being had returned and when Annie Besant spoke in Todmorden early in 1887 on 'Socialism and the Poor', she was heard by 120 people and no questions were asked. Social conflict in Todmorden was not at the time between classes, so much as between rival religious groups.

Changed Role at Manchester

If Todmorden was allowed to drift, but employed greatly reduced capital, Manchester had to find remunerative outlets for the balance of the Partnerships' very substantial resources. At the end of 1865 the balance of accounts kept at Manchester was £706,346, excluding £60,000 in 'real estates near Manchester' and £42,000, the attributed value of property and securities held towards Rostron's debts. There is a gap in the surviving business records regarding Manchester Accounts for the next four years. From 1870 a Manchester Balance Sheet and Statement of Reductions and Accumulations to Capital is available for each year to 1888.[11] At the 31st December 1869, when this series of records begins, the capital employed in Manchester Accounts was £527,590. The difference between this total, and £706,346 at the end of 1865 is accounted for principally by a transfer of £350,056 from Manchester to the Todmorden business, partly to meet losses there but mainly to meet substantial partner's drawings. Meanwhile between 1865 and 1869 the Manchester Accounts benefited from the realisation of part of the Rostron securities and from gains (less losses) on the activities pursued in Manchester.

By 1870 a pattern of activity had developed in Manchester that was to remain for the next twenty years until the Fielden Brothers Partnership ceased. Manchester was a trading office which sold cloth to the Manchester merchant houses, or, on a consignment basis, to agents abroad. It also managed the cotton purchases for the spinning operations in Todmorden. These were traditional activities that had been pursued in Manchester since the early years of the Fielden business. They absorbed capital, especially in the consignment business, but the outcome, in terms of proceeds of sales, or costs of cotton, passed to Todmorden. Manchester now received commission for its trading services and incurred expenses for rent, salaries, taxes, porterage and the like. In most years the income from commissions (paid by Todmorden) was about the same as the expenses.

But Manchester now became more than a trading office, rather a Partnership private bank. In this role Manchester managed that part of the total Partnership capital that was not being used in the other main businesses — that is, Todmorden, Fielden Brothers & Co., which after Thomas's death returned to the Partnership, and the property portfolio. Thus capital required in these businesses, or surplus to their requirements, was moved out of, or into, the Manchester Accounts. When the Partners wished to withdraw part of their capital, these sums were transferred from Manchester to Todmorden and thence into private accounts. Again as the private bank Manchester managed the substantial railway share portfolios of the Partners, receiving dividends, paying calls, selling and buying shares as the Partners determined. The net proceeds of this railway share activity was brought into the Manchester Accounts each year, as a new contribution to Partnership capital, or taken out as a drawing.

A substantial part of the capital employed in Manchester was used to support a large portfolio of loans, some on mortgage terms, some without apparent collateral, with interest being paid, usually at 5 or 4½ per cent, to the Partnership. As a private bank, the Manchester office managed the cash balances and bill transactions of the Partnership. Another significant Partnership asset managed from Manchester was the interest in the Pernambuco Gas Company, still valued in the accounts at £147,000 in 1870. Completing the Manchester activities, was the management of the Partnerships property portfolio (£60,000 in 1865, and probably about the same in 1870). This involved financing acquisitions and improvements, negotiating sales and collecting rents; the proceeds of this activity passed into the Manchester Accounts although the capital represented by the real estate was treated separately.

All these activities were conducted from offices and a warehouse in Norfolk Street, the old place in Peel Street having been given up in the 1850s. Most probably little beyond routine was decided there without the approval of Samuel Fielden, who would visit from Todmorden frequently, probably at least once a week, attending Lancashire and Yorkshire Railway meetings at the same time. But the staff were competent, reliable and trusted employees, Thomas Hodgson, the cashier, George Mattinson, the chief clerk, Walter Beard, and John Cocks the market men. Managing the property, as an agent rather than employee, was John Mallinson, a Manchester solicitor, a nephew of old Joshua Fielden's wife and brother of the second wife of John Fielden Junior, probably used because of these family connections but perhaps the more conscientious and reliable in consequence.

Table XIX shows the Manchester Capital Employed over the last period of the Partnership and how it was gradually reduced by net transfers, mainly withdrawal through Todmorden. No attempt was made to calculate gross profit on the Manchester Accounts; rather, as a balancing item, each year's gains and losses were assessed. Interest receipts were a principal component of these but the annual figures are heavily influenced by property transactions. It is clear that over the period Manchester activity added to the Partnership wealth. There is not a single year when losses including expenses, exceeded gains. But the surplus, amounting to about £324,000 over a nineteen year period, was a poor return on the capital tied up in the Manchester Accounts. Comparing the surplus with capital employed, the average return was

Table XIX: Fielden Brothers: Manchester Business
Capital Employed & Gains & Losses 1870-1889.

	Capital Employed (start of year) £000	Net Transfers by Partners[1] £000	Manchester Gains & Losses[2] £000	Gains & Losses as Per Cent of Capital
1870	528	(51)	54	10.2
1871	531	32	8	1.5
1872	571	(86)	26	4.6
1873	511	(24)	22	4.3
1874	513	(96)	13	2.5
1875	430	(45)	22	5.1
1876	407	(72)	32	7.9
1877	367	(56)	24	6.5
1878	335	(23)	15	6.5
1879	327	(44)	8	4.5
1880	291	(17)	12	2.4
1881	286	(23)	14	4.9
1882	277	(28)	10	3.6
1883	259	(31)	11	4.2
1884	239	(58)	11	4.6
1885	192	(12)	14	7.3
1886	194	(12)	6	3.1
1887	188	(55)	5	2.6
1888	138	6	17	10.6
1889	161			

Source: WYAS, Manchester Accounts C353/255.
Notes:
1. Net Transfers by Partners is the outcome of several items: transfers to or from other Partnership businesses (Todmorden Spinning and Weaving, Fielden Brothers and Co.); drawings by the Partners made by transfers to Todmorden; the proceeds of Partners' railway share transactions (dividends, net purchases/sales); the rents from Partnership properties after paying for repairs.
2. Manchester 'Gains and Losses' or 'Reductions and Accumulations to Capital' is the difference between opening and closing capital employed after taking into account net transfers by Partners. Thus it includes various sources of income: namely interest; commissions; the results of adventures in trade; recovery from suspense accounts; income from property sales. Against these would be operating expenses; write-offs of bad debts or to suspense accounts; expenditures on property purchases, and improvements.

**Table XX: Fielden Brothers: Manchester Business
Employment of Manchester Capital 1871-1889 (£000).**

	Capital Employed (start of year)	Pernam- buco Gas	Adven- tures Outwards	Loans & Mort- gages	Country Trade Accounts	Sundry[1]
1870	528	—	—	—	—	—
1871	531	147	107	241	5	31
1872	571	145	101	278	13	34
1873	511	134	96	183	18	80
1874	513	134	96	183	18	80
1875	430	134	83	191	9	96
1876	407	130	45	245	5	5
1877	367	118	45	216	7	19
1878	335	116	55	141	6	49
1879	327	114	58	138	8	17
1880	291	112	61	133	4	17
1881	286	108	63	98	13	9
1882	277	93	65	81	6	41
1883	259	83	50	85	5	54
1884	239	73	41	66	6	73
1885	192	59	43	66	6	65
1886	194	35	40	69	7	41
1887	188	15	36	68	6	69
1888	138	9	34	94	5	(4)
1889	161	13	25	113	4	6

Source: *WYAS*, Manchester Accounts, C353/255.
Notes: 1. Sundry includes Cash and Bills Receivable, advance payments for cotton shipments, and Waterside Private A/C (ie sums owing by the Partners to the Partnership Manchester Business).

about 5 per cent, more or less what could have been achieved had the money been placed in good railway shares. Table XX illustrates how the Manchester capital was distributed between its main employments. As the capital diminished, it was gradually withdrawn from all its outlets. The 'Sundry' uses are variable, principally because the cash balances were variable and particularly because at certain times the partners, as individuals, appeared to be borrowing, rather than withdrawing, their own capital, no doubt for temporary and convenient purposes at year-end.

Manchester Commercial Activities

Manchester now sold Waterside cloth, and at times yarn and warps, to the Manchester trade. It negotiated the price, effected the deliveries, and collected the receivables, all on behalf of Waterside. The office and warehouse, in Norfolk Street, would not hold stocks but rather samples. Over the years the firm dealt with most of the Manchester trade houses, at any time twenty or so. No house seems to have been dominant in Fielden's business; some drop out over the years but others appear. John Rylands, A & S Henry, Daniel Lee, Kershaw Sidebottom, Schuster Brothers, Steinthal, Behrens, Schaub, Hodgkinson Grindrod are names that figure in the list of County Trade Accounts, who were owing Fieldens money for goods received at the year end. Receivables of this kind were a modest item in the Manchester Accounts and there is no record of bad debts.

The consignment business — described as 'Adventures Outwards' — remained a feature of commercial activity at a slowly declining level. It was not opportunistic but an established part of sales activity. The 'adventure' element — the risks and opportunities — would be diminished given swift communications by ship or cable. Capital would be tied up for shorter periods in each transaction. Returns would be cash or bills, rather than produce. But many of the risks remained — failure of an agent, delays in remittances, loss on foreign exchange, physical damage to inadequately insured goods. Nonetheless the business must have been remunerative or it would not have been retained. No doubt it relied on the reputation of Fielden cloth in particular destinations and on long-standing trading connections. The benefits, in terms of realisations compared with the Manchester market, probably accrued to Todmorden, rather than Manchester. Other than commissions, Manchester got little out of it.

In the early 1870s the adventures were directed to Fielden's traditional markets in South America, and the newer markets in the east, where different branches of Jardine were agents in Calcutta, Shanghai and Hong Kong, and other agents were active in Singapore, Manila, Batavia and Bombay. For whatever reason these accounts were closed and Fieldens by the 1880s had ceased to consign to agents in the markets of India and the Far East. South America remained important and cloth was consigned, as in the past, to agents in ports all round the continent, from Pernambuco, to Arequipa and Tacna. Rio de Janeiro, in particular, was the largest market, especially in the later years. Some agents remained on the books throughout the period, others changed their names or partners, others dropped out and were replaced. Some went bankrupt and left bad debts. The bias throughout was to agencies of Manchester or Liverpool houses, managed by young men or partners

The Manchester Royal Exchange. Tuesday was the most important day and the great majority of businesses, whether directly engaged in cotton manufacture or associated with the industry, would be on the Exchange, either with their own partners/salesmen or through agents. In 1874 the Exchange had over 6,600 members.

Rio de Janeiro remained the most important South American port to which Fielden cloth continued to be consigned throughout the nineteenth century.

who would be known and trusted by the Fieldens or their staff. This remained an area where knowledge of the man was the all-important ingredient to low-risk and successful business.

The Manchester office continued to buy cotton on behalf of Todmorden, no doubt on close instructions from the mill managers as to quality and with Samuel Fielden's authority as to price and coverage. In August 1889, at Whitby for his health, and shortly before his death, a sharp letter from Mrs Sarah Fielden instructs the Manchester Office that 'Mr Fielden has no intention of going with the Liverpool cotton market until he is obliged.'[12] As always the coverage decision was taken at the top. Part if not the whole of Todmorden's cotton needs continued to be covered with the long-standing broker, Colin Campbell in Liverpool. By the 1880s Todmorden was using the futures market to establish forward prices, normally against foward sales of yarn or cloth. Thus in November 1888, the business owned 2,920 bales of cotton, although using only 170 bales weekly at the time: it had 420 bales in stock, 1,500 bales bought forward and 1,000 bales in futures as price cover; these would be sold for actual cotton at a negotiated differential, or merely liquidated, before the futures contract matured.[13] Another change had entered buying practices for a while. Probably to cheapen costs, and also to use surplus capital, the Partnership began to purchase a proportion of its requirements direct from shippers at United States ports; between 1876 and 1880 about half the usage was bought on c.i.f. terms at origin, with a saving against Liverpool (partly cheaper finance, partly margins). These purchases were made through a Liverpool agent, R. Fraser and Sons, by-passing Campbell. For some reason the practice, unusual in the Lancashire industry, ceased in the 1880s.[14]

(Above).
Sam Mendel (1810-1884), the colourful Manchester merchant specialising in the plain cloth trade with India and markets in the East. A bold dealer, willing to trade on a large scale, he made huge profits in the years before the Cotton famine. Thomas Fielden was a close friend and Mendel came to his funeral in Todmorden in 1869. Fielden Brothers made substantial loans and participated in some of Mendel's trading ventures. They seem to have avoided any problems but Mendel died penniless in 1884.

Fieldens as Financiers

Fielden Brothers, with their large surplus capital, had been lending money to other business men at least in the 1840s. They ceased to do so when Partnership capital was reduced but returned to the practice in the late 1850s. If they debated the question of what to do with their funds, this would seem a safe and expedient means of employing them. If the loans could be placed with reliable parties, and adequate security or collateral negotiated, the capital would be secure and would yield a steady return, 5 per cent or thereabouts. The loan portfolio was a personal one; those who borrowed were known to the Fieldens, business associates, life-long friends, some family. One significant borrower was Sam Mendel, the colourful Manchester trader who was closely involved with Thomas Fielden. In 1870 Fieldens were lending him £10,220 and jointly involved to the extent of £8,362 in consignments to Jardine Mathieson in Hong Kong and Shanghai. Loans to Mendel rose to £40,000 in 1871 and £50,321 the following year, significant amounts to a trader whose bold, if not reckless style was a feature of the Manchester market at the time. When Mendel was buying he would clear the market of its stock of grey cloth and put manufacturer's agents under contract for months ahead. Anyone harassed with stock could turn to Sam Mendel and a bid would be made. But he made his mark as a speculative dealer and if for a time showed great wealth — in the boom years after the Indian mutiny his profits were said to be £250,000 a year — in the end he gave it all back and died penniless in 1884. Fortunately he repaid his Fielden loans in 1876.[15]

Another prominent Manchester figure to whom the Fielden's loaned money was Sir James Watts, Lord Mayor in 1855 and 1856, and well established as a home trade dealer in fancy goods and small wares. He had built palace-like warehouses in Portland Street in 1856 at a cost

Portland Street. The Tidmarsh drawing catches the atmosphere of commercial Manchester in the later nineteenth century. Portland Street became the important centre for large textile warehouses, the most magnificent being that of S & J Watts (now the Britannia Hotel) built 1855-1858. Fieldens made loans to Sir James Watts and the Watts Partnership and possibly helped to finance their warehouse, although a building so grand was not their own style; Fieldens' offices were in Norfolk Street near the Exchange.

probably exceeding £100,000. The Fieldens financed Sir James' company to the extent of £40,000 when the warehouses were built, with a further loan of £25,000 secured on Watt's home, Abney Hall. The Watts mortgage and other Watts loans passed from the Partnership to Joshua Fielden personally in 1879 as part of the capital he withdrew at that time. Sir James Watts died in 1878, leaving less than £20,000. [16]

Over the period Fieldens made loans to many others. Lord Brothers in Todmorden were borrowers in the early 1870s. Long-standing business friends like Jonathan Mellor borrowed on mortgage throughout the period; he and his younger brother were cotton manufacturers in Bury and Heywood, but, as a young man, Mellor had been closely involved with John Fielden in the Ten Hours Movement and in Fielden's election campaign in Oldham. Contemporaries in business, and friends as they were, the Mellors had not the Fieldens success: Jonathan Mellor left £71,000 when he died in 1890. [17] In the 1870s large sums were loaned, at call, to Warner and Page, the Manchester stockbroker with whom the Fieldens were closely involved, Thomas Warner being a neighbour of Thomas in Crumpsall. John Robinson Kay was another borrower who, like the Mellors, had known the Fieldens since the 1820s, and like them had started putting-out to hand-loom weavers in Bacup; Kay was a fellow-director of the Lancashire and Yorkshire. Robert Whyatt, the occupier of Bowker Bank print works also borrowed as did, at one time or another, the Ramsbotham family, whether James or his children, to support their business actitivities. Finally, there were safer ventures, it may be supposed, like the Southport Pavilion and Winter Gardens Company (loaned £34,145 in 1879 rising to £38,350 in 1883) or the Manchester Warehouse Company (loaned £17,219 in 1885). Most of the loans continued over the years until the Partnership eventually closed the Account. Occasionally, small bad debts are recorded and written off in the Manchester Accounts, (Robert Whyatt seems to have failed, for instance), but these apart there is no indication that loans did not receive whatever interest was agreed, and were not repaid in full.

Pernambuco

The Manchester Accounts list the Pernambuco Gas Company as a principal asset. It seems to have been an excellent investment, although the returns from it were erratic and no doubt uncertain, from time to time. Fielden Brothers provided a manager for the enterprise; in the late 1880s this was one George Windsor, who so impressed his employers that on his return in 1894 he was made Secretary and subsequently General Manager at Waterside. The Manchester Accounts received an annual fee or commission of £500 from Pernambuco to cover the management services provided. But that apart, this was a free standing business.

In 1870 the Fielden interest in the Gas Company was valued at £147,117. By 31 December 1879 this value was reduced to £107,872 and a year later, at the end of 1880 to £93,130. Finally, when the Partnership ended in 1889, the Pernambuco venture was valued in the Manchester Accounts at no more than £13,285. Only two Pernambuco Gas Company accounts survive, for the year to end March 1880 and the subsequent year. They show clearly that the conservative value Fieldens attached to their venture was the balance of their original investment, reduced by the surpluses received from Pernambuco, but augmented by 5 per cent interest on the reducing balance. Thus at the end of December 1880 this balance was £93,130. In the quarter to 31 March 1881, Pernambuco was charged £2,433 for materials and salaries but remitted £6,758. This reduced the balance to £88,805 to which was added a quarter's interest at 5 per cent, leaving a balance of £90,022 at 31 March 1881.[18] In this way, by 1889, Fieldens recovered practically the whole of their original investment plus interest at 5 per cent on the reducing balance. Moreover they still owned a valuable asset; the book value, for instance in March 1881, was shown as £174,114 showing a surplus in Fielden's favour of £84,092. This book value rested on an undepreciated value of fixed capital put at £146,567, but there were other assets which brought the total to £174,114; these included stocks of coal and cannel, stores and coke, and unpaid gas bills from the government (street lamps), public establishments, and private consumers. The ultimate value was to be a matter of negotiation between Fieldens and the Pernambuco authorities in the 1890s. Whatever the problems at the outset the venture did not go sour; the Fieldens timing was good; they got out before default, regulation and expropriation overtook many similar investments in South America.

Fielden Property

The Manchester business — or John Mallinson — managed the property portfolio, and the rents and expenditures of a capital nature passed through the Manchester Accounts. But the investments in property were a separate Partnership enterprise, never part of the Manchester business. From their value of £60,000 in 1865, by the end of 1878, in a statement of the Partnership capital at that time, Estates near Manchester were valued at £154,376 a significant item (Table XXI).

Table XXI: Fielden Brothers: Partnership Real Estate 31 December 1878.

Queens Park Chester	£21,000
Manchester Residential Estates (Hope, Longsight, Plymouth Grove)	£67,383
Rosebank Estate (from Rostron assets)	£29,755
Norfolk Street office and warehouse	£36,238
	£154,376

Source: WYAS C353/255, Manchester Accounts; *Longden MSS* Partnership Accounts for 1878.

The land at Chester was ripe for building development, and could eventually be sold at enhanced value. The Manchester residential estates were in fashionable and convenient parts of the city where house property would be let at good secure rents to the rising middle class; the Hope Estate was in Eccles; Plymouth Grove and Longsight were all near Victoria Park in Rusholme, close to the relocated Owens College and the nucleus of the Manchester Infirmary. Indicative of the kind of property, were the nine houses built by the Partnership in Plymouth Grove in 1878 and 1879 at a cost of £7,526; a further house was purchased in the same area in 1886 for £1,350. William Gaskell, friend of Samuel Fielden, minister of the Unitarian chapel in Cross Street, Manchester, and husband of Mrs Gaskell, novelist and biographer of Charlotte Bronte, were typical of the residents of Plymouth Grove at the time.[19] Close to the Royal Exchange in the commercial area, Norfolk Street had been acquired by the Partnership to house its Manchester activities; it was transferred to the Estates Account, whereupon Fielden Brothers Manchester became a tenant, sharing the building with others. Rosebank was a legacy of the Rostron involvement, made up of mills, farms, and dwelling houses in Edenfield, near Manchester.

The total rental income of these properties was about £6,000 a year, and although varying from year to year, largely because expenditures on repairs (as distinct from improvements) were offset against rent, income remained at about this level until the Partnership ceased in 1889. As a yield on a portfolio valued at over £150,000 the income does not seem exciting. But the investment was safe and the income secure, and the values, for the most part, would be appreciating. This was especially true of Norfolk Street which, valued at about £36,000, was yielding rents of about £2,100 at the time: the Rosebank estate paid rents of about £1,400 on a value close to £30,000, a low yield but a better yield than on the residential properties in the middle class suburbs of Manchester.

The Estates Account was part of the Partnership capital. The Partners individually owned property , including mills, in Todmorden and as their lifestyle changed, substantial landed estates elsewhere. Collectively they also owned the Waterside and Robinwood mills, and farms and cottages in Todmorden valued at £39,557 in 1865, but as the revaluation made in 1889 was to show worth much more than that (Appendix II note 3, Appendix III); the collective Todmorden property also remained outside the Partnership. Another joint property investment was the so-called London Bridge estate. This had been acquired by Thomas Fielden, no doubt as a result of his involvement with the Southeastern (formerly London and Greenwich) Railway. On his death in 1869 it passed to Samuel, John and Joshua together. They shared the rents which in 1884 amounted to £2,783, a major tenant being Guys Hospital. Parts of the estate were then sold, principally to the Postmaster General, for as much as £51,000, which the brothers shared. On Joshua's death in 1887 his interest was bought by Samuel for £30,000 indicating the substantial value of the property, still outside the Partnership capital.

Fielden Brothers & Co.

The Liverpool operation, associated as it was with Pickersgill in New York, had become moribund in the 1860s and was closed down on Thomas Fielden's death in 1869. It had ceased to be part of the partnership in 1851, and from 1852 its capital was part of Thomas's personal wealth. On Thomas's death, when the greater part of his estate passed to his three nephews, the capital in Fielden Brothers & Co. passed back to the Partnership, and the business was moved to London. The

London office, eventually in East India Avenue, was a modest affair. William Pickersgill seems to have pursued a banking and investment business there. Some services were performed for Manchester, some for Waterside, and some for the Fieldens in their personal capacity. The expenses of London were shared, accordingly, with Manchester and eventually, with Waterside and the partners privately. In total in the 1870s they were about £1,200 per year, a principal item being the salary of Theodore Lodge, the confidential clerk, who was receiving £300 per year. His salary was raised to £500 on Joshua Fielden's instruction in 1879. By the 1880s London expenses had fallen below £1,000 per year. Whatever capital was employed in London in the early 1870s, this was to be substantially reduced. £60,000 was to be transferred to Manchester between 1875 and 1878. At the end of 1877 Fielden Brothers & Co. still used £81,299 of the Partnership capital, and a year later £56,949. Most probably William Pickersgill was using this capital together with his own to trade or speculate in stocks and shares. There is no consecutive record of the outcome but including interest on the Partners' capital, and after allocated office expenses, the Partnership took a loss of £2,855 in 1877 and £3,040 in 1878. In the 1880s activity in London faded away; William Pickersgill continued to come in from his Bexley estate occasionally but the office was mainly used by Theodore Lodge to manage the accounts and property affairs of the Fieldens as Partners, and private men; this activity was to continue until Lodge's eventual retirement in 1897.[20]

The Course of the Partnership

The main series of Partnership accounts, the Private Ledger at Longden, written in Joshua Fielden's hand from 1851, came to an end in 1865. A comparable statement of Partnership capital and its employment, profit, and drawings and the share of individual partners survives only for 1877 and 1878. The statements for these years, prepared by Theodore Lodge, seem to have been retained by Joshua Fielden because they describe the position immediately before he left the Partnership. Similar statements must have been prepared annually but they have either been lost or destroyed.

Table XXII brings together the available information about the capital and income of the whole Partnership, in the last period. Some general statements about the course of the Partner's affairs can be made, in part reiterating what has been noted in the account of individual sectors of Partnership activity. Firstly, as has been seen, Partnership capital was deployed conservatively and the income generated was not comparable with that achieved in earlier periods. Thus the core spinning and weaving business certainly became a drain on capital and the profits and rents from the other employments, that is Manchester, Fielden Brothers & Co. and Property, were little better than 5 per cent. The objective, it might be said, was to conserve capital and achieve a modest but safe return; there is no indication of any interest in seeking new areas of business, assuming risks to build an even greater fortune. Secondly, reflecting age, affluence, the absence of any spirit of enterprise, and as the years went by, the attitude of the young fourth generation, capital was steadily withdrawn by the individual partners and used to finance a variety of private endeavours, railway investment for rentier income, philanthropy, and perhaps especially lifestyle. This will be apparent when the lives and lifestyles of the third generation are described in Chapter 6. But, substantial as the drawings were, their effect on the Partnership was partly offset not so much by the modest income that capital earned as by the fact that the Partners paid into the Partnership as capital introduced all the proceeds of their transactions in railway shares, that is dividends and the balance of purchases and sales. The net drawings, accordingly, were not such as to erode the Partnership to insignificance, but they had reduced its capital by the late 1880s to less than half its peak, and it was of course, by then being employed

Table XXII: Fielden Brothers: Partners Capital, Profit and Drawings 1865-1889 (£000).

Year Ending	Partners[1] Capital	Todmorden[2] Spinning & Weaving	Manchester[2] Accounts	Property	Fielden Brothers & Co	Other Employments	Profit[4]	Drawings[5]
1865	1,117	233	748	60	(private)	75	73	41
1866	1,126*	307	—	60	(private)	—	35*	26
1867	1,059*	398	—	60	(private)	—	(50)*	17
1868	1,105*	474	—	60	(private)	—	65*	19
1869	1,044*	291	528	60	(private)	—	67	128
1870	1,028*	257	531	89	—	—	44*	60
1871	1,038*	218	571	—	—	—	30*	20
1872	922*	191	511	—	—	—	22*	138
1873	928*	176	513	—	—	—	30*	24
1874	909*	219	430	—	—	—	38*	57
1875	918*	291	407	—	—	—	25*	16
1876[3]	857	265	367	—	—	—	39*	100
1877[3]	812	173	335	127	81	96	27	72
1878[3]	762	148	327	154	57	76	8	58
1879	633*	133	291	—	—	—	15*	144
1880	635*	118	286	—	—	—	21*	19
1881	624*	87	277	—	—	—	30*	41
1882	638*	100	259	—	—	—	15*	1
1883	640*	104	239	—	—	—	25*	23
1884	622*	115	192	—	—	—	20*	38
1885	548*	93	194	—	—	—	8*	82
1886	557*	69	188	—	—	—	13*	4
1887	529*	71	138	—	—	—	17*	45
1888	571*	80	161	—	—	—	20*	(22)

Source: Longden MSS, Private Ledger, Partnership Accounts for 1877 and 1878, Stock Account; WYAS, Manchester Accounts; Odiham MSS, Personal Ledgers.

* Estimated

Notes:

1. Partner's Capital is estimated except for 1865, 1876—1878, and included Todmorden and Manchester Capital and estimates for Property, Fielden Brothers and Co. (after 1869) and Other Employments. It includes Joint Freehold Properties in Todmorden owned outside the Partnership Capital (Appendix III and Table XVIII refers).
2. Todmorden and Manchester Capital derived from Tables XVIII and XIX.
3. 1877 and 1878 data based on surviving Partnership Accounts at Longden.
4. Profit estimated except for 1865, 1877 and 1878. Otherwise based on Tables XVIII and XIX and rents as stated in Manchester Accounts, with allowance for income on other Capital.
5. Drawings are based on the Stock Account and the Personal Ledgers at Longden and Odiham, (the two coincide), adjusted for the Partner's railway share account transactions which were added to the Partnership Capital each year.

far more conservatively. By this time the greater part of the individual Partners wealth was outside the Partnership, in the form of landed estates and property or railway shares and other investments. Thirdly, the brothers were happy to retain the Partnership form, rather than form a limited company; they had no wish to market their shares, introduce other capital, and, no doubt, were not concerned to limit their exposure, in control and rich as they were.

Major withdrawals of capital related to significant collective and private activities — collective like the Fielden public buildings in Todmorden, private like the purchase of the Grimston estate by John Fielden in 1872. But two events in particular changed the Partnership. The first was the death of Thomas Fielden at the age of 79 in December 1869. Perhaps that marked the end of the old Fielden Brothers in at least two respects. Thomas had been an enterprising spirit, restless in searching for new outlets for the profitable use of surplus funds; secondly, he was tireless, dedicated, simple and plain ; there was no show of great wealth in his lifestyle. Although involved to the end,

(Above).
Thomas Fielden (1790-1869), the last and probably boldest of the second generation. He had often said during periods of bad trade that while present at the birth of the cotton industry he feared he would be present at its demise. When he died in 1869 the circumstances of the industry were changing. Thomas had hoarded his wealth and left a huge fortune, £1,300,000. He had no children and a large part of his estate passed to the three brothers of the third generation, thus securing their fortunes.

(Right).
Funeral Arrangements 1869. Thomas Fielden was buried at St. Mary's Church in Todmorden with a carefully planned Victorian funeral. Joshua seems to have made the arrangements, allocating carriages for the principal mourners, nominating the bearers, those who would receive gloves, and those to whom funeral cards would be sent.

Thomas's active role was probably limited after 1860. His funeral brought together most of the key associates of the Fieldens in their high period — the Campbells, the Pickersgills, the Mellors, Sam Mendel, Thomas Warner, Robert Whyatt of Bowker Bank.

Thomas's personal estate was £1,226,000. Of this £580,111 was his share in Fielden Brothers, the remainder private wealth of which £626,000 was invested almost entirely in railway shares or in Fielden Brothers & Co. Just how his private wealth had accumulated to such a figure is rather a mystery. His drawings over the years had not been large since he lived frugally; he re-invested all his dividends, and at the time of his death some of his railway shareholdings, especially those in the Lancashire and Yorkshire, were showing large capital appreciation. His personal share in Fielden Brothers & Co. may also have yielded large profits, especially from the Cotton Famine. Thomas's will made provision for his widow but left the balance of his estate including his real estate (the valuable property at London Bridge and various properties in Manchester and North Lancashire — the Middleton Towers estate which he had bought in 1853) to be shared equally among the three nephews, Samuel, John and Joshua. The Partnership capital, accordingly was not disturbed, and the nephews took the balance of their inheritance in railway shares. Outside his will Thomas had recorded his private wish that on his death legacies were to be given to a host of Fielden relatives, nieces and nephews mainly descended from either his sisters or his aunts: tracing some of these, living in humble circumstances, was quite a task. These legacies usually £10,000 or £5,000, together with further provision for his widow and small bequests to long-serving Fielden employees (John Bone, of the Manchester office received £1,000, the rest were £100 or £200), accounted in total for £192,000. This provision apart, and with duty paid £36,000 on the whole estate, on Thomas's death his nephews were enormously rich, whether their wealth was within the Partnership or privately held.[21]

The second significant event was the withdrawal of Joshua from the Partnership. In 1868 he had been elected to Parliament and, once he had established Nutfield Priory in Surrey as the home for his large family, only an occasional visitor to Todmorden or Manchester. He was to retire from Parliament in 1880 but his health deteriorated before this. He was to blame failing health and inability to contribute to Partnership affairs as the reasons for his decision to withdraw his capital in October 1879. Certainly his involvement was much diminished and he was deeply concerned at Fielden Brothers poor financial performance. His capital in the business was not increasing at a healthy rate, but even diminishing with the losses at Waterside in the late 1870s. So Joshua withdrew, taking out his residual share in the Partnership, namely £115,000. This he took in the form of income yielding assets, namely the Watts loans and mortgages, and various other loans the Partnership had made. Samuel and John were almost certainly offended by Joshua's withdrawal from the responsibility of what they may have regarded as a sacred trust. Their views were not recorded, or if they were, no record survives. Joshua wrote apologetic letters, pleading his health, much improved now the cares of his involvement were removed, and emphasising 'we may not be partners, but we are still brothers.'[22]

After 1879 the Partnership was Samuel and John, and mainly Samuel, reflecting his comparatively low drawings: at the end of 1879, of Partnership capital (including Todmorden properties) estimated at £633,000, about £570,000 would be his share. The Partnership capital, diminished but still substantial, was held in low risk assets; where the risk was greatest, namely in Todmorden, the asset values were heavily written-down, almost to insignificance. But the part of the business that mattered most was Todmorden; the remainder, Manchester Accounts, property, were less strategic, easy to sell or relinquish, not involving the livelihood of large numbers of people. Without Todmorden, Samuel and John could readily have wound up the Partnership. But some future for Todmorden had to be secured, if only to keep the mill-hands in work. By 1887 with Samuel, aged 70 and failing in health, and John, a part-cripple aged 65, that future depended on the fourth generation. If Todmorden was not to be closed, or sold for bricks and mortar, a Fielden had to be found either to manage it actively or be, at least, its nominal head. The older Fieldens were concerned; their dependants in Todmorden, workpeople and tradesmen alike, were also deeply concerned.

Whatever family discussions took place were not recorded. Thomas Fielden, Joshua's eldest son, had decided in 1879 that Todmorden was not for him. Samuel's only son, John Ashton Fielden, approaching thirty in 1888, had made it clear that he had no wish to live in Todmorden or manage the mills, whatever his eventual financial stake. Whether under pressure or not, a family member now came forward who was willing to take on the Todmorden role. This was Edward Brocklehurst Fielden, second surviving son of Joshua. Edward, trained as a civil engineer, was living at the time at Headington near Oxford, recently married, and although employed by Thames Conservancy, able to find the time and the means to manage a small farm and become Master of the South Oxfordshire Hunt. He clearly enjoyed the lifestyle of a country gentleman, but his ability and energy, as well as his circumstances, required more significant involvements. In the summer of 1888 and after much discussion with his uncles, and his family generally, visits to the mills and to other mills in Lancashire and talks with managers about the future, he accepted the challenge of Todmorden; he believed there was a reasonable probability of earning a fair dividend, 'with strict economy, and energetic management,' and he wanted 'to keep the old business going'.

With Edward's commitment to lead the Todmorden business, the second Fielden Brothers Partnership could be wound up. The ongoing activity was to be Todmorden Spinning and Weaving, and its associated commercial functions in Manchester, buying cotton and selling cloth. To limit risk for the future, a private limited company was now formed to own this span of activities, Fielden Brothers Limited. A share capital of £130,000, split into 130 shares, mainly owned by Samuel (81 shares) and John Fielden (41 shares) with the balance of the shares owned by senior managers took title to the appropriate assets from the Partnership; these included buildings and machinery valued at £80,000 and working

Edward Fielden about 1890. The Fielden Brothers Partnership found it difficult to engage the fourth generation of the family. A solution was only found shortly before the death of Samuel, the senior Partner, in 1889. A limited company, Fielden Brothers Ltd., was formed, with a greatly reduced capital, and Edward Fielden became Chairman. He was a younger son of Joshua, youngest of the three brothers of the third generation, qualified as a chartered engineer but had already adopted the lifestyle of a county gentleman. Master of the Foxhounds for the South Oxfordshire at the time, living in Headington near Oxford, he agreed to take on the Todmorden role, but certainly intended to remain a country gentleman.

capital of £50,000. What happened to the other assets of the Partnership, in Manchester Accounts, the properties, any capital in Fielden Brothers & Co., or in other employments is not clear. The records of the time have not survived; surmise would suggest that they passed to the two Partners, Samuel and John, in proportion to their respective equity, either as cash, loans or property; Samuel, for instance, seems to have taken all the property while the shares in the Pernambuco Gas Company were divided between them and like the other assets, and their personal wealth, were part of their estates when they died, as was their share capital in the new company, Fielden Brothers Limited.

Fielden Brothers Limited was incorporated on 14 October 1889. The old firm of Fielden Brothers now ceased to exist. The 'vast and complicated business', as it had been described by the *Manchester Guardian* had shrunk back to its original core activity, itself struggling and marginal and much diminished in stature and performance. But provision had been made that would secure the continuation of the Fielden presence in Todmorden and Fielden participation in the cotton trade. Welcoming the new company, the local press called its formation with a directorate of 'new blood' of 'the highest importance for Todmorden — the commencement of a new epoch and a new start in the commercial race.'[23] Whether it met these expectations or not, the new company was to carry on, not without some success, for another seventy years.

JOHN FIELDEN'S FAMILY TREE
(The third and fourth generations)

John Fielden (1784-1849) m.1 (1811) — Ann Grindrod (died 1832)
m.2 (1833) — Elizabeth Dearden

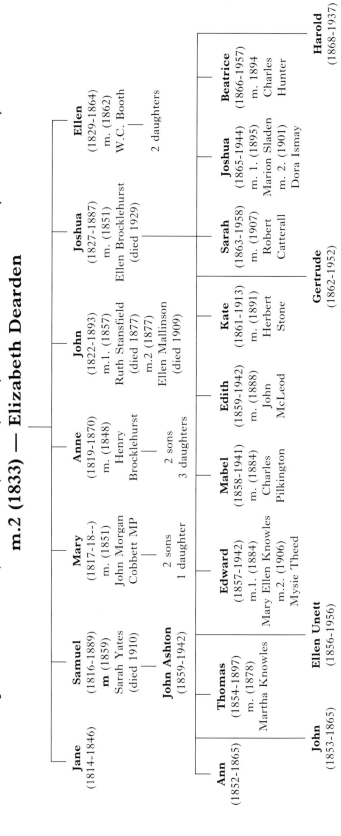

6

THE THIRD GENERATION
1851-1889

The four brothers of the second generation had brought the Fielden family power, fame and fortune. When three of the brothers, Joshua, John and James died within a few years of each other, about 1850, their shares of the Fielden wealth were distributed widely: that of Joshua went to his two children, Jane and John; that of James was partly shared among many descendants of his sisters; John's estate made full provision for his wife and his three surviving daughters as well as his sons. Thus when John's three sons, Samuel, John Junior and Joshua, the dominant figures of the third generation, succeeded to their inheritance, their wealth was small compared to what it subsequently became. Their uncle Thomas, of course, without children, was there in the background. By the early Fifties he was worth upwards of £320,000, and the three brothers, as the years went by, could regard their uncle's wealth as their own. For the time being, however, they had to prove themselves by taking the business forward and building a new and greater capital. It was only by the mid-Sixties, and when their uncle died, that they became rich men. Thus, throughout the Fifties, industry and application seem to have characterised their lifestyles. They were, one would suppose, completely determined to match the achievement of their father and their uncles.

Young Sam

Even before the death of his father and uncles, Samuel had established a strong, controlling presence at Waterside and the outmills, where he was confident, assertive and strict, especially with regard to mill-management, engineering matters and factory discipline. At this stage, while his uncle Thomas remained fully active, he concerned himself less with the commercial side. He had an important single interest outside Todmorden, namely the affairs of the Lancashire and Yorkshire Railway Company. The family had been closely involved with the Company from the start; they were large shareholders and Thomas had been a frequent spokesman at Proprietor's meetings, indeed constantly a thorn in the Chairman's flesh, as one account described him, whether resisting extensions to the network or irksome rules regarding passengers. Dissatisfaction with the management of the Company, the fall in its share price and poor dividends, brought a shareholders revolt in 1850 in which the Fieldens were prominent. A new Board was elected in September, Samuel Fielden becoming a Director, as he was to remain for the rest of his life.[3] His regular attendance at meetings, usually several times a month, added to the recognition he had already attained in Lancashire for the role he played in continued agitation for Ten Hours after his father's death, and his association with John Bright in the agitation for the abolition of church rates. He came to regard himself

Samuel Fielden (1816-1889), at about the time of his marriage in 1859. Since 1845 he had been the driving force in Fieldens' business, certainly in Todmorden, and while a private man he was a well-known figure in Lancashire because of the family name and reputation, his place as a Director of the Lancashire and Yorkshire Railway Company, and his public role in maintaining the Ten Hour Movement.

(Above).
Hunts Bank (later Victoria Station) in central Manchester, was the terminus of the Lancashire and Yorkshire Railway Company and the site of its head office. Given their deep involvement with the Railway (and especially Sam, a Director for forty years and the largest shareholder, and subsequently his nephew Edward, who was to become Chairman in 1918) the Fieldens were frequent visitors to Hunts Bank over at least a hundred years.

(Right).
Todmorden Station from Dobroyd.
Samuel, as a Director, would have local responsibility for the Lancashire and Yorkshire Railway in Todmorden. The Station master and staff would probably be appointed by him. The main station building dates from the early 1860s as shown in this early photograph. The Dobroyd warehouses of the Waterside Mill of Fielden Brothers are shown in the foreground.

as the representative of factory people in the North of England. The strength of his feeling on the rights of working-men and the responsibility of employers, for instance, is revealed by long impassioned letters he wrote to the Times, notably in February 1852. He became known as a strong Liberal in politics, but he never sought public prominence.

While Samuel was seen as a proud and independent man, his manner at this time was described as modest, and disposed to stay in the background; he was not unlike his Uncle Thomas, unassuming and unostentatious for a man of his wealth. He was not eloquent but his interventions in debate were nevertheless incisive and telling. Contemporaries in Manchester recall his 'strong clear mind' and eagerness 'to have it out;' when roused in argument Young Sam could be direct and cutting and some were inclined to take offence at his sharp tongue and abrasive manner on these occasions.[4]

Samuel had inherited shares in the Lancashire and Yorkshire. He continued to add to his holdings, reinvesting dividends, and drawing from Fielden Brothers to make new purchases. His income at the time from railway investments was of the order of £1,500 yearly. Apart from the affairs of the Partnership and Railway, his main interest, then and subsequently, was the Centre Vale estate which he had inherited from his father. Drainage, tree and shrub planting, improving the buildings, all attracted expenditure, as did the adjacent farm, throughout the 1850s. He retained the passionate interest in sport he had shown in his youth; he still enjoyed skating where he was enthusiastic and accomplished. Now he did much to encourage the local Cricket Club whose ground was part of his estate and where he became President. He remained fond of grouse shooting and with his brothers continued to maintain Higher House Moor, south of Todmorden, which would be shot for

Cricket at Centre Vale, 1864. As a young man Samuel Fielden was passionately interested in cricket as his letters reveal, and did much to encourage the game. He played himself but, as owner of Centre Vale after his father's death in 1849, he leased part of the estate to the local club. Clearly at first, cricket was a genteel affair; factory working hours did not permit much spectator participation although later in the nineteenth century, popular interest in the game became as strong in Todmorden as anywhere in Lancashire. Chapel and neighbourhood teams were feeders to the town's club, and its achievements were an important focus for the local community.
(From a lithograph by William Dewhirst).

(*Above*).
Sarah Jane Yates (1819-1910), about the time of her marriage to Samuel Fielden in 1859.

(*Top*).
Joseph Brook Yates (1780-1858), eldest son of John Yates, minister of the Unitarian Chapel in Paradise Street, Liverpool. Educated at Eton he became a successful West India merchant but also a leading reformer in Liverpool, active supporter of its literary and scientific institutions, and with his brothers, an important philanthropist. He employed Decimus Burton to design and build his mansion at West Dingle where his second daughter, Sarah, would grow up.

a few days each August. The Personal Ledger gives no indication of extravagance or travel. He remained unmarried until 1859; in March of that year, at the age of forty-three, at Childwall Church, Liverpool, he married Sarah Jane Yates, herself forty, the daughter of Joseph Brook Yates. On 11 December 1859 their only son, christened John Ashton Fielden, was born at Centre Vale. At the 1861 Census Samuel and Sarah Fielden, their infant son, a butler, cook, and five maids were living at Centre Vale, while a coachman and gardener and their families were at nearby cottages on the estate.

Samuel Fielden must have been a frequent visitor to Liverpool both in his youth and in the Fifties, in connection with the cotton market and no doubt the affairs of Fielden Brothers and Co., although technically this had ceased to be within the Partnership. Almost certainly he met Sarah Yates through Daniel Campbell. Joseph Brook Yates and his family lived at West Dingle, a large classical villa built for them by Decimus Burton in 1824. Dingle and the adjacent Toxteth Park were the dignified parts of Liverpool where the successful commercial and professional classes made their homes. Colin Campbell, who retired in 1839 and died in 1851, lived there as did his brother, Daniel, initially in South Hill and later in the prestigious Fulwood Park. The Campbells and the Yates would have known each other well, partly through their commercial activities but also because of Colin's standing as an eminent mathematician, and as close neighbours.[5]

The Yates were a distinguished and influential Unitarian Liverpool family and the marriage would be regarded as no ordinary match, linking as it did two of the most successful dynasties in Lancashire. Sarah's grandfather, the Reverend John Yates (1755-1826), had been a prominent dissenting minister of the Key Street and then Paradise Chapels in Liverpool, active with other prominent families, like the Roscoes and the Rathbones, in the campaign against the slave trade. Joseph Brook Yates, his eldest son (1780 -1855), was a West Indian merchant, a scholar and antiquary, and leading reformer. He was a patron and long-serving President of the Liverpool Literary and Philosophical Society, and a founder of the Southern and Toxteth Hospitals. He had married an Ashton who was widow of a Bostock, both important South Lancashire families. His brother, James (1789-1871), followed his father as a Unitarian minister, but was also a scientist and Fellow of the Royal Society. Another brother, John Ashton Yates (1781-1863), was MP for Carlow and author of pamphlets on trade and slavery. A third brother, Richard Vaughan Yates (1785-1856), also a successful merchant, was an important Liverpool philanthropist; he founded Harrington School, supported the Liverpool Institute, advanced the idea of a University in Liverpool, and created Princes Park at his own cost. There were also several sisters who strongly supported their brothers in all their endeavours and were themselves independent benefactors. The family were prominent Liberals.

Joseph Brook Yates had several children. Sarah's eldest sister, Elizabeth, had married Samuel Thompson, a partner in the largest Liverpool private bank, Arthur Heywood, Sons and Co; Heywoods eventually became part of Martins Bank. When Samuel Thompson died in 1892, he left £1,134,000. His eldest son Henry Yates Thompson, Sarah's nephew, born in 1838, went to Harrow, became head of school and classics prize-winner, and then was to distinguish himself at Trinity College, Cambridge as well as in later life. He, and his younger brother, the Reverend Samuel Ashton Thompson-Yates, an important benefactor to Liverpool University, remained close to their aunt Sarah, and indeed their uncle by marriage, and their younger cousin, throughout their lives.[6] Samuel Fielden was eventually to make Henry executor of his will.

Sarah's background thus introduced new influences and connections to the Fieldens and especially to Samuel. They shared a sincere Unitarian faith and liberal political views, but their personal characteristics were harmonious; they were both serious and earnest, strong and very definite in their opinions, aloof and demanding, but committed to helping those less fortunate than themselves. The association of Sarah's public spirit, interest in education and philanthropic tradition with Samuel's wealth was to have important results.

John Junior

Young John, along with his younger sister Ellen, continued to live with his brother at Centre Vale in the early Fifties. He was less serious, less assertive, but approachable, outgoing and gregarious. When he joined the business in the 1840s John had worked with his Uncle Thomas in Manchester as a cloth salesman. This remained his role as a Partner in the Fifties although he did not live in Manchester and probably was not there every day. The records in the Personal Ledger for the period show a hardworking fairly frugal lifestyle. Like Samuel, if on a smaller scale, he was adding to his holdings in the Lancashire and Yorkshire Railway. His principal interest, outside the business, seemed to have been the Lumbutts estate he had inherited from his father; here, year by year, he was spending money on improving farms and cottages and the mills, while the rents were part of his income.

Finding a marriage partner was another challenge. Surviving letters indicate John's strong interest in the opposite sex. Whatever his status and opportunities, in the end his passion was engaged by a local girl, Ruth Stansfield, four years younger than he, living at Carr Laithe, a farm on the Centre Vale estate, and working with her sisters as a weaver in a Todmorden mill. Ruth, recorded in the portraits the Fieldens had made, was beautiful. Perhaps both Samuel and John pursued her; John was successful and the union of status and actual and potential wealth, with simple honest beauty - the master and the mill-girl - took place in February 1857. There were many such unions in Lancashire and Yorkshire in the period; some were successful, others not. This one, childless, was to last for just 20 years.

When John Fielden and Ruth Stansfield were married, £69 was distributed as a wedding gift to the workpeople in the Fielden mills, perhaps a shilling or sixpence a person. But otherwise the marriage was a quiet affair. The couple made a home at Ashenhurst, an old property with a commanding view from the hillside over the growing town. John's

(Below).
John Fielden (1822-1893), second son of John MP, quickly became a popular and well-known figure in Todmorden, if not elsewhere. Early letters show his strong interest in the opposite sex but finding a marriage partner was probably not easy. He was thirty-five when he married in 1857.

(Bottom).
Ruth Fielden, neé Stansfield (1827-1877), a portrait made in 1851 and probably commissioned by John Fielden. After a long courtship they were married, not in Todmorden, but in Hammersmith, West London, with Sam and John's sisters, Mary and Ellen, as witnesses.

(Right)
Carr Laithe, a small farm which was part of the Centre Vale estate, where Ruth Stansfield was born and grew up.

(Below right).
Ashenhurst, in Stansfield township, overlooking Todmorden, was the first home of the newly-married John and Ruth Fielden in 1857.

(Below).
Ruth Fielden. This portrait was made after her marriage with John Fielden when the couple would be living at either Ashenhurst or at Dobroyd House. It shows Ruth as a simple, homely, beautiful wife, not in a grand but rather a domesticated setting.

personal cash drawings from the business were now to rise quite sharply as he improved Ashenhurst and enlarged his household; in 1860 his personal spending exceeded £3,000. In 1861 the Census takers showed him to be living with Ruth and two servants at Ashenhurst, with a coachman nearby. Shortly thereafter, following the death of Mrs James Fielden, his aunt by marriage, John and his wife moved to the more convenient and substantial Dobroyd House, close to Waterside. No doubt already at this time his thoughts had turned to the hillside above Dobroyd as the place for his future home.

Ellen Fielden, the unmarried sister of Samuel and John, probably continued to live at Centre Vale until Samuel's marriage: she then went to Waterside House. In 1862 she married William Booth, a sporty but impoverished North Yorkshire squire, and moved to his home near Catterick; their marriage yielded two daughters, but Ellen, always frail, died in childbirth in 1864. Looking after the interests of the daughters became a particular concern of John, who maintained a close relationship with Booth, or Uncle Billy, as he became known to the next generation, for the rest of his life.

Joshua, the Family Man

Joshua had married Ellen Brocklehurst in May 1851. The young couple made their home at Stansfield Hall, then a fairly small but historic Tudor house in a prominent but convenient position overlooking the heart of Todmorden. Joshua bought the Hall and adjacent land and Hollins Farm nearby for £4,500 just prior to his marriage. As soon as he and his wife moved in, they began making extensive alterations and repairs which cost about £3,300 over the next two years.

Joshua became a partner in Fielden Brothers in 1852 and seems to have taken charge of the counting house. Many of the business letters of the period - dealing with quite mundane matters - are in his hand, as are the financial ledgers including the Private and Personal Ledgers. But this would not be challenging work and Joshua was never happy with his role in the firm, nor did he have the appetite for either technical or commercial management. Indeed the likelihood is that he, unlike his brothers, but like the next generation, increasingly found Waterside and Todmorden dull, boring, stifling, in fact a backwater. His participation in the later stages of the Ten Hour Movement, both before and after his father's death, no doubt had whetted his appetite for politics and public life and gave him the confidence to believe that his

(Top).
Joshua Fielden (1827-1887), probably aged about thirty.

(Above).
Ellen Fielden (1831-1929), gave birth to thirteen children at Stansfield Hall between 1852 and 1868. Here she is still the young mother but she retained her looks and her figure, and throughout her life, the respect and affection of her family and all who knew her.

(Left).
The newly-married Joshua and Ellen Fielden came to live at Stansfield Hall in Todmorden. As their family began to grow the Hall was enlarged, but this watercolour painted by Ellen records the building in 1856.

John and Ann Fielden, the eldest children of Joshua and Ellen Fielden, both died in 1865 and were buried in the same grave at the Unitarian Chapel. Ann was frail and sickly from birth; Johnny was killed in an accident at school. He was said to have the looks of his grandfather John MP and his uncle John. His father had Foley, the sculptor, make a bust at a cost of £80; the likeness was such that Joshua wrote, 'we almost fancied we could call him and he would answer.'

intellect, appearance, voice and bearing, as well as his pride and ego, fitted him to be a public man. He was to seek opportunities for such a role, but for the present, at least, his ambitions were contained, and the counting house at Waterside was his place.

Meanwhile, the first of thirteen children, a daughter, Ann, was born in March 1852. A son John came in 1853 and thereafter sons and daughters were to follow almost at annual intervals until 1868. Stansfield Hall proved inadequate for the rapidly growing household and was substantially extended by building a new east wing between 1854 and 1858; new stables were also built, the works at this time costing over £6,000. Joshua maintained detailed accounts of his personal and family expenditure during the 1850s, some of which survive.[7] Housekeeping rose from £1,214 in 1855 to £3,348 in 1861. Joshua was also spending on the mill and farm properties he had inherited, paying calls on railway shares, and contributing to the joint activities that the Fielden brothers pursued. His total outgoings between 1855 and 1861 exceeded £36,000, a substantial sum. About half of this was met by drawings from his Partnership balance, the rest from a variety of other sources of income including rents, dividends on his railway shares, the Trustees of his wife, and exceptionally, legacies to himself and his wife which were £8,700 during the period. Despite his substantial outgoings, given the high profits of the Partnership his equity there grew from £22,195 in 1852 to £113,093 in 1861. In the latter year he valued his personal estate at £132,379 including £17,553 in railway shares, and other minor assets on top of his Fielden equity. His brothers, who had spent more modestly, had larger equity in the Partnership at this time; both then and subsequently they regarded Joshua as extravagant.

As he grew older and with his fortune more secure, Joshua began to devote more time to public affairs. Railway politics and local government provided immediate opportunities. His public role in Todmorden is discussed later. He became prominent at shareholder's meetings of the Lancashire and Yorkshire, notwithstanding his brother's position as a Director. He was especially vociferous in 1860 in criticising a proposed line extension from Rochdale to Bacup, and in 1864 in opposing development at Fleetwood. Some began to describe him as a ranter; he spoke with a deliberate manner but at length, and clearly loved the sound of his own voice. But in 1861 he was still mainly a family man. At the Census in that year, the Stansfield Hall household, Joshua and Ellen and seven children, included two nurses, a cook, three maids and a coachman. It was to grow further and become far grander in the following years, but in size, and no doubt goings-on, it would be in sharp contrast to the childless household at Ashenhurst and the rather austere and serious household at Centre Vale. The three brothers of the third generation were very different in character and style; already these differences were evident and they were to become more conspicuous in the future.

Meanwhile, in 1862, Cotton Famine in the town regardless, Joshua decided Stansfield Hall had to be further enlarged. Rather than rely on local skills, in search of prestige and quality he decided to employ an architect of national standing and distinction. He went to John

Gibson, a pupil and assistant to Sir Charles Barry, who had established his own London practice and acquired a growing reputation. In the 1850s he had designed several country houses, and churches, especially in Warwickshire, as well as buildings in the City of London. Later he was to become architect to the National Provincial Bank.[8] Gibson was a close friend of John Foley, the sculptor, who had been commissioned to make a statue of John Fielden MP. It was probably Foley who introduced John Gibson to Joshua Fielden, but it could have been the other way round.

(Above).
John Gibson (1817-1892), pupil of Sir Charles Barry and rising Victorian architect, was invited to Todmorden in 1862 to design the enlargement of Joshua's home, Stansfield Hall. The family liked him and were impressed with his work and he went on to design a whole series of Fielden buildings in the town and elsewhere, over a period of fifteen years.

(Above left).
Stansfield Hall, greatly enlarged by Gibson in 'a convincing Gothic Revival Style' during the Cotton Famine, to cope with the needs of Joshua Fielden's large household.

(Left).
Fielden Terrace, also built by Gibson for Joshua about 1863, was intended to conceal the somewhat squalid Meadowbottom and provide a dignified approach to Stansfield Hall.

Gibson came to Todmorden in 1862 with a brief to build a large west wing to Stansfield Hall, approximately doubling its size. He designed the enlargement in what was described as 'a convincing Gothic Revival style,' solid and dignified but with touches of flamboyance, the whole new wing sitting well with the older parts of the house. A two-storey building at the rear containing a billiard room and laundry was linked to the house by a covered bridge, crossing the drive which ran alongside the back of the house. A gatehouse was built at the entrance to the drive, and to hide the comparative squalor of Meadowbottom from the eyes of visitors a dignified row of cottages, Fielden Terrace, was built close to the entrance. The cost of all this was substantial but unrecorded; taking into account income and drawings, Joshua spent £46,000 through his Personal Account in 1863-65 of which probably £30,000 was on Stansfield Hall. What the people of Todmorden thought of all this at the time is not recorded; on the good side it provided some work at a time of desperate distress. Meanwhile Joshua Fielden must have been pleased and impressed by Gibson's high quality work, likewise his brothers. A personal friendship was formed and this was the beginning of a lifetime association that was to leave a distinctive mark on Todmorden and to yield some of Gibson's most renowned buildings.

Todmorden

At the beginning of the nineteenth century, a small centre was beginning to emerge where the three stream valleys converged, but the greater part of the population of the three townships, 8,453 in 1801, was scattered over the surrounding hillsides in farms and cottages: Todmorden and Walsden township was in Rochdale Parish in Lancashire; Stansfield and Langfield belonged to Halifax and Yorkshire. The growth of Fielden Brothers and many smaller enterprises had changed all this. By 1861 the population of the townships had reached 21,703, and although the hillsides were still well populated, increasing numbers of people were living in crowded streets straggling along the bottom of the converging valleys close to the mills. A significant town centre had now developed where the three townships and valleys met: a church and chapels, the railway station, a market place of sorts, shops, public houses, mills and congested housing.[9] The whole district came to be called Todmorden.

There was no local government of the new community, merely such authorities as had managed the affairs of the old townships, concerned mainly with highways and the poor law. As in similar new towns, many problems were now emerging. Foremost was what could be described as the sanitary condition: there were no drains, no collective provision to remove the accumulations of ashpits, middens and privies. To those properties which had access, the river afforded relief: the streams were the receptacle of every kind of solid and liquid waste, not merely from households but from factories and their steam-engines, slaughter-houses and the like. Seasonal floods could be relied upon to sweep much of this away, but not all. Flooding had probably always occurred but now, as river beds were choked, it became more frequent and a source not merely of discomfort and expense but of disease. As the population in the valleys grew water supply became a problem, left to the property-

owner to resolve for there was no community supply; in many cases the available supply was inadequate and polluted. The roads and streets were unpaved and unlit. There was no covered market; the working population shopped on Saturday evenings from stalls in the open street, in pitiful conditions during wet and cold weather; the fortnightly cattle market was also held in the street, in the town centre. Smoke pollution worsened year by year. Market forces, preoccupied with cheapness, governed the types and form of houses that were built, and many, accordingly, were back to back, unhealthy and unsanitary, as close to the mills as possible. Public space for recreation or for burial did not exist. There were no adequate public halls, no library, and other than the chapels few institutions to stimulate knowledge or learning.

Filth and squalor became serious. The town lacked dignity; it was a poor place, falling behind its neighbours. And it was unhealthy; cholera, typhus and smallpox were dangerous hazards. But it was a low-cost place to do business. The prevailing view was summed up by the local newspaper: 'it is impossible that we can live as Arcadians and as a commercial and manufacturing people at the same time. Taste and comfort, even health itself, must all give way to the great necessity of productive work.' Describing Bacup, another similar Lancashire community, a local businessman had said, 'here we build as we like and do as we like: there is such a disposition among the manufacturing community lately to save and to get, that they forget the comfort of those about them.' This could equally have been said of Todmorden.[10]

The Fieldens had shown no concern and for many years had acquiesced in the condition of Todmorden; whatever the squalor, it was not different from other new urban communities. They believed in small

An early photograph of Todmorden taken in 1866 shows the Waterside weaving sheds, Dobroyd Mill and the congested town centre. The Unitarian Chapel is conspicuous in the right background, and the centre distance, the newly-enlarged Stansfield Hall. The absence of smoke suggests the photograph was taken on a sunny Sunday afternoon. 'Lancashire towns' a contemporary had written 'are generally regarded by those who, most of all, have the power to improve them, merely as places of business, as places endurable because they are money-making'.

government; part of their objection to reform of the Poor Law had been the loss of local control and the expense implicit in the provision of workhouses. There was another difficulty in doing something about the condition of Todmorden; improvement meant expenditure and some form of rate which would fall on property and business and impair Todmorden's competitiveness. The Fieldens, like the Brocklehursts, were afraid of local authorities who could 'order us to set our pockets wide open'. Moreover many of the potential Todmorden ratepayers, those who owned or tenanted the hillside farms and cottages, or lived in the outlying districts straggling along the valleys, had no interest in contributing to the cost of improvements in the centre of the town from which they would derive no benefit.

Thus in the Fifties there were only modest Fielden initiatives for the benefit of the town. In 1854, Samuel Fielden proposed the rebuilding in a substantial way of Stoodley Pike, the moortop monument that commemorated peace after war, and served as a distinguishing landmark in the upper Calder Valley. All the brothers contributed £50 to this initiative along with other subscribers, and Samuel cleared off the balance of £212 needed to complete the work which cost £812; the obelisk form adopted probably reflected Samuel's freemasonry. In March 1860, Samuel presided at a public meeting called to consider the provision of a public illuminated striking clock at St Mary's Church in the centre of the town; he promised financial support for the new Church clock and for planting trees and shrubs in the churchyard; the brothers gave £20 each and Thomas Fielden promised to top up what was raised by public subscription to whatever sum was required; in the end he gave £38.

A public clock was a convenience. Educational improvement was more important and urged on by Lindsay Taplin, the newly appointed Unitarian Minister, Samuel and Joshua Fielden took the lead in reviving the Mechanics Institute in 1859, raising funds to provide a meeting room, lectures and classes and a library. They enlisted support for the Institute and called on their acquaintances outside Todmorden to give illuminated lectures and addresses. Unlike other manufacturing towns, however, Todmorden lacked the will to use the Institute properly; by 1869 it could be described as 'a ritual of patronage', attracting poor attendances, and it withered away through lack of interest closing in 1872. Regretting this at the time, the local newspaper called the town 'a dumb dog', but Todmordians were more inclined to look to the chapels and the friendly societies for their stimulus and improvement.

All this was to change: by 1860, the Fieldens probably came to regard the backwardness of the town not so much an inconvenience, as an embarrassment, a matter of pride, and even a menace. They knew that something had to be done: if they did not provide leadership, and given their conspicuous economic power in the community they were the natural leaders, there was 'the penalty of refusal; to be governed by someone worse than themselves.'[11] In 1860 their relative ascendancy was at its peak; apart from their wealth, they were employing directly and indirectly at least 20 per cent of the working population and individually and as a Partnership accounted for about 13 per cent of the rateable value of the three townships, 25 per cent of that of Langfield.

The brothers now took a strong initiative in securing local agreement to apply the Local Government Act of 1858 to Todmorden, chairing and addressing public meetings to this end. Todmorden then followed many other urban localities in setting up a collective authority, the Todmorden Local Board; when the new Board was elected in July 1861, John became Chairman and Joshua a member. The Local Board marked the beginning of a period of active Fielden involvement in the government of Todmorden. Samuel stood aside, but John came into prominence as a benign impartial Chairman who was to represent the family in its dealings with the local community, and Joshua found a public arena where he could use his talents and energy, and develop his political skills. A few years later the two younger brothers were made magistrates in 1865, joining the local gentry on the bench along with two of the few other prominent local manufacturers, Abraham Ormerod (a magistrate since 1856) and George Hinchliffe.

Famine Relief

Although the Local Board was elected in 1861 with powers to borrow capital and collect rates in order to carry out sanitary improvement and necessary public provision, the onset of the Cotton Famine with its threat to the town's livelihood deferred any major initiatives. A limited start had been made on paving and lighting. The rise in cotton prices began to affect local mills in October 1861 when short time working began. By July 1862, two to three day working was fairly general and in August most mills closed; the most acute period of the Famine followed. Fielden Brothers were making a generous provision for their own workpeople; some of the larger local companies were able to give some assistance, but there was a huge increase in the numbers who, deprived of normal sources of livelihood and, in most cases, with great reluctance, had to look to the Guardians for relief.

The Guardians were struggling, both to administer relief on a sharply rising scale, and to pay for it. In the two weeks to mid-December 1862, the Guardians paid out £761 to 3,126 persons, compared with £131 a year earlier. Many ratepayers were now unable to pay their poor rates and went into arrears, or were excused. At the time, of 9,360 persons employed normally in Todmorden mills, 3,262 were wholly unemployed and 4,702 working three days or less. A local Relief Committee had also been set up in August, mainly made up of clergy and tradesmen, providing initially bread, oatmeal and soup and other relief in kind. In November the Fieldens intervened. They were not happy with the way the Guardians were administering relief — too few relieving officers, humiliating delays — nor with its adequacy. In particular they saw the separate Relief Committee as slow and ineffectual, lacking influential heavy-weight participation, and perhaps distributing relief unfairly. Joshua had galvanised the Mechanics Institute to provide 'mental culture', free reading, lectures and classes in warm well-lit rooms during the harsh winter months. A large public meeting chaired by John was held on 20th December where it was agreed that a new Relief Committee would be elected, which must be free from 'bias and mischief.' John

Fielden chaired the new Committee, Abraham Ormerod, and George Hinchliffe were vice-Chairmen, and several smaller employers joined a collective endeavour to protect those most harshly affected. Fielden Brothers, who were by far the largest poor-rate payers, promptly gave £500 and promised to add 10 per cent to all contributions raised in the neighbourhood. With Joshua and the Rev. Lindsay Taplin as members the whole operation now acquired much more vigour and was able to use locally-donated funds and the contributions from the Lancashire and Mansion House Relief Funds. In the end the Todmorden Committee distributed, mainly in kind or in shop notes, over £6,000.

The worst of the Famine was over by the spring of 1863. More people were at work for part of the week; for those out of work, relief and assistance was more efficiently administered and there were more diversions from idleness. What Todmorden did not engage in, unlike other Lancashire towns, was public works, to take advantage of government loans for the purpose. For whatever reason — parsimony, in all likelihood, for it cannot have been lack of need — the unemployed were not given work in any significant way in road and street improvement, let alone creating parks or laying drains. A bridge over the canal was the exception. The ratepayers, it was said, could not stand 'the expense of improvements.' John Fielden took issue with this view but did not prevail.

Local Board elections in mid 1863 attracted keen attention. There were no politics, merely factions: those for improvements, and those concerned to limit expenditure. When re-elected, the new Board did very little for the time being. In October 1863, meanwhile, the Relief Committee suspended its activities. Its members had become concerned with encouraging dependency, or as John Fielden put it, 'with making people careless as to whether they got work or not'. Joshua added that 'if people would work, they could get work.' And some manufacturers employing hands, it was said, were paying low wages because their hands could get relief as a supplement. The Relief Fund was finally wound up in April 1864. Employment conditions were greatly improved; the Guardians were then paying out £105 in a fortnight, one-seventh of the relief given during the worst phase of the Famine. There was a setback in the autumn and the number of wholly unemployed again increased before normality returned in 1865.

The Brothers Fielden

The Cotton Famine had made the brothers truly rich, although this was a closely kept secret. The emergency had deferred the questions of town improvement. Effecting improvement through local government and rate-funded expenditure was a necessary approach which, under Fielden leadership, the town would now slowly follow, but the three brothers could also act on their own. They shared the Fielden heritage and the tradition of benevolence established by their father. Now they were to improve the town by their joint philanthropy. In doing so they were probably strongly influenced by what the Crossley brothers, the successful carpet manufacturers, had done in Halifax, where individual and joint enterprise had given the town its Square Church, the Crossley

Orphanage, the Peoples Park, model dwellings, splendid villas and in 1863, Sir Charles Barry's Town Hall, opened by the Prince of Wales. The philanthropy of the Crossleys had been partly matched by that of Edward Akroyd, their Halifax contemporary, who used his large inheritance to build model villages at Copley and Akroydon (1862) and the magnificent George Gilbert Scott All Soul's Church in 1858. The various works of these competing families attracted much attention at the time.[13]

Where could the Fielden brothers begin? Together they had inherited responsibility for the old Unitarian chapel. Thus throughout the Fifties they had paid and shared all the costs of maintaining and heating the building, and paying the minister, He was not over-rewarded; James Taylor, the Unitarian parson at the time of John Fielden's death, received £60 per year, although he probably enjoyed a rent-free house at Waterside. A new appointment was made in 1856 and no doubt, at the time, it was the Fieldens who chose the incomer. If they chose, they chose well for Todmorden. The new minister, one Lindsay Taplin, a young unmarried man, was to stay in the town for 23 years; during that period he devoted not only remarkable energy to the advancement of Unitarianism but to many issues affecting the public well-being. Although beholden to the Fieldens, he was strong enough to take an independent line on many occasions during his Todmorden career.

(Above).
All Souls, Akroydon, designed by George Gilbert Scott and completed in 1859 at a cost close to £100,000, for Edward Akroyd the Halifax worsted manufacturer. Like the Crossleys, his bold philanthropy was a model for the Fieldens.

(Above left).
Square Church, Halifax, the first philanthropic initiative of the Crossley family, to be followed by many others in the early 1860s.

All the Fieldens, at the time, husbands and wives, were Unitarians, and they were receptive when Lindsay Taplin, in 1864, pointed to the inadequacy of the old chapel and the need for a more commodious new building. A minute in Joshua Fielden's handwriting, dated August 1864, records the Brothers Fielden's resolve 'to build a new Church at a cost not greater than £6,000 for 500 persons.'[12] As the proposal developed, it changed in character. It was not just the need for a larger church that motivated them, but also, perhaps, the wish to proclaim by a striking building the legitimacy of Unitarianism, which remained a subject of abuse and criticism from proselytes of competing Protestant sects. The Fieldens saw other opportunities: the new church would be a memorial to their father; it would be a Fielden church, and provide a permanent symbol of their name and benevolence and their higher aims. To do this it had to be in a prominent position and built with distinction, to the highest standards, regardless of expense. A grand building, the brothers felt, would arouse a feeling of reverence. As the first public building of quality, it would enhance and dignify Todmorden and uplift its inhabitants.

Lindsay Taplin, chosen by the Fieldens as Unitarian minister in 1856 remained in Todmorden until 1881 and was honoured by the town when he retired. His ministry, featured by zealous advocacy of Unitarian beliefs, was a controversial one. He took a high profile in relief work in the Cotton Famine, in the small-pox epidemic of 1874, and in the activities of the School Board to which he was elected. Not everyone agreed with his views or activities and he attracted both strong support and active criticism. He took the initiative in urging the Fieldens to build a larger church.

(Right).
The Unitarian Church, completed in 1869 at a cost of £35,835, shared by the Fielden brothers. Their original intentions were for a building to take 500 persons at a cost not greater than £6,000. John Gibson probably encouraged them to build a monument for posterity.

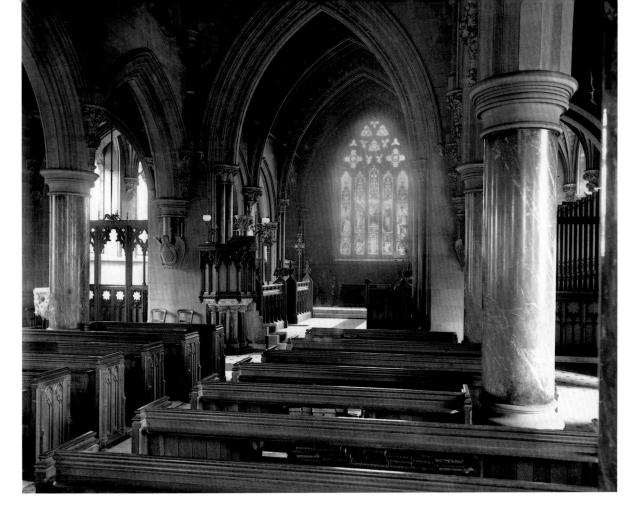

So John Gibson was now engaged early in 1865 to build the Unitarian Church. Samuel Fielden laid the first stone in December 1865: at this stage, as he told his audience, the estimated cost was £12,000. When the Church was opened in 1869 Sam absented himself but his brothers filled in and Joshua, in particular, was able to use the grand occasion to proclaim the Fielden involvement and the Unitarian message. Joshua spoke at length on the brothers' motives. Explaining the paradox between the beautiful new Church, with its elaborate carvings, lavish marble, splendid font and stained glass window, and their father's simple plain chapel, he said that they had decided not to 'follow in the steps of their forefathers' but they had come to the conclusion 'that there was nothing inconsistent in building such a Church .... and holding the purest and most God-like faith.' That point settled the building had been begun and 'had grown more and more elaborate than had been at first contemplated.' 'None of us regrets what has been done .... if there is anything to be entered upon so as to leave its mark upon the sands of time, it is a building for the worship of the Almighty.' They had created a beautiful building, Joshua said, 'out of their abundance' and he exhorted the congregation to match their contribution, by giving their time and labour and energy 'to bring men out of vice, to hear the lessons of virtue which will have to be taught.' William Gaskell, of Cross Street Chapel in Manchester, the most distinguished Unitarian minister in the North West, and friend of Sam Fielden, preached a most eloquent

Unitarian Church interior: elaborate, lavish, splendid and vastly different from the simple plain chapel of the 1820s. At the opening ceremony Joshua said the Brothers had created the building 'out of their abundance'; William Gaskell spoke eloquently to a huge congregation 'of a building so beautiful and so completely in harmony with our bright and happy faith,' but Sam and Sarah Fielden, the truest Unitarians, absented themselves.

William Gaskell (1805-1884), minister of the Unitarian Cross Street Chapel in central Manchester from 1828 to his death. A man of great gifts, he was an inspiring preacher and teacher and worked tirelessly for the poor of Manchester; his wife was the novelist Elizabeth Gaskell. Samuel Fielden first met him when Gaskell visited his school at Stand in 1828. The association was maintained and Gaskell preached at the opening of the Unitarian Church in Todmorden in 1869. At a ceremony in Manchester Town Hall to mark Gaskell's fifty year ministry in 1878, attended by over 1,000 people, Samuel Fielden spoke eloquently of his achievements and led the contributions to his testimonial which was used to endow a Gaskell scholarship at Owens College. Gaskell, Sam said, 'has been a steadfast upholder of our principles, and has never made an enemy of those holding different opinions,' not something that could be said of all Unitarian Ministers.

and appropriate sermon; all admired the splendid building and its many refinements in both materials and workmanship. It did not, perhaps, represent the simple piety of Methodist Unitarianism — as did the old chapel — but it did reflect the wealth and taste of the new generation.

The new Unitarian Church cost £35,835, shared equally among the brothers. Subsequently, as owners, the brothers shared the costs of maintaining the Church and the old Chapel, now a Sunday School, including the Minister's salary and any capital works like heating, or a new organ. The annual costs varied between £600 and £1,200. Lindsay Taplin if paid £120 a year on his appointment in 1856, was receiving £300 in the year of his departure, 1879. The brothers were also making modest contributions to other Lancashire Unitarian congregations: Accrington received £50 in 1868, Rawtenstall and Padiham £100 each in 1872, for example. In 1881 the brothers withdrew from their annual commitment as owners of the Church, which had become a source of friction with the leaders of the congregation. By then only Sam was a regular worshipper, and possibly he, his wife, and Joshua, who had left the town, but remained concerned, sought to interfere too closely in its affairs. John had become an Anglican and broken the connection. The outcome was that the brothers together in 1882 set up a Trust and endowed it with railway shares, to the value of £7,500. The Trust's income would then be the continuing Fielden contribution towards the running costs of the Church and particularly the minister's salary. Thereafter Sam and Sarah Fielden continued to worship at the Church. Joshua made occasional visits notably at the anniversary celebrations in June 1884 when he recalled his father's commitment to Unitarianism. If there were a few disagreements with the aging patrons, the Unitarian community remained profoundly grateful; here, above all, the Fieldens could look for friends. Thus on their deaths, all three brothers were memorialised, although in subtly different terms, by plaques within the Church; John was noted for his benevolence, faithful work and genial kindness; Joshua benevolence, faithful work and interest in its services; Samuel for generous benevolence, faithful work and constant interest in its services. Joshua and Samuel were to be buried beside the Church. And when the Unitarian Sunday School — the old chapel — was extended in 1899, the contribution of the brothers was again recorded.[14]

While the Unitarian Church was being built, John Gibson was given another task by the brothers. He had built Fielden Terrace for Joshua outside the approach to Stansfield Hall. He was now to design similar workmen's cottages at Robinwood where the brothers owned the mill together, as well as a manager's house. Robinwood Terrace provided twelve well-built houses, each with three bedrooms, piped water, drains to the river but not at the time expensive water-closets. This was to be the only Fielden experiment in improved housing, modest compared with the model villages or larger developments round their mills of the Crossleys and Edward Akroyd in Halifax or Titus Salt in Saltaire, Hugh Mason in Ashton, the Gregs at Styal, and the Fieldens old friends and debtors, the Mellors of Bury. The brothers shared the cost of £5,890;

Robinwood Terrace, built by John Gibson for the Fielden Brothers. This was their only initiative in improved work peoples housing, although the Partnership owned many cottages near their mills. Like the larger scale schemes in Halifax, Saltaire and elsewhere, the houses at Robinwood were beyond the means of the ordinary millworker.

(Below).
Todmorden Town Hall. After many years of anticipation John Gibson was commissioned to build the Town Hall in 1870. This was an artist's drawing for approval. Construction took four years and the magnificent building was opened in April 1875. It cost £54,000. The Bridge Street United Methodist Chapel behind was built at the same time but finished without a spire.

they were fine houses, but if let at economic rents, the Robinwood houses were beyond the means of ordinary workpeople; the typical worker's cottage in Todmorden at the time would cost £100 to £150 to build and be let at a rent of two to three shillings weekly.

Apart from the Unitarian Church, the most significant mark of collective Fielden philanthropy in Todmorden was to be the Town Hall. By mid-century the lack of an adequate public hall was increasingly recognised. A Todmorden Town Hall company had been formed in 1860 to which the Fieldens, with others, subscribed share capital. Land in the heart of the town where the three valleys converged was acquired, an architect's design accepted, and some building work commenced. Title to part of the land was then contested but the company ran out

of money in the Cotton Famine and failed. The site, with its incomplete building work, became a conspicuous eyesore, as it remained throughout the 1860s. In 1866, it seems on the urging of Thomas Fielden, the brothers bought the site for £5,500 and other necessary plots of land that had been in dispute previously. The local press revealed their intention to build a public hall for the town and some preliminary plans were prepared. Some years then elapsed. Finally, involved as they were with John Gibson, and delighted with his work, they commissioned him to design and build a suitable Town Hall. Contracts went out in 1870 and work started in June 1871; the fine classical building which resulted was completed and opened in April 1875. Built to a high standard, with lavish external and internal decoration, the building cost £54,000, the brothers sharing the expense between them.

The opening ceremonies, although marred by heavy rain, brought large crowds and distinguished visitors to Todmorden. John Foley's statue of John Fielden MP, commissioned in 1861 with the proceeds of a public subscription throughout Lancashire, and completed in 1863 at the cost of £1,000, but put in store until a suitable site could be found, was placed along the side of the new building and formally unveiled by Lord John Manners. The whole occasion was an opportunity to eulogise John Fielden and, to a lesser extent, the family, and call for the continuance of 'good feeling and social harmony within the community.' Speakers from Rochdale urged others 'who are very wealthy but keep their wealth in their pockets' to follow the Fielden example. If the bonds of dependence and deference were weakening at the time, this was an occasion to remind workpeople 'to remain united to their masters, pulling together heart and soul.' Samuel Fielden and his wife could not face the occasion and were absent. Joshua, in particular, while apologising for 'my elder brother who ought to have been here,' became

(Top).
The opening of the Town Hall, although marred by rain, was a great occasion in Todmorden. Sam and Sarah Fielden again were absent.

(Above).
John Fielden's Statue was formally unveiled at the Town Hall opening. It had been commissioned from Gibson's friend John Foley in 1861, financed by the proceeds of a public subscription, but put in store until a suitable site could be found.

(Right).
The Town Hall in the 1880s. Statues for the niches were never commissioned; that of John Fielden was moved to Fielden Square in 1890.

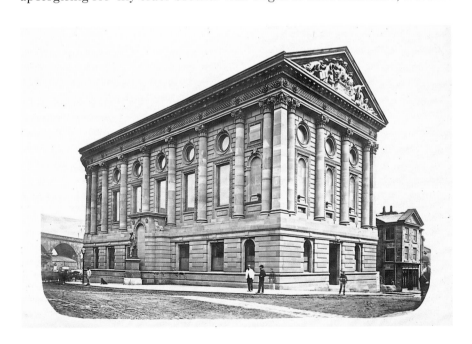

180

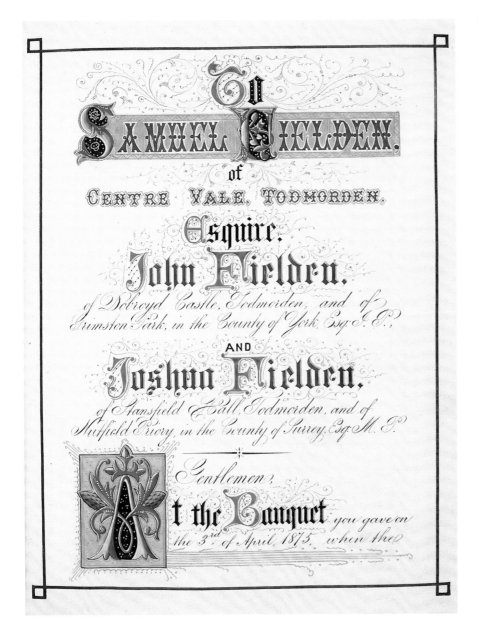

TO
SAMUEL FIELDEN,
of
CENTRE VALE, TODMORDEN.
Esquire.
John Fielden.
of Dobroyd Castle, Todmorden, and of Grimston Park, in the County of York, Esq I.P.,
AND
Joshua Fielden.
of Stansfield Hall, Todmorden, and of Nutfield Priory, in the County of Surrey, Esq M.P.

Gentlemen,

At the Banquet *you gave on the 3rd of April, 1875, when the*

The Memorial Address presented by Todmorden's leading citizens to the Fielden brothers following their gift of the Town Hall in 1875. This was Samuel Fielden's copy which, given his aversion to show and his cool relationship with the Local Board, he declined to accept. As his wife said after his death, 'he hated to be thanked for doing good.' The Address lay in the Local Board and then the Corporation offices until 1926 when it was sent to his son, John Ashton Fielden.

the family spokesman, and enjoyed himself to the full, recalling the Fielden history and success, and reminding his audience that 'some are and must be greater than the rest.'[15]

The people of Todmorden were rightly grateful for the splendid and much-needed building; after all, they had acquired a magnificent hall 'without a penny of cost to the inhabitants.' The Fielden's generosity 'exceeded anything that could be expected: we should be profoundly and eternally grateful,' said Abraham Stansfield, the local poet and prophet. Not everyone saw it that way: the *Rochdale Observer* called for 'more public spirit, more willingness to do things as a community.' In Rochdale, the Town Hall had cost £145,000 but the people of Rochdale had paid for it and had 'more right to be proud.' Todmorden

Thomas Ashton (1818-1898),
contemporary, competitor
and friend of the Fieldens.
The Ashtons of Hyde, from
humble beginnings,
developed a huge cotton
spinning and weaving
business. Thomas Ashton,
apart from being head of the
concern, was a prominent
Unitarian and Liberal. He
engaged the Fielden family in
the cause of Owens College
and its enlargement, to which
Sam and Sarah in particular
were to give generous
financial support.

people were 'mean, late and reluctant' about public improvements, 'too happy to look to the Fieldens rather than themselves.' In the end, warned the *Observer,* 'the Fieldens would get tired, and the town would resent their giving.'[16] But for the present all was thankfulness; £600 was raised for a portrait of Thomas Fielden and the three brothers were eventually presented a handsome address, each copy signed by 364 leading inhabitants. A Trust, mainly of Fielden family and associates, was set up to manage the Town Hall's use; eventually in 1891 the then Trustees gave the Hall to the people of Todmorden, namely to the Local Board. The building remains, a conspicuous, majestic and enduring monument.

Another joint Fielden philanthropy, but outside Todmorden, was support for Owens College. Almost certainly the initiative here came from Samuel who himself became involved through his association with Thomas Ashton of Hyde, like Sam a large and successful cotton manufacturer, a Unitarian and a Liberal, a kindred spirit in many ways. Thomas Ashton had also been at school with John Fielden, Junior at St Domingo House in Everton. The history of Ashton Brothers in many ways paralleled that of the Fieldens. It was said of Thomas that he crowded his life with public activities and especially with the affairs of Owens College which had been endowed by John Owens, a Fielden business associate in the 1830s. The College had moved from central Manchester to the Oxford Road site where large extensions took place in 1870. Thomas Ashton appealed for support throughout the Lancashire business community. He could certainly turn to the Fieldens; they had each given £100 in 1852 to the enlargement of the original Owens College; they now gave £1,000 each to the new extension. In total Ashton's appeal realised £200,000.

The brothers together, although probably again under Samuel's leadership, also conspicuously supported the National Lifeboat Association, a popular Victorian charity, with appropriate drama. A Fielden contribution of £2,500 in 1875 financed, among other boats, the *Thomas Fielden,* launched at Holyhead in the following year. This boat, was launched sixty-four times and saved 137 lives before it was replaced with a new boat of the same name in 1891; the various rescues performed were well publicised in Todmorden. The Royal Albert Asylum in Lancaster, opened in 1873 to care for idiots and imbeciles from the northern counties, also benefited from the Fieldens. Here the initiative was taken by Mrs John Fielden and the brothers each gave £500.

Town Government

Meanwhile, with the Famine over, the collective town authority could get down to its responsibilities. The Fieldens apart, the members of the Local Board were mainly tradesmen and smaller manufacturers, preoccupied not so much with improvement as controlling expenditure. They wanted to move slowly; in February 1866 John Fielden was complaining, as Chairman, at the poor attendance at meetings, so bad that 'he could spend his time more profitably.' By September 1866, Joshua was roused sufficiently to attack the Board for its neglect and constant postponement of necessary improvements, in scathing terms. He moved a motion 'that the question of the sewerage of the district be immediately taken into consideration by the Board.' He was at his most eloquent in arguing the benefits, the need to control cholera and typhus, the fact that the whole district would gain as the development of the town would be encouraged, and that 'future ratepayers would bless them for it.' Caution prevailed nonetheless: an amendment to defer consideration of the drainage question for twelve months was carried by six votes to five. Joshua was not constrained so easily. He threatened a deputation of 'several influential inhabitants' to the Home Secretary to petition for a Commissioner to carry out the necessary works at the expense of the Local Board. He had the support of the local press which complained of the failure to carry out improvements that should have been done thirty years ago; the *Advertiser* concluded that 'nothing is as profitless as dirtiness.'

A limited drainage proposal, covering only the centre of the town at a cost of £3,000, came forward in January 1867. Joshua's allies in the local press again attacked the dilatory Board — 'all had not been done which might have been, there was economy which became parsimony.' Todmorden was lagging behind in public provision; it was a place where 'people only see, think and feel cotton.' The plea was always the same: poor trade; the cost of improvement; who was to pay; and the habit of looking to the Fieldens. The Cotton Famine, of course, had depleted savings and amassed debts throughout the community. Progress was very slow and it was not until the following year that the drainage project was approved. Another concern, however, led to speedy action; there was a shortage of houses, resulting in overcrowding, rising rents and demands for higher wages. The solution proposed was to relax by-law standards and again permit back-to-back housing with communal privies; Joshua was opposed but the Board agreed.

Joshua ceased to be an active member of the Local Board on his election to Parliament in October 1868. John remained the impartial, genial chairman, anxious to avoid controversy, disposed to be passive rather than give a strong lead. Bit by bit the town moved forward. In March 1869 land was bought for a market place, including the cattle market that hitherto had been held in the street, with all its consequent filth and obstruction. The main sewer began to be laid in September. That month also brought controversy about proposals to build a market hall at a cost that could go up to £7,000, the amount that Bacup had spent. In 1869 dissatisfaction at the extravagance of the Local Board, and the waste of public money, led to attempts to form a Ratepayers Association, 500 people attending a public meeting on the question. John and Joshua Fielden were present, and urged the market hall proposal: the meeting voted it down by a majority of two to one. As one dissenter argued 'where would it end; we have lighting, footpaths and a sewer; before the market was finished, someone would likely want water-works, others a cemetery.'

So the local controversy continued. Fear of spending money remained the predominant attitude in a town that was still recovering from the Cotton Famine and struggling to maintain its trade; the decade of the

Peter Ormerod (1811-1884) and his older brother Abraham were contemporaries and local rivals of the third generation Fieldens. They grew up at Todmorden Edge, close to Edge End, and went into cotton spinning at Gorpley Mill in 1824 and expanded by acquiring Ridgefoot (1842) and Hollins and Alma Mills (1866). Although Ormerods became a large concern (48,000 spindles, 1276 looms in the 1880s) they never enjoyed the business success of Fielden Brothers and left modest fortunes by comparison. In the 1840s they were active in opposing the Ten Hours legislation; they had also been prominent in supporting the new Poor Law in the 1830s. The Ormerods were the principal shareholders in the Todmorden Gas Company, competitors to Fielden's gas. Peter Ormerod clashed frequently with John and Joshua Fielden on the Local Board and was the leader of those opposed to significant expenditure on town improvement.

(Right).
Sourhall Hospital. A serious smallpox epidemic in 1874 highlighted the need for an isolation hospital. Pressed by Samuel Fielden who paid for the nursing staff at first, this was the town's modest response. The building was an old hillside factory that had stood vacant for many years. The purpose-built Fielden Hospital replaced it twenty years later.

sixties had seen no growth in population in Todmorden and Walsden. The conflict of interest between the congested centre and the outlying districts continued to paralyse initiative. In September 1872 the Local Board decided not to have a free library, largely because of resistance from the fringe ratepayers. 'We only go slowly in Todmorden,' complained a witness to the Rivers Pollution Commission in 1873, 'in most things we are ten years too late.'[17]

After appalling floods in July 1870, when the Fieldens launched a Relief Fund with their own contribution of £300, drought returned in September 1871. Lack of water prevented the newly completed main drain from functioning properly. An injunction was imposed preventing the Local Board from emptying its contents into the river below the town without prior treatment of the contents; a standstill resulted, lasting for many years. Cholera and smallpox returned to the poorest streets, supplied by inadequate unclean water and polluted by the foul stench from the river. The local press repeated the litany of complaints, and saw the town as 'merely a collection of dwellings' with no public spirit, no community feeling, 'where each owes something to the rest.' Many of the improvement issues came to the fore again with a serious smallpox epidemic in October 1874. There were several deaths and no means of isolating those affected. Panic struck the town and feeling turned against the Local Board for its impotence. Lindsay Taplin took the lead; those not allowed to go to work, or fearful of doing so, should be paid their wages (this the Fieldens, and some others, did); above all there must be an isolation hospital. Samuel Fielden was roused to speak in public; those, like the Ormerods, he claimed, who opposed a hospital were 'afraid of losing their own money'; he would instruct the local doctors, 'to take all steps necessary to isolate cases and he would pay the expenses for a fortnight.' An old mill, at Sourhall, in a hillside situation, now became the isolation hospital. The Local Board had to pay for it, although at first Samuel Fielden paid for nurses, doctors and equipment. Sourhall Hospital remained in use for many years thereafter, although the need for it diminished.

Sourhall Hospital

Despite the smallpox epidemic, things seemed to stay the same — no functioning sewer, inadequate and contaminated water, stinking night-soil carts, filthy putrid rivers, as was the complaint. The first report of the Medical Officer of the Board in April 1875 was an appalling account of sanitary squalor, poverty and neglect, and its consequences for health and mortality. Local Board elections took place in 1875 and the improvers then had their say; their priority was 'a proper system of scavenging.' Slow progress began to be made. The Local Board's area was enlarged; in 1877 the assessed rateable value had risen to £66,500 and the Board was spending the proceeds of a higher rate 1s 8d, partly to service increased debt, partly for improved services. But the town was not doing well with closed mills, short-time, empty property, and rumblings about wage reductions at the end of the year.

The autumn of 1877 was marked by a succession of severe floods, prompting correspondence from Joshua Fielden and other prominent ratepayers. Samuel Fielden, whose property at Centre Vale was affected, launched an aggressive criticism of the Local Board for its slow piecemeal approach. To him the Board did not lack 'powers' so much as 'pluck'; they were falling down on every aspect of their responsibility. The Board did act the following year, with extensive works to deepen and enclose the river bed in the Burnley valley, to which Sam Fielden contributed directly; in all he spent £3,300 to the Board's £1,800. His impatience with the Board, chaired by his brother, continued and was to lead to further angry incidents in the next decade. In 1878, a year of acute depression, the Board finally approved plans for a Market Hall, but not before a large public meeting saw many objections on grounds of cost. In Burnley it was pointed out £60,000 had been spent on the market ground and hall; in Todmorden they were looking at £7,400 in total and hoping that the income from rents would make the project self-financing. The much needed building was eventually completed and opened by John Fielden in 1879; Sam Fielden did not attend the formal opening or the jollification which followed.

This seemed to end the positive active association of the Fieldens with local government. Thereafter, notwithstanding John's continued nominal chairmanship of the Local Board, there were to be disputes over gas and water, and angry confrontation with Sam over the Board's alleged neglect of its responsibilities and over incorporation. The remarks of the *Rochdale Observer* came true; the people of Todmorden, after looking too much to the Fieldens, came to resent Fielden giving and Fielden dominance; the Fieldens themselves grew tired of the popular attitude of waiting for the Fieldens and became almost hostile to the town, as the incidents with Sam Fielden were to reveal. But these incidents apart, life in Todmorden, notwithstanding trade depression, became less harsh; real incomes and living standards were rising as the cost of provisions fell and a widening variety of goods became available. By 1875 Saturday became a half-day; participation in sport increased; the chapels, the Co-op and voluntary organisations of many sorts, became more prominent; the town matured and stood on its own feet eventually taking pride in collective provision rather than squabbling. New, quite independent, families emerged to prominence: the next generation of Ormerods, the Hoyles and many others. The Fieldens moved into the background; age, their private lives and other interests were, in any event, taking them away from the affairs of the town; with the death of the third generation they would become only a memory.

The Workhouse Again

In 1867 another long-standing issue of town government had resurfaced. Todmorden, led by the Fieldens, had made an impassioned, dramatic and successful stand against the introduction of the new Poor Law in 1838. For many years thereafter the townships of Todmorden and Walsden, and Langfield, where the Fielden influence was strongest, remained outside the Todmorden Union. Eventually, the Union was properly constituted, with all the townships represented, but no hated workhouse, humiliating the deserving poor, was built; instead, as in the Famine, outdoor relief continued and traditional poor-houses made some squalid and unsatisfactory provision for the destitute old, infirm and mentally deficient.

The first local initiative to change this situation came in January 1867 when new legislation was under discussion; at a meeting in Hebden Bridge the view was expressed that a workhouse should now be built to cater for the aged and infirm poor; it was argued that if the Guardians did not proceed, the government would build a workhouse at local expense. The three Fielden brothers, anxious to scotch these murmurings against the triumph of 1838, called a meeting in Todmorden where they were joined by the Lord family and many of their Waterside workpeople. Samuel now came forward and spoke powerfully, insisting that the existing poor houses were quite satisfactory and that there was no need for a Union workhouse built at great expense, which would be a curse, a calamity, an injustice and a cruelty to the poor. He recalled the rout of the 'Malthusians' thirty years earlier, and expressed himself forcibly and personally against those who were now taking a different view; if these 'dirty rascals' persisted in their 'vile attempt', he said in a domineering way, they would be 'marked men'. Joshua spoke at length in the same vein but was less personal and vehement. He saw no need to spend £10,000 on a new workhouse into which the poor would be forced, at greater expense to the rate payers than outdoor relief. To great applause he declaimed, 'Let our hatred of a Union workhouse be handed down to our children. Let us never be so disgraced.' Even the mild John Fielden said that 'strong language was necessary.' Samuel's resolution was carried by acclamation. A deputation was appointed, led by Samuel, to make representations on the issue to the Guardians. As magistrates John and Joshua were ex-officio Guardians.

There were clearly those who saw this as an issue with which the Fieldens were obsessed. The Chairman of the Guardians, George Hinchliffe of Stoodley Lodge, a rival millowner and member of an important old family from lower down the valley and also a magistrate, defended himself strongly, against 'weak and childish' and 'unworthy' attacks, and 'a miserable attempt at intimidation.' Joshua's claim that a workhouse would 'imprison people for being poor', was exaggerated 'claptrap'. How could it be that 'any expression of opinion different from

Todmorden Workhouse, completed in 1878 after over forty years successful local resistance, led with great energy and emotion by Samuel Fielden and his brothers, following their Father's example from 1837.

or opposed to the opinion of the Messrs. Fielden,' could make him, in Samuel Fielden's 'outrageous' words, a 'dirty rascal' or 'a marked man.' Others came out in support of Hinchliffe, suggesting that the Fieldens real concern was 'the pockets of the ratepayers'. It was not right that Samuel Fielden could take, 'a dogmatic and magisterial tone as if he and his brothers had the absolute government of the town and district vested in their hands.' There were legitimate grounds for concern, not merely with the small unsegregated poor-houses or the fact that 'waifs and strays' had to be sent to the poorest lodging house, but at the lack of a fever hospital. The Fieldens were not the only friends of the poor.

Fielden opposition to any government attempt to force a workhouse on the Union nevertheless continued. In July 1867 the three brothers led their deputation to Whitehall, carrying a petition signed by 4,946 persons representing that the issue should be left to the Guardians as the best people to make a judgment. The deputation seems to have had its effect since the government proposal in their Bill to take powers to impose workhouses against the wishes of the Guardians was withdrawn. But the Earl of Devon emphasised that not all Todmorden's needs were being met — apart from the aged poor, there were orphans, idiots, and vagrants to provide for. The Guardians, in response, visited the three poor-houses and were shocked by the squalor they found. A committee urged that the aged poor should be brought to one place and put in the care of a married couple rather than be left to look after themselves. The problem with this was cost and money, in a year of poor trade. Nothing was done but the problem returned in 1869. Influenced by a committed local officer, the Local Government Board now threatened to dissolve the Todmorden Union, attaching its townships to the Rochdale or Halifax Unions, unless a workhouse was built. The Board could not accept that the circumstances of Todmorden were unique or different to those of six hundred other Unions. Again the Fieldens led objections and a new petition with 3,456 signatures was raised, urging that Todmorden's circumstances were special and unique and a workhouse was not needed.

To provide for the sick and infirm aged poor, the Fieldens offered to build at a cost of £3,000, three cottage hospitals at their own expense. Whitehall saw this as inadequate and unacceptable, not least since the Fieldens rather than the Guardians would retain control of the hospitals; under threat of dissolution, the Guardians then agreed to build a workhouse. But deliberately they were dilatory and negotiated endlessly with John Fielden for a site to show they were trying, without intention to complete. In 1873 Whitehall lost patience. A renewed Fielden offer to build cottage hospitals was rejected, and divided Guardians finally went ahead to buy land and proceed with a workhouse. One objective of delay had been accomplished; the Todmorden Union in 1873 had the lowest poor rates in Lancashire; its 2s in the pound compared with 4s in Oldham, 4s.5d in Preston, 2s 9d in Burnley.

In the end, with a minimum of fuss but without enthusiasm, the Guardians built a workhouse on the Langfield hillside. John Fielden argued for a small inexpensive building, taking not more than 100 inmates and costing £4,500, but when it was completed, in 1878, the new workhouse cost £10,280: it was extended a few years later. The Fieldens had made this a main issue, following the example of their father. They now had to accept defeat but it was honourable defeat; most people in Todmorden agreed with the position that they had taken.

Sam and Sarah

But to go back to private lives, Samuel and Sarah Fielden had become greatly attached to their home at Centre Vale, as they were able to fashion it into a place of pride over the years. John Gibson enlarged the mansion in 1872. Gradually, as nearby property became available, the estate was

Centre Vale in the late nineteenth century. Samuel Fielden inherited the property on his father's death in 1849, greatly enlarged and improved the estate and employed John Gibson to extend the mansion in 1872, when the Fielden School was also built in the grounds. When Samuel died in 1889 his wife Sarah remained at Centre Vale until her death in 1910. Her son John Ashton Fielden then sold Centre Vale to Todmorden's Mayor for £10,000, perhaps a quarter of its commercial value, and after heated debate the estate became the town park.

Samuel Fielden, in his early 60s, a portrait by the court photographer in Wiesbaden about 1879. The most significant of the third generation of the Fieldens, but his role as senior partner of the family business, his serious stand on many public issues, his sense of public duty, and his philanthropy, was obscured by his overbearing, irascible and intolerant temperament. In this photograph, he seems confident, self-assured, and friendly, but already, to many of his townspeople, he was 'Black Sam.'

extended; the works of improvement continued with gate-houses and drives, flood control works, extensive hot-houses; in particular, to complete the enlargement, the adjacent Ewood Estate with its separate mansion was purchased for 12,000 guineas in 1876. The whole estate then extended to 75 acres and Sam, it was said, worshipped the place; Centre Vale had beauty, dignity and privacy. The couple rarely entertained; both rather formidable personalities they cannot have been easy company and had few friends in the town. Samuel had his cronies, among them the prominent local doctor, Charles Thorp, and the solicitor William Sager; they were his frequent partners at billiards. Sarah had her paid companion Annie Bentley, sister of Alfred Bentley, Fielden Lecturer at Owens College and later Registrar of the Victoria University of Manchester. For a while the Bentleys lived at Stones, a Fielden property. No doubt Sarah's relatives were also visitors. The two led active lives, he with the Fielden Partnership, his railway work and managing his investments which he enjoyed; she in her educational work. Sam followed national affairs closely; in 1877 he was writing to *The Times* regarding his father's and Lord Shaftesbury's respective roles in the Ten Hours Movement; his letter encouraged a leading article in response.

Together Sam and Sarah would plan their inconspicuous but sustained philanthropy. Both remained active Unitarians, regular in their worship and consistent in their support. Together they enjoyed their holidays; visits to Scotland, to the Shetlands, stays on the Yorkshire coast, and more ambitious tours to Germany, Paris, frequently to Italy and to Egypt. When in London, like other members of the family, they stayed at the Burlington Hotel close to Bond Street, 'a discreet hotel of irreproachable standing', which Florence Nightingale and Cecil Rhodes used.[18] Apart from the August shoot on Higher House Moor (in August 1864 for instance, he led seven guns including W.C.Booth and William Pickersgill to shoot 150 brace on the first day), Sam seems to have had no taste for country sport. He did not hide his political preferences. Centre Vale was used on a number of occasions for Liberal demonstrations. He contributed to the local party and he was willing to support financially Liberal candidates in local constituencies; this he did, for instance, in the general election of 1880 when he gave £250 towards the expenses of successful candidates in South East Lancashire and a similar sum to the Northern Division of the West Riding.

Sam and Sarah's only son, John Ashton Fielden, born in 1859, grew up at Centre Vale. Not much is known about his boyhood. No doubt he played with his cousins at Stansfield Hall since although their educational paths diverged, he remained on close friendly terms with them in the 1880s and 1890s. But the Yates influence was a strong one; John Ashton's middle name was that of his maternal grandmother; the choice of school, Harrow, was clearly following his older cousin, Henry Yates Thompson, and there he would mix with the sons of the landed aristocracy, old wealth, as well as the offspring of successful industrialists and bankers. John Ashton did not achieve his cousin's distinction, either at Harrow between 1874 and 1877, or subsequently at Jesus College, Cambridge, nor did he maintain any close subsequent association either with his school or university. Whatever influences he acquired from his education, led him away from Todmorden and the family home. Like his father he was fond of cricket, and had joined the Todmorden Club in 1875; while at school and university he returned for the vacations when he played with the Todmorden Club, joining the first team, for instance, on its annual Grimston game in July 1878. But from 1880, when he left Cambridge, he seems to have spent very little time at Centre Vale.

His father had given him an allowance of 400 guineas a year, rising to £500 a year in 1884, when £4,000 nominal of railway shares, (costing £6,958) were purchased in his name. Much of 1881 and 1882 passed with his Booth relatives in North Yorkshire; in 1884 he spent several months in Germany and in 1885 he made an extensive trip to North

Henry Yates Thompson (1839-1928), nephew of Sarah Fielden, brilliant classics scholar at Harrow and Trinity College, Cambridge, visited America in 1863 and wrote a diary commenting on the Civil War. In later life he was a Director of the Lancashire and Yorkshire Railway and a Governor of London Hospital, as well as owner of the Pall Mall Gazette and a collector of illuminated manuscripts. He remained close to his Fielden relatives, was Executor of Samuel Fielden's estate, and probably a strong influence on John Ashton Fielden.

America, a trip his older Fielden cousins had already made. On his return, his father gave him independent means with a gift of £51,000, and a further £5,000 at the end of 1886, anticipating his later inheritance. John Ashton was to invest this shrewdly in home and foreign railway stock and in good mortgages, creating an adequate income for himself. He now had to decide where he was going to live and what he was going to do with his life. Unmarried as he was, he took a small house at Bottisham near Cambridge and then bought a larger home, Lawrence Court in Huntingdon, for £2,800 in 1890. Thereafter he was to make only infrequent visits either to Manchester or to Todmorden, spending most of the rest of his life in the eastern counties, which, no doubt, he had come to know while at Cambridge.

While he held strong political views, Samuel chose to play no public role in Todmorden. He never joined the Local Board and although he became a Magistrate he never sat on the bench or used the letters J.P. Increasingly, a very private person, he now sought neither prominence nor recognition. He shunned display and grand public occasions. It was said of him that 'there was probably nothing so distasteful as publicity.' Although he laid the corner-stone at the new Unitarian Church in 1865, he was absent at the ceremonies which marked its formal opening in 1869, although he of all the brothers took the closest interest in its affairs. More conspicuously he absented himself from the opening of the Town Hall in 1875, pleading his wife's health and taking off to Rome and Naples. The full account of the opening in the local press was despatched to him there without delay. His absences on these occasions were seen as disrespect by the townspeople. Thus the whole town knew of the Fielden philanthropy and there were many public expressions of gratitude and deference. It was probably Sam more than his brothers who had initiated this giving while as an individual he showed significant private philanthropy to the town. Yet this did not bring him affection or even respect; rather he was described as 'aloof and cynical'. Characteristically, when a memorial of thanks for the gift of the Town Hall, signed by the leading townspeople, was presented in 1876, Sam declined to accept his copy. His strict, if not harsh reputation would be known from Waterside but was to be publicised throughout the town by a number of incidents during his life, incidents which reflected his increasingly autocratic and intolerant personality. What prompted his fierce temper is not clear; it may have been related to the worsening business situation at Waterside. But as one incident followed another, and as he was slighted, his outbursts became more extreme.

The first public incident in 1867 concerned the Workhouse issue, already described. Sam's dictatorial tone to those who differed from the Fielden position was firmly rebutted. His impatience and temper showed itself again during the smallpox epidemic in 1874. But these outbursts apart, if Sam took a low public profile and left the prominent local role to his brothers, in effect to the mild and friendly John, his personal characteristics did not stay hidden. He had a memorable clash with the police in December 1875. An exchange of words with an officious police-constable, late one evening in the centre of Todmorden, with Samuel apparently the worse for drink, led to Sam striking the

Abraham Ormerod (1805-1888), like his younger brother Peter frequently took issue with the Fielden position. As Todmorden's senior magistrate, Abraham found Samuel Fielden guilty of assaulting a policeman in 1875 and fined him £6. There was no love lost between the families.

constable with his walking stick after pulling his whiskers. No doubt after some anxious debate, he was summonsed. The case duly came before the magistrates, to be heard by Abraham Ormerod and George Hinchliffe, neither warm to the Fieldens; Hinchliffe, in particular, would remember the abuse of 1867. Brother John, a senior magistrate, was present in court but left the bench. Samuel defended himself in a packed court room with a Manchester barrister and several witnesses, local friends and cronies. But with little hesitation the magistrates rejected Sam's evidence — he denied striking the constable, supported by witnesses — and unanimously found him guilty of assault fining him £3 with costs. After all, if a man of Samuel's wealth and power could get away with assaulting the police, where would stand their authority in the community at large. To Samuel, the outcome can only have been humiliating; it left its scars, and thereafter people in the town became inclined to laugh at him, ridicule him, although not, needless to say, to his face.

Another ill-advised public encounter took place outside Todmorden in January 1876, about the same time. At the shareholder's meeting of the Manchester, Sheffield and Lincoln Railway, Samuel, presenting himself as the largest railway shareholder in the kingdom, took strong issue with the Chairman over the appointment of his son to the Board of the Railway, probably with good reason. But the Chairman, Sir Edward Watkin MP, a well known Manchester man and son of a cotton merchant who had probably known Sam all his life, came back hard: 'I respect the aristocracy — the real aristocracy — but those men with their money bags, those mere plutocrats, I do not. They have inherited all the selfishness and meanness of their fathers, but none of their talent and ability.' The two were well-matched: of Watkin it was said that 'everywhere he went controversy and acrimony reigned, fuelled by a blunt and aggressive personality which was intolerant of criticism.' Sam did not let go, pursuing his dispute in July at a general meeting of the South Eastern Railway where Watkin was also Chairman and his son an engineer, and writing to the railway press. John Cobbett and William Pickersgill, themselves shareholders, appeared to have supported him at the meeting, but the redoubtable Watkin again pushed them aside for 'trifling with the meeting.' All this was fully reported in Todmorden. Watkin, notorious for his conflicts of interest, was later described as 'the Railway Machiavelli'; but he seems to have got the best of Sam in these encounters. [19]

Within Todmorden, Sam can hardly have made friends by the manner in which he exercised his ownership of the piece of ground at the perimeter of the Centre Vale estate which had become the town's cricket field. He loved the game and was committed to it as enjoyable sport, public pleasure and a desirable social diversion for a population that laboured long hours for low wages in the mills. In its early days, the town's Club had paid only a nominal rent, and that often many years late. Sam had told them, 'to pay all your accounts before you think about rent.' He had encouraged young people to join the Club at a very low subscription, 2s 6d a season; he had paid for improvements to the ground, proper drainage, providing a boundary wall and a pavilion. But he wanted to rule the Club as its President, not be 'merely a dummy,' and sought as in other affairs to be tediously punctilious and correct about its procedures. Thus over many years he publicly interfered, sought to impose changes which many found objectionable, or refused suggestions others made; a proposed reward for a bowler who performed a hat-trick, for instance, was dismissed as 'simply ridiculous.' He would conspicuously withhold his agreement that the ground could continue to be used for each new season until the appropriate formalities were pursued.

He first took umbrage in 1875, objecting to rowdy youths under the age of fifteen being members and giving notice to quit when his views were not met. He did not relent when a deputation led by brother John called on Centre Vale: his consent to use the ground was given only as the new season was about to begin. In June 1881, having belatedly agreed to let the Club use his ground for the year, Sam threatened 'to close the ground' unless he was given a satisfactory assurance that the engagements made with him would be carried out. At the Club's annual meeting in October 1885, with Sam Fielden as President in the Chair, a member had the temerity to suggest, 'if the Todmorden club had the

Samuel Fielden's Cricket Letters. A long correspondence survived with Sam quarrelling with the club almost annually on some detail of procedure or practice and threatening to terminate its lease of 'his ground.' It was all very tedious and made him a laughing stock in the town.

ground on the same conditions as other clubs there would be no need to ask for it every year as we have to.' Sam, who had objected to the club reducing subscriptions to increase membership, and to the low standard of play — they were 'nothing but hard hitters like the boys in the road; it is not cricket,' — responded 'I tell you, you'll not have my ground, I have done with the club and you can do as you like.' He then stormed from the meeting, repeating his threat. It was, for those involved, tedious and time-consuming. The bark was worse than the bite. An apologetic deferential deputation to Centre Vale gained consent for the ground for a further year. Cricket in Todmorden continued and flourished. But a critical question to those running the Cricket Club was their President and renewing the yearly tenancy of their ground. They were probably too careless about the necessary courtesies; in one season they failed to send him the fixture list until most matches had been played.

Sarah Fielden must have supported her husband's stand on many issues. His relationship with Joshua was very distant by the Eighties and by then he had little respect for the genial, easy-going John, his lavish lifestyle, his politics or his religion. The lack of respect between the two became conspicuously public in Sam's conflict with the Local Board where John was the long-serving and much esteemed chairman. Sam now became outspokenly impatient with the Board, not for spending money but for its timidity, lack of initiative, and neglect of its responsibilities. He used one issue to focus his contempt and impatience — Scrapers Lane. This was a hillside track way adjacent to a farm he owned; it became overgrown and obstructed and following complaints in 1879 the Local Board ordered Samuel and other adjacent landowners to repair it, as was within its power. The expense was trivial but Samuel refused, arguing that the road was an ancient 'pack and prime way,' in effect a public road which the public authority had to maintain. The issue dragged on and eventually went to the County Assizes with the full apparatus of the law. On a majority vote by the jury Samuel won; the Local Board was humiliated, with legal costs of £648, a significant sum, falling on the ratepayers. Samuel had made his point. Somewhat unwisely, he was later to tell the townspeople, 'Our family have made money in the country and I shall willingly spend some of it in trying to make the Local Board do its duty.' This was plutocracy with a vengeance. Open criticism in the local press now described Sam as a 'misanthrope.'

The second public clash with the town's authorities was more significant. During the Eighties, civic pride and the example of other communities encouraged the Local Board, which then had a population of 24,280 and rateable value of £92,581, to consider incorporation as a Borough. Eventually a petition to central government was prepared, signed by 2,400 people, which outlined the achievements of local government in the town and made the case for greater powers and higher status. A large public meeting was held in April 1886. Sam was roused to intervene. His entry to the meeting was greeted with 'general applause and laughter.' He asked 'what advantage was to be gained' and turning to his brother, in the chair, and referring to his indirect ambition to be Mayor, said 'he could not conceive that the Chairman wanted some more grand paraphernalia like those of the High Sheriff.' To Sam, 'the Local Board is bad enough, a Corporation would be worse.' The meeting did not agree with him and carried the incorporation proposal with acclamation. It was felt at the time that Sam's opposition was more apparent than real, or 'of a trifling character' as the *Manchester Examiner* described it. Sam, it was said, 'mostly sings a good deal better than he plays.'

But by June it was evident Sam meant what he said. Through his solicitor, William Sager, he organised local opposition. The local press, echoing the town's establishment, said his stand 'would not increase his popularity: he has set himself determinedly and at all costs, to overthrow and bring to naught the aspirations and desires of the great majority of ratepayers.' At the public enquiry in October Sam put his case trenchantly. Castigating the Local Board for its lack of progress, he referred to his brother, 'whom I am ashamed to say is Chairman.' He then argued that incorporation was merely a matter of pomp and show, would be a costly thing which the town, with its industry struggling in long recession, could ill-afford. He was supported by farmers in the outlying districts who had resisted the Board throughout, and interestingly by his old enemy in controversy, George Hinchliffe of Stoodley Lodge, then aged 76. One after the other of the town's leading citizens including brother John and nephew Thomas, now the local MP, William Ormerod, Caleb Hoyle and others, argued for Borough status but the petition was rejected, along with similar petitions from Haslingden and Rawtenstall. Sam's view might seem to have prevailed and Todmorden had to wait a further ten years for incorporation. To rub salt into the wound, he was successful in establishing that the full costs of the incorporation hearings were met by Local Board members out of their personal means, and not from rate revenues.

That was the end of any respect most in the town had for Sam, Black Sam, as he was now called, a figure to be feared, ridiculed, even hated. And despite her good works the proud image of his wife did not help. She did not mix with the town and on her public appearances, at the School Board or on visits to shops, was brusque in her manner, too definite and intransigent in her views, and insistent on appropriate deference to 'the Mrs Fielden.' In 1887 she was publicly to refer to many of her colleagues on the School Board, as 'half-educated men', whose 'great object is to keep the rates down' and who 'look a great deal more after the expenditure than after the instruction.'[20] Sam's position, towards the end of his life, led to some public expression of resentment and ingratitude towards the Fieldens, their dominance, their wealth, even their philanthropy. Thus in 1887, when he sent his solicitor William Sager to express opposition to the Local Board's renewed intention to acquire the town's three separate gas undertakings (one of them being owned by Fielden Brothers), his announcement was greeted with cries of dissent and loud groans. Brother John, still Chairman of the Local Board, and chairing the meeting, gave no expression of opinion. But Sam's opposition prevailed. In November 1889, with Samuel in bed with

William Sager (1850-1899), son of a grocer and publican in Church Street, Todmorden, qualified as a solicitor. His rivals, the Eastwoods, served the Local Board and the Magistrates, but Sager became Clerk to the Poor Law Guardians. He won the friendship and confidence of Samuel Fielden, was his regular companion, and acted for him in local affairs and his quarrels with the Local Board, not least his opposition to Todmorden's Incorporation in 1886. Like other Todmorden solicitors, Sager died rich leaving £62,331 at the early age of forty-nine.

his final illness, he again sent Sager to urge the town, at a public meeting, to acquire the Todmorden Waterworks Company which he and others had financed as a private venture, in frustration at the vacillations of the Local Board. He believed strongly the town needed and should own a proper water-supply and was probably haunted by his own failure a decade or so earlier to implement a proposal for a Fielden-financed scheme to provide enough water from Stansfield Moor. He now offered financial help to facilitate a public scheme. Another Fielden, no relative, objected to the Fieldens 'again dangling money in front of us', there was bitter insulting language, and the large meeting, chaired by John Fielden, voted to reject Samuel's proposition. Again, John said nothing, but the occasion was remembered thereafter, not least by Samuel's son, John Ashton, and the Fielden attitude and sense of obligation to Todmorden was never the same. Todmorden, it was to be said later, 'had done for itself so far as the Fieldens were concerned, for all time.'[21]

Samuel died a week after this last event, a death that was hardly mourned in the town, unlike that of his brother John, four years later. He had a very private funeral, three carriages only, no ladies present, no flowers. The Yates were represented, the Campbells, and the Cobbetts, while William Pickersgill sent his apologies. His grave, adjacent to his brother Joshua, and similarly in Egyptian form, adjoined the Unitarian chapel which he had done so much to build and to support and at which he and his wife continued to worship. Leading freemasons of the town later honoured him, by a visit to Stoodley Pike. In contrast to the fulsome eulogies that followed the later death of brother John, local comment was very guarded and restrained — like his father, it was said, he had 'a dogged nature': he 'acted regardless of public opinion', and 'was very firm on matters upon which he took a strong stand. He never hesitated to express his vigorous convictions in forcible and uncompromising terms. He pressed his views with a force that would have been better to restrain.' The best that some could find to say, was that Sam was not always understood by his fellow townspeople. Others, privately, were blunter in their resentment of his overbearing bullying manner, outspoken contempt for others, and dictatorial attempts to get his own way in the town as in his business. It was as Black Sam that many remembered him.

His death, and that of his brother John four years later, marked the end of conspicuous Fielden influence in the town and a changed relationship. But while Samuel was not loved, and not respected but even feared by many, he was the most significant of the third generation, the most able, the most business-like, the most serious and high-minded. He cared deeply for Fielden Brothers and its workpeople; he remained loyal and devoted to his church, continuing to worship there quietly until his death. He was concerned that wealth should be 'rightly gotten and rightly used.' He hated self-aggrandisement and self-indulgence; with his wife he believed that those who were rich and successful had the obligation, 'the plain duty,' to support deserving causes that would benefit the less fortunate. 'He loved to do good, he hated to be thanked for doing it,' recalled Arthur Fox the Unitarian Minister, referring to

Sam's genuine kindness. Below the hard shell was a deeply religious man, of an emotional nature, moved to tears by children singing a favourite hymn or by the fatal injury of a workman at his mill. Doing good by philanthropy was a source of great satisfaction. the more so because it was private and anonymous. What the brothers had done collectively was one thing; his own later years had been featured by a stream of giving to public institutions and to communities outside Todmorden with which he and his wife were associated.

One institution which benefited was Owens College in Manchester, later the Victoria University. The Brothers Fielden had already responded to appeals in 1852 and 1870. Acting individually, Samuel was to go further in 1871 when he endowed with £700 a lectureship in Mathematics and in 1874 made a further gift of £5,500 to make this a permanent Fielden Lectureship. Some years later he was to give £1,000 towards a New Buildings Fund.[22] After Sam's death his wife was to make a distinguished contribution to the teaching of education at what had then become the Victoria University of Manchester.

Samuel had been a Director of the Lancashire and Yorkshire Railway for close to 40 years, as well as its largest shareholder. Thus his philanthropy towards the end of his life became involved in two communities which were in large part creations of the Railway. The one was Horwich, near Bolton, which in 1885 became the location of the Lancashire and Yorkshire's Engineering Works, and grew very rapidly to a town of 15,000 people. The other was Fleetwood which, having failed as a packet port for Ireland and Scotland, eventually became a minor port and fishing centre developed by the Railway. Sam had bought property in Fleetwood on a large scale in 1874 and 1875 as an investment, when the Lancashire and Yorkshire pushed ahead with development of the port. His donations to the town came late in his

Owens College. The Fieldens contributed to the enlargement of the original Owens College in Central Manchester, and then to its move to larger buildings in Oxford Road in 1870. Subsequently Samuel endowed a Fielden Lectureship in Mathematics and at the end of the century his wife Sarah made the important contributions to the development of the teaching of education in what had become the Victoria University of Manchester.
(From a drawing by H.E. Tidmarsh).

life and were continued by his widow. In 1887 he bought the Whitworth Institute for £1,100, and the building then became the Fielden Public Hall and Library; Fleetwood was grateful, celebrated the occasion and named its promenade the Fielden Esplanade. Mrs Fielden, in opening the new library, said her husband 'hated to be thanked for a good action ... his desire was to assist a town that was striving to help itself.' Some years later, in 1899, the Fielden Seaman's Rest was built at Fielden expense, opposite the dock. Sam also bought Fleetwood a lifeboat; his wife subsequently provided a cottage hospital. In Horwich, Sam Fielden financed the Mechanics Institute which opened in 1888. After his death his widow paid for a large extension, the Samuel Fielden wing, at a cost of £7,000, providing a large hall, library and reading rooms; this was opened in 1895. Henry Yates Thompson, also a Director of the Railway, was a generous benefactor to Horwich at the same time.

Finally, Samuel's Private Account shows regular giving to a host of charitable institutions — hospitals, churches, schools, orphanages. Particular mention may be made of the Lancashire Unitarian Missions, the Manchester Discharged Prisoners Aid Society, the Chester Cathedral Restoration Fund, the Manchester College for Women, the Manchester Warehousemen and Clerks Orphans School, the Railway Benevolent Fund, the Manchester Royal Eye Hospital, the West London Hospital, Guys Hospital and many others. In 1881 he and his wife gave £500 to relieve hardship in the Shetlands following a disastrous storm there: at the time donations like these were seen as huge sums of money.

Of all the three brothers of the third generation, Samuel gave most away during his lifetime — probably of the order of £90,000 — and drew least of his wealth to support his own lifestyle. While comfortable and well-supported, life at Centre Vale bore no comparison with what his brothers were to spend on houses, country estates and yachts or other pleasures. Samuel's total drawings from the Partnership between 1865 and his death were of the order of £380,000 but these covered his major joint and personal philanthropy, his gifts to his son, and the purchase of many property assets like his Fleetwood Estate, and Joshua's share in the London Bridge estate in 1887; he also bought Todmorden property adjacent to Centre Vale and in the centre of the town (the Queen's and the White Hart Hotels) and continued to add to his railway share portfolio. What may be termed lifestyle personal and household expenditures, were not more than £3,000 to £4,000 per year; his total expenditure on Centre Vale was not more than £35,000. The lower level of his drawings left Samuel with the largest equity in the partnership. At the end of 1878, prior to Joshua's withdrawal, Samuel's share was £562,671, compared with John's £84,701. His partnership stake would be at least £450,000 when the Partnership was dissolved shortly before his death in 1889.

Most of Sam's wealth, however, lay outside the Partnership. Part was in privately owned property in Todmorden, in Fleetwood, Manchester, and in the London Bridge Estate. But in particular he had accumulated a huge investment in railway shares, derived from his father, his own modest purchases in the 1850s and 1860s and his large inheritance, with his brothers, from Thomas Fielden. Thus in 1870 his holdings were valued at £262,725 of which £116,945 were in the Lancashire and Yorkshire. Such an investment would, of course, generate substantial dividends; in the boom of the early 1870s the Lancashire and Yorkshire, for instance, paid 7.5 per cent while over the period 1861-1890 its dividends averaged 5.5 per cent. Samuel did not need the dividends for income; he re-invested them in new railway share purchases year by year; thus between 1871 and 1888 he received £380,489 in dividends but made net purchases of £366,595. At the time of his death his share portfolio was of the order of £700,000 yielding variable dividends around £25-£30,000 annually.[23] He claimed to be the largest railway shareholder in the country.

Samuel left real and personal estate of £145,566 and £1,168,615 respectively. Duties paid accounted for no more than about £15,000. Because of the size of his personal estate, and his modest lifestyle, compared to his brothers, Sam came to be regarded as a miser. That he had been careful in his investments and meticulous in managing his affairs there can be no doubt. He was the only one of the three brothers to make significant bequests to charity on his death, a total of £30,000, mainly to the hospitals, schools, and other institutions (including £2,500 to the Unitarian Church) he had recognised in his lifetime. Samuel made full provision for his wife, (an annuity of £3,000 and a £20,000 lump sum) and bequests to his nieces and nephews, to his cousin, Jane Ramsbotham, to personal friends like Alfred Bentley and his sister Annie, and to long serving Fielden employees in Todmorden and especially Manchester. But the residual estate, of the order of £1 million, with the property, and the shares in Fielden Brothers Limited, and Pernambuco Gas, went to his son, already well-endowed, and living as a single man in Huntingdon. Thus John Ashton Fielden, a millionaire by inheritance at the age of 30, was the chief beneficiary of the Fielden fortune. The way in which he used his wealth would probably not have

Fielden Hospital, opened in 1894 without ceremony, provided the town with a much-needed isolation hospital. Its provision was Samuel Fielden's wish and the cost, £6,000, was met from the estate.

disappointed either Samuel or Sarah, had they been alive to witness it. One of his first acts, after his father's death was to press forward with the Fielden Isolation Hospital, on the Langfield hillside, as his father had instructed in 1888. John Fielden provided the land for a nominal sum and the building was completed in 1894 at a cost of £6,000, paid out of Sam's estate. This was his last act of philanthropy 'for the people of Todmorden'; characteristically, John Ashton Fielden insisted that at the opening there was to be 'no display, no banquet, no speeches, no newspaper reporters present — everything is to be done as quietly as possible.' This was just as his father would have wished.[24]

Sarah and Education

As a young woman with a privileged but enlightened background, Sarah Yates had become involved in young children's education in Liverpool, teaching herself and contributing financially. At the time she spared no pains to gain a full knowledge of educational methods, both in the United Kingdom and abroad. After her marriage, she continued this activity in Todmorden where the need was no less. With one or two assistants she started a school in two cottages in Prince Street, Cobden, itself a crowded district of workpeople's housing near the town centre. The school was well attended and attracted good teachers; in 1866, sixty of its eighty pupils passed their examinations with credit. Commenting on the annual treat in January 1871, the local paper reported the high standards attained and the well spoken neat appearance of those at the day school and the young girls aged thirteen upwards who attended the evening school. In the town, it was regarded as a privilege to attend the school.

Sarah's initiative was encouraged and supported publicly when her husband financed the building of the Fielden School by Gibson in 1872 at the edge of Centre Vale at a cost of £7,807. Sam may not have shared her enthusiasm but he was broad-minded and sympathetic. Mrs Fielden's school then took its place alongside Todmorden's other schools in the educational facilities available. There were the Fielden Factory schools for half-timers maintained by the Partnership, the National schools, and the Board schools, which the School Board formed under the Education Act of 1870 was eventually to build. From inadequate facilities the district moved forward quickly: by the late 1880s there were over twenty-seven schools. Attendance was not compulsory until 1880 and school pence had to be paid until 1891. Sarah was elected to the School Board in 1874 and as a member until 1886, she was in a strong position to influence the development of education in the town. Her comments on local attitudes to education at the time were clear enough: 'the moment they can go to work, they go — only the better class stay later;' the fact that many children only came to school when they were able to begin working half-time at the age of nine; and that half-timers came dirty and inclined to insubordination but had a vigour and a zeal that others lacked. In her visits to local schools she was scathing in her criticisms of the shortcomings of individual teachers; there were those who preferred to resign rather than be bullied by Mrs Fielden. She seems to have taken a particular firm stand within the School Board on religious

Sarah Fielden: a portrait about the time in 1870 when she was developing her role in education, both in her own school and on the local School Board. A formidable personality, she got her way on most matters.

instruction and the daily assembly, insisting that neither prayers, nor scripture, nor hymns in the Board schools should offend the faith of any particular branch of religion, and Unitarian belief in particular.

But it was in her own school where she had the freedom to develop a distinctive approach. She was interested in improving the methods of elementary education then in vogue: in particular, the school at Centre Vale gave her a laboratory in which she could experiment and perfect her own teaching methods, In her own words, with regard to 'the crude and stupid methods' adopted in other schools, she would 'get them ended or mended.' In her evidence to the Royal Commission on Education in 1887, Sarah gave a full description of her model school and set out in forthright terms her own strong views on education and those who were teaching. The school received her close personal care; she herself taught for part of each day when she was at home, and doubtless supervised closely the headmistress, assistants and pupil-teachers. At the time there were 180 pupils, some boys but mainly girls, aged between the ages of six and twelve. Fees were 4d per week and the children who attended were probably from better-off homes. Discipline was strong and reliant on personal authority rather than cane or other forms of punishment. 'Any teacher who is obliged to cane a girl is not fit for her work,' she said, and went on, 'I can make them sufficiently unhappy with my tongue, without a cane.' Sarah or her headmistress would personally inspect her girls, or 'her babies' as she described them, for dress and cleanliness and required appropriate courtesy and deference; she hated slovenliness of any kind. But what drew attention to the school was its method of teaching children to talk and read, almost without accent and with appropriate emphasis and understanding; this was achieved by practice and repetition, with constant exercises performed

The Fielden School in Centre Vale, built by John Gibson in 1872 at a cost of £7,807, was run as a private fee-paying school by Sarah Fielden until 1896. Here she developed and demonstrated her innovative teaching methods, apart from imparting wholesome education to many hundreds of students. The school was given to the town by her son in 1896.

201

in response to signals from the teacher. Many educationalists visited the school to observe and learn from its practices. Many young teachers were trained there. Sarah's views on the training of teachers and on the government's policy towards education — the inspectorate, the grant policy and other issues — were expressed in blunt and critical terms to the Royal Commission. Typically her views were overstated, too definite and decided, too unqualified and stimulated resistance rather than support. She and her husband were alike in these respects: she

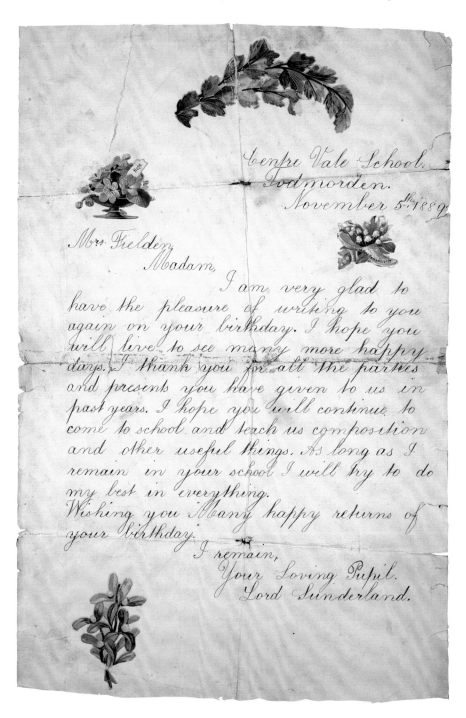

A pupil writes to Sarah. She ran a good school with firm discipline. In deference, and to prove their handwriting skills, all the children had to write individual letters on her birthday.

Sarah Fielden: a portrait from later life, probably about 1900 when she was eighty. This was the time when she became a leading benefactor to Manchester University, endowing the Fielden Demonstration School and a Chair in Education.

was sure of her position and unsympathetic to other views.[25]

Sarah gave up the school in 1896 after her husband's death and with advancing years. The building passed to her son, John Ashton, who gave it to the Borough Council in 1898 to be used for educational purposes; eventually it became the Fielden School of Art. Meanwhile Sarah, to further her own life's work, and her concern with the training of teachers, turned to the University in Manchester. There she endowed a Chair of Education in 1898; a house and land was bought for £1,150 in nearby Lime Grove and a demonstration school opened called the Fielden Upper School; when the School was later conveyed to the University Sarah provided an endowment of £4,000. Some years later in 1908, she bought a large house and grounds in Victoria Park to which the School moved and became able to extend its facilities. Sarah's total benefactions to the University were £9,000. In 1906 she received the honorary degree of D.Litt.

After Samuel's death in 1889, Sarah lived on in Centre Vale with her younger companion Annie Bentley. When she died in July 1910, aged ninety, after many years of infirmity, she was generously treated in obituaries, not so much as a warm friendly approachable person but as a devoted teacher, a pioneer in educational methods and a formidable doer of good. She was, in fact, after John's wife Ellen, who died at Dobroyd Castle in 1909, the last of the Fieldens to regard Todmorden as their home. Sarah was buried beside her husband at the Unitarian Church; a solemn funeral brought back to Todmorden her son and his many cousins, Joshua's children, and various relatives from Liverpool. The home and park which she and her husband had created and loved was then acquired by the town of Todmorden at well below its commercial value, an appropriate final act of philanthropy to mark Sam and Sarah who, of all the Fieldens, had improved the town and community by their urge to do good.[26]

John, King of Todmorden

John's personality was different from his older and younger brothers. They were both aloof and exclusive although their style and manner was not the same: the one was private and overbearing; the other self-important and vain. John had no airs; he enjoyed prominence but, probably to the delight of his audience always presented himself as a simple modest man, not given to making speeches. 'I am not a talking man,' he was fond of saying, 'I have not got the gift of the gab, I try to work another way.' He was remembered for 'his amiable disposition and his vein of sunny humour which made him universally beloved. Wherever he went his was a welcome presence and he had the fine tact of making everyone at home with him and with one another.'[27]

His huge local popularity and esteem notwithstanding, John was, perhaps, the least significant of the brothers. Samuel was a powerful personality, a respected businessman, and a notable philanthropist. Joshua's ambition led him, unsuccessfully, to seek a role on the national stage. John was content to be Mr John, King of Todmorden, Chairman of the Local Board, Magistrate, President or Patron of this and that club or society. His leadership was convivial and benign rather than clear and strong; he was a consensus man who, enjoying the approval and respect of his fellow-townsmen, would follow rather than direct. He was an easy-going partner at Waterside where his masterful brother exercised control. Philanthropy was not to him, as to Sam, a plain duty; considering his wealth as an individual his gestures in that direction were modest. He was happier using his wealth to make a prominent mark and achieve social standing. The town liked his social prominence; everybody looked up to him and took pride in his status and conspicuous possessions.

His first grand gesture with the large wealth he had acquired after the Cotton Famine was Dobroyd Castle. John, and his wife Ruth, were

John Fielden, about 1870. The Stevenson portrait, captures Todmorden's leading citizen for over thirty years and the most popular and respected member of his family.

then living at Dobroyd House, close to the Waterside Mill. A story prevailed in Todmorden that John had promised Ruth, before their marriage in 1857, to build a castle on the hill. Be that as it may, in 1865 his uncle Thomas — probably at John's request — had bought the Stones Estate and the Friths Estate, several farms and cottages on the hillside ledge above Waterside, and the Friths mill and cottages in the Dulesgate valley, paying £22,000 for the whole. John Gibson meanwhile was building the Unitarian Church and had clearly won the confidence and friendship of the brothers. In 1866 John commissioned Gibson to build a castle at Dobroyd.

The objective, it was stated at the rearing ceremony, was a building 'to immortalise the name of Fielden,' which would be 'the most

Dobroyd Castle. As the Unitarian Church progressed John Gibson was commissioned to build John Fielden's castle overlooking the town and its valleys on the Dobroyd hillside. For his client's approval, Gibson produced this illustrative painting.

commanding object in the neighbourhood.'[28] Gibson followed his commission; he designed a huge castle on a prominent site, building it over three years without regard for expense, not least so far as the interiors were concerned. The completed building attracted attention in the Architectural Press at the time, especially for its fine saloon and its imposing staircase. In total it had sixty-six rooms, apart from its large stables for seventeen horses, conservatories and the like, and its model farm. It never attracted praise as a building of distinction; much of the comment, then and subsequently, was critical of its pretension and taste. Mark Girouard dismissed it as 'little more than a castellated villa with remarkably unappetising detail.' But from a distance it stood as a prominent, not unattractive, hillside feature. When the Castle was finished in 1869, it had cost £71,589, much more than was spent on the Unitarian Church, or subsequently the Town Hall. The 1871 Census records John and his wife in residence; there were five maids, a footman, porter and groom living in the Castle, and a gardener, coachman and butler with their families living in houses on the estate. An establishment of this size seems to have been maintained throughout John Fielden's lifetime, whether the Castle was occupied or not.

John and Ruth Fielden were childless, but the household at Dobroyd was enlivened by a nephew and a niece whom John virtually adopted. His sister Ann had married Henry Brocklehurst in Todmorden in 1848; both she and her husband died in 1870, leaving five young children. John Fielden was their executor. The eldest son, John Fielden Brocklehurst, born in 1852, had a successful military career, commanding a Brigade in the Boer War and becoming a royal equerry; he was made a Baron in 1914. The second son, Henry Dent Brocklehurst, born in 1855 married into the Lascelles family, and eventually settled in Sudeley Castle, Gloucestershire. The youngest children, Ernest, then aged nine

(*Left*).
Dobroyd Castle: a view of the saloon or entrance hall, lit from above, which was the one feature of the building to attract favourable comment from the architectural press of the time. Note the monogram of John and Ruth Fielden on the facing wall.

(*Below*).
Dobroyd Castle: a plan of the ground floor. The building had sixty-six rooms offering generous accommodation for John and his wife, childless, but looked after by eleven indoor and outdoor servants.

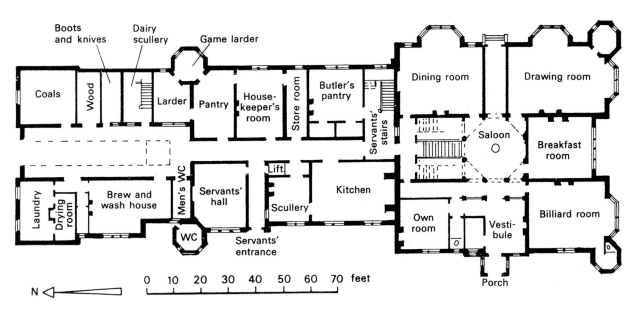

Boots and knives · Dairy scullery · Game larder

Coals · Wood · Larder · Pantry · House-keeper's room · Store room · Butler's pantry · Servants' stairs · Dining room · Drawing room

Saloon · Breakfast room

Laundry · Drying room · Brew and wash house · Men's WC · Servants' hall · Lift · Scullery · Kitchen · Own room · Vesti-bule · Billiard room

WC · Servants' entrance · Porch

0 10 20 30 40 50 60 70 feet

N

Dobroyd Castle, photographed about 1870, shortly after completion. Its cost, £71,859, was much larger than that of the Town Hall.

and Constance, aged seven, came to live at Dobroyd in the early Seventies. As John was to say in his will, they were 'brought up by me.' Certainly young children about the house, other friends and visitors, Unitarian fetes in the grounds, would bring life and activity to the Castle in the years after it was built. Nonetheless, the likelihood is that John was never quite comfortable with the prominent display of wealth that he had imposed on the Todmorden landscape. With his uncle Thomas's death in 1869 his personal wealth had substantially increased. His thoughts turned to something different, a country estate, away from Todmorden, that could place the Fieldens among the landed gentry, give them social position close to the aristocracy. As with many other 'nouveaux riche' of the time, and indeed previous times, the acquisition of land, as an investment, for sport, pleasure and amenity, and above all for status, was the prevailing value. As George Brodrick put it, 'men who have made their fortunes in trade are covetous of land which for them is the sure passport to social consideration.' *The Economist* wrote in July 1870, often quoted, 'it would pay a millionaire to sink half his fortune in buying 10,000 acres of land to return a shilling per cent, rather than live upon the whole without land: he would be a greater person in the eyes of more people.'[29]

The Fieldens had already bought Beachamwell in Norfolk for their cousin-once-removed. Close to home, John Foster of Black Dyke Mills

208

at Queensbury near Halifax had bought Hornby Castle in North Lancashire and its estate of 11,000 acres for £205,000, Francis Crossley, Somerleyton in Suffolk, in each case in 1861. John probably did not search for a suitable landed property for long. In 1872 the Grimston estate near Tadcaster came on the market. Offered by Lord Londesborough, Grimston featured a magnificent Decimus Burton mansion, built in the attractive local limestone, a park of 600 acres, and several tenanted farms and cottages, the whole estate extending to 2,875 acres. Set in the Vale of York, close to many other country seats of the nobility and gentry, it was both prestigious, and convenient. Not surprisingly at the time there was keen interest to buy the estate. At the auction in July 1872, after an opening bid at £150,000 a succession

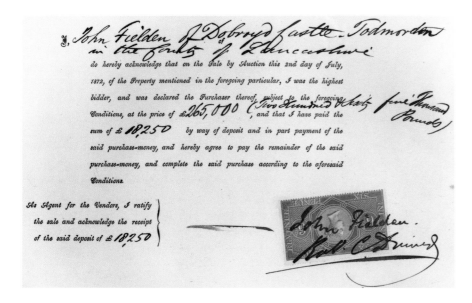

(Above)
Grimston Park, a splendid house near Tadcaster, built by Decimus Burton, situated in an attractive park, the whole, with tenanted farms, making an estate of 2,875 acres. This illustration is taken from the agent's particulars of sale.

(Left)
Grimston: the confirmation of purchase. There was keen competition for the property and the price was a high one, nearly forty years purchase of the rental income. Ten years earlier Queen Victoria had bought the Sandringham estate of 7,700 acres at what was regarded as an inflated price of £219,000, about thirty years purchase.

209

of bidders quickly pushed the bid to £220,000, comfortably above the reserve of £200,000. At this stage things went quieter as two determined personalities competed with each other, the one, John Fielden, and the other William Henry Foster, then master of Black Dyke Mills, whose career and circumstances closely paralleled that of the Fieldens. For twelve minutes they sparred until Fielden bid £265,000. That was enough to secure Grimston Park, nearly forty years purchase of the rental income. Foster's son, Robert, was to buy Stockeld Park nearby some years later.[29]

Grimston was bought at what, with hindsight, was the peak of the nineteenth century land market; thereafter values fell as depression and competition of imported grain severely affected farming incomes, rent payments and land values. That did not matter to John at the time or subsequently; he was now the owner of a beautiful estate. Over the years he was to fill the house with fine furniture, paintings, books, porcelain and the like, and make his home a source of great pride as well as comfort. He had joined a different class to the small millowners and tradespeople of Todmorden; county society welcomed him to their homes, to the hunting field, to their functions. Hardworking Todmorden, or the deferential element there, was enthralled by the status their senior citizen had acquired; parties of Fielden employees, of Unitarians, of townspeople generally, visited his estate on annual outings; the Cricket Club played annual matches in the Park; Grimston became part of Todmorden.

John's enjoyment of his estate and its accompanying status was marred by an accident on the hunting field in 1873. A kick from a horse left him with a crippled leg and a wheel-chair, although it did not impair his activity as a squire, or in Todmorden. More serious perhaps was the reaction of his wife Ruth to the enhanced way of living. The course of their marriage — the master and the mill-girl — was not publicised in Todmorden. Portraits of Ruth present her as a beautiful and then dignified woman. She had many friends, not least in the Unitarian congregation, for her warmth and simplicity. When Dobroyd Castle was opened, the local press commented that she 'bore her honours meekly'. She probably did not enjoy the lifestyle, surrounded by servants, at Dobroyd and would find the grandeur of Grimston, mixing with the county families, even more alien. Rumour and gossip had it that she took to alcohol in her unhappiness. She died in February, 1877, aged fifty, (of jaundice, according to the doctors) and was buried at the old Unitarian chapel. The funeral, described as 'a quiet and spontaneous display of respect' brought most of the family together; the Ramsbothams came from Crowborough, Joshua was represented by his sons, and John Gibson attended as a friend. Lindsay Taplin's address was a masterpiece of tact; carefully chosen words that would offend neither Ruth's friends on the one hand, nor the Fieldens on the other. The following Sunday, he spoke of 'one whose noble simplicity and unaffected tenderness and truthfulness, it was a privilege to know.' 'Ruth,' he said, had 'a heart full of goodness, charity and unassuming modesty.'

Within eight months, on 25 October 1877, John had remarried. His

Ruth Fielden. This carte-de-visite photograph, probably dates from the 1870s, when Dobroyd Castle was complete and when John Fielden had bought Grimston. Ruth is older, more severe. The last few years, before her death in 1877, would be a desperate trial for a simple plain person like Ruth, expected to behave as mistress in large households, and a difficult period for John Fielden her husband, anxious to impress the county society he had joined. Their relationship is not recorded, but the inference is that they became alienated.

new bride was Ellen Mallinson, also aged fifty, daughter of Richard Mallinson, Rector of Arkholme in North Lancashire. As a further indication of his concern with status, he chose for the ceremony, St. George's, Hanover Square, a long way from Todmorden, but a church where many of the rich and famous in society chose to be married, as well as the tradesmen and house-servants of Mayfair. Samuel Fielden was present and signed the Register; Joshua was represented by Thomas, his eldest son. The Mallinson connection went back at least forty years when John's uncle Joshua had married Else Mallinson, then from Horton-in-Ribblesdale. Ellen, the new Mrs Fielden, had been close to John and indeed to Ruth for some years before their marriage. Her brother, a Manchester solicitor, John Mallinson, was over many years employed by the Fielden Brothers to manage their property interests.

Ellen Fielden was a handsome woman and a strong personality, stronger than her husband. She would manage his household and take care of the Brocklehurst children. She quickly persuaded him to become Conservative in politics, Anglican in religion. The couple began to worship at St Mary's. Mrs Fielden's particular gesture to Todmorden was the Fielden Temperance Hotel, in Fielden Square, built for 'a very fine purpose, no less than that of practising temperance, and total abstinence too,' as the local Almanac put it. The building, opened in December 1880 by the Bishop of Manchester, cost John Fielden £4,000; it was never a commercial success, and by 1884 part was being let to the Conservative Association who eventually bought the whole building, for half its cost, as a Conservative Club. Partly under his wife's influence, John began to spend more time at Grimston, where he was host to grand parties, and shoots. The couple were also frequent visitors to London, staying at the Burlington, dining well and seeing a light play or music hall. Occasionally they made trips abroad. Their wedding at St George's,

St. George's Hanover Square, the fashionable church for society weddings where John Fielden married Ellen Mallinson eight months after the death of his first wife, Ruth. The Fieldens knew the church from its proximity to the Burlington Hotel where they stayed when in London. Sam Fielden signed the register.

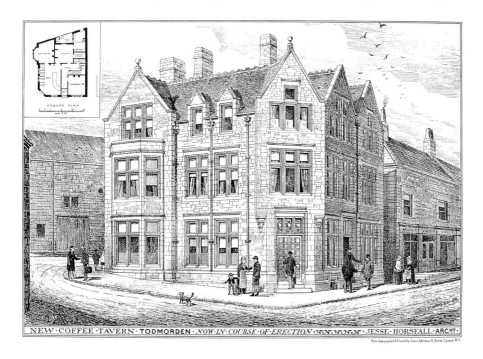

NEW·COFFEE·TAVERN·TODMORDEN·*NOW·IN·COURSE·OF·ERECTION*······JESSE·HORSFALL·ARCHT·

The Fielden Coffee Tavern, built by John Fielden in 1880 for his second wife, Ellen Mallinson. A vicar's daughter, she was a strict Anglican and strong on temperance, unlike her easy-going husband.

John Fielden made himself available as patron or president or chairman to many Todmorden organisations and events. Here he joins a number of other prominent local personalities to lend distinguished patronage by presence at a performance of *Uncle Tom's Cabin* by Harriet Beecher Stowe. By comparison his brothers were regarded as aloof.

Hanover Square, had hit the right note. Thomas Fielden, Joshua's oldest son was married there in 1878 and four years later, a proud John Fielden gave away Constance Brocklehurst in the same church where she married Charles Fitzwilliam, fourth son of Earl Fitzwilliam of Wentworth Woodhouse, and captain in the Royal Horse Guards. Their match, probably enormously pleasing to John, almost certainly resulted from Grimston socialising; both his brothers and their wives were present. Charles Fitzwilliam went on to become a crown equerry and the couple's son, whose grandmother had been born at Dawson Weir, became the ninth Earl.

But John's regular presence in Todmorden continued to be noted throughout the 1880s, entertaining his tenants, attending the Bench, chairing the Local Board, presiding at the Agricultural Society's annual show, or the Musical Society's annual Messiah and visiting the mill, rewarding a pensioner, hiring a young man for the office or raising someone's pay. The managers at Waterside received their annual gifts

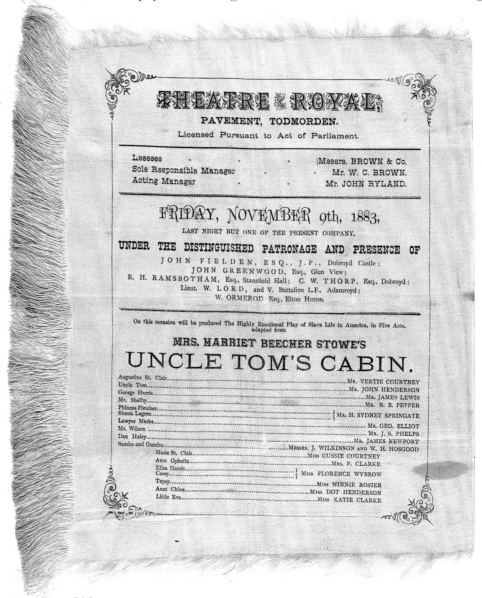

THEATRE ROYAL;

PAVEMENT, TODMORDEN.

Licensed Pursuant to Act of Parliament.

Lessees	Messrs. BROWN & Co.
Sole Responsible Manager	Mr. W. C. BROWN.
Acting Manager	Mr. JOHN RYLAND.

FRIDAY, NOVEMBER 9th, 1883,

LAST NIGHT BUT ONE OF THE PRESENT COMPANY,

UNDER THE DISTINGUISHED PATRONAGE AND PRESENCE OF

JOHN FIELDEN, ESQ., J.P., Dobroyd Castle;
JOHN GREENWOOD, Esq., Glen View;
R. H. RAMSBOTHAM, Esq., Stansfield Hall; C. W. THORP, Esq., Dobroyd;
Lieut. W. LORD, and V. Battalion L.F., Adamroyd;
W. ORMEROD Esq., Elton House.

On this occasion will be produced The Highly Emotional Play of Slave Life in America, in Five Acts, adapted from

MRS. HARRIET BEECHER STOWE'S

UNCLE TOM'S CABIN.

Augustine St. Clair	Mr. VERTIE COURTNEY
Uncle Tom	Mr. JOHN HENDERSON
George Harris	Mr. JAMES LEWIS
Mr. Shelby	Mr. R. B. PEPPER
Phineas Fletcher	
Simon Legree	} Mr. H. SYDNEY SPRINGATE
Lawyer Marks	
Mr. Wilson	Mr. GEO. ELLIOT
Dan Haley	Mr. J. S. PHELPS
	Mr. JAMES NEWPORT
Sambo and Gumbo	Messrs. J. WILKINSON AND W. H. HOSGOOD
Marie St. Clair	Miss GUSSIE COURTNEY
Aunt Ophelia	Mrs. F. CLARKE
Eliza Harris	
Cassy	} Miss FLORENCE WYBROW
Topsy	Miss MINNIE ROSIER
Aunt Chloe	Miss DOT HENDERSON
Little Eva	Miss KATIE CLARKE

Waterside.

January 31st 1887.

Dear Richard Ramsbotham,

Engage this lad, if you
think he is suitable, after having
seen him. —

Yours Truly

John Fielden.

—"—

To have 5/6 p: week to begin with.
J.F.

Feby 1/87 -

Engaged him on the above named
terms — as he seems to be a likely sort
of boy.

poor writing

3 Raglan Street.
Todmorden.

January 28th 1887.

To Messrs Fielden Bros.

Sirs.

Having heard,
you were in want of an office.
boy, I beg to apply for the situation.
I am 15 years of age, and passed
the 5th standard two years ago.
Since that time I have been
employed at Messrs Lord Bros sizing
and warp dressing room, If
you could give me a favourable
consideration, I would do my
utmost to give satisfaction in
whatever duties I had to perform.

Yours Obediently.

John William Greenwood,

from the proceeds of Grimston shoots, pheasants, rabbits and the like. Although he was warmly received on his visits the town probably begrudged the fact that it saw less of him; he had to remind them on one occasion that 'whenever I am at home, I am at Todmorden.' There were sharp comments that in 1887, for instance, on the occasion of the Queen's Jubilee he gave land for a school in Tadcaster but nothing to mark the occasion in Todmorden.

He had however continued to invest in Todmorden property, rounding off his Langfield estate in Lumbutts, and in a period of bad trade in 1882 building a road to Cragg Vale over the moor. At his own expense, some £4,000, he had employed Gibson to build a school in Lumbutts, opened in 1878. His property investments were mixed; the farms and houses on what was now the Dobroyd estate were well-let, often to wealthy tenants like the millowners Peter Ormerod and Caleb Hoyle; Friths Mill, an old cotton spinning place, was let with greater difficulty, for some years as a brewery until, in 1878, a rising local firm, Luke Barker and Sons bought it, built weaving sheds and turned it into a substantial cotton manufacturing mill. John could not resist bargains when Todmorden mills, shops or cottages came onto the market in periods of depressed trade. Thus in 1876 he bought Lineholme Mill and its

Applying for work at Waterside. The letters speak for themselves. J. W. Greenwood eventually became manager at Robinwood but proved inadequate and was replaced in 1908 by John Midgley from Lumbutts.

213

machinery, and twenty-eight cottages in the Lineholme area for £5,600, but that became an encumbrance. He bought well in York Street in the town centre in 1878 but in the same year he paid £7,450 for Hollins Mill buying from a bankrupt concern; that was not so far-sighted and the mill could not find tenants until 1890 and then at rents as low as £200 per year; the property was eventually sold, after John's death, for £2,400. John also bought property in Cheetham Hill, Manchester, probably on the initiative of his wife who was living there prior to their

(Above)
Hollins Bottom Mill was one of John Fielden's bad investments; he bought it at auction in 1878, the owners being in bankruptcy, but as the cotton trade continued to struggle, he could not find tenants for many years and then only at a low rent. The mill still stands.

John Fielden became High Sheriff of Yorkshire in 1885, regarded as a very proud honour. Here he is seated in his coach, having spared no expense to get the turn out right. His irascible brother, Sam, impatient with the Todmorden Local Board, said in public that John 'was so exhausted by his duties as High Sheriff, that he had fallen asleep as Chairman of the Local Board.'

marriage: he had inherited the Wellfield estate nearby on the death of his uncle Thomas in 1869.

Perhaps for many the greatest moment came when John was made High Sheriff of Yorkshire in 1885. In Todmorden this was regarded as a dignified honour indeed, not merely to its senior citizen but to the town itself. To mark the occasion a grand pageant based on the story of Robin Hood was staged at Grimston in September, 'a magnificent spectacular display' as it was described, with many well known county families participating and enjoying John's indoor and outdoor hospitality. This was repeated on three days before many thousands of visitors, all at the expense of the new High Sheriff. Brother Sam did not approve: 'John,' he said in Todmorden, 'was so exhausted by his duties as High Sheriff, that he had fallen asleep as Chairman of the Local Board.' Given his prominence, name and wealth, and once he became known as a Conservative, John Fielden had many invitations to stand for Parliament, which he always declined. He knew that was not his scene; he enjoyed the platform but as a diffident courteous chairman and never as a public speaker.

With his investments in property, the improvements to his Todmorden and Grimston estates, the purchase of art and furnishings for his homes, and his grand lifestyle generally, John spent freely. On his death the contents of two homes were valued at £14,169. Between 1866 and 1879 his drawings from Fielden Brothers were no less than £666,000; philanthropy in Todmorden accounted for not more than £30,000 of

A Grimston Park Wedding. John Fielden and his second wife Ellen sit, surrounded by their tenants, estate workers and friends and family of their agent, Edmund Harrison, at his wedding in October 1889. This was the kind of occasion John would enjoy. His nephew Thomas and his wife Martie, who became owners of Grimston on John's death are also in the photograph, as is Uncle Billy (W.C. Booth) who had married John's sister Ellen in 1862, (she died in 1864).

John Fielden, crippled by a kick from a horse in 1873, subsequently walked with difficulty with a stick and was usually in a wheel-chair.

Kirkby Wharfe Church at the edge of the Grimston Park.

this. In the following decade to 1889 his drawings were £196,000. Throughout this period, like his brothers, he was receiving substantial railway dividends which partly offset these drawings, but on balance he took £675,000 out of the Partnership in the period.

Increasingly feeble in his last years, John died in Todmorden at Dobroyd in July 1893, aged 71. The eulogies were obsequious and extravagant: 'let us call him by the highest title that gratitude and admiration can suggest,' said the Todmorden Almanac, he was 'one of the brightest and best the world ever knew — one who worked hard to amass wealth that he might be a father to the people by whom he was surrounded. He leaves behind him the enviable reputation of a thoroughly good man, loyal, chivalrous, unaggressive; all snobbery, affectation, vanity and mere show were abhorrent to his refined nature.' It was his modesty, geniality and approachability rather than his generosity that probably most commended him and accounted for his popularity. His personal giving to the local institutions and causes he favoured was typically modest: £62 to Lumbutts Chapel, £76 to the Parish Church organ, £61 to pay off the Musical Society debt. Yet he, more than his brothers, got most of the credit for Fielden philanthropy to the town; he was the most highly regarded because he was the most human, the most visible. The more the town feared or hated Black Sam, the more they loved his friendly unassuming brother who was 'rich but not dictatorial, influential yet respectful of the opinions of the most insignificant, never ill-natured or malevolent.' In contrast to the death of Sam, the town now went into deep mourning. To its sadness, or that of the local elite, John had decided, probably to please his wife, that he wanted to be buried in Grimston rather than 'among his own people,' in Todmorden, the place of his birth, where he had said he was 'at home,' and with his brothers. On the day of the funeral, as the coffin moved to the railway, 'everyone turned out to do honour to the dead,' 'anxious faces full of grief' lined the route; this was for the townspeople 'a moment of sore strain,' when 'only lamentation was the occupation of the crowds.' So the train with his coffin made its way down the valley and Todmorden lost its favourite son. John Fielden's grave, and that of his second wife, are in Kirkby Wharfe church, near Grimston, along with those of members of her family, as well as other Fieldens of subsequent generations who lived at Grimston. In Todmorden, apart from the plaque in the Unitarian Church, a stone cross erected in St Mary's churchyard, a stained glass window in the chancel, and the bold outline of Dobroyd Castle above the town, are his monuments.

John Fielden left a personal estate of approximately £476,000, mainly in railway and other stocks and shares including his shares in Fielden Brothers Ltd; additionally his share in the Pernambuco Gas Company was valued at £75,000. His real estate, at Grimston, in Todmorden and in Manchester was also about £280,000, a very substantial sum although its probate value at his death was much less than its cost.[30] Duties paid were no more than £20,256. His wife was very well provided for, a lifetime interest in Dobroyd Castle, £70,000 and an annuity of £4,000 yearly. She lived at the Castle until her death in 1909. Unoccupied, save for a caretaker, and hard to let, it was then valued only at £3,825 and

The Graves at Kirkby Wharfe Church. John Fielden, although he died at Dobroyd in 1893, chose to be buried at Grimston, to the disappointment of many in Todmorden which he had said was his home. He had become an Anglican, influenced by his wife, and he probably thought that he would cause less offence by being buried at Kirkby Wharfe, rather than the Anglican church in Todmorden which would certainly have offended the Unitarians there. His second wife, Ellen, and some of her Mallinson family are also buried here, as are Thomas Fielden (1854-1897), who inherited Grimston from his Uncle John, and his family.

(Below)
Mrs Ellen Fielden (nee Mallinson), John Fielden's redoubtable second wife, was well provided for on his death in 1893. She continued to live at Dobroyd Castle until her own death in 1909; thereafter the Castle was only used occasionally.

when it was eventually sold out of the family in 1942 it realised £10,000. Grimston went to Joshua's eldest son, Thomas, as had been planned for many years. The Dobroyd estate and other Todmorden properties would eventually pass to Tom's brother Edward; the Lumbutts mills, farms, and cottages also passed to Thomas, while Joshua's other two sons, Joshua and Harold received the Crumpsall estate and minor Langfield properties respectively. Thomas and Edward were to share the interests John had retained in former assets of Fielden Brothers, namely Pernambuco Gas and London Bridge land. Significantly, John's shares in Fielden Brothers Limited were distributed among Joshua's eleven children.

From his personal estate, John left substantial legacies to all Joshua's sons and daughters (the sons got £20,000 each, the daughters £10,000), to his surviving sister Mary, the widow of John Cobbett, and to the Brocklehurst children of his sister Ann, including Ernest and Constance whom he had brought up, and to the Booth daughters of his sister Ellen. He left smaller legacies to other relatives and friends and sums ranging from £500 to £150 to long-serving managers at Fielden Brothers. The sister and brother of his late wife Ruth received £300 each. Fifteen servants at Grimston and Dobroyd were also remembered. Nothing went to charity.

(*Top*)
Joshua Fielden about the time of his election to Parliament in 1868. At the time he was still living in Stansfield Hall in Todmorden, but in 1872 moved with his large family to Nutfield Priory in Surrey, hiring a special train for the purpose.

(*Above*)
Ellen Fielden, about 1870. Her thirteenth child, a son, Harold, had been born in 1868. In a birthday message to his wife at the time, Joshua quoted Proverbs to his wife: 'many daughters have done virtuously but thou excellest them all.'

Joshua and his family

Although he was active, Joshua was unfulfilled by the dull routine of Todmorden, life at the mill, the petty affairs of the town. Given his ample wealth he could break away. Throughout the early 1860s his thoughts turned to wider horizons, in fact to Parliament and to what he termed 'the work of the nation'. He never missed an opportunity to find a platform and exercise his public speaking skills with long carefully prepared speeches. At Unitarian meetings, at the Local Board, or at the Mechanics Institute he had, for the most part, respectful audiences, even when his tone was patronising. He did not always go down well. Lancashire's attitude to the American Civil War was staunchly in favour of the North, and against slavery: Samuel probably held that view, Joshua not. A public meeting on 6 June 1863 gave him the opportunity to make his position clear. To him the war was not worth pursuing: the North was seeking 'territory aggrandisement and power', and a stalemate would result. His views were not well received and he gave offence by referring to many in his audience as 'poor wretches.' An anonymous response in the local press followed: 'Mr Fielden — our rude manufacturer — has so short a time been accustomed to his wealth and has so recently thrust himself into his honours that he does not know how to use them. ....he will learn better than to insult working men for their poverty and for holding unpopular opinions.'

Joshua had the wealth, the local position and above all the name that would assist his political ambition. Perhaps he felt he needed to associate himself with a national issue to acquire a wider prominence; his father had done that out of deep conviction with the Anti-Poor Law campaign and the Ten Hours Movement. In 1859 at a time when many successful cotton-men were joining the Lancashire Reform Union, he committed himself publicly to what had been his father's radical position on widening the franchise. But the issue he chose to pursue most vigorously was repeal of the malt tax, in effect the tax on beer. He wrote pamphlets and made many speeches on the subject. It was hardly a momentous issue, not comparable to Ten Hours, and it was not one that attracted support from social reformers. In April 1864 Joshua arranged a large meeting in Todmorden on the malt tax, getting brother Sam to chair it; he spoke at length but roused the local clergy to oppose him; given the levels of drunkenness, they and others were not likely to favour a proposal that would cheapen the price of beer. Joshua was commended for his braveness but told that 'brave men are not always the wisest.' In February 1865 he joined a deputation to the Chancellor on the subject and was described as 'the most elaborate of the speakers,' speaking again 'in an eloquent and flowery manner' at a large public meeting on the subject in London. He attracted the attention of *The Times* which found his arguments 'quite disgraceful.'

The General Election of 1868 was to provide Joshua with his opportunity to break into national life. His malt tax campaigning may have attracted attention but in seeking a candidate the conservative gentry of the Eastern Division of the West Riding were probably more attracted by his wealth and above all the Fielden name. Described by his sponsors as 'able, straight-forward and thoroughly English,' he was persuaded to run as a Conservative, although he admitted 'never having been one,' and adopted in July 1868. He subsequently fought a vigorous campaign, giving his long, forceful speeches throughout the constituency. Opposition to disestablishment of the Irish Church, repeal of the malt tax, and resistance to central government taking powers from local authorities, were his main themes. He enjoyed the platform and the controversy, not least rebutting the conflict between his Conservative candidature and the radical politics of his father. Thus, he repeated his strong support for the wider franchise, as was 'justly due to working people,' there being 'nothing to fear by adopting such a course.' He was attacked as a dissenter who nonetheless favoured the union of church and state, a Radical yet an admirer of Mr Disraeli, as a former Chartist (his father had supported the Charter), and as a Unitarian and non-believer in the divinity of Christ. He was prickly and sensitive, taking affront at remarks by C.B. Dennison, the other Conservative candidate 'who lacked the manner and courtesy of a gentleman', and in an unguarded moment had described Joshua as 'a parrot that was a beggar to talk.' At one stage Joshua threatened withdrawal. He was finally elected in December 1868 with a narrow majority of 88 votes over his nearest Liberal opponent, Isaac Holden, the Bradford wool-comber. On his return to Todmorden, although this was not within the constituency, there was great rejoicing. Todmorden itself felt honoured by the election of one of its principal sons whom, given its memory of Honest John, the town now chose to regard as a Tory Radical.

Following his election, while absent for much of the year, Joshua did not at first leave the town. His family was completed with the birth of his youngest son, Harold, in 1868. Sadly in 1865 his first daughter Ann and his oldest son, John or Johnny, both died, the latter from an accident at his school in Lancaster; they were buried in a simple grave close to that of their grandfather at the old Unitarian chapel. The large family — in 1868 four boys and seven daughters — were close and happy, and Joshua was a caring and affectionate father, although strict in admonishing and punishing. This, of course, was now a very large household; in 1871 Stansfield Hall had a governess, three nurses, a butler, two footmen, a housekeeper and eight maids, a coachman and groom, making a total of eighteen servants in addition to the family. They amused themselves by various activities, not least musical evenings when the children would sing, recite, play the piano or the fiddle, and act small plays. All would go regularly to the Unitarian Church where Ellen, in particular, was appreciated for her attractive and gracious personality and tranquil influence. The family filled two pews in both the old chapel and new church. The boys had ponies and would ride round the mills or Fielden farms with their father; they all became good horsemen. In winter, skating on mill dams was a regular pastime. As they grew older they would join their uncles and family friends at Higher House Moor on the Twelfth; in 1871, for instance, young Thomas shot six brace as part of a large party that got eighty brace before lunch. They would be familiar figures in Todmorden until they went away to school. There were regular visits to Macclesfield. Ellen had remained close to her sister

Mabel Fielden, born in 1858, with her governess, Miss Aspinall.

(Right)
A class at Wellington College in Berkshire, founded by the Prince Consort and highly fashionable at the time, where Joshua Fielden sent three of his sons.

(Previous page — top)
Young Thomas Fielden, aged about ten, in 1864.

(Centre)
Una, or Ellen Unett, the oldest surviving daughter of Joshua and Ellen Fielden. Something of a favourite as a child, and the centre of everyone's affections thereafter, she remained unmarried and died, aged a hundred, in 1956.

(Bottom)
Edward Fielden, born in 1857, with his mother.

Martha who had married Charles Phillips MD in 1860; in 1865 Joshua encouraged Phillips to move to London to pursue his career which he did successfully, becoming family doctor to Joshua's household.[31] Three of the Fielden boys, Thomas, Edward and eventually Harold, after Field House preparatory school, near Brighton, were to go to Wellington College in Berkshire, newly established and still developing its facilities but, with its patrons drawn from the Royal Family, the Church and the Aristocracy, fashionable and prestigious at the time, although leaning to the military rather than the manufacturing connection for its pupils. No record survives of the girls education.

As Joshua's active interest in the business or in the affairs of the town diminished, residence in Todmorden lost its appeal. It was inconvenient and scarcely fashionable for a man of his wealth and ambition. He began looking for a suitable place in the south. Nutfield Priory, in the Surrey heathlands close to Reigate, was near to the Pickersgill's country place at Netherne and they may have drawn the property to Joshua's attention. The house had been built between 1855 and 1857 for Henry Gurney, partner in Overend, Gurney and Co., and became available following the dramatic failure of that bank. It stood on a splendid hillside site in an adequate park, and with tenanted farms the estate extended to 328 acres. In April 1870 he took the whole family down to Surrey to look round their prospective home; a special train of twelve coaches with boxes for the ponies was commissioned for the purpose. Joshua probably paid about £40,000 for the property in September 1870; he immediately commissioned John Gibson to rebuild the house on a much larger scale, to provide thirty bedrooms, seven bathrooms, schoolroom, nursery, billiard room, conservatory and the like. Elaborate interior decoration and expensive materials suited Joshua's flamboyant taste; a particular feature was the grand staircase flowing down to the Great Hall with its organ, minstrel gallery and huge stained window, almost a memorial, whose scenes reminded the household and visitors of the family association with the cotton industry, the Ten Hours Act and

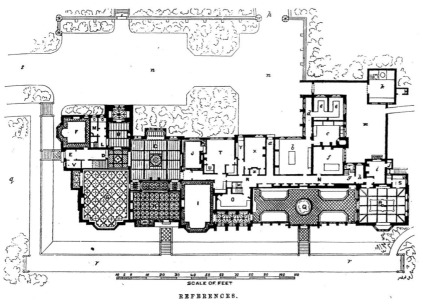

Plan of Nutfield Priory, as
enlarged and rebuilt by John
Gibson after 1870. The plan
shows the ground floor.
There were thirty bedrooms
and seven bathrooms on the
first floor.

(Below)
The Hall at Nutfield Priory.
Whatever impression was
made, visitors were strongly
reminded of the Fielden
heritage by the stained glass
window.

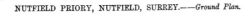

SCALE OF FEET

REFERENCES.

A. Entrance-porch.
B. Vestibule.
C. Hall.
D. Principal staircase.
E. Garden entrance.
F. Boudoir.
G. Drawing-room.
H. Library.
I. Dining-room.
J. Own room.
K. Safe.
L. Servants' stairs from basement (to open front door).

M. Lavatory, &c.
N. Corridor.
O. Gun-room.
P. Groined cloisters.
Q. Old conservatory (re-arranged).
R. Billiard-room.
S. Lavatory, &c.
T. Butler's pantry.
U. Glass.
V. Hats, &c.
W. Servants' stairs.
X. Housekeeper's room.

Y. Stores.
Z. Lift.

a. Servants' entrance.
b. Kitchen.
c. Scullery.
d. Passage.
e. Larders.
f. Servants' hall.
g. Men-servants' stairs.

h. Entrance.
i. Knives and boots.
j. Men's W.C.
k. Brewhouse and washhouse.
l. Steps to vaults.
m. Courtyard.
n. Entrance courtyard.
o. Steps to high ground.
p. Back road.
q. Croquet-ground.
r. Terrace and flower-garden.
s. Principal entrance (roadway).

NUTFIELD PRIORY, NUTFIELD, SURREY.——*Ground Plan.*

Honest John. Pevsner described the house as 'dull and mechanical', and with its prominent tower, 'an elephantine pile'; to Lionel Fielden it was 'extremely hideous'; Girouard found it 'big and charmless.' The local press at the time, however, took a different view, opining 'altogether the seat is quite a Paradise,' and Girouard had to admit the setting was superb with an immense view from the terrace over a lake and woods, planted with 'every rare tree' that Joshua could find. Adding the cost of rebuilding and furnishing to the purchase price, Nutfield was a major outlay; Joshua's drawings from the Partnership between 1871 and 1873 were £108,000. He moved in at Christmas 1872 and his family were to remain there for another fifty years.[32]

Meanwhile Joshua also rented a place in town, at least for the parliamentary session. For many years this was in Queen's Gate, South Kensington, and later in Grosvenor Square in Mayfair. He was a member of the House of Commons during the period in parliamentary history dominated by Gladstone and Disraeli at the height of their powers. He was not inhibited in parliament; in his frequent interventions he was probably regarded as precocious and over-persistent. He followed Disraeli on one occasion, and on others he was followed by Gladstone, who charged Joshua with misquoting him and referred disparagingly to his youth. On a number of occasions he moved the adjournment of the House or postponement of a Bill but his motions were as a rule lost by large majorities. He caught the derisory attention of the press in 1870, not least when he criticised a proposal to reduce the stamp duties on newspapers. 'His greatness has not attracted the attention it deserves' said one critic, 'we have a leader whose lofty intellect and acute perceptions may bring us happily to the path in which we should walk and refine and elevate our tastes to his own sublime standard. Perhaps by and by we shall find this modern Joshua ordering the sun to stand still on Todmorden and the moon on the valley of Hebden Bridge.'[33]

Although Joshua spoke on a variety of issues, his major concerns were the Poor Law and the malt tax; on these he seems to have made virtually the same speech on several occasions in his first few years, attracting little support. His parliamentary career did not flourish; in the election of 1874 he was returned with a larger majority of 792, but he received no recognition in Disraeli's Conservative government. Thereafter he was much quieter, speaking only rarely.

His visits to Todmorden, once he left Stansfield Hall, had become less frequent although he continued to preside at the annual meetings of the Mechanics Institute until it closed. In December 1871 he presided at the first meeting of the Todmorden Working Mens Conservative Association where he was joined by other prominent Conservatives in the town, members of its elite. On this occasion he described himself as 'a public man, a person of position and property and independence': that was probably a fair description of how he saw himself. His last big occasion in Todmorden was the opening of the Town Hall when he led for the family and performed well before a large audience. He spoke again 'very earnestly and at great length' as President of the Conservative Working Mens Association in January 1876 when he urged the town's working men 'to improve their minds.' But he was losing touch with the town and with Fielden Brothers; the fact that the firm was not doing very well was an additional source of worry. To cap it all, his health, hitherto regarded as very robust, was giving cause for concern; in August 1876 the Todmorden press described him as 'very seriously ill for some months.' He was much better by the end of the year and spent the winter in Cannes. With failing health, and his ambitions unrealised, the years after 1875 must have been difficult and disappointing. Appropriately, after speaking only once in 1876 and not at all in 1877, his last speech in parliament was in February 1878 on the Factories Bill; he was then able to remind the House that after his father's successful campaign to restrict the hours of labour, the factory towns had enjoyed more prosperous times, 'the masters having made larger profits and the workmen having been better off, enjoying more leisure and better health and higher wages than ever before.'[34]

There were family occasions that gave him pride. His eldest surviving son Thomas, down from a brief undemanding spell at Trinity College, Cambridge following Wellington, was given a splendid twenty-first birthday at Nutfield in 1875, with many visitors, parties and feasts for servants and tenants, and appropriate speeches. He then made a trip round the world at a cost of £987, setting an example which became part of a young Fielden's education thereafter. In 1878 Tom was to marry Martha Knowles, second daughter of Thomas Knowles, who had been elected Conservative MP for Wigan in 1874. Knowles, like Joshua, had accumulated great wealth, in his case as a colliery proprietor as well as a cotton spinner; he was chairman of the Mining Association, where he resisted as 'a revolutionary measure' proposals to make employers liable to compensate workmen for injury. The two became friends in much the same way as John Fielden and John Brocklehurst in 1832. Tom and Martha were married in style (following their Uncle John) at St George's Hanover Square; the couple then went to live at Stansfield Hall where the intention was that Tom would become the first of the fourth generation to join Fielden Brothers. Children quickly followed, with two daughters and a son, John, born at Stansfield Hall by the end of 1880. Tom's income in 1879 was £2,824 including £1,528 from Joshua, £500 from Thomas Knowles and £787 railway dividends; his outgoings were £1,677 and he put the balance, £1,147, in a private account with the Partnership.

Although he was active in the town during the few years he lived there Tom did not take to the routine of Todmorden life and by the end of 1881 he was renting Stockeld Park, near Wetherby, where farm management (buying cows, lambing ewes and experimenting with incubators to hatch chicks) and the pleasures of hunting and shooting, the activities of the volunteers, large family parties, as well as his several young children, kept him busy over the next several years. Tom, a confident outgoing friendly person, clearly got on well with the local county families. When rent day approached in April 1884 he wrote to his father reminding him about the quarterly cheque and reporting with regard to Joshua's grandchildren, that 'all the chicks are flourishing.' Stockeld was not far from Grimston Park and Tom and his wife were frequent visitors there for shooting and social events. The logic of

(Top)
Thomas Fielden, about the time of his marriage to Martha Knowles in 1878.

(Above)
Martha Knowles, or Martie, as her family knew her. Daughter of Thomas Knowles, wealthy colliery proprietor and MP for Wigan, she met Thomas through her father's friendship with Joshua Fielden.

Stockeld Park near Wetherby in West Yorkshire. Thomas and Martha Knowles lived in Todmorden after their marriage in 1878 but decided they did not like the place or, for Thomas, the routine of the mill. They rented the Stockeld estate in 1881, and raised their family there, with Thomas deeply involved in farm management, hunting and shooting.

moving to Stockeld was clearly the understanding that in due course he would inherit Grimston from his childless Uncle John. In 1886 Stockeld was bought by Robert Foster of the Queensbury family that had lost Grimston to John Fielden's higher bid in 1872, and Tom and his family moved to Walton House in nearby Boston Spa. Tom also took a lodge at Amulree in Perthshire where the Knowles family had a large grouse moor. This was the place where each August for many years from 1883 he took his growing family and where he was joined by his brothers and friends, to enjoy excellent shooting and fishing, deer-stalking and the like.

Joshua did not encourage his son to remain involved with the family firm. Indeed the two seemed to have influenced each other, possibly sharing the view that the business was going downhill. It must have been that concern, as well as absence from Todmorden and the state of his health, that prompted Joshua to withdraw from Fielden Brothers in October 1879; having withdrawn £269,000 on balance between 1865 and 1879, his share in the Partnership was then only £115,000, which he took out mainly in the form of mortgage loans made by the Fieldens to the Watts and others. By that time too it was clear his parliamentary career had failed. Family apart, he must have been bored for there is little evidence of other involvements, political, business or intellectual. In 1876 he was elected to the Royal Thames Yacht Club renting a yacht, the *Helen,* to sail the Channel; in 1877, after illness, he took a Mediterranean cruise. The following year he purchased the steam yacht *Zingara* for £15,000. This huge ship, 186 feet long and weighing 450 tons, was to be another source of expense; in 1879, for instance, yacht expenses were £5,438, and subsequently not less than £3,000 a year, for crew, fuel, supplies, repairs. Once the novelty of ownership and sailing had worn off, the yacht was a doubtful asset. There are records of trips with family and friends (John Gibson and William Pickersgill joined them on occasions), along the south coast, and round the Mediterranean. But Ellen did not like the yacht, preferring to travel overland to meet her husband in the South of France; Joshua's own interest faded and the yacht was sold in 1882, for £10,200. A villa at Beaulieu, near Nice, was then purchased for £30,000; Joshua and his wife were to spend winters there regularly for the rest of his life.

Joshua's brothers had been concerned at his extravagance and the high level of his drawings from the Partnership. When he withdrew in 1879 he promised not to become a borrower from Fielden Brothers. Once he had settled at Nutfield, his annual outgoings seem to have varied between £20,000 and £30,000 a year, An account which survives for January — June 1883 shows personal and household expenditure of £6,775 (housekeeping £2,409, stables £414, gardens £1,013, wife and children £1,862, travel £707); extensions at Nutfield and purchases of works of art (a Constable was bought for £945) as well as expenditure at Beaulieu took the total to £11,346. In the second half of the year he spent £16,060, including the purchase of further property at Nutfield. He had not the income to sustain regular spending quite on this scale. Interest on his mortgage loans and rents from property in Todmorden and Lancashire (Middleton Towers and other estates inherited from Uncle Thomas) and from the London Bridge estate were about £4,000 in 1883 and railway share dividends reached £16,100. The balance was met by repayment of mortgage loans and over the year Joshua was able to add to his railway share-holding which by then was close to £400,000.[35]

Photographed by Lock & Whitfield.
Copyright.
178, REGENT ST LONDON, · 109, KING'S ROAD, BRIGHTON.
Printed by the Woodbury Mechanical Process.

Joshua Fielden, about 1880 when he retired from Parliament and withdrew from the Fielden Brothers Partnership.

Self regard and vanity had always been characteristic of Joshua; as he grew older he became increasingly proud, and quick to take offence. He seems to have fallen out with the leading personalities in his constituency, primarily over the sharing of 1874 election expenses with his fellow candidate, a dispute that dragged on for years afterwards. Be that as it may, he stood down at the 1880 election, probably wisely since the Liberals won large majorities in his constituency, and that was the end of his parliamentary career. Perhaps there was some flickering of interest a few years later in 1884, when the name Fielden was again mentioned as a possibility in the Barkston Ash constituency and more especially in the Northern Division of the West Riding , the Bradford area, which had a large Liberal majority. Those approaching him were flattering — the Fielden name was 'a household word' — but pointed out that the expenses of an election would be £2-3,000. Joshua made it clear he was interested only in a winnable seat. His proud and touchy response to approaches at the time, both from Barkston Ash, Bradford and also North East Lancs, stifled them.

After 1880, with failing health and disappointed expectations Joshua's life was mostly downhill. He and Ellen now spent long periods in the South of France. Brighton and Torquay were other favourite resorts. There were infrequent visits to Todmorden, and 'the happy valley' as he described it, notably in June 1884 when Joshua addressed his 'old friends,' namely a large Unitarian meeting commemorating their 60th Anniversary. He kept in touch with the Church there, sending modest

annual contributions. He became interested in the history of the Fielden family, commissioning Fishwick to research the genealogy, briefing the author of the account in *Fortunes Made in Business,* and starting, if not completing, his own account of his father's life. There is little evidence that he had much to do with his brothers, but the marriage of his daughter Mabel to Charles Pilkington, the fifth son of Richard Pilkington, co-founder of Pilkington Brothers, St Helens in May 1884, was an opportunity for a grand family occasion at Nutfield. The two had probably met at a Knowles family function in Cheshire. All the Fieldens came to the wedding, including Sam and Sarah, John and his wife, and many other friends including the Pickersgills and Gibson. A servants ball to which local tradesmen were invited rounded off the occasion.

Mabel was the only one of Joshua's seven daughters to marry during his lifetime. His own career disappointments may have been assuaged when his son Tom was successful in winning the Middleton Parliamentary seat at the second attempt in the General Election of July 1886 standing as a Conservative. The large constituency included that part of Todmorden that was in Lancashire, as well as manufacturing villages around Rochdale and Oldham. It was a marginal seat but one where the Fielden name in particular must have been worth many votes. When he first ran in 1885, when he lost narrowly, Tom probably knew little about politics nor was he a practised public speaker, but he had a straight-forward honest style and a genial hearty approachable manner with the gift of making friends. His father supported him on the platform in Todmorden both in 1885 and 1886, although he was not well-received. Tom and his wife Martie were tireless in becoming known in the constituency; at his second election he had a majority of 318 votes. Following Tom's election Joshua made his last public appearance, addressing a large enthusiastic victory meeting in Rochdale.

If Thomas was well established, Joshua's other sons had not entirely secured their careers by 1887 when their father died. His second son, Edward or Ted, frail as a boy, after Field House and Wellington, studied in France briefly and visited the United States, crossing the continent in 1878. An account of his trip survives: the Atlantic crossing took only eight days; after New York he sailed to Albany, visited Niagara and took the train to Chicago where he visited the stock-yards. He then spent six days crossing the Great Plains, the Rockies and the Sierras on uncomfortable trains to reach San Francisco, quite an adventure at the time; the record does not describe his return journey. He then took indentures with a leading Chartered Civil Engineer, Sir John Hawkshaw, and in 1881 was working hard on drainage and flood control in the Severn estuary, living in lodgings in Corsham near Bristol. His father had given him an allowance and he was able to buy a horse and hire a groom, and hunted regularly in November and December 1881, and again in January from Stockeld. He was a regular visitor to Stockeld where he met Martie's sister Mary Ellen, and later her parents, Mr and Mrs Knowles. 1882 was an active year, with work at Bristol on the one hand and regular visits to Yorkshire, to London, to Macclesfield, to the Knowles home at Darnhall in Cheshire and to Nutfield, taking in Henley Regatta,

Goodwood, Cowes on his father's yacht, Lords, Todmorden for the Twelfth when seventy-six brace were shot at Higher House, the St Leger, to name the most prominent events. At the end of the year, having qualified as MICE, he joined the Thames Conservancy as Assistant Engineer at a salary of £150 per year and took lodgings in Oxford. His work did not interfere with another active social year, 1883, beginning with a huge Knowles family party centred on the Grand National in March. In August he spent two weeks at Amulree and in November began serious hunting with the South Oxfordshire.

In May 1884 he became engaged to Mary Ellen Knowles whom he married at Winsford, Cheshire on 30th September. The other Knowles daughter, Elizabeth, had married John Harwood Banner, a successful Liverpool businessman and politician; Banner gave Mary away and the two sisters and their husbands, as well as Tom and Martie, remained close thereafter. Mary inherited, in trust, a substantial sum from her father while Edward received a marriage settlement of £27,265 worth of railway shares yielding about £1,000 a year; clearly the couple were not badly off. Ted had found a house, Bury Knowle with a large park, in the attractive and fashionable village of Headington, near Oxford and moved there following his marriage. He and his wife quickly settled down and apart from his work, and the management of an adjacent farm he now bought for £4,000, Ted continued to hunt regularly with the South Oxfordshire, mix socially in the district, and involve himself in county affairs, county politics and local government. His first son, Edward Anthony was born in 1886. There was no let-up in the family visits, including Todmorden where he stayed at Dobroyd, continued to shoot on the Twelfth, and was well received when he spoke for Thomas in his election campaign. He became Master of the South Oxfordshire Hunt early in 1887, and seemed securely established there. But that was not to be. His business-like qualities became apparent in winding up his father's estate; he in particular became involved with

(Top)
Edward Fielden, a serious young man in his mid-twenties, working as a Chartered Civil Engineer with the Severn Conservancy. He had lodgings in Bristol. Later he joined the Thames Conservancy and moved to Oxford.

(Above)
Mary Ellen Knowles, younger sister of Martha Knowles, married Edward Fielden in 1884. Two sisters, both with large inheritances, had married two brothers, both with large expectations.

(Left)
Mary Ellen Fielden at Dobroyd Castle in 1888. She and her husband stayed there whenever they were in Todmorden, but their home at the time was in Headington outside Oxford.

Harold Fielden. After Wellington College and Emmanuel College Cambridge, where he did not take a degree, he joined a crack cavalry regiment, the Seventh Hussars, in 1890. He was to serve with distinction in the Boer War.

the Todmorden properties and as the year progressed, with the family firm. In 1888 as noted in Chapter 5 he committed himself to provide leadership of the Todmorden business on behalf of the fourth generation who would eventually own it.[36]

Joshua's third son, Joshua, Jossy or Jos as the family called him, born in 1865 was more of a problem. Against his father's wishes and not being fond of the classroom, he left home instead of going to Wellington and probably found work as a hunt-servant before subsequently studying to be a vet. In 1883 he was living near to Ted, hunting with the South Oxfordshire, and working in the kennels at Stadhampton. On his twentieth birthday he went round the world like his older brothers. Thereafter, until his marriage in 1894, he stayed close to Ted, attended the family occasions, and developed the passion for hunting which was to be the main interest and occupation of his life; he was a youthful master of the Fitzwilliam Hounds from 1892 to 1895.[37] Harold, the youngest son, went from Wellington to Emmanuel College, Cambridge; he was a proud young man, greatly admired by his parents and sisters. On his twenty-first in 1889 he was given £1,700 and a gold watch; a big party at Tom's town house was followed by the theatre. Later Harold committed himself to an appropriate career for a younger son of his means, namely a crack cavalry regiment, the 7th Hussars, which he eventually joined in April 1890.

Joshua had increasing bouts of illness in 1886: he died at Cannes on his sixtieth birthday in March 1887. Many of the family were there and the death was not unexpected. The body was brought back to Todmorden for a solemn and elaborate funeral at the Unitarian Church, attended only by male relatives, Fieldens and Brocklehursts, and close friends. Samuel did not attend, because of illness, although his son, John Ashton did. To the Unitarians and to many in the Fielden mills, the first death among the brothers, seemed a particularly sad event, no doubt because of their concerns about the family's involvement in the future. Samuel later sharply reprimanded the Fielden managers who had gone to great lengths to make a collection from the workpeople, to receive the coffin on its arrival in the town and place it in the church where it was surrounded by a profusion of wreaths.[38] Joshua had written a note in September 1883, expressing his wish to be buried at the south end of the Church 'at a point from which one can see Stansfield Hall through the archway under the tower.' His wishes were complied with.[39]

His will had been carefully prepared in 1883 and provided for the understanding that Thomas would eventually inherit the Grimston Estate from the childless Uncle John. Edward, accordingly, was to inherit Nutfield (subject to his mother's lifetime occupation) and Joshua's other properties in Todmorden and Lancashire went to his other sons, Joshua and Harold. Their value for probate was considerably less than their cost; Stansfield Hall, for instance was valued at only £10,675, notwithstanding the huge expenditure in 1861-63, and Nutfield at £50,700.[40] His personal estate was £503,598, principally in railway shares, and mortgage loans. After providing an annuity of £5,000 for his wife (to satisfy which £125,000 was set aside) this was distributed

Nutfield Priory,
Redhill,
Surrey.

30 Sep/83

I wish to be buried at the south end of the walk which goes in front of the Todmorden Unitarian Church at a point from which one can see Stansfield Hall through the archway under the tower.

Joshua Fielden.

To my Executors.

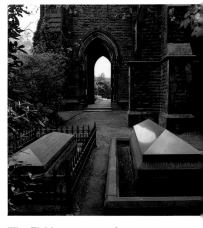

The Fielden graves at the Unitarian Church: Joshua, Samuel and Sarah.

(Left)
Joshua's burial wish, to be brought back to Todmorden, was fully respected at his solemn funeral in 1887.

among his children. Their individual shares (the sons got about £60,000 each, the daughters £20,000) may have seemed large at the time but were eroded subsequently by inflation and taxation and would not support a high lifestyle. Certainly they were subsequently to feel poor compared with their cousin John Ashton. Joshua left nothing to charity and had given very little to charity during his lifetime. Nor did he remember the Unitarian Church.

Todmorden obituaries remembered him as a politician of courage and persistence who had opposed with determination unpopular questions like the Union workhouse and who did much to bring about 'a toleration and expansion of conservative views' within the town. In particular he advanced the memory of his father, while endeavouring to establish that there was no dichotomy between his own conservative position and his father's principles. Above all the honour of a seat in Parliament gave Todmorden 'a measure of dignity that otherwise it might not have been enabled to boast.' There was talk in the town of raising a public subscription to pay for a statue which would occupy one of the niches in the Town Hall but in the end the initiative petered out. To many in the town, although not at the church or the mill, Joshua was a rather proud and self-important figure, reserved, aloof, sometimes patronising and patrician and tending to look down on those less fortunate than himself. His wife, whose portrait was hung in the Town Hall, attracted warmer feelings. Whatever his vigorous ambition and the early promise of his career, in the end he failed on the larger stage and his closing years were a disappointment, marred by ill-health and culminating in premature death. He used his wealth selfishly and extravagantly. His memory quickly faded but Stansfield Hall and the Unitarian Church in particular, stand there as reminders of his strong, if brief, presence.

The Other Joshua Fielden

The history of the third generation is mainly that of the family of John Fielden MP. But there were others: his older brother, Joshua who died in 1847, had two children; Jane who married James Ramsbotham in 1837 and eventually went to live at Crowborough Warren, the house in Sussex bought for her use by the executors of her father's estate; and John, who after his marriage to Sarah Cockcroft, went to live at Wenning Cottage and then at Greenbank, near Caton, in North Lancashire (Pages 106-107).

Joshua's children, with their properties and the income from the investments held by their father's executors, were well provided for. James and Jane Ramsbotham raised a large family at Crowborough, nine sons and two daughters. James 'a very free and affable man,' was well known and liked in Todmorden and returned there frequently. The couple kept in touch with the moneyed branch of the family, attended weddings and funerals, James shot with his wife's cousins, and so on. The Fieldens helped as they could: they gave Ramsbotham children business; share transactions went through Ramsbotham and Ross in the City, legal business through Ramsbotham and Cooke of Lincoln's Inn; a Canon Ramsbotham officiated at John Fielden's second marriage in 1877. Richard Hugh Ramsbotham, Jane's sixth son, born in 1848 and educated at Lancing and Cambridge, returned to Todmorden in 1870, and later took charge at Waterside for nearly twenty years, living at Waterside House and then at Stansfield Hall, and appearing at many public meetings as a Fielden surrogate and prominent local conservative. He married a relative of Thomas Fielden's wife, Agnes Hoyle. But he was neither dedicated or competent and he did not survive the change in ownership and control at Waterside in 1889 and thereafter left Todmorden. Some obligation was felt towards him because he received a legacy of £5,000 from the will of Samuel Fielden (his mother Jane received £10,000). The relationship with the Fieldens did not end happily; in 1890 all Jane's children, with the exception of Richard Hugh, brought an action in the High Court against the Trustees of her estate.

The case was settled out of Court, John Fielden paying £10,000 to Jane's family. Richard alone, thereafter, remained on friendly terms, living in the area and continuing to shoot with his second-cousin Edward from time to time.[41]

John Fielden, Jane's brother, had died at Caton in 1852, aged thirty-two, and was buried at Todmorden Old Church. His widow, Sarah, had the care of two small children, Mary Alice, and Joshua, born in Todmorden in 1848; they grew up, it was recalled, happily, in Caton. But the Fieldens in Todmorden, exercising their responsibilities as executors and their family concern, wanted the best for the fatherless son. That was to be Eton, a quite new departure for the family, and young Joshua went there in 1861, no doubt to make a gentleman of him. Large a departure from his simple upbringing as this must have been, and if at first he was lost and lonely, he was subsequently to recall it as a happy period. He then went to Magdalene College, Cambridge in 1867. Charles Stuart Parnell was a student of the same college from 1865; he subsequently referred to 'the sons of moneyed parvenus from the North of England' who 'tried to liken themselves to country gentlemen and succeeded in looking like stable-boys.'[42] Whether or not Joshua was regarded in this way, he was happy at Cambridge as at Eton. In 1867 his mother had remarried to John Pilkington, a cotton manufacturer, of Westhoughton near Bolton. Living with his mother and her second husband at Lostock Grange, their home, memorialised on his coming-of-age by the mill workers in Lostock, and pursuing and marrying Frances Thom, daughter of John Thom, a dye-stuff trader of Chorley, who became his wife in 1875, Joshua was well-settled. His daughter, Constance Mary, was born at Caton, in 1876.

To set up young Joshua the Fieldens had bought the Beachamwell Estate in Norfolk in 1851. It was completely alien to him. The argument was used that if Norfolk was good enough for the Prince of Wales — a reference to Sandringham — it was good enough for a Fielden. Whatever pressures eventually persuaded him to leave Lancashire were not recorded. Probably having let the estate for many years, when the squire of Beachamwell was asked to take his turn as High Sheriff in 1884, Joshua felt he had to leave Caton to live in Norfolk. He spent the rest of his life there, unhappily, for he found it an unfriendly place, flat and boring; in his loneliness he took to drink, encouraged by an unscrupulous butler. He was probably also short of money when rents from the estate began to fall. He visited Egypt in 1887 and later made a voyage on a sailing ship to Australia, taking his wife and daughter, perhaps to break his drinking habit. He eventually died at Beachamwell in 1892, a comparatively young man aged forty-four. His wife lived there for the rest of her life, eventually taking to the place, and his daughter, having married Patrick Villiers-Stuart in 1908, became a well known lady in Norfolk society, and a national authority on gardens on which she wrote extensively. If Joshua had more or less lost touch with the Fieldens and Todmorden, his daughter Constance, who was status conscious and mixed with the best families, later tried to revive the family connection. She was a regular visitor to Grimston, and to Condover in Shropshire where Edward Fielden was living after 1896;

Joshua Fielden of Beachamwell (1848-1892) half-cousin of the third generation Fielden brothers, whose father had been encouraged to leave Todmorden and for whom the Beachamwell estate in Norfolk had been bought. Obliged to live there, probably against his will, he died unhappily in 1892.

she also visited John Ashton Fielden who, close to Peterborough, was her nearest relative. But ownership of the odd farm or cottages apart, this branch of the family had moved far and permanently away from its roots in Todmorden.[43]

The Third Generation in Retrospect

Having described the lifestyles and achievements of the third generation, their careers can be reviewed, for they, more than any of the Fieldens, had wealth and power at a time and on a scale that made them stand out; the second generation was too busy making wealth to enjoy it or use it; the fourth were more ordinary members of what was by then a very large rentier class.

The three sons of John Fielden were among the richest people in mid and late-Victorian England. Theirs were among the truly great business fortunes of the period. In each case, by the 1880s, their real and personal wealth comfortably exceeded £500,000, an enormous sum then, an enormous one now, in today's equivalent, say at least £30 million. They were very rich by the standards of Lancashire and Yorkshire where individual fortunes of £100,000 were exceptional; there were not so many millionaires, or even half-millionaires, in nineteenth-century Lancashire and Yorkshire; according to one study, eleven of the former, thirty-nine of the latter.[44] Two of the three brothers were half-millionaires, the third a comfortable millionaire and in the aggregate their real and personal estates exceeded £2.7 million. Their wealth for the most part, exceeded or matched the richest of their contemporaries: Hugh Mason of Ashton who died in 1886 left £291,000; John Brocklehurst had left £800,000 in 1870; Thomas Ashton of Hyde £526,000; John Platt the machinery maker of Oldham, £800,000; John Bullough of Accrington, pioneer of the ring spindle in Lancashire, left £1,228,000 in 1891; and John Rylands, who died in 1888, left the largest cotton fortune to that time of £2,575,000. Contemporary Yorkshire fortunes included Titus Salt, £400,000, Samuel Lister of Manningham, £634,000; Francis Crossley £800,000 in 1872, and William Henry Foster of Black Dyke Mills £1,180,000 in 1884.

Although their father was also wealthy, until late in life, his lifestyle, and that of his brothers, was simple and unostentatious. His three sons did not grow up in a rich household although they had personal possessions, like horses, and opportunities to travel, which set them apart in Todmorden. But when they had made their own fortunes, by the mid-1860s, and on the death of their uncle Thomas, they were 'nouveaux riche', that is, in possession of wealth that far exceeded their family's experience. Managing, enjoying, using that wealth was for them, and those close to them, a completely new venture. It would be wrong to attribute their wealth to outstanding business enterprise. If they did not inherit more than a small part of the wealth they eventually achieved, they inherited a concern which had efficient capacity, experience and connection to benefit from the Lancashire cotton boom of the 1850s; they were helped too by the commercial skill and wisdom of Thomas Fielden. Finally, as a climax of fortune building, they made large profits from the Cotton Famine, as did many others in Lancashire. The brothers were happy to present themselves not merely as manufacturers, but as merchants, and merchants not merely of Manchester and Liverpool but of New York. They, especially Joshua, were proud of their heritage and especially their father's achievement, and concerned that along with the genealogy, it should be put on record and appropriately memorialised: it was this heritage, of course, that distinguished them from mere wealth. But unlike many others, having made their fortune, the Fieldens held onto it, did not give it back. Profitable new business enterprise eluded them, indeed was not pursued, since rentier income yielded a cash flow which not only supported free spending and philanthropy but enabled their wealth to go on increasing. In this respect, in handling their own wealth, and that of their relative's trusts for which they were executors, managing it and investing it, the Fieldens were shrewd and well-advised; they were good custodians of their own and their family's assets.

Their wealth, of course, gave the brothers complete ascendancy in Todmorden. There no one could approach their circumstances. The old gentry, John Crossley of Scaitcliffe, William Greenwood of Stones, who died in the 1860s, each left less than £6,000; James Taylor of Todmorden Hall left about £35,000 in 1872. Of those who were successful at the time in cotton manufacture and held onto their fortunes, the Ormerods, Abraham and Peter, left respectively £48,000 and £52,000; Edward Lord, senior partner in the Fielden off-shoot, Lord Brothers, was worth £80,000; and George Hinchliffe £56,000. Other sizeable Todmorden fortunes included A.G.Eastwood, long established solicitor, who probably through judicious buying and selling of property, was worth £159,000 in 1911 when he died; John Arthur Ingham, landowner and cotton manufacturer left £114,000 in 1900; and Caleb Hoyle, cotton manufacturer and first mayor, left £228,000 in 1914. But most of the local cotton manufacturers of the mid-nineteenth century who were contemporaries of the third generation Fieldens left less than £30,000, and the majority less than £10,000. And most households in the town would have little wealth and family incomes below £100 or even £50 per year.[44]

It is not difficult, accordingly, to appreciate the dominance of the Fieldens in Todmorden by the 1860s. A large part of the community, directly or indirectly, was dependent on their business success and goodwill. Deference to their wishes would be the normal condition. But the Fieldens inevitably moved away from the town and the townspeople, in body and spirit. Todmorden became dull, dirty, backward and undignified; its inhabitants, 'poor wretches,' or narrow, small-minded and 'half educated.' Joshua and his family moved completely away. John, who of all the brothers, valued his local status and the esteem and gratitude of his fellow townsman, chose to separate himself by the demonstrable ascendancy of Dobroyd Castle, and by the status of a large Yorkshire country estate which he was proud to introduce to his Todmorden people. Samuel and his wife, chose to make themselves aloof and private, and as age increased his bad temper, he was roused, on more than one occasion, to demonstrate his impatience and his contempt for the leaders of the local community. He, of the three brothers, was described as the plutocrat, perhaps unfairly, although he did at times use his name and wealth to try to impose his will on others and in doing this he did not always succeed.

The Fieldens were remembered for their philanthropy; both collective and individual. But of the three brothers only Samuel, perhaps influenced by his wife, was genuinely philanthropic: he felt some sense of duty. Compared to their wealth, the family philanthropy was modest; nor was it comparable with that of some contemporaries, notably the Crossleys in Halifax, the Ashtons or Hugh Mason in Tameside, or the widow of John Rylands in Manchester, let alone the great Victorian philanthropists such as Thomas Holloway, Samuel Morley or Josiah Mason, all successful manufacturers.[45] The philanthropy and the Fielden homes left a conspicuous and impressive mark on Todmorden which would probably have been a poor place without them. The Fielden buildings were not merely an attempt to embellish the town with family memorials, but also to augment its inadequate facilities and improve its condition. Philanthropy won gratitude at the time, but also encouraged a dependence, too great a tendency among townspeople to look to the Fieldens, to wait for the Fieldens, rather than do it themselves. And in the end there were those in the town who became resentful of Fielden giving, while the Fieldens grew tired, lost any feeling of obligation or need for social reconciliation. If philanthropy had a role, the Fieldens felt their true obligation was to give people work and livelihood, to keep their mills going; this they did and continued to do long after the third generation was gone; this, they felt they owed to Todmorden. It was their fulfilled responsibility as employers rather than as philanthropists that helped to keep Todmorden free of social or class conflict.

Philanthropy aside, the Fieldens use of their wealth was conventional. The mill towns of Lancashire and Yorkshire all featured fine mansions built for successful businessmen in the mid-Victorian period. Samuel, it has to be said, lived comfortably but in some respects, modestly. He allowed his wealth to accumulate rather than show in property and possessions but it was unfair to call him a miser. Joshua lived as did his rich contemporaries, with a fine house, beautiful furnishings and gardens, a farm, a town house and the pleasures of London, a yacht, and the south of France. He encouraged his children to enjoy these things too, and especially hunting, fishing and shooting. John was especially concerned with status and recognition. But in buying land, a large and prestigious country estate, at Grimston, he was doing no more than many of his rich contemporaries.

Although the third generation enjoyed its wealth, and gave part of it away, it was able to bequeath huge wealth to the next, the fourth generation. Such inheritance taxes as there were in the 1880s or early 1890s had trivial impact. The next generation, accordingly, could inherit a comfortable lifestyle, enjoying and expecting to enjoy the amenities of a large house and of a landed estate, and generally, to have adequate private means to live without working. Unsurprisingly, given their inheritance, public school education and upbringing, they were unlikely to want the responsibility of a failing old business in a small drab Pennine

mill-town, or the challenge of using their fortunes in new forms of enterprise. They, or many like them, have been described as 'the children of affluence, tired of the tedium of trade and flushed with the bucolic aspirations of the country gentleman.' The decline in the industrial spirit which this generation showed has attracted plenty of scholarly interest.[46] Of course, the Fielden fortune was unequally distributed, with John Ashton Fielden, inheriting a super-fortune that placed him among the richest two or three hundred in the country, and the many children of Joshua, his cousins, coming into more modest but still significant wealth. All could pursue a rentier lifestyle at the turn of the century, in a gilded high noon. It was eventually to be disturbed by many developments, inflation, taxation, death duties, the fall in the income from assets such as land or railway shareholdings, the fall in the value of the assets themselves. The story of the fourth generation is that of a generation that saw the secure, serene world of its youth and early middle-age disappear, and that struggled to maintain its lifestyle, or even appearances, and to keep the values and conventions that became threatened on all sides. But that is not how the future seemed in 1890.

The Fourth Generation of the Fielden Family, mainly the eleven surviving children of Joshua and Ellen Fielden, all born at Stansfield Hall, are brought together in this group photograph at Nutfield, probably on the marriage of Kate Fielden to Herbert Stone in 1891. Ellen Fielden sits with her seven daughters of whom at the time three were married: Edith (MacLeod), Mabel (Pilkington), and Kate (Stone) are together at the front. The eldest daughter Una, who never married, sits next to her mother. The three older sons are recognisable at the rear, Thomas (with his wife Martie), Edward and Joshua, while the youngest son, Harold, stands near his mother in the centre. The group also includes the husbands of the three married daughters, Herbert Stone, Charles Pilkington and John MacLeod. John Ashton Fielden stands on the right behind MacLeod and in front of Joshua. The elderly gentleman on the left is Francis Dicken Brocklehurst, older brother of Ellen; she was aged sixty at the time.

235

INDIAN SUMMER
Fielden Brothers Limited 1889-1939

The New Company

Before committing himself to become chairman of the new limited company with its Todmorden manufacturing and Manchester commercial operations, Edward Fielden had been able to take stock of the old concern in 1887 and 1888. His involvement coincided with the death of the long-serving mill manager, John Howarth, and his replacement by the younger Thomas Wrigley, a member of the wider family, also a lifetime employee, and most recently in charge of Robinwood. The two new men seem to have prepared some ambitious plans between 1888 and 1889 to restructure and modernise the business, including a complete rebuilding of Waterside with a new spinning mill, and enlarged weaving operations. Samuel Fielden, curbed this enthusiasm, while admitting that changes were needed. 'The old concern may be rotten and require a thorough overhauling to get it right,' he wrote in July 1888, 'and a radical change in the system in which the business is conducted is an absolute sine qua non,' but, he warned, 'it is easier to be fault-finders then fault-menders.' What did come out of these plans was the replacement of the old engines at Waterside with two large modern steam-engines christened *Sam* and *John;* these were to be commissioned in November 1889.

Within a few weeks of the incorporation of the new company, in October 1889, Samuel died. Of his eighty-one shares, sixty-one passed to his son, John Ashton, the remainder being shared equally between

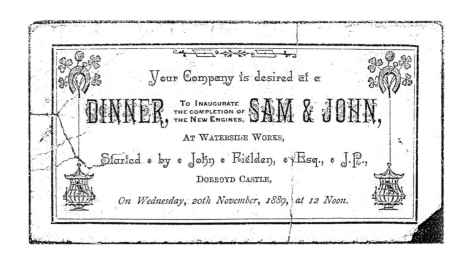

The commissioning of new steam engines at Waterside was a public relations event, the message being confidence in the future under new management.

Edward and his three brothers. With the ageing John Fielden increasingly feeble, the fourth generation was now in control. On John's death in 1893, his holding passed substantially to his eleven surviving nephews and nieces, that is Joshua's surviving children. The division of the shareholding at this time can be summarised as follows:

Table XXIII: Fielden Brothers Ltd: Ownership of Shares 1894.

John Ashton Fielden	63 shares
Edward Fielden	11 shares
Thomas Fielden	11 shares
Joshua Fielden	10 shares
Harold Fielden	10 shares
Ellen Fielden (Joshua's widow)	5 shares
Seven daughters of Joshua Fielden, that is, sisters of Edward.	14 shares
Fielden Managers etc.	6 shares
	130 shares

Source: *WYAS*, C353/5

The family owned the business, but John Ashton Fielden, given the support of the shareholding managers, had the controlling interest; this he retained until his death in 1942. Edward's own interest was modest but that of his brothers and sisters, in the aggregate, substantial. And while John Ashton, with his huge inheritance, in no way depended on dividends from Todmorden, that was not true of Edward's family; to a varying degree, but especially with regard to his sisters, it was important to them that their shares held or increased their value, and especially that in due course they paid a useful dividend. There were neither ambitions nor resources to enlarge or develop the business; indeed any investment would have to be funded from cash flow generated within the business or from asset sales. The business, in short, had to be run for profit — there was no longer, in Edward's terms, 'room for philanthropy,' that is acceptance of the losses that had been a feature of the past twenty years. Edward had a particular interest in restoring profitability and dividends; his own payment as Chairman was to be at the rate of £100 per 1 per cent dividend. There was also a concern to preserve the role of Fieldens in Todmorden where at this time they had been leading employers for a century. But this was secondary; to keep going, the business had to be profitable.

John Ashton became a member of the new Board but except in the very early period had no wish to attend meetings, whether in Todmorden or Manchester. He was happy to leave things to Edward. The same was true of his holding in the Lancashire and Yorkshire Railway — over £200,000 — where he asked Edward to take what had become the family's seat on the Board. The two rarely met; Edward adopted the routine of advising John Ashton of the annual results, and consulting him on issues of importance, mainly dividend policy, asset sales and key management changes. He was left free to get on with the challenge he had accepted. He saw his role as that of non-executive Chairman: setting policy and objectives; approving capital expenditure and the use of cash; controlling the cotton price exposure and supervising the performance of management. The key managers were given shares and joined the Board. At the outset they included Richard Ramsbotham and Thomas Wrigley from Todmorden, the commercial managers in Manchester, Walter Beard and John Cocks, together with trusted advisers like Thomas Hodgson and Theodore Lodge. Board meetings were monthly and clearly taken seriously, at least in the early years. Edward made regular visits to Waterside and to Manchester, easier when he moved his family to Shropshire in 1894, and when he joined the Board of the Lancashire and Yorkshire Railway Company in 1899. Apart from the understanding of the business which he acquired, and his role as surrogate for the main shareholders, he had a strong presence which commanded immediate respect. There is no doubt that those running the operation in Todmorden or in Manchester would want to please him and meet the objectives he set.

The Return to Profitability

It became clear to Edward in 1889 that the trading losses of the 1880s would have to be staunched without delay; his managers would get that message. The business had too much spinning capacity and was selling surplus yarn against Oldham prices, probably at a loss. If the old dilapidated spinning mill at Waterside could not be rebuilt, then it had to be closed. This happened in 1891, when long-serving staff in the Mechanics Department were also laid off; the Department, where wages were £3,600 a year, was closed in 1894. Edward wanted to close Lumbutts at the time and concentrate spinning at Robinwood and weaving at Waterside. John Fielden who owned the mills at Lumbutts would not agree but the rent charged on the buildings and machinery

Waterside Mill. The old spinning mill had closed in 1891 and the Mechanics Department in 1894. Some of the premises were let out but a fire in 1901 destroyed many of the oldest buildings. From 1891 Waterside was purely a weaving operation.

there was re-negotiated for a term of seven years from 1891 at £200 per annum; John Fielden also agreed to improve the steam-engine and shafting at Jumb mill at his own expense, charging interest at 5 per cent on his investment. This gave the Lumbutts operation a further lease of life, strengthened when the company was able to justify further reductions in its rate assessment on the grounds of the extra cartage costs the operation required; installation of a turbine instead of old worn-out water-wheels, also helped.

Robinwood and Waterside were the main problems. Edward Fielden was frustrated by the continued poor results of the business at a time when other businesses, locally and across Lancashire, were making at least modest profits. A profit of £4,379 in 1892 was followed by losses of £7,199 and £10,118 in 1893 and 1894. These would have been critical but for £20,000 realised on the sale of the company's old gas plant to the Todmorden Local Board at the end of 1892 (Table XXIV). The cash received encouraged payment of a 4 per cent dividend, as well as substantial investment in close to 1,000 new looms, replacing the oldest at Waterside, in 1893 and 1894; some £14,000 was spent in these years. Nevertheless the operating losses remained deeply disappointing and Edward began to take the view that his problem was not equipment and mill structure so much as the competence of management; to get the business right he needed a change of management across the operation and at Waterside in particular.

Some of the senior people he inherited had already gone. Richard Ramsbotham, a member of the family, the general manager, was not

Weaving at Waterside, inside the new shed built in the 1840s. This is one of the few surviving photographs of the interior of Waterside Mill: it was taken in 1912.

239

happy with the new organisation; he retired from the firm in June 1891. Harry Hoyle, also family, had been told there was 'no hope for him' and left at the end of 1889. William Hollinrake, the long serving cashier and secretary at Waterside, left in 1893. Edward's perceived problem by 1894 was the firm's senior manager, Thomas Wrigley, who had been given overall responsibility in January 1892, with a three-year contract, and the mill-manager at Waterside, John Lord. Wrigley was warned in 1894 that the cost of weaving had to be reduced and that radical changes would be made if improved results were not achieved. Edward had written on 27th July, 'We are working much too expensive a system,' and he threatened to put to the shareholders 'whether to try fresh management or close the place.' To John Ashton Fielden in December 1894, he was more blunt; in the last five years he believed they had 'brought the equipment into the front rank and our quality has immensely improved.' He went on, 'the management is poor and must be changed. I believe even at present prices we could make a fair profit anyway others can.' Fielden now took harsh decisions. John Lord, Unitarian warden, leading figure at the Cricket Club, and all his life a loyal deferential Fielden servant, was dismissed for an apparent offence in borrowing company tools. Wrigley was dismissed in January 1895, on the grounds of inadequate performance; he went with the greatest reluctance, having to vacate the company-owned Waterside House and in the end he was given six months notice.

John Ashton Fielden supported these moves. 'Richard Ramsbotham must attend to his work or go', he had written in December 1889, 'he seems to think he can do just as he likes at Waterside.' Of Wrigley, he wrote 'I have never been a believer in him as I consider his ideas are far too antiquated to be of any use at the present time and as he has now been given a fair trial without satisfactory results I think it is best to get rid of him at once and try and get a good modern man in his place. If this does not do, we must as you say, shut up shop, but it would be an awful loss'. Wrigley's dismissal would be the talk of Todmorden at the time, possibly even across the industry since he had received many accolades for improvements in ring spinning. Edward, it would be said, was a hard master who meant business; to him it was a matter of the firm's survival.

After Wrigley left, George Windsor, recently returned from twelve years in Pernambuco, became Secretary at a salary of £300; he was to remain at Waterside in that role and later as General Manager until 1927. He was no cotton man, rather an upright reliable and trustworthy custodian, and Edward clearly had doubts about him from time to time, although in the end he came to rely on him absolutely and reward him generously. New manufacturing expertise across the operation now became an urgent need; it was introduced in 1895 by George Coates, manager of a successful weaving business in Rawtenstall, who, at the outset, gave two days a week. Edward was keen that good young men should be introduced at both Todmorden and Manchester, to provide for succession; one such, John Rothwell joined in 1898 to manage the weaving mill at Waterside.

Edward Fielden was monitoring the working expenses of the three

A ropeway connected the two spinning Mills at Lumbutts to minimise the cost of moving prepared cotton from the Upper Mill to Jumb. Although the Mills were small, they were efficient and their labour costs were not uncompetitive. Getting workpeople as well as the cost of carting coal and cotton became part of the problem of keeping them going in the twentieth century. Edward Fielden wanted to close them but they survived until 1926.

mills closely and carefully, paying particular attention to labour costs per pound of yarn, coal prices and usage, waste losses in spinning and weft or cop waste in weaving, the cost of stores and repairs. He demanded control and improvement. Certainly the costs at Lumbutts fell over the period and were generally lower than those of Robinwood although that mill did two thirds of the spinning. At both mills total costs per pound of yarn were around 2d which was typical for the industry. By 1908, for whatever reason, a decision was taken to part with J.W. Greenwood, the long-serving mill-manager at Robinwood, and he was dismissed by Coates, a difficult and delicate task as a letter written at the time makes clear. 'I have been convinced for a long time he was the wrong man,' he wrote, 'but being such an old servant it was very difficult to take action. It is one of the unpleasant duties you have to put up with in situations such as ours.' John Midgley, who had followed his father and grandfather at Lumbutts and was credited with the success there, was

241

Robinwood became the main spinning site when Waterside closed and as Lumbutts faltered. All its old throstle frames were progressively replaced with ring spindles, and electric power introduced to all machinery by the 1920s. Robinwood could spin 3 to 3.5 million lbs of cotton a year.

moved to take charge of Robinwood in his place, being succeeded at Lumbutts by his brother Luke. The change was seen as a very sensitive affair and there was continuing concern at Midgley's lack of tact with the workforce. Edward Fielden still regarded Lumbutts as unwanted despite the low costs: in 1908 he decided that no further capital expenditure would take place there and the mills would have to close after any serious breakdown. As he saw it, Robinwood would make Waterside's warp requirements, and some of its weft; the rest could be bought cheaply outside. The particular problem at Lumbutts was getting workpeople; mill-workers now wanted to live in the town with its amenities and the Fielden-owned cottages near the mills were occupied by pensioners beyond working age. These problems notwithstanding, Lumbutts still survived another eighteen years.

Edward Fielden had taken, from the start, close personal control of the overall cotton exposure, in much the same way as Sam Fielden or John and Thomas Fielden before him. He received regular reports of cotton purchases, stocks and cloth sales; he appears to have been willing to authorise outright positions long or short, and continued to use futures for their flexibility in varying the position, or cover as it would be called. The matter was regularly discussed at Board meetings in the early years. In November 1892, for instance, the Board decided to be overcovered by 4,000 bales, probably six months usage; the decision may have been a good one since cotton prices rose modestly in 1893, although the business made a loss in that year. In January 1897 Edward censured

LYDGATE

Table XXIV: Fielden Brothers Ltd: Profit and Dividends 1890-1913.

YEAR	Manufacturing Profit	(£000) Interest/Rent	Total Profit	Dividends %
1890	—	—	(0.3)	—
1891	(1.3)	1.3	—	—
1892	3.8	0.6	4.4	—
1893	(8.1)	0.9	(7.2)	4
1894	(12.2)	2.1	(10.1)	—
1895	3.3	1.3	4.6	—
1896	—	1.5	(1.5)	—
1897	—	1.9	1.9	—
1898	2.4	2.2	4.6	—
1899	3.1	2.8	5.9	—
1900	(2.4)	2.6	0.2	—
1901	(0.7)	2.3	1.6	—
1902	1.6	2.3	3.9	—
1903	(8.0)	2.6	(3.4)	—
1904	(6.9)	2.5	(4.4)	—
1905	14.9	3.0	17.9	5
1906	8.9	3.7	12.6	6
1907	9.8	3.0	12.8	6
1908	9.6	3.4	13.0	6
1909	6.9	3.3	10.2	6
1910	5.3	3.1	8.4	6
1911	7.0	2.7	9.7	6
1912	17.5	2.9	20.4	9
1913	11.0	3.7	14.7	9

Source: WYAS, C353/1.

Beard for failing to cover a sale of 5,000 pieces to Rylands, leaving the firm uncovered when policy was to be overcovered. In 1903 Beard was reprimanded again for buying 400 bales without consultation or his approval. Although the company took losses on its futures holdings in many years, these were only a part of the total cotton exposure and no conclusion can be drawn as to whether use of futures or a variable coverage policy helped or worsened the overall performance. Subject to Edward's control, Manchester bought the cotton although the mill-managers in Todmorden would select and approve samples. In Manchester, Beard remained in charge of cloth sales, and represented the firm on the Exchange. All sales were now being made to the Manchester trade; critically, authority to make sales that did not cover production costs remained with Edward.

The years after the prolonged trade depression of the 1870s and 1880s eventually brought resumed expansion in Lancashire and some years of exceptional prosperity. Fielden Brothers Limited results to some extent mirrored the industry although compared with other firms they under-performed; the period 1900 to 1904 was difficult as for the rest of the industry, but 1905 was an excellent year when a profit of £17,928 was the best result since 1871. A long run of profit years followed, up to and through the Great War. Clearly the experience with the ring spindles installed in the 1880s had been satisfactory, given low counts of yarn, and a further 16,000 ring spindles went into Robinwood in 1908-10, at a cost of £17,000, replacing thirty-year old throstles; fourteen experimental automatic looms were also put into Waterside at this time.

The Manchester Exchange, 1904. Walter Beard was the chief Fielden representative there for many years.

Lancashire was now enjoying its last great boom; in 1907 cotton consumption reached 1985 million pounds; in 1913, 2178 million pounds: these figures compared with an average of 1460 million pounds in the 1880s. Fieldens, still using about 3 to 3.5 million pounds, remained a significant firm, but had obviously not shared in the expansion, but to some extent Todmorden had. 1907 saw the opening of a new multi-storey spinning mill, built in the Oldham style in the Burnley valley: Hare Mill, close to Centre Vale. Its 80,000 spindles represented an investment of £80,000, not very different to what such a facility would have cost in the 1830s. Opening the mill, in a confident mood, the town's mayor could say there was 'almost unlimited room for growth in the cotton trade'; his fears were for 'an abundant supply of cheap cotton.'

Dividends of 10 to 20 percent were not untypical for shareholders in Lancashire mill companies at this time. Fieldens felt able to declare a dividend of 5 per cent in 1905, the first real dividend since that of 1894 derived from a windfall. Dividends followed at 6 per cent in subsequent years reaching 9 per cent in 1912 and 1913, two excellent years when the business did better than many others. 9 per cent was yielding Edward a useful fee of £900 on top of his dividend while the managers also benefited from the improved results. Apart from their salaries they received individual bonuses for each per cent in dividend paid; thus in 1913 Windsor got a bonus of £25 for each per cent, Coates the same. In 1913 Windsor was paid a salary of £600, as was Beard in Manchester; Coates took £480, John Midgley and John Rothwell each received £312 and the young Ernest Witham, warehouse clerk, but later General Manager, got £78. Coates retired in 1913; he had helped to turn the business round and left proven managers in charge.

Another change was taking place in the company. Its old assets were now being run profitably. While year by year sums were set aside for depreciation, cash flow was augmented by occasional asset sales, and although substantial dividends and bonuses were paid, generally low expenditure on buildings or machinery left surplus cash which could be invested in a portfolio of 'safe' securities, railway debentures, industrial blue chips, consols and the like. As this policy, starting in

1898, was continued, the company's dependence on cotton manufacturing profits, important as it remained, was reduced and interest on investments as well as rents from farms and cottage property in Todmorden assumed a significant scale. Thus by 1913, the company's assets were £179,603, financed by share capital of £130,000 and retained earnings and other resources of £49,603; investments were then valued at over £60,000; of profits of £14,750, £1364 came from rents and £2,288 from interest or dividends. Everything in the balance sheet, investments, stocks, fixed assets had all been written down very prudently; as Edward wrote to John Ashton in January 1913, 'the machinery, property etc., are all at prices that would be easily realised.'

Edward, after a difficult start as a custodian of the family interests, had done all that they could expect. One may suppose his sisters were extremely grateful for their dividends; two were spinsters and not all those who had married enjoyed large incomes. John Ashton Fielden had expressed his appreciation of his cousin's achievements in various ways. Writing in November 1896, when he made Edward a loan of £70,000, he said, 'I shall not push if there is no dividend as I think we all ought to be very grateful to you that the place has not been sold for bricks and mortar as it would have been if you had not taken it in hand.' When he learned of the 1905 profit he replied, 'I never thought it possible with the present mills: I have considered for many years that Fielden Brothers was kept going rather than throw the mill-hands out of work.' A year later he was concerned the position of the firm was precarious 'as it hangs on your life. No-one else could keep it going: if you were out of it the only course open would be a sale.' In January 1908, when the company was well in profit, he was trying to sell some

Todmorden about 1900, looking down the Calder valley towards Halifax: an industrial town at its maturity. Many new enterprises had risen since the 1850s and Fielden Brothers, although still important in the town were no longer as ascendant as they had been. The Fielden family had ceased to play any part in the town's affairs. Todmorden people saw nothing ugly about their home town; by 1900 many improvements had been made and the valley setting remained beautiful. Life for the millworker offered unpretentious but inexpensive enjoyment outside clearly defined working hours. By the turn of the century, although working hours were still fifty-eight a week, real wages were much greater and holidays had become an annual event.

245

of his shares, partly because of his fear of what would happen if Edward gave up. He wrote, 'when you look back in what state the company was in when you took over the management out of kindness to the Fielden family, its present state must be very pleasing to you.' Edward did, apparently at the time, contemplate looking for a successor but not for long; that issue and the composition of the Board generally, became more serious a few years later.

Wartime and between the Wars

The Great War did no harm to the Company's profits. Margins steadily increased and the steep rise in cotton prices and world-wide shortage of yarn and cloth that developed in 1918 and 1919 resulted in a sharp appreciation in the value of stocks and a period of busy working throughout Lancashire at quite exceptional margins, perhaps the best in the industry's history. Many established owners of cotton firms sold out at this time, and their businesses were refloated at vastly increased values to new owners. Not surprisingly 1918 and 1919 were among the most profitable years in Fieldens' history; to their credit, neither John Ashton or Edward Fielden, others of the family, or the managers, contemplated floating the company. The period of exceptional profit was short-lived; 1920 saw a collapse of prices and heavy write-downs of stock; at the end of the year Edward was worried about large stocks of piece-goods sold at high prices but not taken up by customers. But the results were good, and Edward gave credit to Windsor; 'he has done splendidly for us during the last year. I cannot speak too highly of him,' he wrote. The post-war boom in Lancashire was over in 1921, cotton consumption fell dramatically, and although it recovered in the subsequent years, especially in 1925, the onset of starkly changed world markets for Lancashire cloth was casting its shadow, a shadow that was to deepen as the decade progressed. The huge markets for plain cloth in India and China were now being supplied to an increasing extent from manufacturing in these countries — mills built, equipped and often managed by Lancashire firms — while both in these markets, and elsewhere, Japan emerged as a most formidable competitor. Exports of cloth, which had been 7 million yards in 1913 averaged 4 million yards in 1922-27 and fell to only 2 million yards in the worst years of the Thirties.

Looking at Fieldens results, profits held up well through 1922, collapsed in 1923 and 1924, but recovered strongly in 1925. It was not until 1928 that the inter-war slump is reflected in the results; thereafter the manufacturing activity barely broke even until trade began to recover in the late 1930s (Table XXV). A number of points may be made. Most obviously, unlike hundreds of enterprises throughout Lancashire, and especially the re-capitalised mills, the firm survived this period of recession and contraction. Although it experienced periods of short time working, the scale of activity, measured by consumption of cotton, remained stable throughout at around 3 million lbs yearly; similarly employment in Todmorden was maintained at about 700 persons. The mills in Lumbutts were closed in 1926, their output being largely replaced by enlarged output at Robinwood and regular purchases of

George Windsor (1860-1931) had joined Fielden Brothers as manager for nine years of the Pernambuco Gas Company. On his return to Lancashire he became Secretary at Waterside in the 1890s and General Manager in 1913, remaining with the company until his retirement in 1928. Although no cotton man, he was a strong reliable personality who handled sales and purchases prudently and ran a tight manufacturing operation which made good profits in the best years and survived the bleak periods. He became a leading figure in the political, religious and educational life of Todmorden.

Table XXV: Fielden Brothers Ltd: Profit and Dividends 1914-1939

	Manufacturing Profit	(£000) Dividends, Interest and Rent	Total Profit	Dividend %	Retained Profit
1914	6.6	3.0	9.6	7	16.0
1915	11.1	3.9	15.0	9	20.5
1916	12.9	3.3	16.2	10	23.3
1917	17.4	2.5	19.9	10	29.3
1918	75.1	2.0	77.1	10	92.8
1919	76.0	3.4	79.4	25	103.8
1920	43.9	3.2	47.1	20	84.0
1921	24.3	3.9	28.2	20	94.9
1922	16.3	4.7	21.0	25	102.4
1923	3.1	4.8	7.9	15	55.0
1924	7.4	4.1	11.5	17	41.5
1925	35.7	3.5	39.2	30	56.6
1926	8.4	5.2	13.6	15	30.2
1927	12.1	4.4	16.5	12.5	25.6
1928	2.5	4.0	6.5	5	21.7
1929	3.3	4.3	7.6	5	21.3
1930	0.8	4.5	5.3	5	19.4
1931	1.7	4.8	6.5	5	18.7
1932	2.4	4.0	6.4	5	8.6
1933	2.8	3.8	6.6	5	8.8
1934	3.0	4.1	7.1	5	10.0
1935	4.0	4.1	8.1	6	12.1
1936	12.6	3.2	15.8	10	18.4
1937	15.0	3.4	18.4	10	19.1
1938	19.2	4.0	23.2	10	22.9
1939	20.1	2.7	22.8	10	25.2

Source: WYAS, C353/1.

cheap weft on the market. In 1930 and 1931, Robinwood used about 3 million lbs of cotton and in 1937 and 1938, when 10 per cent more time was worked, about 3.5 million lbs.

In particular years the profits benefited from sale of Waterside properties, old offices, warehouses and the like, to the Railway or local Council, at a useful surplus on book value. But these windfalls apart, the profit record reflected careful and efficient management and trading by a stable team, led by Windsor with Rothwell and Midgley running the two mills and Greenhalgh, who succeeded Beard, handling the cloth sales; all these managers enjoyed large salary increases and bonus payments in the post-war boom period. This team and their subordinates, under Edward Fielden's leadership, took advantage of the opportunities the market gave and survived the bleakest periods. Labour relations remained stable; the firm had abandoned its resistance to trade unions and now recognised the Weavers Association, belonged to the local and industry-wide Employers Associations and paid at the wage-rates they negotiated. The huge cash-flow in the best years was used partly to strengthen the business and broaden the conservative trading base; thus in 1920 the Manchester offices in Norfolk Street were bought

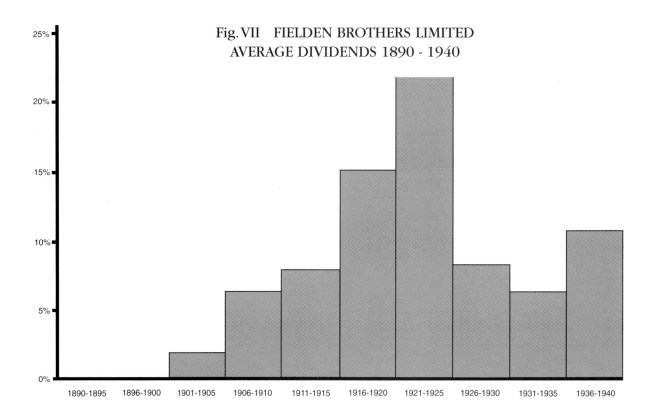

Fig. VII FIELDEN BROTHERS LIMITED
AVERAGE DIVIDENDS 1890 - 1940

from John Ashton Fielden for £23,400. Apart from the rental income from tenants, Norfolk Street eventually proved a most valuable asset. Investment in the manufacturing facility continued in all but the worst years. Thus conversion of Robinwood to ring spindles was completed in the mid-1920s and in 1922-1925 electric power replaced steam at that mill; it then had 31,000 ring spindles, equal in productivity to about 46,000 mules. The complete commitment to rings made Fieldens unusual, if not exceptional, among Lancashire businesses at the time. At Waterside steam engine boilers were replaced, new warehouses built and in 1936 and 1937, 240 Northrop automatic looms replaced the old sheeting looms in the old shed. In total over £60,000 was invested in buildings improvements and new machinery in the period, not unenterprising given the general circumstances. The conservative approach that had always been a feature of Fielden financial management, certainly since the 1840s, was reflected in heavy write downs (by over one quarter) of buildings and machinery in Todmorden in 1932 and provision of a large investment fluctuation reserve which more than covered the loss in value of railway shareholdings in the 1930s. A valuation of Todmorden cottage property at this time showed its value to be well above that in the balance sheet. Edward Fielden could continue to say that the assets of the business were worth comfortably more than their book value.

Dividends remained the chief call on the company's profits. Over the fifty years 1890-1939, close to £500,000 was paid in dividends (before tax) on shareholders capital of £130,000. The dividend payments were unbroken from 1905 and between 1919 and 1927 averaged 20 per cent; after 1927 they remained at 5 per cent until the profit improvement of the late Thirties. These were years when many cotton firms, like many other enterprises, including especially the merged railway companies, on which those who lived on the returns from share capital relied, were paying no dividend at all. The LMS Railway Company for instance, important to the Fieldens since its stock replaced their holdings in the old Lancashire and Yorkshire, after paying 7 per cent on the merger in 1922, averaged 3½ per cent between 1926 and 1930 and paid no dividend during the period 1931 through 1935. Robson's sample of cotton spinning firms, show dividends averaging 20 per cent in 1919 and 40 per cent in 1920 but paid an average dividend of only 1.86 per cent in the period 1927-1935. Fielden Brothers Limited, of course, spread the bounty of the short boom years over a long period by holding large retained profits which financed cash balances, short term loans or stocks, and were drawn down to pay the shareholders when profits fell (Table XXV).

Lancashire had enjoyed an Indian summer in the early years of the century and then a brief illusory boom in 1918-1920: it might be said that looking at the whole history of the Fielden enterprise, after the long period of stagnation following the Cotton Famine, the fifty years to 1939 were the firm's Indian summer.

Edward Fielden, a portrait from the 1920s. He was Chairman of Fielden Brothers Ltd from 1889 to 1939 and would take pride that the company had kept going and remained profitable when so many in Lancashire had failed. He was concerned with the interests of the shareholders but also the workpeople and, indirectly, others in Todmorden who depended on the company. Whatever time he gave to Fieldens, where he was held in high respect, he was MP for the Exchange Division of Manchester, Deputy Chairman of the LMS Railway Company, and Chairman of Finance at Shropshire County Council. He still found time to ride to hounds.

THE INHERITORS
The Fourth Generation 1889-1939

John Ashton Fielden

John Ashton Fielden, educated at Harrow and Cambridge is here probably in his late thirties in the 1890s. He thought Todmorden was damp, dirty and dull and found homes in the Cambridge district. Very rich, handsome, devoted to shooting and fishing at both of which sports he excelled, he never married. In later years his tendency to avoid conversation or contact with young women, led to gossip that he had been jilted at the altar as a young man.

When John Fielden of Dobroyd Castle and Grimston died in 1893, John Ashton Fielden became head of the family. One of the richest men in the country, unmarried, he was still living at Lawrence Court in Huntingdon; he also seems to have rented rooms off St James Street in London and later in Cavendish Mews and belonged to the Carlton Club. Managing the very large fortune he had inherited would take some of his time. He had a huge holding in railway shares which he wisely reduced in order to diversify into other investments including gilts and foreign shares, home rails were now ceasing to be the attractive investment they had been and many more alternatives were available. He had property acquired by his father in Todmorden, Fleetwood and Greater Manchester (formerly part of the old Partnership) and the London Bridge estate. Over the years much of this, but not London Bridge, was to be sold piecemeal; thus in 1900 he sold the Rosebank estate, part of the Rostron assets acquired by the Partnership when that business associate had failed in 1862, for £22,000.

Todmorden was a minor concern. For a while he was President of the Cricket Club; he warned its committee not to take for granted his willingness to let them use 'my cricket ground,' but gave them less trouble than his father. His gift to the town of his mother's school has been described. Following his mother's death in 1910, he sold his parents' home, Centre Vale, to the town. This was a curious transaction since for whatever reason the estate was not offered to the Corporation of Todmorden, but advertised in the Manchester press. The Mayor of the time, Edward Lord, saw the advertisement and approached Fielden's solicitors; a quick deal was made, to which no conditions were attached, at a price of £10,000, in effect an act of charity. Much argument ensued in Todmorden before the estate, which had become the property of the Mayor, became the town's park with the cricket field being finally leased to the Club.[1] His majority stake in Fielden Brothers Limited apart, that was John Ashton's final link with Todmorden and after his mother's death there is no evidence that he visited the place for the rest of his life.

Part of his father's estate had been the half-share in the Pernambuco Gas Company, the other half-share belonging to Uncle John. On John's death his nephews, Thomas and Edward received his share which John Ashton had an option to buy. In 1894 he exercised that option for £60,000 confirming the reputation he had acquired with his cousins for being sharp, business-like and punctilious. He wrote them a brusque letter objecting to their discussing the question with others: 'I wish to know by what right this has been done. You have quite exceeded your powers in doing so without my permission.' Tom, characteristically, was emollient. 'My dear Johnnie,' he replied. 'We accept your offer,' 'Yours Ever,' and P.S. 'Capital day with the hounds but very cold.' John Ashton then sold the Company to the Pernambuco municipality for £120,000. Thus ended what had been a bold and lucrative investment for the Fielden family, almost certainly the initiative of old Thomas.[2]

What was John Ashton to do with his wealth? His future life style was probably clear in his mind; that of a quiet bachelor country gentleman enjoying the amenities and management of a shooting estate so soon as a suitable property could be found. But that would absorb a small part only of his huge wealth and large, virtually untaxed, rentier income. Philanthropy was another outlet and in the event the one he pursued; it was the tradition of his parents, and of his mother's family in particular. His father had given Todmorden a much-needed isolation hospital. John Ashton now did the same in Huntingdon at a cost of £10,000 in 1892. What became his lifelong concern for hospitals assumed a much more significant turn a year or two later with his large anonymous gifts to the London Hospital in Whitechapel.

How he became involved with this huge institution is not clear. It was the largest hospital in London and in Great Britain, wholly maintained by charity, in the heart of the densest and poorest districts of the East End. Serving 160,000 outpatients and 13,000 in-patients yearly from immigrant Jewish communities on the one hand, and Cockney Irish dockers on the other, the Hospital desperately needed financial help. John Ashton's distinguished older cousin, Henry Yates Thompson, owner of the *Pall Mall Gazette,* was a Governor and probably made the connection. Sydney Holland, later Lord Knutsford, the so-called 'Prince of Beggars', who as Chairman of Governors was in charge of the fund-raising activity, tells another version in his book

London Hospital in Whitechapel, was the largest hospital in Great Britain, at the heart of the poorest districts in London's East End. It was maintained entirely by charity.

(Opposite above)
Debden Hall in North Essex,
appears a quite unsuitable
stately home for a rich
bachelor. John Ashton
bought it for its shooting in
1900 and with his friends
shot 7,000 pheasants in the
first season, but he quickly
tired of the place and sold it
in 1902.

(Opposite below)
Holmewood was a Victorian
country house, on the
outskirts of the village of
Holme south of
Peterborough. John Ashton
bought the estate in 1902 and
spent the rest of his life
there. To his tenants he was a
strict but generous squire.
White he imposed many
restrictions, forbidding
garden bonfires for instance,
all the cottages were well
maintained and the occupants
were relieved of their rents
when times were hard as
in the Great War.

In Black and White.[3] John Ashton had a major abdominal operation in 1893, performed by Frederick Treves the distinguished surgeon. Treves suggested he do something to help the Hospital (to which he was attached) and subsequently, accordingly, Fielden asked Sydney Holland to call on him. Holland goes on:

'He asked me to write down what I wanted. This was a pretty large order and I began at £100 and went up to an Isolation Block costing £22,000. He drew out his cheque book and gave me a cheque for £22,000, saying 'That will help you with the Isolation Block.' I said 'I have no words to thank you.' He replied 'I do not want any thanks, keep my name entirely secret, pay it into your bank and give your cheque to the Hospital' — and that was the beginning of a long friendship.'

Fielden gave another £5,000 at the time which paid for balconies outside the wards, and then a further £10,000 to complete the Isolation Block which subsequently became Fielden House. In 1910 he sent a Christmas box of £3,000. Another large gift was made in 1929: £12,000 to purchase a gramme of radium for cancer treatment. During his lifetime, his gifts amounted to some £84,500.[4]

In 1900 he believed he had found the country place he was looking for when he bought Debden Hall, near Saffron Walden in Essex, a huge rambling old house in a large park and an estate of 4,000 acres. What he paid is not clear but the land market would be a great deal lower than when a Fielden bought Grimston in 1872. He began buying adjacent land and within a year had 5,300 acres in a ring fence. For a while he was happy there, killing 7,000 pheasants in the 1900-01 season. But Debden was cold and badly lit (he sought advice from his cousin Edward on installing electricity), and quite unsuitable for a single man, not given to large scale entertaining. Within a year he began looking for something else, which he found when the Holme estate came on the market in 1902. He was fortunate to sell Debden within £500 of his reserve.

The Holme estate, when he bought it, was 6,362 acres, south of Peterborough, some 1,700 acres fenland, part of the former Whittlesea

Mere, the rest higher ground. Apart from twenty tenanted farms it had a park of about 680 acres and excellent shooting both in the park and in coverts on the farms. The country house, Holmewood, had been the home of the Wells family since the eighteenth century; they had rebuilt it in red brick in 1874, without any distinction. The estate village of Holme was adjacent, with a halt on the main London — Peterborough line of the Great Northern Railway nearby. About 800 people lived in the village and on the estate farms. With a gross rental of about £6,700 yearly, Holmewood had been tenanted for some years before John Ashton bought it for a rumoured £90,000, that is, very cheaply. In February 1903 he could write 'it is a very nice place and seems to suit me very well.' He planned, he said, 'to settle down here for good.' At times subsequently he had his doubts; in 1908 he complained the place was 'too low and damp' and his doctors said he must leave as soon as he could find another. In the event, whatever his health problems, he stayed at Holme for the rest of his life.[5]

As a man of abundant wealth, he became an excellent squire and landlord. He was respected rather than popular; like his father, private, shy, aloof, somewhat eccentric, increasingly prickly as he got older and began to complain of his health. Children, it was recalled, ran to hide when they saw him approaching, on foot or on his bay gelding. He enforced strict rules about permitted days when the villagers could hang their washing to dry; there were occasions when he would shoot down offending washing with his twelve bore. But the estate (hedges, ditches, drains on the fen, roads, farm buildings, cottages in the village) was always immaculately maintained by a diligent well-paid force of craftsmen, who lived in the village. New pumping stations were built on the fen at the landlord's expense. When times were difficult for his tenants — as they were for much of the time — they were told to pay the rent when they could, and if the squire's pheasants damaged their crops, they could expect to be fairly compensated. There is no doubt that he took great pride in his property and his good relationship with his tenants and estate-workers. He sold 2,200 acres to Peterborough in 1918 but otherwise the estate remained intact.[6]

John Ashton lived quietly with a handful of servants. Many stayed with him over forty years as did some of his keepers and outdoor staff; his paid employees usually numbered over one hundred. He rarely entertained and apart from a few shooting friends, hardly mixed with local society. He became a JP in 1903, but never sat on the bench. In 1908 he became High Sheriff and if at first that was 'a great bother' he seems to have enjoyed it in the end, 'doing a proper job,' with his hire carriage, 'a very good turn-out,' which was painted blue and gold with the Fielden Coat of Arms; he suggested Edward Fielden take the same carriage when his turn for High Sheriff came up. He was patron of the living at Holme but never attended church, claiming to be a Unitarian. Apart from occasional cricket matches (the MCC sent a team one year), there were no village social functions in the park. He did not travel and hated motor transport; when he did travel it was by rail frequently exercising his right to stop fast trains at the local halt. His great pleasure was his shooting; he was never a hunting man and refused

John Ashton Fielden was an excellent shot over a lifetime. This photograph catches him at his favourite sport, probably in the 1920s. He had five gamekeepers and the Holme estate abounded with pheasants although none of the tenants dare take them. Hundreds of rabbits were killed on each shoot, and a couple would then be thrown into every cottage doorway.

to let the local hunt cross his land. His game books survive, meticulously recording each of the three drives on the several shoots on the estate each year from 1904, the number of birds, the weather conditions, more or less the same guests. In 1911-12, for instance, a total of 4,338 pheasants and 10,258 rabbits, apart from partridge and wood pigeons, were killed. John Ashton was an excellent shot, bringing down the birds at the end of the line that others had missed; he had won trophies for clay-pigeon shooting in his youth and at Holmewood he would practise his shooting aiming at flies on the wall of the house with an air-gun. The huge harvest of dead birds were hung in the game-larder and despatched by rail in baskets to Smithfield. No doubt John Ashton shot on other estates in the season but there is no indication that he shot grouse, in Todmorden or elsewhere, although he owned Higher House Moor. His other sporting interest was fishing and most years in the spring he rented a Scottish lodge, usually in Ayrshire, occasionally in the Highlands, to fish the salmon, again it seems alone.

This was his life for forty years. There would be rare visits to London or to Manchester to manage his business affairs but, eschewing the telephone, much of his business would be conducted by correspondence. He was strict in attention to detail like his father, and sensitive to any liberties or oversight. He fell out with the long-serving Lodge who felt he should have discretion to sign cheques, and Lodge then retired in 1897 after a lifetime with the Fieldens, a career that led him from Liverpool to the City of London and many confidential visits to Fielden homes, since he was privy to their most personal affairs. The offices in East India Avenue were then closed and John Ashton's affairs put in the hands of solicitors.

Staunchly Conservative in his political views, there is no doubt that as one of the propertied few John Ashton felt uncomfortable in a popular democracy which for the first time was giving ascendancy to the property-less man; he felt threatened by the politics of envy and redistribution. He was unhappy at the return of the Liberal Government in 1906 and the increased Labour membership of the Commons: 'they will simply take away all they can from everyone who has anything — to keep all the lazy roughs who don't want to work.' In 1911 he was more forthright; 'this damned government has brought us to Socialism and I fear it has come to stay.' Not merely Conservative but deeply patriotic, John Ashton felt keenly about the cause in 1914; 'I am of no use except for money,' he wrote 'which is however useful in many ways in wartime.' His old house in Huntingdon became a hospital full of wounded soldiers, 'a good matron' having been sent up from Whitechapel. He sought the advice of London Hospital on how he could help; the result was the purchase for £21,000, in November 1914, of a large steam yacht, the *Paulina,* and its fitting out as a hospital ship. Queen Alexandra, closely associated with the Hospital, and with military nursing, offered to have it called after her and for a while the yacht was renamed *The Queen Mother.* It carried thousands of wounded soldiers across the Channel throughout the war, one of seventy-nine similar ships in this service. One of the few surviving pictures of John Ashton, taken in December 1915, shows him sitting with the crew while a signed address honours his generosity; at the end of the war he sold the yacht. He repeated this form of philanthropy in the second world war. Giving £50,000 outright to the Treasury, he told a reporter 'money is the only weapon an old man like me can fight with.' In 1940 he paid for two Spitfires, and another two when these were lost, and gave six ambulances to the Red Cross. Many other wartime appeals benefited from his generosity, particularly those directing help to Russia. In 1942 he made a personal gift of £1,000 to Winston Churchill. He invested sums as large as £40,000 and £50,000 in the War Savings campaigns in Huntingdon and at the

The SS *Paulina* was the hospital ship bought by John Ashton Fielden at the suggestion of London Hospital in November 1914. He paid for it to be fitted out to carry wounded soldiers across the channel, and for all its expenses in this task throughout the Great War. The ship, or steam yacht, was sold after the war.

John Ashton Fielden was photographed with the crew of the *Paulina* in December 1915. The crew, who were servicemen, gave him an illuminated address.

(Left)
The Spitfire *'Holmewood'*: John Ashton bought four Spitfires in 1940 and 1941, two in replacement of two that were shot down; he also gave six ambulances to the Red Cross and large sums to War Savings or direct gifts to the Treasury. Aged eighty-two in 1941, he was determined to use his money to support the war effort. Repeating his words from 1914, he said, 'money is the only weapon an old man like me can fight with. Our young pilots are grand and I am proud to be able to help to give them their machines.'

time he died his house was being used to accommodate people blinded in bombing raids on Coventry and East London.[7]

Throughout the period up to the 1900s, John Ashton maintained his connections with his family, that is his Fielden cousins on Joshua's side. Certainly in the Eighties and Nineties he attended family occasions at Nutfield and Grimston, weddings, funerals, reunions and parties at Christmas or on other occasions. Whenever one of Joshua's daughters was married, John Ashton, even if not present, sent a handsome gift, usually a diamond bracelet. But as cousins were married, and middle age succeeded youth, the visits became infrequent, and eventually ceased. His friendly if sparse correspondence with Edward, mainly about the affairs of the Todmorden business, but also on personal matters from time to time, became his main link. He probably felt uncomfortable at his huge wealth relative to that of his cousins. When Edward asked to borrow £70,000 in 1896 he had no problem in making the loan, on slender collateral. They were gentlemen and cousins and they could trust each other. Years later, in 1907, and after the death of Edward's first wife, John Ashton, too shy to write himself, instructed his solicitor to write advising Edward that he released him 'from all liability in respect of his loan.'[8]

Thomas, Edward and Family

Thomas was the oldest of the fourth generation; he inherited Grimston from uncle John in 1893 and was proudly set up there. Even at the time the rental of the tenanted farms was probably insufficient, in amount or certainty, to meet the expenses of the large house and estate but Thomas had his inherited wealth, probably about £120,000, while his wife Martie had received a comfortable legacy on the death of her father, Thomas Knowles, in 1883. Tom enjoyed Grimston, the farms, the hunting, the game, hosting shooting parties each autumn. His growing family, relatives and friends, continued to visit Amulree in Perthshire each year, for the grouse, deer-stalking, fishing in the loch. They were also regular visitors to Nutfield; a record survives of a family party on Boxing Day 1891 when all the family — brothers and sisters and in Tom's case his small children — entertained each other with solo songs, duets, monologues, tableaux, recitations, and the like, printing a programme for the occasion.[9] There were similar family parties at Grimston some years. Tom's other large concern was his Middleton constituency, politically very marginal, where popular and well known as he was, he remained vulnerable to the national swing. Thus he lost his seat by 116 votes in 1892 but regained it in 1895 with a majority of 865. He and his wife stayed in London during the Parliamentary session, when he rented various houses, for many years in Cavendish Square and then Portland Place. There is no record that he ever spoke in Parliament, sought any prominence or had any political ambition; he was happy to be a country gentleman in politics and a reliable conservative vote for the government of the day.

When in town during the season, Tom and Martie mixed in society; Martie was presented to the Queen in May 1889, and in March 1890 *The Queen* reported Mrs Tom Fielden's attendance at the first of Her

⋅❀ PART I. ❀⋅

DUET ... ...
Mrs. Tom Fielden & Miss Lorna Fielden

TABLEAU ... ... { "Where are you going to my pretty Maid"
Miss Bee Fielden & Master Jack Fielden

SONG ... ... A day's ride
Mrs. Ed. Fielden

MONOLOGUE ... ...The Woman of Courage
Miss Beatrice Fielden

SONG ... ...Leonore
Mrs. Stone

READING ... ... The pied piper of Hamlin
Mrs. Fielden.

TABLEAU ... ...Day of Rest
Miss G. & Miss S. Fielden

⋅❀ PART 2. ❀⋅

RECITATION ... ... The Well of St. Keene
Mrs. Stone

DUET ... ...
Mrs. Tom Fielden & Miss Fielden

DIALOGUE ... ...If I was a Woman
Mr. & Mrs. Pilkington (by special request)

SONG ... ...
Mrs. Macleod

TABLEAU ... ..." Mary, Mary, quite contrary "
The Misses Fielden

RECITATION ... ...
Mr. Macleod

BRITANNIA'S REALM.

Boxing Day at Nutfield 1891. Ellen Fielden, her children and grandchildren entertained each other in a carefully planned programme.

(Below)
A Group at Amulree, Perthshire, where Thomas and Martha Fielden rented an estate and visited once or twice a year with friends for fishing and shooting. Tom stands behind Martie and his children, three boys and three girls. Ellen Fielden, grandmother to the children, has joined them on this occasion which was probably about 1890. Tom, who was epileptic like his younger brother Harold, collapsed and died when shooting grouse at Amulree in 1897: he was only forty-three. His oldest son, John, born at Stansfield Hall in 1880, on the right of the group, inherited Grimston Park on his father's sudden death.

Majesty's Drawing Rooms of the season; on this occasion, she was accompanied by her sister Mrs Edward Fielden.

Tom, although robust and vigorous, was probably epileptic like earlier members of the family and like his younger brother. He had a fit during the vote-counting at Rochdale in 1886 and this was a recurrent condition. Edward's diary records Tom having a convulsive fit in 1888 and again at Amulree when fishing on the loch in the summer of 1890; the latter occasion seems to have been painful and nearly fatal, since Tom threw his shoulder and fell into the loch, being retrieved with difficulty. On another occasion he had turned giddy while deer-stalking and fallen twenty feet over a precipice, lying unconscious for several hours before he could be recovered from a narrow ledge. In the end he probably died of heart failure caused by a fit; when shooting grouse at Amulree in October 1897 he was found dead in the butts. He was forty-three, in his prime, and left a young family of three girls and three boys, his eldest son John being a seventeen year old schoolboy at Eton. Thomas was buried at Grimston. Martie carried on to raise her family and run the house and estate until her death in 1916. Young John Fielden served in the Royal Scots Greys in the Boer War, was caught in the siege of Ladysmith, but returned to Grimston in 1902 and apart from involvement in the Great War, lived as a country gentleman there for the rest of his life.

Meanwhile, as described in Chapter 7, Edward Fielden took his responsibilities for the business in Todmorden seriously. He was not going to live there but in 1889 he began his regular visits that continued over fifty years, once or twice a month, sometimes overnight, sometimes over a weekend. He stayed in Dobroyd Castle which became his property on his uncle's death in 1893, although John's widow remained in occupation until her death in 1909. He was recalled for walking up and down the steep hill-side, and if he was there for the weekend he would walk around the farms which he had inherited, with his agent John Horsfall or in later years Edward Stott. Teddy Fielden, as Todmorden knew him, became a well known figure in the mills, less so, perhaps, in the town, although many would know him there, since he it was who maintained the Fielden presence. Thus, while he had become an Anglican, he was a regular patron of Unitarian events, President of the Cricket Club, the Agricultural Society and the like, as well as active politically.

In 1889, however, Edward was well established in Oxfordshire; settled into local society, narrowly failing election to the County Council, he became a magistrate, and a popular Master of Foxhounds over seven years from 1887, managing to hunt a regular three times a week. But Headington and Oxfordshire were not going to remain his home. They were not convenient for the Todmorden involvement and in any event, with his inheritance from father and uncle and his wife's wealth, Edward could think of something grander. In 1893 he was looking at country estates in the Midlands and as far north as Darlington but in the end settled on Shropshire; his wife Mary probably wanted to be closer to her family roots, while Shropshire, with its many country estates, its pastoral pursuits, and its relative convenience, was attractive. Edward, to get the feel of the County, rented Longford Hall near Newport in August 1894. As in Oxfordshire, he quickly joined local society and was hunting and shooting from Longford within a few weeks of moving there. Other than Todmorden he had no purposeful involvement at this time beyond his family and his sporting pursuits. In 1895 apart from his regular hunting, (thirteen days in January), shooting and ferreting, he had five weeks fishing in west Scotland in April and May, long stays at Nutfield and the big wedding of his brother Jos to Minnie Sladen at St George's, Hanover Square in the summer.

In September 1895 the prestigious Condover estate came on the market following the death of Reginald Cholmondely.[9] After much discussion, especially over how to pay for it, Edward bought it in July 1896, again benefiting from a weak land market, for £120,000. Clearly he was attracted by what Pevsner later called 'the grandest Elizabethan house in Shropshire', its park, and its fine estate of 4,118 acres in the middle of South Shropshire hunting country. But wealthy as he was,

(Above)
Condover Hall, 'the grandest Elizabethan house in Shropshire,' and its park, village and farms making an estate of 4,118 acres was bought by Edward Fielden for £120,000 in July 1896. Whatever its attractions and prestige, the Condover estate was an expensive affair, with as many as fifty indoor and outdoor staff and constant spending on maintenance and improvement: from the start it was beyond Edward's means.

(Left)
The South Shropshire Hunt meets at Condover: like his brothers, Tom and Jos, Edward was a keen huntsman and rode to hounds three or four times a week when he could, for most of his adult life. His eldest son, Antony followed him and became Master of the South Shropshire from 1925 to 1929.

it was beyond his means; the loan of £70,000 from John Ashton Fielden, a bank overdraft and a further loan of £17,000 from his brothers enabled him to complete. Having sold the contents in March 1897, the house had then to be refurbished, provided with modern drains and electric light, furnished in appropriate style and servanted, indoors and out. Many of the farm buildings and estate cottages were run down. It was a heavy obligation although there were the rents from twelve tenanted farms, and the cottage property and the possibility of income from timber and the like.

Edward enjoyed himself putting things right and, not least, developing the timber resources where he built a water-powered saw mill. He and his wife quickly settled down. He was able to keep up his hunting in the season two, three or even four days a week; each year he shot on the estate with his guests who included at different times his brothers-in-law, Banner and Charles Pilkington, Brocklehurst cousins, Dick Ramsbotham, John Ashton and his nephew, Jack Fielden from Grimston, as well as his new neighbours who included the Swires. But if more settled he continued to visit Todmorden, Grimston, Nutfield, Amulree, and indeed enjoy life. In June 1897 the whole family went to London for the Diamond Jubilee. His younger brother Harold seems to have been a frequent visitor during his army leaves. His three sons went to preparatory school in the south of England; the family took seaside holidays at Westgate-on-Sea; his eldest son Anthony went to Eton in 1899. A cloud on the horizon was his wife's recurrent bouts of illness, indigestion, stomach cramps, dizziness, which confined her to bed all too frequently throughout the 1890s; the London doctors could not find a better explanation than 'nervous exhaustion.'

The Condover Accounts show how expensive Edward's lifestyle now became and how extended his finances were (Table XXVI). He was, of course, paying the wages of a huge staff. Although their numbers varied, typically up to fifteen or twenty worked on the estate, the farm or the agents office, while the rest, more personal, could include four keepers, three — even six — in the stables depending on the number of hunters and coach-horses kept, ten or so in the gardens, and ten or more in the house; as a rule the indoor and outdoor staff were fifty people, more or less. The stables, gardens, and shooting involved other current expenses, as did the household, and there were personal expenses for himself, his wife and children. Hunt subscriptions, school fees, and a constant stream of small gifts, donations, subscriptions were other demands on his purse; all these outgoings, excluding the estate, but including interest on part of his debt, averaged about £10,000 a year. His rent income from the estate approached £6,000 yearly but normal estate expenditures, excluding large capital items, averaged about £4,000 and there were interest charges of about £2,000 a year; over the period 1900-1907 the estate ran up a deficit of nearly £3,000. Thus the estate was contributing nothing to the house, and he relied on his own and his wife's income from dividends, fees, other rents. This was variable but clearly inadequate and he had to sell off inherited assets including his wife's holding in Pearson and Knowles and Todmorden property to meet his outgoings; when the need arose he borrowed more. In 1900,

Table XXVI: Condover Accounts 1900-1907.

	1900 £	1901 £	1902 £	1903 £	1904 £	1907 £
ESTATE						
Rentals	5,768	5,760	5,791	5,959	5,988	5,883
Interest Paid	2,255	2,224	2,209	2,220	2,238	2,235
Expenditure	3,448	4,947	4,749	3,818	4,053	3,546
Surplus/Deficit	65	(1,411)	(1,167)	79	(303)	102
HOUSE AND PERSONAL						
Division	1,012	325	282	230	155	—
London	—	873	936	170	136	—
Stables	484	599	650	474	597	711
Gardens	414	507	461	522	530	707
Shooting	360	325	319	373	348	333
Interest	1,688	1,665	1,949	1,671	1,708	1,747
Other items including Household, wife, children travel	6,411	5,256	5,268	5,651	4,461	7,290
Special Items	8,640[1]	—	—	—	—	—
	19,009	9,550	9,865	9,111	7,935	10,788
INCOME						
Mary Ellen Fielden	9,367	9,897	4,096[2]	2,867	2869	1,763
E.B. Fielden	2,080	1,711	2,156	2,531	1,773	4,645
	11,447	11,608	6,252	5,398	4,642	6,408
BALANCE	(7,562)	2,058	(3,613)	(3,713)	(3,473)	(4,380)

Source: Court of Hill MSS, Condover Accounts.
Notes:
1. Loss on Cotton Futures.
2. Following Mary Fielden's death, her estate provided income for her children.

to reduce his debts he seems to have tried his hand unsuccessfully at speculation in cotton futures but his trading losses sharply worsened his position. Money, for Edward must have been a constant anxiety, as it was to be for the rest of his life.[11]

When Tom died suddenly in 1897, Edward became the head of this branch of the family with his brother's children and ageing mother and several sisters to watch. His brother Joshua had married in 1895 but his wife died in 1898 leaving Jos, who had had a serious accident and was not expected to live, with an infant son Lionel, who then went to live with his grandmother and aunts at Nutfield. Lionel Fielden's autobiography, *The Natural Bent,* written many years later, gives a vivid account of life at Nutfield at the time, as well as his father's lifestyle.[12] Jos, who married again in 1901, with Dora Ismay, daughter of Thomas Ismay, founder of the White Star Line, seems to have moved between various rented country houses before settling in 1905 at the beautiful Farnborough Hall in south Warwickshire, and then in 1912 at Kineton House, close to the kennels of the Warwickshire Hunt, not far away; he stayed at Kineton the rest of his life. To say that life was given over to fox-hunting would not be an exaggeration for whether, as Master of the Warwickshire, between 1911 and 1924, or just as a hunt-member, he seems to have hunted four or five days weekly. In 1911 the *Morning Post* was to say of him, 'no-one in Warwickshire excels his horsemanship in the field and devotion to the sport; he is a past master of the art of fox-hunting who lives for nothing else.' According to his son, he was keeping fifty horses and nearly half as many grooms at one time, but generally living a spartan existence, 'largely indifferent to houses, family, food, heat and comfort,' taking a cold bath every morning and preferring cold beef, bacon and marmalade to anything else. Joshua regarded his son's interest in a university education as a waste of time; he saw himself as an old-fashioned squire. He could afford his lifestyle and the costs of maintaining the Hunt, and when he died in 1944 he left £117,000, more or less what he had inherited.

The youngest brother Harold, Captain as he then was, distinguished himself in the Boer War, winning the DSO in 1901. But personal tragedy intervened here through the strain of epilepsy that ran through the family. After a serious fit in 1903, Harold was invalided from the 7th Hussars in 1904 and placed partially incapacitated, both physically and mentally, in the care of a male nurse; he was occasionally brought to see his mother and sisters but seems to have spent the rest of his life in seclusion, in Kent and then at Chilworth Court near Southampton, where he died in 1936 leaving £238,000 to be shared among his family; his will had been made in 1899 before he went to war in South Africa.

Edith Fielden, Ted's second sister, had married, in January 1888, John MacLeod, son of the manse, prominent Glasgow churchman, businessman and Conservative politician, and eventually Unionist MP for Glasgow Central and Baronet. Edith lived in Glasgow for the rest of her life but kept an active contact with her family and with John Ashton who seems to have been closest to her of the several sisters. Her son, George Fielden MacLeod, born in 1895 and educated at Winchester and Oxford, won the MC with the Argylls in the world war, and entered the Church of Scotland, and while at first a brilliant preacher at a fashionable church in Edinburgh, went to minister to the poverty of Govan in 1930 and in 1938 founded the Iona Community; he later became Moderator of the General Assembly and a Life Peer in 1967.[13]

Edith, and her sister Kate, had themselves attracted national attention as prominent leaders in the Women's Anti-Suffrage League. Two of the other sisters married in the Nineties: Kate in 1891 to Dr Herbert Stone, a Reigate general practitioner, and Beatrice in 1894 to William Hunter, a Harley Street physician and consultant and teacher at Charing Cross Hospital; these weddings at Nutfield, Tom giving away his sisters, were again big family occasions. But the other sisters, Una, 'plump and practical,' Gertrude or True, 'pretty and a bit daft,' and Sarah, remained unmarried at Nutfield with their mother. Sarah, as Lionel recalled, was mannish, severe in dress, completely lacking in vanity, but 'the soul of fun' and 'a true Christian.' She became involved in efforts to combat London prostitution and in 1907, aged 44, she married an Anglican priest, Robert Catterall; Catterall had written to Edward asking his permission to marry and Edward gave his sister away. This was the last big Nutfield wedding. Robert Catterall, then vicar of a modest church in Highbury was a forceful and popular preacher, given to open-air services. After the marriage, probably as a result of Ted's influence, he was invited to a living in Middleton, Lancashire and later to Church Stretton in Shropshire; sadly he died in 1914. There were other weddings in the wider family; Constance Fielden of Beachamwell married Patrick Villiers Stuart at St Paul's, Knightsbridge in 1908; and in 1909 Thomas's daughter Marjory married Sir Charles Lowther Bart, distinguished in the South African War, and heir to large properties on the Welsh borders. The latter was a grand family occasion at Grimston, attended by Sarah from Centre Vale as well as by John Ashton, Brocklehursts and Knowles.

Edward's mother, Ellen, provided with a secure income of £5,000 per annum for life, seems to have tired of Nutfield in 1894 and said she was leaving for good. His father's will provided that the estate would belong to Edward when his mother's interest ceased. She looked for a place in London, lived in a rented house in Queen's Gate and then other rented houses for a while, but changed her mind and was to remain at Nutfield with her unmarried daughters for another twenty-five years. Lionel Fielden, devoted to her, wrote of her 'unusual beauty and elegance in silk and lace and diamonds, and unusual serenity — unruffled dignity and complete unselfishness.' As described, life at Nutfield, one of the isolated islands of respectable feudalism, had a regular routine: prayers in the morning room at 8 o'clock read by Ellen with perhaps twenty servants present; followed by breakfast, 'a delicious profusion' of food; reading The Times; correspondence; a ride round the estate in pony and trap with practically every man, woman and child on it known by name, as well as their health and circumstances. Life went on comfortable and secure, 'very slowly, very gently, very serenely.' In 1909 Ellen was writing in the Mothers Union Journal on 'Joy and Love,' making the point that these were virtues which the poor as well as the wealthy could enjoy; in the article she claimed that despite her age — nearly eighty — she could still run upstairs. She was committed to charitable causes, keeping a 'Fresh Air Home' on the estate, a roomy farm-house in which thirty or more slum children were kept throughout the year. In the Great War the estate took Belgian refugees. Her diary at the time is placid and philosophical; it is a storehouse of poetry and prose that reflects her deeply religious and pious view of life, something which some of her daughters shared. She never questioned the source of her wealth, nor did she feel any guilt; to her the poor were poor and the rich were rich, that was their station in life and they lived accordingly. Ellen eventually left Nutfield in 1920, and the house and estate was sold, probably for about £50,000, given the dwindling interest in places of that kind, except for institutions, schools, hotels and the like. Then aged ninety, she took a house in Melbury Road, Kensington and died there in 1929; Edward, like Lionel, was a frequent visitor to the end.

Thomas Fielden had become a Director of the Lancashire and Yorkshire. On his death, Edward was invited to join the Board in his place and so began an association with the railway world that he was to maintain for the rest of his life, modestly rewarding, prestigious and no doubt interesting, but onerous in terms of travel, visits and endless meetings. By 1903 he had been made Deputy Chairman. Meanwhile the Conservative activists of the Middleton constituency were seeking

Ellen Fielden, beautiful, elegant and serene, commanded respect and affection from her family and friends throughout her long life. Here she is photographed in her seventies, probably about 1905.

(Below)
Ellen prepares to ride round the Nutfield estate, which she did as her afternoon recreation most days. She finally left Nutfield in 1920 at the age of ninety and lived in Kensington with her daughter Una until her death in 1929.

another Fielden to carry their standard. Edward would not contest the by-election which followed Tom's death, mainly on the insistence of his wife, but he campaigned for the Conservative candidate. The seat was then won by the Liberals, but Edward ran in 1900 (the Khaki election), addressed endless meetings, campaigned on the issue of the just and necessary Boer war, and against Liberal demands for old age pensions, higher taxes, and the like, and won back the seat by a very tight majority, 136 votes. Edward was a popular candidate with an affable and confident style; his victory was an exciting and proud experience, capped by a huge demonstration in Todmorden in the early hours of the morning.

What was, by then, becoming a full busy life for Edward with many commitments — he was also becoming involved in church affairs (as was expected of the squire of Condover), work for the Shrewsbury Hospital and county government — was tragically disturbed when his wife died suddenly of peritonitis at their London home in Portland Place in May 1902. She was buried at Condover where a memorial window commemorates her. Edward was shattered; he announced his intention to stand down from Parliament, his diary ceased and his life became very quiet for a while. It was this event which prompted John Ashton Fielden some years later in 1907 to release Edward from any obligation towards the loan of £70,000. His solicitor wrote that 'the loan had not been the benefit to you which he desired and hoped it would be at the time it was made.'

No longer in Parliament, Edward married again in April 1906 to Mysie Theed, daughter of William Theed, a fellow MP; young John Fielden of Grimston, his nephew, was best man at the wedding in Chelsea. The couple took a long honeymoon in Canada and returned to Condover. Mysie was recalled as a very handsome woman, beautifully dressed, well spoken. But neither his sons nor the villagers of Condover liked the new Mrs Fielden, patronising and overbearing as her manner was; nonetheless she was Edward's constant companion, usually accompanied by her sister Doll, for the rest of his life. His financial problems were

Edward's first wife, Mary Ellen (nee Knowles) died suddenly and tragically in 1902. He married again to Mysie Theed in 1906 and she, with her sister Doll, was his constant companion for the rest of his life. She is photographed here as mistress of Condover Hall but was not popular either with Ted's children or the villagers and household in Condover.

no easier and in 1906 he had borrowed another £20,000 from brother Jos on the security of Condover. He now settled down to the remarkably active routine he pursued at least for another twenty-five years. At Condover, apart from managing the estate, there was regular hunting, and entertaining both his family and local gentry, and in a different way, at Christmas and the summer, large parties for his tenants and their children.[14] Todmorden and the Castle remained on the itinerary but more of his time went to the Railway, which required regular visits to Manchester and later to London. In 1918, he became Chairman of the Lancashire and Yorkshire Railway Company, and in 1922, following the railway mergers, Deputy Chairman of the LMS. From 1916 he had rented a house at 19 Great College Street, Westminster. This was convenient for railway affairs, the London offices of the Lancashire and

A country house was for entertaining and there were frequent parties at Condover in the years before the Great War. Here is Edward with some of his guests on the terrace overlooking the park.

(Left)
This page from the Condover Visitors Book at Easter 1911, suggests a large party with three of Edward's sisters and their husbands, joining immediate family and friends

Edward Fielden as High Sheriff of Shropshire in 1911.

Yorkshire being lower down the street. This building, Number 10, eventually became the offices of the Railway Company's Association of which Edward became Chairman; subsequently the building was named Fielden House.

Then there was public service in Shropshire. He had been High Sheriff in 1911; subsequently his involvement in county affairs grew and he was to serve as a JP and Chairman of Wartime Tribunals. In 1916 he became a County Councillor — later an Alderman — and from 1920 to 1940 Chairman of the Finance Committee; his budget speeches annually were described as models of clarity and brevity. Most Saturdays over many years seem to have seen him in Shrewsbury, to which he frequently cycled from Condover, either at County Hall, or at the Alliance Insurance company of which he was local chairman. Every Sunday he was at church and his standing as an Anglican was shown by his election to the House of Laity. His drive, stamina and energy were remarkable, as great perhaps as those of his grandfather, John Fielden MP.

Edward was very proper in his relations with his children who viewed him with old-fashioned respect. His daughter Hilda, not easy to control, had married at Condover in 1909. The eldest son, Antony, went to Sandhurst after Eton and joined the 10th Hussars with a long duty in India. The younger boys, Nicholas and Geoffrey, also went to Eton, Nicholas being Captain of Boats in 1908, and all were involved in the Great War, Antony winning the MC at Ypres in 1915. Edward was greatly concerned to give Antony an adequate private income and to set him up as a gentleman; when he married just before the outbreak of the war, he borrowed a further £30,000 on the security of Condover, to provide an appropriate marriage settlement.

For Edward, as for John Ashton Fielden, the world after the war was

Antony Fielden, Edward's oldest son, born in 1886, went to Eton and Sandhurst and was gazetted second lieutenant in the 10th Hussars in 1906. Here he is with the officers of the regiment (second from left, front row) photographed during service in India. Anthony served in the Great War, winning the Military Cross, and retired to manage the Condover estate in 1921.

All Edward's sons, like those of his brother Thomas, went to Eton, as did the boys of the next generation. His second son, Nicholas, was Captain of Boats in 1908.

a different place. The sense of security and supremacy they had enjoyed belonged to the past. It was not merely that the rise of socialism seemed a threat to property and wealth. The proud and powerful position of Britain in the world was gone, despite the clinging to Empire both for status and for trade. The country's industries were in decline, not least cotton textiles and agriculture which were the activities closest to the Fieldens. Their whole status, influence and lifestyle was under attack from economic and social change. Inflation had brought a significant rise in the costs of living on and maintaining a large estate, certainly one employing fifty or more indoor and outdoor staff. Income had not grown with expenses and certainly by the mid-Twenties railway and other dividends were falling, the rents from depressed agriculture were reduced and not always paid, while income was taxed on an unprecedented scale.

John Ashton could take these changes in his stride although they upset him. For Edward they were far more serious; although his income had risen he was now living well beyond his means and getting deeper into debt. His circumstances were helped in 1920 by the sale of Nutfield Priory when his mother moved to London. After many approaches he had again stood for Parliament in 1924 and represented the Exchange Division of Manchester from 1924 to 1935, holding the seat through three elections. He was assiduous in attendance and well liked on the Conservative backbenches although he spoke only two or three times in debates. Parliament gave him the social round and prestige which both he and his wife enjoyed, but added to his expenditure. In 1926 he decided he had to sell Condover and find something more modest. To Antony his eldest son, retired from the army, who was living in the Small House in Condover, married with three sons, hunting regularly and Master of the South Shropshire Hunt in 1925, this was a matter

(Below)
Edward Fielden fought four general elections. He won the Middleton Division as a Conservative in 1900 but retired following his wife's death. Well known in Manchester because of his involvement in railway affairs as well as Fielden Brothers Limited, he was invited to represent the Exchange Division of that city in 1924. Elected then, and again in 1929 and 1931, he finally retired in 1935.

Exchange Parliamentary Division of Manchester.
General Election, Thursday, 30th May, 192[
YOUR VOTE & INTERES[
are respectfully solicited on behalf of
Mr. E. B. FIELDEN
The Conservative & Unionist Candidate
Printed and Published by CHAS. SEVER LT[
40, King Street West, Manchester.

(Above)
Edward could no longer afford Condover in the 1920s: the costs of the estate and household were inflated, agricultural rents were depressed and his income, not itself growing, was taxed. He sold the Estate for a good price in 1926 and moved to the smaller but beautiful and historic Court of Hill estate near Tenbury Wells. He lived at Court of Hill for the rest of his life and was succeeded there by his son and then his grandson.

(Right)
Higher House Moor, on Blackstone Edge at the head of Cragg Vale, had been bought by the Fielden brothers for its shooting in the 1840s. By the 1920s the moor belonged to John Ashton Fielden but it was his cousin Edward who went there most regularly. Here Edward stands with his party probably about 1925.

of some distress; he was managing the estate which he looked forward to inheriting and which he had been promised. Edward was fortunate enough to find a buyer, namely the Cohens of Liverpool who owned the Lewis's chain of department stores; they paid £170,000. This enabled him to repay the £50,000 he had borrowed in 1906 and 1914 and make better provision for his eldest son with a further gift of £20,000. His other sons had to make their own way. Nicholas, having lived in Canada, married Noel Swire in 1921 and settled down in Shropshire, owning local collieries and helped by his wife's money; he was a flamboyant colourful personality, well known across Shropshire between the wars. Geoffrey, the youngest son, made his career as a professional soldier in the 7th Hussars.

Edward now bought a much smaller but beautiful and historic home, Court of Hill, near Tenbury Wells, for £12,500. The house had a beautiful situation on the slopes of Clee Hill; with its gardens, woodlands and home farm, the estate extended to 348 acres.[15] Edward lived there for the rest of his life. He bought a Lanchester to get around more easily, not least for his visits to Shrewsbury and even occasionally to Todmorden. But most of his journeys were still by rail: Tenbury Wells via Worcester to Paddington; Euston to Manchester and on to Todmorden; Manchester to Shrewsbury and so on. He must have been a familiar figure at some of the stations he used. His busy activity and commitment to public life as well as to business, always on the move, again revealed his remarkable stamina; in 1927 he was seventy years old. In 1931 he celebrated his twenty-fifth wedding anniversary to Mysie and invited his family not to Court of Hill but to Todmorden. They did not stay very long — the Castle was not popular with his sons or their wives — but a photograph was taken of what must have been the last large family occasion at Dobroyd. Edward's immediate family spent Christmas at Dobroyd one year in the early Thirties, including a service at St Mary's Church on Christmas Day; however, this was not an experience they repeated. Rarely used thereafter, the Castle was sold early in 1942 for £10,000; the buyer was the government who used the buildings and the estate for an approved school.

John Ashton and Edward, and the Family Firm

When John Ashton told Edward in 1909 that he was forgetting about his loan, the two cousins, affectionate in correspondence but never close, were at the high point of their relationship. He wrote afterwards, 'I am most thankful the loan business is over with. I never signed my name with greater pleasure.' Thereafter their correspondence became less frequent although its friendly tone did not change. Edward told his cousin what he felt he needed to know about the business where the results were pleasing. John Ashton would comment on his personal doings, but increasingly on his health. Entries in his Game Books carry similar comments. The particular complaint seems to have been aches and pains that were variously diagnosed as gout, lumbago, sciatica, rheumatism and the like. Then in December 1917 he had a serious accident when he lost his footing on leaving a train, fell heavily, cut an artery and was badly shaken. Later he became quite deaf. Thereafter he was increasingly anchored to his estate, isolated, irascible and difficult to deal with. His servants and the villagers at Holme took this in good part; after all, he was their squire and the general feeling was that he was never as ill as he made out. Contacts with the family all but ceased and his correspondence becomes curt, brusque, ill-humoured. Possibly his memory began to fade.

Two questions were to change the relationship between the cousins.

To mark the twenty-fifth anniversary of his marriage to Mysie Theed, Edward called his family together at Dobroyd Castle in late August 1931. It was not a popular venue and they did not stay very long; Edward was called to London in the middle of the stay. Here Edward is in the centre of the group. From left to right, back row: Dora (nee Ismay) wife of Edward's younger brother Joshua); Edward's mother-in-law, Mrs Theed; Lorna Anderson (daughter of Thomas Fielden and Edward's niece); Joshua Fielden of Kineton, Edward's brother; and Edward's sisters Mabel (Pilkington) and Sarah (Catterall). Centre row: Ellen Unett or Una, Edward's unmarried eldest sister; Doll Theed (sister of Mysie); Mysie Fielden (nee Theed); Edward, aged seventy-four; Phoebe married to Edward's son, Antony; Virginia, married to Edward's son, Geoffrey. Front row: Noel Fielden (nee Swire), married to Edward's son, Nicholas; Nicholas; Beatrice Caton-Jones (another daughter of Thomas and Edward's niece); and Edward's sons Antony and Geoffrey.

John Ashton Fielden, continued to wear his naval cap. He had a serious accident in 1917 and thereafter continually complained of aches and pains, deafness and in the end failing eyesight. He rarely had visitors at Holmewood and lived quietly with the same servants over many years. His main companions were two cats, Tom and Jim; his main pastimes, apart from his shooting and fishing, were billiards and stamp collecting. He became increasingly solitary, forgetful and concerned about what would happen when he died, in particular to Fielden Brothers and to his own wealth which he had carefully preserved. The break-down of his relationship with Edward Fielden was as much a consequence of John Ashton's irascible personality and loss of memory, as any impropriety on Edward's part.

The one was the succession to Edward as Chairman of Fielden Brothers Limited. John Ashton had already expressed his fears should anything happen to Edward on whom, as he saw it, so much depended. The composition of the Board had changed; Windsor joined, and in particular Emerson, of Grundy's, the company's Manchester solicitor had joined. No-one, however, could have taken Edward's place. In 1912 John Ashton told Edward to find 'a good business man, one who understands cotton spinning in all its branches and lives in or near Manchester.' The war intervened and when the matter was raised again, in 1919, Edward proposed his eldest son, Antony, who needed a career and income on his prospective retirement from the army: 'his income of £2,500 a year was alright before the war but does not go very far in these post-war days,' as Edward put it. John Ashton was much surprised at the suggestion, asking how Antony, with Eton and a crack cavalry regiment behind him, could possibly settle down 'in a very dull place like Todmorden' where there would be 'no society for him and his wife.' He turned the suggestion down curtly; it would be 'a waste of time trying it: a member of the family has to come for good to be any use, to give his life to it.' Edward argued that Antony would be a Director, not a manager, who 'shapes the policy to be followed and vets the results and the human side'; he wanted at least a twelve month trial. John Ashton was firm and forthright, not unlike his parents. 'We have gone through the family and they are all ruled out so we must look outside,' he wrote.

For the mill, where Windsor was ageing and Coates had long since gone, John Ashton felt in 1922 'we must have a young man born and brought up in the neighbourhood of Todmorden: anyone else would be quite useless and not at all likely to stay there any length of time.' Windsor, perhaps had been the exception. Edward favoured the thirty-year old Ernest Whitham, 'with us since he was a boy,' whom he described as 'capable reliable and steady.' Whitham proved to be the successor, but the approaching retirement of Windsor, with his authority and experience, made a successor to the Chairman even more critical. Edward pushed Antony again as well as his brother Nicholas as a Board member. Antony, he said in November 1922, was managing the estate and home farm, while Nicholas had made a success of his coal business and 'had a strong commercial instinct.' The tone of the correspondence became brusque: John Ashton wrote, 'I have told you distinctly on two previous occasions that I will not have Antony on the Board. In spite of this, you again ask me to let him go on and Nicholas as well. For once and for all, I decline to allow either or both of them to go on the Board of Fielden Brothers or have anything to do with it.' That ended the subject for the time being.

By 1924 a friendlier tone returned to the correspondence, with John Ashton expressing his surprise that Edward should again be standing for Parliament but wishing him well and, showing his keen political interest, fulminating against Asquith, the Womens Vote, Baldwin and the Socialists: 'if they get into power again, Heaven help us!' In 1925 he is saying he does not need a dividend, but 'if only a small dividend is paid, you and the others suffer'; he suggested he should not take his dividend. He sent Edward his Olympia show tickets, describes his fishing trips to Scotland, a visit to Una to whom he gave a great shock, a visit by the Villiers-Stuarts from Beachamwell, and expresses his annoyance on hearing that Jack Fielden (of Grimston) was going to marry 'into that awful family,' that is the Selby-Lowndes. He was happy to agree a generous two-thirds pensions for Rothwell, the weaving-master, and other long-servers retiring from the Company: 'they have helped to make the firm what it is.' When Lumbutts closed in 1926 and sixty-two people were affected, a number were moved to Robinwood but many retired on pensions which John Ashton raised from ten to twelve shillings weekly. The two cousins met in London in 1926, probably for the last time; they were both in their late sixties.

Windsor partly retired in 1927 although he continued to control the cotton buying and cloth selling in Manchester — he had gone out to Pernambuco forty-five years earlier in 1882 — and Whitham succeeded. Edward now described him as 'very conservative in his views;' others found him straightforward but cautious and indecisive. John Midgley, with Fieldens all his life, who had done an excellent job at Robinwood, had a problem taking orders from Whitham and chose to go at the age of sixty-three, 'a bit young for a pension,' as Edward put it, but the cousins agreed £450 a year. When Windsor died in 1930 the issue of new Directors and Edward's successor surfaced again. Writing in November 1930 from Holmewood, John Ashton said

'so much is in you, the only active member of the Family. Your sisters have large sums in the firm and if a crash came now it would be a serious matter. I am nearly 71 and my death, as things are now, might put the firm in a very awkward position. To sum up, if you or I or both were to die as things are now there would be no Fielden left to look after the Holdings of the Family. The firm would be wound up by Trustees and Lawyers and with the cotton trade as it is you know what that would mean.'

Edward again suggested his sons, describing Nicholas as 'a first class business man,' and also his nephew, Edward Pilkington, son of his sister Mabel, who was active in colliery companies in Greater Manchester. John Ashton's position on Antony and Nicholas was the same, and he resisted Pilkington who wanted to be paid and was unable to put up £1,000 for shares. 'We need someone in Manchester,' he said, 'who can devote the necessary time.' He told Jack Fielden at the time, 'I won't have any of Ted's sons in the business. I shall make my own arrangements.' His letters in 1930 and 1931, have a litany of complaints of deafness, painful arthritis (he went to London Hospital for a month), septic teeth, rheumatism, stiffness-all-over, his inability to shoot. He objected to Edward's suggestion that Fieldens might make public its financial results: 'I am sure if our fathers had felt that Fielden Brothers business was known in Todmorden, they would have been rabid,' he wrote.

A new problem now entered their relationship, namely Edward's finances. The move to Court of Hill had brought some relief but smaller as the house was, Edward and his wife seemed to have maintained quite an establishment of servants, as many as fifteen in 1927. His Court of

Edward Fielden acquired car and chauffeur in 1928, although he could ill afford them. Here they are pictured at Dobroyd Castle.

Hill Accounts over the years 1927 to 1932 show how his situation changed (Table XXVII). His income from dividends and fees fell sharply. Part of this was Fielden Brothers but, perhaps more serious, was the plight of the LMS where Director's fees were cut and dividends, as with the other railway companies, collapsed. Edward and his wife made economies but not enough to avoid a serious shortfall; their lifestyle had many commitments, including the expenses of a Parliamentary seat and a rented London home. He received further capital when his mother died in 1929, some £77,000 being his share in the sum set aside for her annuity, but he continued to borrow and apart from bank overdraft, the family company, with its substantial cash balances, became a convenient source. For most of the 1920s he had been borrowing sometimes £10,000, sometimes less, from the company. The fact was not concealed in the balance sheet but Edward had not mentioned the loans to John Ashton before 1930. At the time, when told, the latter had readily agreed to the borrowing: 'getting it from Fielden Brothers is quite satisfactory but you should have told me first,' he said. In January 1934 Edward wrote from Great College Street to John Ashton reporting on the year just ended and asking if he could have some more money,

Table XXVII: Edward Fielden's Personal Accounts: Court of Hill.

EXPENSES	1927 £	1928 £	1931 £	1932 £
Household	4,472	3,726	3,771	3,438
Court of Hill including farm	919	682	505	580
Super and Income Tax	—	2,088	1,143	1,551
Stables	299	384	334	232
Gardens	858	934	505	527
Wife	2,109	1,939	1,187	1,223
Motor Car	852	2,152	434	367
Personal	539	353	348	466
Great College Street	591	666	708	605
Division	414	590	1,439	573
Sons's Rent	300	494	494	494
Interest	272	282	635	351
Other including Gifts	2,781	1,204	574	416
TOTAL	**14,408**	**15,494**	**11,319**	**10,823**
INCOME				
Dividends	7,387	5,389	5,113	3,575
Fees	3,629	2,838	2,170	1,953
Other, including rents	5,238	1,390	1,222	546
TOTAL	**16,254**	**9,617**	**8,505**	**6,074**
Balance	1,846	(5,877)	(2,814)	(4,749)
Met by Change in Fielden loan	—	—	(1,000)	(3,000)
Change in Bank Overdraft	1,814	(5,877)	(1,814)	(1,749)

Source: Court of Hill MSS, Account Books.
Notes:

1927   Other Expenses inclue £1,490 removal/furnishing expenses; other income includes £4,000 Condover rents.

1928   New Lanchester Motor Car purchased for £1,777.

1931   Division Expenses reflect General Election of 1931.

Edward Fielden, or E.B. or Ted or Teddy as he was variously known, appears less august as he grew older. Here, about 1930, his robust, relaxed, affable demeanour conceals his financial anxiety which he kept well-hidden. He continued to drive himself very hard with a full portfolio of involvements. Part of his career ended sadly when his relationship with John Ashton broke down in 1934, partly because Edward had been borrowing from Fielden Brothers Limited, partly because he was reluctant to introduce new directors hoping to find a place for his sons. Five years later he was voted out of the Chair of Fielden Brothers, on the instructions of John Ashton, an unnecessary act which caused great bitterness and anguish within the family.

that is an additional fee as Chairman. 'Do you think I might have something more,' he wrote, 'so many investments are paying little or nothing (especially railways) — it's not easy to make both ends meet and every little helps.' He concluded, 'I never hear or see anything of you, why don't you come and have lunch here with us some day.' He got a curt and hurtful reply. John Ashton was 'against any increase in salaries when trade is bad. You should not complain about railways. You have been an insider for 40 years and should have known.' The climax to their relationship occurred the next month when John Ashton learned from Emerson , his man on the Board, of Edward's borrowings. He had clearly forgotten his prior agreement and wrote in outraged terms: 'It is simply disgraceful that you should have used your power as Chairman to borrow money from the company for your own benefit.' At the end of 1933 the outstanding loan was £11,000; this was immediately repaid by Edward, but the damage was done. On 16th

February a letter from Kearsay, Howes and Wilkinson, John Ashton's London solicitors, advises Edward that Mr John Ashton Fielden 'has revoked your appointment as an executor of his will.' That was the end of the relationship; the cousins never met, spoke or corresponded thereafter.

There was another sequel. Frustrated by Edward's stalling and inaction, John Ashton resolved the matter of succession by appointing two new Directors to the Board, W.R. Allen, a former cotton spinner, and E. B. Hardy, a Manchester stockbroker. No-one knew them; they were apparently chosen, or suggested by Emerson, John Ashton's representative. Todmorden cynics said they were chosen at random from people Emerson could see from his office window in surrounding buildings. Writing through Emerson, John Ashton subsequently tried to persuade Edward to resign, but to no avail. Finally, in March 1939, at the AGM, no-one proposed Edward's re-appointment, and Emerson, seconded by Hardy, moved the appointment of W. R. Allen. So Edward was brutally forced out of the Chair, after almost fifty years. Full of affection and regard, Edward's brother and sisters, nephews and nieces — the family shareholders — were outraged and appalled at this 'abominable, evil, inhuman' behaviour, and the appointment of Allen, 'the little rat.' They all rallied round but furious letters to Holmewood brought no response, while attempts to call an EGM and secure the appointment of more family Directors failed. John Ashton was adamant and he had control: the new Directors obeyed his instructions as did Whitham. In his own judgment, he had done what was in the best interests of Fielden Brothers.

So the long relationship ended sadly. The family had split. Edward died, one would suppose a disappointed man, two weeks after his second wife, on 31 March 1942, and was buried at Nash on Clee Hill. Todmorden was well represented at the funeral. His financial problems had pursued him. Particulars of his estate show how his large railway investments, and indeed his property, had lost value. His gross estate was £136,000 but £65,000 was committed to Antony, as compensation for the promise of Condover twenty years earlier. Dobroyd Castle had been sold just before his death, a matter of some concern to Nicholas, who inherited the Todmorden properties. Antony got Court of Hill and when death duties of fifty per cent had been paid, there was very little to distribute, some £13,000. Of Edward's 152 shares in Fielden Brothers — the £100 shares were valued at only £130 for probate — Antony got ninety-one and Nicholas and Geoffrey the remainder.[16]

John Ashton died at the end of October the same year. He had shot his estate for the last time the preceding January, a very cold day as he noted in his game book; 'Fear this is my last season as my eyes are failing me. My last two shots were a real good double!' The party of six killed 282 pheasants on the day. He was buried in a corner of the churchyard at Holme. He had given instructions: 'no music, no hymns, no show, and when the time comes, lay me in the earth outside.'[17] A pheasant, as is remembered in the village, watched the proceedings and called as the body was committed. The whole village turned out but only Allen came from Fieldens and no-one from Todmorden. Only one member of the Fielden family was there, Beatrice Caton-Jones, Thomas's daughter; Beachamwell sent flowers. Many attended from Peterborough and county organisations.

His will was interesting and controversial, reflecting his quarrel with most of his family and his devotion to good causes. Prior to codicils he had intended to leave his cousins Edith, then Lady MacLeod, £80,000, and Gertrude £10,000, and £50,000 each to two of cousin Thomas's daughters, Lorna Anderson and Beatrice Caton-Jones. These and other legacies were all struck out in a codicil dated 8 July 1941 except the bequest to Lorna Anderson: the reason stated was high inheritance taxes. A legacy of £25,000 to John (Jack) Fielden of Grimston had been introduced in May 1940. Otherwise the family were left out. Of an estate of £1,406,841, death duties took £654,153 and of the remainder legacies to the two family members, his doctor, the local MP and a few personal friends, and all his servants, amounted to about £125,000. Apart from £5,000 to Todmorden Unitarian Church, the rest went to hospitals, with three large bequests, £105,000 each, to the Manchester Infirmary, Liverpool Infirmary and London Hospital; the residuary estate which included Holmewood and the London Bridge property went to the King Edward VII Hospital Fund.[17] Jack Fielden could write from Grimston to his cousin Nicholas in January 1943, 'the old boy had gone hospital mad,' and with 'so many penniless Fieldens around.' He had personally got £25,000 free of tax but having been told 'I was to be his heir,' he thought 'they had forgotten to put an extra nought on.' He went on, 'I don't know why he fought with all the family — he got very cantankerous in his old age.' And more cheerfully, although he had shut up three-quarters of the house at Grimston, and reduced his staff by half, he was doing big business selling timber, sand, gravel and stone, had 'a very nice two-year old filly in training' and had 'booked Pat Beasley for the season.'[18]

The will had another aspect that concerned Edward's sons, namely the disposition of John Ashton's 634 shares in Fielden Brothers Limited. The three Directors he had put on the Board, Allen, Hardy and Maitland (Emerson's successor) got 200 each, and the balance went to his Peterborough solicitor. After more than 150 years. control of the old firm had now passed out of the Fielden family.

THE LAST CHAPTER
1939-1960

The Board-room upheavals at Fielden Brothers Limited did not last for very long. Following Edward's death, his nephew, Mabel's son Dennis Pilkington, became a Director; he had discussed the possibility many years earlier (in 1930) but not taken it up, partly because at that time Directors were unpaid. One change, in 1940 following Allen's appointment, had been to pay the Chairman £700 and the Directors 200 guineas a year. In October 1943 Maitland died and Nicholas Fielden, Edward's son, was then invited to join, 'to fill his father's place.' Accepting, Nicholas said he would do all he could 'to prove himself a worthy successor of those of my family whose energy and foresight built up the undertaking.' Nicholas became Deputy Chairman in 1947, and went on to become Chairman following Allen's retirement in 1959. Together with his nephew, John Antony Fielden, Antony's son, who had joined the Board in 1954, he became the main remaining link of the family with the town, having inherited the several farms on the Dobroyd hillside when his father died.

All this turmoil, if turmoil it was, probably had little effect on the fortunes of the business. Profitability had recovered sharply in 1936 when the dividend was restored to 10 per cent. The course of the business

Nicholas Fielden, Edward's second son, became Chairman of Fielden Brothers Limited in 1959 although by then the majority of shares were owned outside the family. Here he is speaking in Todmorden during the war, with Lady Edwina Mountbatten in the background. Nicholas had inherited Fielden properties, mainly farms, in Todmorden and his grandson has retained their ownership.

Table XXVIII: Fielden Brothers Ltd: Profit and Dividends 1939-1958 (£000).

Year	Manufacturing Profit	Interest and Rent	Total	Dividend %
1939	20.1	2.7	22.8	10
1940	62.5	3.0	65.5	17.5
1941	51.7	3.2	54.9	15
1942	47.7	2.8	50.5	15
1943	44.6	2.8	47.4	15
1944	41.3	2.6	43.9	15
1945	30.1	2.8	32.9	15
1946	19.2	2.8	22.0	15
1947	31.5	2.7	34.2	15
1948	77.7	2.4	80.1	15
1949	128.0	3.0	131.0	15
1950	166.3	3.5	169.8	15
1951	216.7	3.9	220.6	15
1952	35.1	4.1	39.2	15
1953	55.2	5.4	60.6	25
1954	56.9	4.9	61.8	20
1955	7.8	3.9	11.7	20
1956	12.6	4.6	17.2	20
1957	43.2	3.3	46.5	20
1958	34.6	2.9	37.5	20

Source: WYAS, C353/1. Court of Hill MSS.

Interior of Waterside Mill, weavers and tacklers celebrating VE Day in 1945.

in the wartime and post-war period is summarised in Table XXVIII. Wartime brought control, but busy working and improved margins. The difficult period immediately after the war was followed by the span of five years when Lancashire participated in the country's export drive, sheltered from overseas and especially Japanese competition, and was able to meet world-wide shortages of cotton textiles, aggravated by the Korean War. Of course corporate taxation took a large share of the exceptional profits made in this seller's market but substantial reserves were built up in the balance sheet and there were handsome dividends to the shareholders over many years; more than half of those benefiting were non-family, indeed recipients of a chance windfall which they had done little or nothing to earn. At this time the Company's management was strengthened by the appointment of Ronald Watson, a competent technical man, who succeeded Ernest Whitham as General Manager when the latter died in 1952.

The company's fortunes mirrored those of the Lancashire industry during the next several years. The story has been frequently told. To quote Singleton, 'after 1950 pre-war trends in the world textile trade reasserted themselves with a vengeance.'[1] The remaining mass export markets were lost during this period, often to protected indigenous producers, while elsewhere low labour-cost countries such as India, Japan, Hong Kong and Pakistan continued to undercut British cloth prices. This was especially the case for the types of drill cloths from low counts of yarn that were a large part of Fieldens production. Cheap Asian cloth invaded the home market and in 1958 the United Kingdom became a net importer of cotton cloth for the first time since before the industrial revolution. By the late Fifties many Lancashire firms were working at well-below capacity. Few were making profits. Fieldens profits were the result not so much of efficient conversion and available cloth margins, as successful forward purchasing on the raw cotton market.

SALES OFFICE:
7 NORFOLK STREET
MANCHESTER 2
TEL. DEANSGATE
3936 (2 LINES)

𝕱ielden 𝕭rothers 𝕷imited.

ESTABLISHED 1782

Cotton Spinners & Manufacturers

WATERSIDE &
ROBINWOOD MILLS
TODMORDEN
TEL. TODMORDEN 823 (3 LINES)

WATERSIDE

TODMORDEN, LANCS.

Fielden Brothers Limited ceased to trade in 1966, the company changing its name to Waterside Plastics Limited. This is the last letterhead of the old concern.

The government's scheme for reorganisation of the cotton industry compelled the Fielden Directors to take stock of their position in 1959. The Waterside manager, Watson, advised them of the realities. He described the mills: of Robinwood he wrote,

'The buildings, although in good condition, are more than one hundred years old. The disposition of the machinery over six floors of small area interferes with the material flow resulting in excessive labour costs for material handling and supervision. Many of the cards and speed frames are nearly seventy years old. The counts are much coarser than was envisaged when the machinery was installed: this means there is a shortage of rovings to supply even the ring-spindles normally running. In spite of all its handicaps the mill is running at good efficiency, about average for a ring mill with old machinery.'

Waterside has a total of 1,023 looms spread over two sheds each more than 100 years old. The pillars interfere with machine layout and, particularly, in the old shed, the weaver's alleys are very cramped and the roof is low. The average level of artificial illumination is far below modern practice. All the looms in both sheds are in reasonably good condition and operational efficiency is high for the class of work and type of machinery.'

Of the 1,023 looms, only about 800, including 240 automatics, were running, mainly on drill cloths and sheetings; the existing equipment precluded production of more expensive cloths for dress-goods, shirtings, furnishing fabrics and the like. About 500 people were employed at both mills.

If Fieldens were to carry on with any prospect of success, replacement of old machinery in both mills would be essential at enormous cost. Such a course would be unthinkable without building new mills. The necessary investment was of the order of £1 million, part of which could attract a government re-equipment subsidy of 25 per cent. Moreover, given the capability to make different types of cloth, they would need a close working arrangement with an established successful marketing organisation. The alternative, which the Government was encouraging, was to withdraw from production completely, scrapping the equipment and closing the mills: compensation in these circumstances, could be of the order of £140,000, as much as the share capital of the company.

The Directors decided, as Nicholas put it, 'to accept defeat, and take advantage of the Government's scheme, and to cease production.' Nicholas was concerned at 'the betrayal of trust to those who have gone before us, their responsibilities for the workforce and community and especially that such a course would terminate the proud honourable Fielden history.' The Directors contemplated maintaining the Company's presence in cotton as a merchant-converter but this was, in the end, ruled out as incompatible with the Government scheme. But the Company would pursue other activities; since 1956 it had invested in a Manchester cloth merchant, Hampson and Hughes, and in a small plastics moulding operation, Waterside Plastics, carried on at one end of the mill. Through its ownership of these subsidiaries, Fielden Brothers remained alive, and would continue to provide employment in Todmorden.

The shareholders accepted these proposals. They were repaid practically all of the value of the original capital at the rate of £99 per £100 share, partly from the Company's reserves, partly from the compensation payments received when spinning and weaving ceased in April 1960. The majority of the workforce was then made redundant; a fifty-eight year old weaver earning £7 or so a week got compensation of about £70. The balance of the compensation proceeds which totalled £135,000 remained in the Company and was used to enlarge and develop the plastics operation. The old shareholders received 99 new £1 shares at the time and retained their equity in the on-going business; its share capital was still £130,000 but in £1 rather than £100 shares. They had a further repayment of capital of 10/- per £1 share in 1962 from the surplus of £65,000 realised on the sale of the Company's Norfolk Street property in Manchester.

In an effort to increase sales turnover to cover high fixed costs, significant investments were now made in plastics plant. The scale of

Waterside, in a photograph taken in the 1960s. After a brief period of busy working and prosperity about 1950, trading conditions in the cotton industry deteriorated sharply and the mill closed its weaving operations in April 1960. Robinwood closed at the same time.

Waterside Plastics made a glass fibre house in the old Fielden Mill. Here it is being moved to a position in the town centre where it was used in the celebrations to mark the 75th anniversary of Todmorden's incorporation in 1971. Waterside Plastics Ltd. was bought out by its management in 1972 and closed in 1990.

(Below)
The old Waterside Mill is demolished but the Unitarian Church, built from the wealth it created, remains.

this investment was under-estimated and sales and margin did not materialise. Faced with heavy losses in the early 1960s the operation was scaled down, indeed efforts were made to sell it as a going concern. At the end of October 1966 Fielden Brothers, no longer involved with cotton, changed its name to Waterside Plastics Ltd. The business continued but was a marginal affair, small profits one year, losses the next. In the end the shareholders sold it to the management, received 60p per £1 share in 1972. Waterside Plastics then traded with modest success, repaying the bank debt it had incurred within three years, and continuing until 1990.

Thus the old company, with its proud history and its capacity to survive, went in the end with a whimper. It had generated enormous wealth for its owners over the years, not least for the fourth and fifth generation. And it had been the largest contributor to Todmorden's economic base for most, if not all, of its history. It left its enduring marks on the town's landscape and architecture, and provided employment, directly and indirectly, for a high proportion of its people. Fieldens made Todmorden, remained a large part of it, and, if now no more than a memory of the past, will continue to be the most important element in the heritage for the future.

An autumn evening on the Todmorden hillside: Stones Grange is seen from Speke Edge, land and farms still owned by the Fielden family.

Appendices

Appendix I: Fielden Brothers: Expenditure on Todmorden Fixed Assets 1832-1854

Period	Land &[1] Buildings (start of period) £	Additions £	Machinery[2] (start of period) £	Additions £	Depreciation[3]	Comment[4]
1 June 1832 -31 Dec. 1835	34,950	5,090	29,260	7,928	Net provision £142	Mainly extensions at Waterside including sizing house, new carding engines, 6,912 mule spindles at 4s 6d.
1836	40,040	1,333	37,046	3,317	Up to 10 per cent on machinery.	Mainly Waterside loom shed and sizing.
1837	41,373	3,349	37,010	5,892	10 per cent on machinery	Extensions at Waterside. New machinery at Smithyholme (carding, drawing, 1,008 throstle spindles at 9s 6d — J. Lord). Private expenditure on Lumbutts dams in 1836-37: £2,151. Private purchase of Mytholmroyd Mill.
1838	44,722	3,486	39,153	4,692	5 per cent mill buildings 10 per cent on machinery	Further private expenditure on Lumbutts dams £640. Private expenditure on Mytholmroyd mill £2,844.
1839	46,664	4,721 Less, 1,403	39,930	4,503	5 and 10 per cent.	Extension at Waterside: new loom shed and engine house. Sale of land to Railway £1,403. Private expenditure at Mytholmroyd £1,188.
1840	48,341	6,697	40,390	5,964	5 and 10 per cent.	Work on Waterside loom shed. Machinery expenditure includes £1,726 second hand purchases.
1841	53,343	8,325	42,332	12,215	25 per cent buildings. 33⅓ per cent machinery.	Completion Waterside loom shed. £3,351 for two 60 HP steam engines at Waterside supplied by Kay of Bury. £7,917 for Mytholmroyd machinery (cotton preparation, carding, drawing, 10,752 throstle spindles at 8s 6d — J Lord).
1842	51,352	—	40,850	—	Buildings revalued for Poor Law assessment: no depreciation. Machinery revalued & written down.	No records of any capital expenditure. Write down of second hand machinery in store.
1843	50,755	2,438	35,038	—	No depreciation at Waterside, 10 per cent on machinery at out-mills	Erection new warehouse alongside the railway at Waterside. No apparent expenditure on machinery.

1844	53,193	3,628	34,341	—	Buildings revalued. No depreciation at Waterside. 10 per cent at outmills	Private purchase of Robinwood Mill. Completion of Waterside warehouses. Regarding machinery "nothing new of any significance."
1845-1847	56,087	6,970	32,992	25,938	5 per cent buildings. 10 per cent machinery.	Private expenditure on Robinwood buildings, waterwheels, steam engines with W. Fairbairn £8,283. Extension to Waterside property. £7,230 expenditure on Waterside spinning, £6,162 on weaving; £5,007 on Lumbutts; £6,054 at Robinwood; £1,485 at Mytholmroyd.
1848- June 1849	56,058	3,743	46,123	7,934	5 per cent buildings; machinery revalued by Tweedale in August 1849 at £61,063, but written down by 20 per cent.	Private expenditure on Robinwood buildings £2,392 Robinwood machinery £7,934 (J. Glee — 4,160 throstles at 6s 0d per spindle, J. Lord — carding, winding etc.).
July 1849- June 1851	55,666	2,408	48,850	8,713	10 per cent machinery.	Waterside machinery £2,210 (4 mules, 2,772 spindles at 4s 6d; 6,000 at 4s 4d; new looms); Robinwood £4,537 (J. Lord — carding)
July 1851- 31 June 1852	58,075	N/A	47,230	4,355	5 per cent buildings, 10 per cent machinery.	Waterside weaving £1,605; Robinwood (18 throstles — 3,744 spindles at 6s 0d — J. Lord) and Causeway.
July 1852— 31 December 1853	54,000	N/A	46,851	8,718	10 per cent Waterside, 15 per cent outmills, (£7,053 in total).	Waterside weaving £1,607; Robinwood £6,943 (J. Lord — throstle spindles at 6s 0d.).
31 December 1854	55,421	778	48,518	1,765	10 per cent (£4851)	Waterside weaving £1,009.

Source:
WYAS C353/132 Machinery Valuation; Rylands MSS.

Notes:
1. Buildings are the Waterside mill complex and associated farms/cottages only. Outmills were private property. Of the Waterside property, approximately £14,000 was farms and cottages. In 1849 the jointly owned land and buildings ceased to be a Partnership asset.
2. Machinery expenditures cover Waterside and outmills.
3. Depreciation shows no consistent practice. In the early years no separate provision was made but a judgement figure offset additions to machinery. Thereafter normal practice was 5 per cent buildings and 10 per cent machinery.
4. Almost all expenditure, including repairs and maintenance and direct labour by Fielden mechanics, was capitalised.

Appendix II: Fielden Brothers: Expenditure on Machinery 1855-1889

Year	Opening Book Value of Machinery: All Mills £	Depreciation at 10% £	Net New Expenditure during the year £	Comment
1855	45,428	4,543	721	
1856	41,614	4,161	2,620	[Waterside new 80 HP engine (£3,099, with millwork £5,542) — not treated as machinery], Waterside spinning.
1857	40,073	4,007	2,036	Waterside spinning.
1858	38,102	3,810	1,071	
1859	35,364	3,536	(127)	Sale of Stoneswood machinery £351.
1860	31,700	3,170	2,750	Waterstalls closed and machinery sold £500. Stoneswood £2,168 (Lord-carding engines, drawing, winding).
1861	31,128	3,128	5,293	Waterside spinning £2,068 (1861-1865 Progressive replacement of old mules at Waterside with self acting mules, up to 800 spindles each, total 23,500 spindles, supplied by McGregor at prices ranging from 4s11d to 3s6d per spindle) Stoneswood £2,168. Sale of old silk machinery at Waterside. Greenwood mill closed; machinery put in Lumbutts mill.
1862	33,445	3,344	2,063	[Waterside buildings (£2,144)]. Waterside silk £1,389.
1863	32,164	3,216	4,372	Waterside spinning £3,771.
1864	33,320	3,332	1,390	Sale of Waterstalls mill. Expenditure mainly Waterside.
1865	31,378	3,138*	3,098	Waterside spinning £2,541.
1866	31,338	3,134	757	
1867	28,961	2,896	188	
1868	26,253	2,625	25	
26,253	2,625	25		
1869	23,652	2,365	359	
1870	21,646	2,165	(270)	Mytholmroyd mill closed. Machinery sold for £839
1871	19,212	1,921	1,411	Lumbutts New Mill (Jumb) £1,389, (6 pairs of mules, for 7,344 spindles, at 3s8d, supplied by McGregor).
1872	18,701	1,870	355	Jumb £1,816, including machinery moved from Waterside, Robinwood, Stoneswood.
1873	17,186	1,719	101	Smithyholme mill closed. Machinery sold for £212.
1874	15,569	1,557	1,049	Mainly Robinwood.
1875	15,061	1,506	5,846	Waterside £3,187 (19 new throstles — 5,776 spindles at 8s3d, Howard and Bullough). Robinwood £2,310 (1875 — 1877:38 new throstles, 7,448 spindles at 8s6d — Leigh and Sons).

1876	19,201	1,920	4,561	Robinwood £3,842.
1877	21,842	2,184	4,390	Robinwood £2,730. Waterside £1,658 (Progressive replacement of Waterside looms begins 1876 and extends though 1887. In total 1,119 looms replaced with new looms supplied by Bracewell and Bulcock, Burnley. Price of new 36" looms fell from £7.15s in 1876 to £6.5s in 1879 and £5.10s in 1886 with credits up to £1.18s for old looms). £1,566 spent on Waterside Steam Engines (Buildings).
1878	24,049	2,405	10,195	Robinwood: £7,402 (38 new throstles, 7,524 spindles at 7s 3d — J. Lord. 36 new throstles — 7,056 spindles at 7s 6d — Leigh and Sons).
1879	31,839	3,184	739	
1880	29,394	2,939	3,532	Stoneswood £1,926 (carding, drawing), Waterside £1,489. £2,174 spent on Waterside Steam Engines (Buildings).
1881	29,987	2,999	846	
1882	27,835	2,783	2,168	Waterside £1,637, Jumb £632.
1883	27,219	2,722	2,473	Robinwood £1,426, Waterside £1,043, Causeway mill closed. Mill demolished 1884-86.
1884	26,970	2,697	2,298	Lumbutts £1,365. Dobroyd mill demolished.
1885	26,570	2,657	4,937	Stoneswood £2,028 (10 new throstles-4,600 spindles at 8s 3d Howard and Bullough). Lumbutts £2,473 (19 frames with 4,864 ring spindles).
1886	28,850	2,885	802	
1887	26,768	2,677	371	
1888	24,462	2,446	712	
1889	22,728	2,273	423	Stoneswood closed. Machinery all moved to Robinwood.
1890	20,878			

Source WYAS 353/132 Machinery Valuation; *Rylands MSS*
Notes:
1. Depreciation throughout at 10 per cent.
2. Expenditure on boilers and steam engines treated as mill property, and held outside the Partnership. Thus expenditure at Robinwood in this category was £1,253, 1866; £1,045, 1867; £1,852, 1877. Expenditure on Robinwood buildings was £9,943 1884-1888. Expenditure on motive power at Waterside was treated as mill property, rather than as machinery at Waterside.
3. Machinery valued at £22,700 (end 1888) and Mills and Property revalued at £159,700, were bought by Fielden Brothers Ltd. from the Partnership or the Partners with effect from end 1889 for £78,000. Given the loss of value, the machinery sale was put at £9,707 with a book loss to the Partnership in 1889 of £11,101.

Appendix III: Fielden Brothers: Capital in Trade and its Financing 1849-1865

Date	Joint[1] Todmorden Properties	Todmorden[2] Spinning and Weaving: Machinery and Working Capital	Manchester Accounts (including property)	Total Capital in Trade	*Financed by*	
					Partnership capital	Private Family Accounts and Loans (net)
	£	£	£	£	£	£
30 June 1849 after restructuring	55,566	61,451	271,279	332,730	73,938	258,792
30 June 1851	58,075	78,905	429,190	508,095	232,553	275,542[3]
30 June 1852	54,000[4]	64,222	390,044	454,266	268,683	185,583
31 Dec 1853	55,421	204,616	314,134	518,750	314,511	204,239
31 Dec 1854	53,429	208,373	339,190	547,563	339,568	207,995
31 Dec 1855	51,649	278,993	302,152	581,151	381,259	199,892
31 Dec 1856	54,655[5]	70,447	546,137	616,584	441,306	175,278
31 Dec 1857	52,087	88,752	536,371	625,123	453,888	171,812
31 Dec 1858	49,600	153,009	547,156	700,165	527,353	172,812
31 Dec 1859	47,173	108,090	643,350	751,468	576,502	174,966
31 Dec 1860	44,977	187,090	669,432	856,522	702,015	154,507
31 Dec 1861	43,770	295,834	590,830	886,664	792,691	93,973
31 Dec 1862	43,650	435,384	500,448	935,832	932,588[6]	3,244[7]
31 Dec 1863	41,776	198,872	805,713	1,004,585	1,018,916	[14,331]
31 Dec 1864	39,933	133,466	879,888	1,013,354	1,044,827	[31,472]
31 Dec 1865	39,557	193,566	808,346	1,001,912	1,007,152	[75,240]

Source: Longden MSS Personal Ledgers.

Notes:

1. The mills, farms, houses and cottages in Todmorden that were owned by the first Partnership, as distinct from privately owned, were now separated from the second Partnership capital in trade. Their value is not included in the column Total Capital in Trade, in the Table. In 1849 the joint ownership was divided in three parts between James, Thomas, one third each, and John's sons Samuel, John and Joshua, together one third. After James' death in 1852, Thomas held four ninths, and five ninths were shared between Samuel, John and Joshua.
2. Machinery at written down value after additions and depreciation each year (Appendix II). Working Capital to include stocks of cotton and cloth etc. and sums owing (receivables) from sales of cloth through Manchester. Stocks of cotton, work in progress and cloth inventory would not normally exceed £25/£30,000, except when the mills were weaving for stock. Receivables were probably an arbitrary item between Todmorden and Manchester.
3. Executors of Joshua Fielden £163,393; Executors of John Fielden £112,149. By 1855 when the Private Family Accounts were still close to £200,000, the principal accounts were still the Executors of Joshua Fielden (£84,467), together with John Fielden's daughters and the beneficiaries of James Fielden's estate — Lacys, Wrigleys and others.
4. The value of Todmorden properties were written down to £54,000 in 1852. Thereafter they were depreciated by 5 per cent annually.
5. £5,517 was spent on Waterside mill buildings/power source in 1856.
6. After provision of £84,549 against the Rostron bad debt.
7. Loans to family members began to exceed Private Family Accounts loaned to Fielden Brothers in 1863 and subsequent years.

Note on Manuscript Sources

There are several collections of manuscript material which are relevant to the Fielden history.

WYAS: West Yorkshire Archive Service, has extensive material received from the Waterside Mill at Todmorden when this was closed. All this material is now held in the Archive section in Halifax Public Library.

Longden MSS: ledgers, letters, deeds, photographs and portraits, diaries and other family papers in the possession of Mrs Ann Stevens and Mr Jonathan Lovegrove Fielden of Longden Manor, Pontesbury, Salop.

Rylands MSS: the Fielden papers in the John Rylands Library, Deansgate, Manchester.

Court of Hill MSS: letters, photographs and portraits, diaries and other family papers in the possession of Mr John Anthony Fielden of Court of Hill, Tenbury Wells, Salop.

Odiham MSS: chiefly personal ledgers and other family papers and photographs in the possession of Mr John Fielden of Poland House, Odiham, Hampshire.

Taylor MSS: letters and other papers relating to John Fielden and Fielden Brothers in the possession of Mr Jack Taylor of Stansfield Hall, Todmorden.

Illustration Acknowledgements

The author would like to thank the following individuals, museums and photographic archives for permission to reproduce their material:

British Library L45/1900: 45, 76, 149; Mr Bill Birch: 211; Mr J. D. Bliss: 256, 257; Board of Trustees of the National Museums and Galleries on Merseyside: 79, 81, 164; Mrs Christine Copping: 187, 188 and elsewhere; Mrs Valerie Hartley: 195; Mr and Mrs John Helliwell: 163; Mr Richard Hill: 164; Mr and Mrs Sam Kelly: 35; Mr A.F. Kersting: 224; Library of Congress: 74, 80, 120; Mrs Evelyn Lord: 279; Mrs Electra May: 231; Metropolitan Borough of Calderdale: 100; National Maritime Museum: 78; Mr Kevin Nichol: 68; New York Public Library: 70; Notman Archive, McCord Museum of Canadian History: 81, 82; Mr Dennis O'Neill: 60, 94; Mr and Mrs Thomas Newell: 212; Mrs Minnie Ormerod: 202; Royal Commission on Historic Monuments: 214, 253; Royal Institute of British Architects: 201, 207, 221: Mr J. Simpson: 125; Mr Jack Taylor: 169, 206; Mr J. Uttley: 62; Mrs Edna Varley: 236.

Members of the Fielden family have made available many of the photographs, paintings and documents which are used as illustrations; Mr Colin Woolf and Mr Roger Birch have assisted in copying many of these. Finally Mr. Robert Jackson has prepared the maps and diagrams.

References

Chapter 1: The Beginnings

1. For accounts of the early business see 'The Fieldens of Todmorden' in *Fortunes Made in Business*, (London, 1884), Vol. I, pp. 413-456; Joshua Holden, *History of Todmorden* (Manchester, 1912), pp. 159-168; H. Fishwick, *The Family of Fielden*, (Rochdale, 1884). A manuscript family history written by Joshua Fielden of Nutfield in 1882 describes the early period; this is in the possession of Mr. John Fielden of Odiham, (*Odiham MSS*). For the industry background at this time there are many sources but especially M. Edwards, *Growth of the British Cotton Trade, 1780-1815*, (Manchester, 1967).
2. *Longden MSS*, bills dated 7 July 1774 and 14 January 1775.
3. B. Jennings, *Pennine Valley*, (Otley, 1992), p. 109; *Odiham MSS*.
4. John Fielden, *Curse of the Factory System*, (London, 1836), p. 22.
5. *West Yorkshire Archive Service (WYAS)*, 353/816.
6. Copy of the *Crompton Census* in Manchester Public Library; Jennings, *Pennine Valley*, p.109.

Chapter 2: The Rise to Prominence

1. W.D. Rubinstein, *Men of Property*, (London, 1981), p.141, for Joshua Fielden's estate. The value of 17s 6d per spindle for the fixed assets of a cotton spinning mill is the figure used in E. Baines, *History of the Cotton Manufacture*, (London, 1835), p.368.
2. *Longden MSS*, Partnership Document dated 3 May 1816.
3. *Longden MSS*, Private Ledger; *WYAS*, 353/132, Machinery Valuation.
4. *Select Committee on Hand Loom Weavers* (afterwards SCHLW), BPP, 1835, XIII, Q18, Q1857.
5. T. Ellison, *The Cotton Trade of Great Britain*, (London, 1886); R. Robson, *The Cotton Industry in Britain*, (London, 1957).
6. *Manchester and Salford Advertiser*, 24th December 1841.
7. *SCHLW*, Q8048-8050, Q 8060; *Select Committee on Manufactures*, BPP, 1833, VI, Evidence of K. Finlay, p.45.
8. Quoted in B.W.Clapp, *John Owens, Manchester Merchant*, (Manchester, 1965), p.46.
9. *Select Committee on Manufactures*, BPP 1833, VI, Evidence of R.H. Greg, p. 675.
10. R S Fitton and A P Wadsworth, '*The Strutts and the Arkwrights*', (Manchester, 1958), p.302; *Taylor MSS*, John Pickersgill to Fielden Brothers 13 March 1826;

A. Redford, *Manchester Merchants and Foreign Trade*, (Manchester, 1934), p.76.
11. *SCHLW*, Q 3291.
12. *SCHLW*, Q48-49.
13. *Rylands MSS*, JF 11 Nov 1819, JF 29 August 1826.
14. *Fortunes Made in Business*, p. 424.
15. *Rylands MSS*, Joshua Fielden to Hebden Bros, 26 May 1812.
16. Alfred, *History of the Factory Movement* (London, 1857), I, p.326. A. Ellis, *The Story of Brown Shipley*, (London, 1960), p.14.
17. *Reports of the Inspectors of Factories* (afterward Factory Inspectors), BPP 1841, X, p. 46.
18. John Travis, Local Historical Notes, (Todmorden, 1905), p. 56.
19. *WYAS* C353/260, Letter Book, 12 January 1861.
20. *Rylands MSS*, JF 25 September 1821, 18 May 1824; John Fielden, *Curse of the Factory System*, p. 31; *WYAS* C353/427; C. Wing, *Evils of the Factory System*, (London, 1837), p 48.
21. *SCHLW*, Q 8072.
22. *Select Committee on Burdens Affecting Real Property*, BPP, 1846, VI Pt I, Q 3496. The weaver's letter is quoted in *Manchester and Salford Advertiser*, 15 January 1842.
23. *SCHLW*, Q 2333.
24. Samuel Fielden, letter to *The Times*, 18 February 1852.
25. John Fielden, quoted by J.T.Ward in his introduction to Fielden, *Factory System*, p.xxvi. Samuel Fielden, *The Times*, 18 February 1852.
26. *Todmorden Advertiser*, 9 April 1875. (Hereafter THBA.)
27. *Longden MSS*, Partnership documents.
28. *Rylands MSS*, TF 29 May 1850.
29. *Calderdale District Archives*, 55.55.
30. John Travis, *Old Todmorden*, (Todmorden, 1901), p. 33, p. 39. for detail on Stoneswood and Smithyholme.
31. *Rylands MSS*, JF 5 May 1818.
32. *Rylands MSS*, document 11 February 1824.
33. *Rylands MSS*, JF 9 January 1822.
34. *Rylands MSS*, document dated 18 April 1826.
35. *SCHLW*, Q18.
36. *Return of Power Looms*, BPP, 1836, XLV, p 151.
37. John Fielden, *Factory System*, p.32. *Todmorden Advertiser*, 9 April 1875.
38. *Rylands MSS*, Invoice 28 February 1811.
39. *Rylands MSS*, TF letters, 26 May and 12 June 1812; *Taylor MSS*, Hebden Pickersgill letters 20 June 1812 and subsequently, to 5 September 1818.
40. *Rylands MSS*, TF 19 August 1814.
41. *Todmorden Advertiser*, 9 April 1875.

42. *Rylands MSS*, various letters.
43. *Taylor MSS*, John Pickersgill to Fielden Brothers 13th March 1826; *Rylands MSS*, various letters.
44. *Rylands MSS*, letter 5 September 1817.
45. *Rylands MSS*, JF 5 September 1817.
46. *Rylands MSS*, 11 August 1820.
47. *Rylands MSS*, 8 July 1822.
48. *Rylands MSS*, 3 September 1826.
49. Quoted by S.D. Chapman. 'Financial Restraints on Firms in the Cotton Industry' *Economic History Review*, XXXII, 1979, p.56.
50. John Fielden, *National Regeneration* (London, 1834) p.18.
51. *Rylands MSS*, JF 29 September 1827.
52. D.C. Platt, *Latin America and British Trade 1806-1914*, (London, 1972), p.56. This paragraph draws on S.D. Chapman, *Merchant Enterprise in Britain*, (Cambridge, 1992), Chapter II. Clapp, *John Owens, Manchester Merchant*, gives an excellent account of consignment business in textiles from a merchants point of view. John Owens was an associate, customer and competitor of Fielden Brothers. V.B.Reber, *British Mercantile Houses in Buenos Aires*, (Harvard, 1979), gives a full description of the operations of houses like that of Hodgson and Green (then Robinson) with whom Fieldens, and Owens, did much business. Wallis Hunt *Heirs of Great Adventure* (London, 1951), describes the history of Balfour Williamson, a Liverpool house who established branches in Valparaiso and Arequipa and with whom Fieldens did business.
53. *Rylands MSS*, TF 19 January 1822.
54. *SCHLW*, Q 8072.
55. John Fielden, *National Regeneration*, p.18.
56. *SCHLW*, Q8050.
57. S.D. Chapman, *Economic History Review*, 1979, p. 63.
58. *Rylands MSS*, JF 23 April 1822.
59. *Rylands MSS*, various letters from James Hodgson; S.D.Chapman, Merchant Enterprise, pp.71-72.
60. *Rylands MSS*, letter J. Hodgson to JF dated 10 September 1831. The letter was received on 9 December, three months later.
61. *Rylands MSS*, JH to JF 5 November 1830.
62. *Bank of England*, Liverpool Letter Books, 3 February 1840.
63. Alfred, *The Factory Movement*, p. 326.
64. *WYAS*, C353/132.
65. *Odiham MSS*, 'John Fielden: a Biographical Sketch,' written by his son Joshua Fielden.
66. John Travis, *Historical Notes of Todmorden and District*, (Todmorden, 1896), pp. 299-301. Linda Croft, *John Fielden's Todmorden*, (Todmorden, 1994), p. 7 for reference to Samuel's estate.
67. The Fielden family relationships are set out most fully in Fishwick, *The Family of Fielden*.
68. John Travis, *Historical Notes*, p. 24.
69. *Longden MSS* for Sam Fielden's school bills. *Rylands MSS*, JF to Samuel 21 October 1829.
70. Much of this account is based on family correspondence between John Fielden and his children or between the children. Many of these letters are in the *Rylands MSS*, some in the possession of Mr John Fielden of Court of Hill, Tenbury Wells, (*Court of Hill MSS*), and others, held by Mr J. Taylor of Todmorden, (*Taylor MSS*).
71. Early Todmorden Unitarian involvements are described in A.W.Fox, *Annals of the Todmorden Unitarian Congregation*, (Todmorden, 1924) pp. 1-31; H. McLachlan, *The Methodist Unitarian Movement*, (Manchester, 1919). Joshua Fielden described his father's early religious beliefs in a speech at the Unitarian's sixtieth anniversary. (THBA, 25 June 1884).
72 *Odiham MSS*, 'John Fielden of Todmorden, His Times and Work', draft thesis by Charles Biggins. Holden, *History of Todmorden*, pp. 196-199; Mc Lachlan, *Methodist Unitarian Movement*, pp 106 -110.
73. *Manchester Public Library*, 736/1-9; *Taylor MSS*, JF 4 July 1831.
74. *Todmorden Political Union 1831-32*, (British Library); J. Travis, *Todmorden History*, pp. 4-9; Linda Croft, *John Fielden's Todmorden*; Chapters 2 and 3 deal with this period in detail.
75. E.L.Woodward, *The Age of Reform*, (Oxford, 1938), p.128. *Manchester Courier*, 9 June 1849 (obituary).
76. The fullest account of Fielden's political life is S.A.Weaver, *John Fielden and the Politics of Popular Radicalism 1832-1849*, (Oxford, 1987). Weaver gives a full bibliography. The Manchester press quotation is taken from Weaver p. 47.
77. *Longden MSS*, 1832 Election Address; Alfred, *The Factory Movement*, pp. 325- 331.

Chapter 3: A Vast and Complicated Business

1. *Return of Power Looms*, p. 151.
2. V. Gatrell, 'Labour, Power and the Size of Firms in the Lancashire Cotton Industry', *Economic History Review*, XXX, 1977, pp. 95-138.
3. *WYAS*, C353/132; Wing, *Factory System*, p. 48.
4. Information from Mr J. Uttley of the Mytholmroyd Historical Society.
5. James Montgomery, *The Cotton Manufacture of the United States compared with that of Great Britain*, (Glasgow, 1840), pp. 114-125; A. Ure, *The Cotton Manufactures of Great Britain*, (London, 1836), Vol 1, p. 345, p.314, p.316. £500 investment per Horsepower is stated by Ure p.414.
6. Fieldens wages from *Longden MSS*; comparisons from J. Chadwick, 'On the Rate of Wages in the Manufacturing District of Lancashire, 1839-1859' *Journal Royal Stat. Soc.*, XXIII, 1860, p.23 and G.H.Wood, 'Wages in the United Kingdom in the Nineteenth Century: Part XV, The Cotton Industry', *J.R.S.S.*, (73), 1910. For equipment and employment at Quarry Bank Mill see Mary B. Rose, *The Gregs of Quarry Bank Mill*, (Cambridge, 1986), p. 69. The industry figures are from E. Baines, *History of the Cotton Manufacture*, (London, 1835), pp. 383, 414, 431. The 1836 figures for Fieldens are based on Wing,

Factory System, p. 48. and *WYAS*, C353/132, Machinery Valuation.

7. Fieldens costs from *Rylands MSS*, 'Return of Yarn Produced and Wages Paid 7 July-28 September 1842,' and from *Longden MSS*. Other figures from T. Ellison, *Cotton Trade*, pp. 68-69; J. Montgomery, *Cotton Manufacture*, pp. 114-125; John Fielden, Hansard 1844, 73, col 1235 (he was quoting from W. Kenworthy, *Inventions and Hours of Labour*, Blackburn, 1842) F. Merttens, *Cost of Labour in the Cotton Industry*, Transactions Manchester Statistical Society, 1894.

8. *Rylands MSS* for correspondence describing Manchester business at the time. I am grateful to Mr. John Simpson of Helmshore for information about Richard Rostron who grew up in Edenfield where his father had a small cotton mill and a calico-printing works. *Bank of England*, Manchester Letter Book, 20 July 1840.

9. Rhodes Boyson, *The Ashworth Cotton Enterprise*, (Oxford, 1870), p. 29. gives these figures; they are taken from evidence to the Lords Committee on *The Burdens affecting Real Property*, BPP, 1846, VI i, Q335 and 330-2.

10. *Taylor MSS*, John Pickersgill to John Fielden, 21 April 1838.

11. The sections on Wildes Pickersgill and on the financing of North American trade draw on a substantial literature but especially, S.D.Chapman, *The Rise of Merchant Banking,* (London, 1984); R.W.Hidy, *The House of Baring in American Trade and Finance*, (New York, 1949); E.J. Perkins, *Financing Anglo-American Trade, the House of Brown 1800 - 1880*, (Harvard, 1975); N.S, Busk, *Anglo American Trade 1800 - 1850, (New Haven, 1925).*

12. *Rylands MSS*, announcement of the Partnership. Mr Kevin Nichol of Todmorden has the original Partnership document.

13. *Bank of England*, Manchester Letter Book, 11 December 1839.

14. J.B.Riggs, *The Riggs Family of Maryland*, (Baltimore, 1939), describes the family relationships.

15. Rhodes Boyson, *The Ashworth Cotton Enterprise*, Oxford, 1870, pp. 30-33.

16. *Court of Bank of England*, Minutes, 30 March 1837 and subsequent weeks for the Bank's handling of the Wildes problem.

17. Sir J. Clapham, *Bank of England*, (London 1935), pp. 158-161. The Panic of 1837 and its effect on W. & J. Brown is described in Ayton Ellis, *Heir of Adventure, The Story of Brown Shipley*, (London, 1960), pp.38-50.

18. *Rylands MSS*, Letter JF to Governor of the Bank.

19. *Court Minutes*, 6 July 1837.

20. *Rylands MSS*, JF to Daniel Bowman, 7 July 1837.

21. The document is in the possession of Mr J. Taylor of Stansfield Hall, Todmorden.

22. D M Williams, 'The Function of the Merchant in Liverpool Import Trades, 1820-1850'. MA Thesis, Liverpool University 1963 is the source for this paragraph. See also *Business History*, VIII, 1966, pp.

103-121 and J. R. Harris, '*Liverpool and Merseyside*', (London, 1969), pp.183-207. J.R. Killick, 'The Cotton Operations of Alexander Brown 1820-1860', *Journal of Southern History*, XLII, 1977 pp. 169-194. describes a cotton procurement and exporting activity — that of the Browns — that was probably similar to that of Wildes Pickersgill, if on a larger scale.

23. *Bank of England*, Manchester Letter Book, 10 December 1839.

24. Clapp, *John Owens*, p. 105.

25. *Bank of England*, Liverpool Letter Book, 3 February 1840.

26. *Rylands MSS*, John Pickersgill to JF, 15 October 1837; *Taylor MSS* John Pickersgill 21 April 1838.

27. *Rylands MSS*, Return of Accounts in Ledgers of Wildes Pickersgill and Co., 30 November 1841.

28. *Taylor MSS.*, Documents written by John Fielden dissolving the Partnership.

29 T Ellison, *Gleanings and Reminiscences*, (Liverpool, 1905), p.238.

30. *Bank of England*, Liverpool Letter Book, 6 January 1842, 13 May 1842.

31. *Bank of England*, Manchester Letter Book, 11 July 1843.

32. A.P. Lower, *Great Britain's Woodyard*, (McGill, 1973), and *Colony to Nation*, (Toronto, 1977), pp. 212-213, for the timber trade. *Taylor MSS*, Memorandum by John Fielden on the whaling company.

33. *Bill of Entry Records*, Liverpool Central Library.

34. R.S.Albion, *Square Riggers on Schedule*, (Princeton, 1938); C. Cutler, *Queens of the Western Ocean*, (Annapolis, 1961), for the history of sailing packets. The Economist, 31 August 1844, has a timetable and there were many advertisements in the Liverpool press of the period.

35. Particulars from *Liverpool Register of Shipping*, Merseyside Maritime Museum. Lower, *Colony to Nation*, p. 232 describes emigration to Canada on the timber ships as does T. Coleman, *Passage to America*, (London, 1972). For the organisation of trade and shipping in Liverpool, S Marriner, *The Economic and Social Development of Merseyside*, (London, 1982), pp. 34-35. For the ships, D.R. Mc Gregor, *Merchant Sailing Ships 1815-1850*, (London, 1984), and Esther Wright, *St. John Ships and Builders*, (Woodville, Canada), 1976.

36. *Rylands MSS,* TF 16 December 1838.

37. *Longden MSS*, Private Ledger.

38. *Bank of England*, Manchester Letter Book, 28 April 1841.

39. *Rylands MSS.*

40. *Factory Inspectors*, BPP 1842, XIX, XXII.

41. *Hansard*, 1846, (83), col. 1057.

42. *Manchester Spectator*, 9 June 1849; *Annual Register*, 91, 1849, p.243.

43. *Report of Poor Law Commissioners*, BPP 1847, XXVIII, p.267.

44. *Rylands MSS*, JF 23 March 1841.

45. *Hansard*, 1841, (59), col. 572.

46. William Dodd, *The Factory System*, (London, 1842), p.144.

46. William Dodd, *The Factory System*, (London, 1842), p.144.

47. *WYAS*, C353/307, 7 March 1842.

48. Dodd, *The Factory System*, p.144; *Rylands MSS*, 17 November 1840

49. *Rylands MSS*, 'Return of Yarn Produced and Wages Paid 1842'.

50. *Court of Bank*, 9 June 1842, for Fielden's letter and Court Response. Fielden's draft letter is also in the *Rylands MSS*.

51. *WYAS*, C353/132. For the Ashworths, Rhodes Boyson, *The Ashworth Enterprise*, p.34.

52. *Hansard*, 1844, (73), col.244.

53. *WYAS*, C353/307.

54. J. Jarrett, *The Fielden Trail*, (Otley, 1988), quoting letter Mary Fielden 10 May 1836, p.34.

55. *Taylor MSS*, Samuel Fielden 12 June 1840; *Rylands MSS*, Samuel Fielden 18 July 1845.

56. *Taylor MSS*, John Fielden Jnr, 22 July 1845.

57. *Taylor MSS*, Joshua Fielden, 23 April 1845.

58. *Longden MSS*, Private ledger.

59. *National Buildings Record*, SD 920257, for the history of Robinwood Mill. Information on the Ramsbotham family from J. Travis, *Historical Studies*, (Todmorden, 1911), pp. 6-12, and Mr J. Lampitt of Harrow.

60. *WYAS*, C353/13, C353/132.

61 *Calderdale Archives*, 46; *WYAS*, C353/132. Information about Lumbutts Mills from Mr Dennis O'Neill of Todmorden.

62. *Factory Inspectors*, BPP 1842, X, p.55; *WYAS* C353/132.

63. *WYAS*, C353/132.

64. Much of the account that follows is based on family correspondence in the *Rylands MSS*, *Court of Hill MSS*, and in the *Taylor MSS*. Mr J Lampitt of Harrow has given me helpful material on the Ramsbotham family, I have also been able to draw on the *Odiham MSS*, Personal Ledger I.

65. Family participation is described in J.T. Ward, *The Factory Movement*, (London, 1962).

66. *Annual Register*, 91, 1849, p. 243.

67. There are many accounts of the agitation against the new Poor Law in Todmorden, admirably summarised in Croft, *John Fielden's Todmorden*, Chapter 4. Chapter 5 deals with local Chartism.

68. *Memorials on the Ten Hours Bill*, BPP, 1847 XLVI; *Rylands MSS* John Fielden Jnr., 5 June 1847.

69. *Bank of England*, Manchester Letter Book, 5 September 1839. Thomas Fielden is described in the *Manchester Sphinx*, 8 January 1870.

70. R. H. Greg, *The Factory Question*, (London, 1837), p. 69. *Memorials on the Ten Hours Bill*, BPP, 1847, XLVI. Fieldens problems with the bailiffs were described in *Hansard*, 82, vol. 1199, 30 July 1845, and the Manchester incident in *The Manchester Guardian*, 7th March 1844.

71. Much of what I have written about the family of Joshua Fielden is based on the recollections of Mrs Patricia Nemon (neé Villiers-Stuart), his great-great-granddaughter. Mr Douglas Wilson of Todmorden has helped me with his knowledge of the Cockcrofts, and the Mallinsons.

72. *Taylor MSS*, John Pickersgill, 6 November 1835.

73. The relevant wills are in Somerset House and the Public Record office. The following paragraphs also rely on the *Longden MSS*, Private Ledgers, and the *Odiham MSS*, Personal Ledgers.

74. Rhodes Boyson, *The Ashworth Cotton Enterprise*, p.31, pp. 70-71.

Chapter 4: Boom and Famine

1. *Factory Inspectors*, BPP, 1852-53, XL, p.21. Rhodes Boyson, *The Ashworth Cotton Enterprise*, p.32.

2. J. Watts, *The Facts of the Cotton Famine*, (London, 1866), p.344.

3. *Factory Inspectors*, BPP 1854, XIX, p. 62; Clapham, Bank of England, pp. 228-230 for the crisis of 1857.

4. WYAS, C353/260, Letter Books. On 1 June 1858 Campbell was instructed to despatch 400 bales weekly by rail. Fieldens were using at this rate in January and February 1859 but by May (letter to Campbell 19 May) they were asking for 350 bales a week. (In the first five months of 1857 usage had averaged only 294 bales weekly).

5. *WYAS*, C353/710, document dated 8 July 1859. *WYAS*, C353/260, Letter Books, 12 January 1861. Rhodes Boyson, *The Ashworth Cotton Enterprise*, Chapter V.

6. There are many accounts of the Cotton Famine. Contemporary works include J. Watts, *The Facts of the Cotton Famine* (London, 1866) and R.A. Arnold, *History of the Cotton Famine*, (London, 1864). W.O. Henderson *The Lancashire Cotton Famine* (Manchester, 1934) has been revised in D.A. Farnie, *The English Cotton Industry and the World Market 1815-1896*, (Oxford, 1979), Chapter IV, and D.A. Farnie's contribution to B.M. Ratcliffe (Ed) *Great Britain and Her World 1870 — 1914, Essays for W.O. Henderson*, (Manchester, 1975). A vivid account of conditions in Lancashire is given in Norman Longmate, *The Hungry Mills*, (London, 1978).

7. *WYAS* C353/260, Letter Books, 19 and 31 December 1860.

8. *Longden MSS*, minute of 11 August 1862. For the Brocklehursts see C.S. Davies, *History of Macclesfied*, p. 136. see also *Factory Inspectors*, BPP, 1863 XVIII p.20. *The Economist* 22 November 1862 describes how many Lancashire mill owners were supporting their workpeople. The article urged masters 'to seize this opportunity of cultivating a friendly relation with their workpeople' drawing on 'the ties of Christian neighbourhood'. Rhodes Boyson, *The Ashworth Cotton Enterprise*, p. 81 for another mill-owners reaction to the situation.

9. *WYAS*, 353/349. Mill Diaries for 1863, 1864, (virtually day-by-day descriptions of mill activity). *WYAS*, 353/132, Machinery Valuation.

10. *Report on Sizing Processes used in Cotton Manufacture in Todmorden*, BPP, 1872, LIV.

11. *WYAS* C353/260, Letter Books, 3 August 1864, 26 January 1865.

12. Rhodes Boyson, *The Ashworth Cotton Enterprise*, p.68. Watts, *Cotton Famine*, p. 342.

13. I am indebted for these quotations from Dun to Professor Stanley Chapman.

14. *Fortunes Made in Business*, Vol. 1, p.421.

15. Sam Mendel attended Thomas Fielden's funeral in 1869. His business style and general character is described in a memoir in *Manchester City News*, 15 November 1913.

16. The earliest surviving detail of Manchester loans is in *WYAS*, C353/255, Manchester Accounts for 1870.

17. E.M. Sigsworth, *Black Dyke Mills*, (Liverpool, 1958), pp. 223-225.

18. The investment is not recorded in the *Longden MSS*, Private Ledgers, but features in WYAS, C353/255, Manchester Accounts for 1870. The concession and project is described in *The Journal of Gas Lighting*, Vol. VI, 3 February 1857. For the Consular *Report on Pernambuco 1864* see BPP 1865, LIII, p. 33. A more general account of British overseas investment of the kind is given by J.F.Ryppy, *British Investments in Latin America 1822-1949*, (Minneapolis, 1959).

19. *Longden MSS*, Private Ledger, entry for 1862 gives particulars. The Rostron properties are described and valued in *WYAS*, C353/255, Manchester Accounts for 1870.

20. Henry Houldsworth, quoted in V.Gatrell, *Economic History Review*, XXX, p. 117.

Chapter 5: Maturity and Decline

1. D.A. Farnie, *The English Cotton Industry and the World Market 1815-1896*, (Oxford, 1979), p. 204.

2. T. Ellison's comments and calculations of mill margins are taken from the *Commercial History and Review* published each year by *The Economist*. Ellison, *Cotton Trade*, Chapter IX, and Supplementary Chapter I, describe conditions in this period.

3. D.A.Farnie, *Cotton Industry*, Chapter 5, fully describes the industrial background.

4. Rhodes Boyson, *The Ashworth Cotton Enterprise*, p.6; *Dictionary of Business Biography*, notes on John Rylands, Frank Hollins and Henry and Joseph Lee. The best account of Rylands is D.A. Farnie, *John Rylands of Manchester*, (Manchester, 1993).

5. *Worralls Cotton Spinners and Manufacturers Directory*, various editions; *WYAS*, C353/390 for Fielden data. Samuel Fielden's comment is quoted by *THBA*, 26 August 1881.

6. *WYAS* C353/370/371, Mill Diaries for 1878 and 1879.

7. *Longden MSS*, J.A.Fielden/E.B.Fielden correspondence. Thomas and John Ashton Fielden's attitudes were not untypical of the third or fourth generations of successful business dynasties. Chapter VI returns to the subject but H. Berghoff 'Public Schools and the Decline of the British Economy 1870-1914,' *Past and Present*, 1990, pp. 148-167 explores some of the influences.

8. *WYAS*, C353/526, (Ledgers), and C353/380 onwards (Board Room Diaries), for particulars of cotton usage and mill operation, during this period.

9. The account of industrial relations relies heavily on the local press, *THBA*, from which reported statements are quoted. Individual references are not given. A. Fowler, *The Barefoot Aristocrats*, (Littleborough, 1987), has the background.

10. *Taylor MSS* and *Rylands MSS* for the wage lists.

11. *WYAS*, C353/255, *Manchester Accounts*. The succeeding sections are based on the information given in these accounts.

12. *WYAS* 353/291, Letter from Mrs Sarah Fielden 13 August 1889.

13. *WYAS* 353/291, Board Room Diary 15 November 1888.

14. Details in Manchester accounts, *WYAS* C353/255.

15. Samuel Mendel's life is described in *Manchester City News* 15 November 1913.

16. *WYAS* C353/255 and *Odiham MSS*, Personal Ledger 6 p. 99 for particulars of the Watts loans; *Manchester Courier* 13 April 1878 for the obituary of Sir James Watts; Somerset House for particulars of the will. On the warehouse in Portland Street see D. Farnie, 'The Commercial Development of Manchester in the late Nineteenth Century,' *Manchester Review*, 1954 -56, p.329.

17. The Mellor loans are recorded in the Manchester accounts. The will is in Somerset House.

18. The detailed accounts for the Gas Company are part of the Manchester Accounts for these years.

19. G.S.Messinger, *Manchester in the Victorian Age*, Manchester, 1985, p.100 and following.

20. *Longden MSS*, Partnership Accounts for 1878 and 1879; Manchester Accounts, WYAS C353/255.

21. *Longden MSS* for details of Thomas Fielden's gifts and railway shares. His will is in Somerset House.

22. The settlement with Joshua Fielden is in the *Odiham MSS*, Personal Ledger No. 6, p.99. Joshua Fielden's letters to his brothers are in the *Longden MSS*.

Chapter 6: The Third Generation

1. This chapter draws on a number of general sources: the Personal Ledgers (*Odiham MSS*) record details of the income, drawings and expenditure of the family from 1849 until their deaths or withdrawal from the Partnership; the *Manchester Accounts* (*WYAS* C353/255) record railway share transactions which mostly went through the Partnership; the Todmorden press, *Todmorden and Hebden Bridge Advertiser* (*THBA*) from 1853, *Todmorden and District News* from 1861, *Todmorden Historical Almanacs* 1867-1913, record many local involvements of the Fieldens; the *Longden MSS* includes some Private Accounts of Joshua Fielden; A.W.Fox, *Todmorden Unitarian Congregation*, especially Chapter V, is a valuable commentary on the Fieldens. The manuscript diaries of Edward Fielden from 1881 are another source. Individual references in the text are as few as possible and refer to particular rather than to these general sources. The whole chapter has been greatly helped by the background provided by A. Howe *The Cotton Masters 1830-1860*, (Oxford, 1984), John K. Walton, 'Lancashire, a Social History', (Manchester, 1987) and Patrick Joyce, *Work Society, and Politics*, (London, 1980).

2. *Longden MSS*, for details of John Fielden's will.

3. For the affairs of the Railway at this period John Marshall, *The Lancashire and Yorkshire Railway*, (Newton Abbot 1970), Vol. 1; and PRO, Rail 343, Minutes of the Board and Committees.

4. Young Sam is recalled in the later obituaries, especially *Manchester Guardian*, 11 November 1889. As a director of the Lancashire and Yorkshire Railway Company at this time, he is described in an article in *THBA*, 3 September 1902.

5. *J.A. Picton, Memorials of Liverpool*, (London, 1875) Vol. II, pp. 467-468, comments on Colin Campbell, and the part of Liverpool where he lived. There is an engraved portrait of Colin Campbell in *Transactions Historic Society of Lancashire and Cheshire*, 14, 1862,

6. There are many references to the Yates family, including the *Dictionary of National Biography* and especially, S.A. Thompson-Yates, *Memorials of the Family of John Yates*, (Private, 1890). T. Kelly, *For Advancement of Learning*, (Liverpool, 1981), records their involvement in higher education.

7. Joshua Fielden's household accounts are in the *Longden MSS*.

8. For John Gibson see *Journal of the RIBA*, 7 November 1908. 'One Family, One Architect,' *Country Life*, 6 February 1986, describes his association with the Fieldens.

9. The growth of Todmorden is described in E.M. Savage, *The Development of Todmorden 1700 to 1896* (Todmorden, 1987). The many booklets published by John Travis, and especially *Chapters in Todmorden History*, (Todmorden, 1901), record events in the town and particulars of the history of different cotton businesses. See also Holden, *History of Todmorden*, and Jennings, *Pennine Valley*.

10. Quoted by Howe, *Cotton Masters*, page 140. Bacup, a nearby manufacturing village at about this time is described in William Lee's *Reports to the General Board of Health* on the *Sanitary Condition of Bacup*, (London 1849, 1850); conditions in Todmorden would be much the same.

11. Howe, *Cotton Masters*, p. 142.

12. *WYAS*, C353/818.

13. For the Crossleys see E. Webster, *Dean Clough and the Crossley Inheritance*, (Halifax, 1988); for Edward Akroyd, E. Webster, *Transactions Halifax Antiquarians Society*, 1987.

14. The Fieldens relationship with the Church over this period is described in Fox, *Todmorden Unitarian Congregation*, Chapter VII.

15. *THBA*, 9 April 1875.

16. Quoted in *THBA*, 16 April 1875.

17. Report of the *Rivers Pollution Commissioners*, BPP, 1873, XXXVI, p. 146.

18. The 'dingy Old Burlington,' 'a discreet hotel of irreproachable standing,' used by Florence Nightingale and Cecil Rhodes, is described in the *Survey of London*, Vol. XXXII, p.504.

19. For Sir Edward Watkin see *Dictionary of Business Biography*, Vol. VI, p. 683.

20. *Royal Commission on Education*, BPP, 1887, XXIX, Q 26082 p.380.

21. The expression was that of the Mayor in 1911, Edward Lord. (*THBA* 16 June 1911).

22. *Annual Report of Owens College 1885* lists the many benefactions over the period including those of the Fieldens (pp. 349-354).

23. Particulars of Samuel Fielden's railway share holdings from *Longden MSS*, papers on the estate of Thomas Fielden; and *WYAS*, C.353/255 Manchester Accounts.

24. For Samuel Fielden's estate see *PRO IR26-4172* — folio 751. His will was dated December 1879, ten years before his death. The instructions of John Ashton Fielden regarding the opening of the Hospital were given in a letter from J.F. Horsfall, Todmorden estate agent, to E.B. Fielden (*Longden MSS*)

25. Sarah Fielden received full obituaries in the local press. The *Manchester University Magazine 1906*, and E. Fiddes, *History of Owens College*, (Manchester, 1937) describe her links with the University. Her evidence to the *Royal Commission on Education* in 1887 is the best statement of her views. 'A Day in Life of a Pupil' an oral history recorded by Mrs E.M. Savage of Todmorden describes Centre Vale School around 1886. Finally Mrs Fielden wrote and published as pamphlets her own *Notes to Teachers*, 1900, outlining her methods of teaching Reading and Arithmetic.

26. The sale to the town was not without controversy. *THBA* 1911 had many reports on the argument about the use of the estate which the Mayor, in order to expedite matters, had bought in a private capacity. One strong faction wanted part of the estate to be a cemetery, something the town lacked.

27. Fox, *Annals* p.4; *TBHA*, 9 April 1875

28. *THBA* 14 May 1868, on the occasion of the rearing ceremonies at Dobroyd; Mark Girouard, *The Victorian Country House*. (London, 1979) p.404; the building is described in *The Builder*, 1869, p. 883, p.946 and 1875, p. 953.

29. On the interest of wealthy and successful businessmen in landed estates there is much literature but especially F.M.L. Thompson, *The Rise of Respectable Society*, (London, 1988), Chapter 5, and his earlier *English Landed Society in the Nineteenth Century*, (London, 1963), Chapter X. See also his article 'Life after death: how successful nineteenth century businessmen spent their fortunes', *EHR*, XLIII, 1990. The Brodrick quotation is from J.F.C. Harrison, *Late Victorian Britain*, (London 1990) p. 30. On land values, F.M.L. Thompson, The Land Market in the Nineteenth Century, *Oxford Economic Papers*, IX, (1957). On Grimston Park see Christopher Hussey, *English Country Houses 1800-1840*, (London, 1955), and articles in *Country Life*, 12 October 1901 and 9-16 March 1940. The auction sale is reported in the *Leeds Mercury*, 6th July 1872, and the sale particulars are in *British Library Maps* 137 c 1(7).

30. Details of John Fielden's estate from a document prepared by T. Lodge (*Longden MSS*). Further details, including real property valuation, in *PRO IR 26-4654* Folio 2939.
31. *Court of Hill MSS*, Diary of Joshua Fielden, 1865.
32. Nutfield Priory is described in *The Builder*, 1874, p. 53: N. Pevsner, *The Buildings of Surrey*, (London, 1963, p.62); Mark Girouard, *The Victorian Country House*, (London, 1879), p.415, and Lionel Fielden, *The Natural Bent* (London, 1863), pp. 13-14. *British Library Maps* reference 137 b7 (16) has the particulars of the estate as it was when offered for sale in 1868; at that time, having failed to reach the reserve of £42,000 it was withdrawn.
33. *Hansard* for the period has many references. Press criticism was reported in *THBA* 13 May 1870.
34. *Hansard*, 1878, vol. 237, col. 1470.
35. *Longden MSS* has some Personal Accounts from this period and these are the basis for this paragraph.
36. This paragraph is based on the Diaries of Edward Fielden, for this period part of *Court of Hill MSS*.
37. *Court of Hill MSS*, Diaries of Edward Fielden. Joshua's son, Lionel Fielden, was to describe his father in *The Natural Bent*, especially Chapter One.
38. The reprimand is in the Board Room Diary for 1887, *WYAS*, C353/291.
39. *Longden MSS*.
40. Particulars of the estate in *PRO IR26-3823*-Folio 1069.
41. This paragraph draws on information provided by Mr J. Lampitt of Harrow.
42. Quoted by Robert Kee, *The Laurel and the Ivy*, (London, 1993), p. 37.
43. This paragraph is based on the recollections of Mrs Patricia Nemon, née Villiers-Stuart.
44. Some of these business contemporaries are described in the *Dictionary of Business Biography*. Information on their estates from Somerset House and from Todmorden Almanacs. On nineteenth-century wealth generally, W.D. Rubinstein, *Men of Property*, (London, 1981). and his article in *EHR*, 1977.
45. Wills of Todmorden people were reported in the Todmorden press or Todmorden Almanacs, otherwise information in Somerset House.
46. David Owen, *English Philanthropy 1660-1960*, (Harvard, 1965), describes the nineteenth century philanthropists.
46. W.D. Rubinstein, 'Capitalism, Culture and Decline in Britain 1750-1900', (London, 1993), deals with the subject, following M.J. Wiener, *English Culture and the Decline of the Industrial Spirit 1850-1980*, (Cambridge, 1981). H. Berghoff and R. Moller *English and German Entrepeneurs, 1870-1914, EHR*, XLVII, 1994 has a full list of the extensive literature; the quotation comes from their article.

Chapter 7: Indian Summer

This chapter draws heavily on three main sources. The records of Fielden Brothers Limited in *WYAS* include Board minutes and the Company's accounts as well as miscellaneous correspondence/papers, wage books, sales ledgers, letter books and the like. Secondly, papers at Longden include correspondence between Edward and John Ashton Fielden, partly about the affairs of the Company and management changes; there is also some correspondence in Edward Fielden's letter book with Samuel Fielden, Thomas Wrigley, George Coates and Walter Beard. The Court of Hill MSS includes company accounts and mill accounts for Robinwood Mill, and the Diaries of Edward Fielden for the period until 1906; his subsequent Diaries, except for the period 1907-1915 are at Longden; the Diaries note his visits to Todmorden and occasionally record discussions with management. I have avoided making particular references to these sources to support individual statements or quotations in the text. There is, of course, an abundance of literature on the Lancashire cotton industry during this period but especially D.A Farnie, *Cotton Industry*; B. Elbaum and W. Lazonick (eds), *The Decline of the British Economy*, (Oxford, 1986); R. Robson, *The Cotton Industry in Britain*, (London 1957); B. Bowker, *Lancashire under the Hammer*, (1928), and L. Sandberg, *Lancashire in Decline*, (Ohio, 1974)

Finally I have been able to draw on the work of Mr Steve Toms of the University of Nottingham who has analysed the performance of Fielden Brothers during part of this period, comparative to that of other Lancashire companies. He has published in *Textile History*, 24, 1993, and *Accounting Business and Financial History*, 4, 1994. His papers 'Progress of a Pennine Cotton Enterprise: Fielden Brothers Ltd, 1889-1914,' and 'Financial Performance of the Lancashire Textile Industry 1880-1914,' and 'The Progress and Profitability of Ring Spinning in Lancashire Cotton, 1873-1914,' are in draft.

Chapter 8: The Inheritors

The Diaries of Edward Fielden 1881-1906 and 1916-1939, his correspondence with John Ashton Fielden, and his personal papers and account books, at Longden and Court of Hill, are the main sources used in this chapter. On John Ashton Fielden I am grateful to Mr J.D. Bliss of Holme for his family recollections and for the opportunity to examine the Holme Game Books and to Mr Richard Hill of Peterborough for allowing me to study his box of Fielden papers. There are good obituaries in the Peterborough press. Lionel Fielden, grandson of Joshua of Stansfield Hall and Nutfield, in his autobiography, *The Natural Bent*, has vivid reminiscences of his family, not always accurate in matters of fact but good on character and atmosphere. A good account of the lifestyle and circumstances of Edward's eldest son, Anthony Fielden, and his family between the wars is given in Philip Fielden, *Swings and Roundabouts*, (1991).

1. Details of the sale and surrounding controversy in *THBA*.
2. *Longden MSS*.
3. Lord Knutsford, 'In Black and White,' (London, 1924), p. 323. The London Hospital Archive has a written appeal for 1898 written by Sydney Holland, which vividly describes the work of the hospital and its needs. Interestingly, Mrs Joshua Fielden of Nutfield, from 1899, gave £10 yearly.
4. Fielden House is now used for private wards.

5. Holmewood and Holme are described in the *Victoria County History for Huntingdon*, III and in papers (RB/5/4) in Huntingdon County Record Office. The house is now owned by the British Sugar Corporation and is described in an article in *Hunts Post*, 22 June 1976.

6. Much of this comment is based on conversations with Mr J.D. Bliss of Holme.

7. Obituary notice *Peterborough Advertiser* November 1942.

8. John Ashton Fielden's letters to Edward Fielden at the time, *Longden MSS*.

9. Gertrude Fielden's Scrapbook, *Longden MSS*, refers.

10. There are papers regarding the history of Condover in Shrewsbury Library and the Shropshire County Record Office as well as the account in *Victoria County History*, Salop, VIII. The house is described in *Country Life* 26 March 1898 and 1 June 1918, and in Pevsner, *Buildings of England: Shropshire*, (1958), p. 112.

11. *Court of Hill MSS*, Condover Accounts 1900-1907.

12. Lionel Fielden, *The Natural Bent*, (London, 1963), especially Chapter 9.

13. A full obituary of Lord Macleod is in the *Manchester Guardian*, 29 June 1991.

14. Miss J. Wood of Condover has helped me with recollections of this period.

15. Court of Hill is described in *Country Life*. 18 October 1946.

16. Details of Edward Fielden's will and estate in *Court of Hill MSS*.

17. The will is in Somerset House and a fuller version with Mr Richard Hill of Peterborough.

18. John (Jack) Fielden's letters to Nicholas Fielden dated 12 January 1943 and 10 March 1944 are in the *Longden MSS*.

Chapter 9: The Last Chapter

1. John Singleton, *Lancashire on the Scrapheap*, (Oxford, 1991), p. 147, and his article 'Showing the White Flag,' *Business History,* 32, 1990, pp. 129-145.

2. The account of the closing years of Fielden Brothers Limited draws on records in *WYAS* and on the *Court of Hill MSS* which has papers discussing the decision to close in 1959. I have been greatly assisted by Mr Joseph Hirst of Todmorden who was Company Secretary at this time.

Index

Page numbers in italics
refer to the illustrations